D0978187

Perspectives on Pedagogical Grammar

THE CAMBRIDGE APPLIED LINGUISTICS SERIES

Series editors: Michael H. Long and Jack C. Richards

This new series presents the findings of recent work in applied linguistics which are of direct relevance to language teaching and learning and of particular interest to applied linguists, researchers, language teachers, and teacher trainers.

In this series:

Perspectives on Pedagogical Grammar

Edited by

Terence Odlin
The Ohio State University

CAMBRIDGE
UNIVERSITY PRESS

Published by the Press Syndicate of the University of Cambridge
The Pitt Building, Trumpington Street, Cambridge CB2 1RP
40 West 20th Street, New York, NY 10011-4211, USA
10 Stamford Road, Oakleigh, Melbourne 3166, Australia

First published 1994

Printed in the United States of America

Library of Congress Cataloging-in-Publication Data

Perspectives on pedagogical grammar / edited by Terence Odlin.

p.   cm. – (The Cambridge applied linguistics series)

Includes index.

ISBN 0-521-44530-2 (hc). – ISBN 0-521-44990-1 (pb)

1. Language and languages – Study and teaching.   2. Grammar,
Comparative and general – Study and teaching.   I. Odlin, Terence.
II. Series.

P53.P446   1993

418′.007 – dc20   93–7885

                                                           CIP

A catalog record for this book is available from the British Library

ISBN 0-521-44530-2   hardback
ISBN 0-521-44990-1   paperback

Contents

Contributors

Vivian Cook, University of Essex, Colchester, England
Ruqaiya Hasan, Macquarie University, New South Wales, Australia
Philip L. Hubbard, Stanford University, Stanford, California
Tim Johns, University of Birmingham, England
David Little, Trinity College, Dublin, Ireland
Peter Master, California State University, Fresno
David Nunan, Macquairie University, New South Wales, Australia
Terence Odlin, The Ohio State University, Columbus
Gillian Perrett, University of Sydney, New South Wales, Australia
Russell S. Tomlin, University of Oregon, Eugene
Paul Westney, Universitat Tubingen, Germany
Virginia Yip, Chinese University of Hong Kong

Series editors' preface

The place of grammar in foreign and second language learning and teaching has long been a hotly debated issue in applied linguistics. Opinions vary as to the merits of different linguistic theories, the relationships between theories and pedagogical grammars, and the derivability of one from the other. In addition, the findings from second language acquisition research have raised questions about psycholinguistic constraints on the learnability of any grammar, the scope of rule-based and instance learning, the role of positive and negative evidence, and relationships among implicit and explicit learning, memory, and knowledge.

These are some of the issues addressed in this collection of original papers, *Perspectives on Pedagogical Grammar,* edited by Terence Odlin. The book includes work by individuals with extensive experience in linguistics, applied linguistics, and language teaching, with most authors drawing on their expertise in two or all three of these areas. The contributors, who work on four continents, reflect the diversity of theoretical orientations and positions on the issues that characterize the field today. They have dealt with what is often quite complex material in an accessible way, and they have shown once again how the flow of insights between linguists and language teaching is rarely unidirectional.

The Cambridge Applied Linguistics Series publishes theoretically motivated, data-based work in applied linguistics, especially work which relates theory to practice. That orientation is reflected in this book, which moves from approaches to linguistic analysis for pedagogical purposes to matters of classroom implementation and evaluation. We think it will be of interest to linguists, applied linguists, and language teachers working in a wide variety of theoretical frameworks and social contexts.

Michael H. Long
Jack C. Richards

Preface

Although predictions can go wrong for many reasons, it does seem likely that future historians of twentieth-century thought will see grammar as an area which showed important advances. A great deal of evidence suggests real progress: the highly detailed descriptive grammars now available for English and several other languages, the historically oriented grammars of scholars such as Otto Jespersen, the increasing number of grammars for languages rarely described before, and the insights resulting from work on language typology and language universals. In pedagogical grammar there has also been considerable progress, as seen in work on second language acquisition and English for specific purposes. Despite such advances, however, language teaching has not yet benefited as much as it should. For some teachers, grammar is an unreliable tool, and for others it is a source of fear. A fundamental assumption of *Perspectives on Pedagogical Grammar* is that language teaching will not make significant advances beyond those already seen until more teachers become convinced of the importance of grammar and until they find ways to employ it more effectively. This volume aims to convince more practitioners of the importance and the potential of improved grammar teaching.

Since *Perspectives* is informed by recent insights from linguistic theory, it will also be worthwhile for researchers interested in complex problems such as the relation between syntax, lexicon, and discourse. The theoretical stances taken in the chapters are quite diverse; such pluralism is especially desirable, I feel, since controversies abound. For some readers, this pluralism may seem disconcerting, as it challenges the assumption that we now have an adequate framework (and one accepted by all right-minded people) to understand the most crucial problems in the learning and teaching of second languages. Such a framework may in time come, but there are now many more questions than answers. Although the lack of a straightforward theoretical program may make this volume difficult in some ways, I have tried to ensure that each chapter is accessible to readers who have only a little background in linguistics. Where the style in some parts had to be technical, the glossary should provide help.

Readers especially attuned to style may note some of the hobgoblins catalogued in the less enlightened prescriptive manuals: for example, some contributors to *Perspectives* may use *which* as the pronoun in a restrictive relative clause, as I did in the first sentence of the preface, and some may use *hopefully* as a sentence adverb, as I do in the next sentence. Hopefully, most readers of this volume recognize that such matters have little to do with the great difficulties that second language students must overcome. The introduction to *Perspectives* expresses my belief that prescriptivism has a real place in language teaching; however, grammar has gotten a bad name from attempts at over-regulation.

Along with the contributors to the volume, friends and colleagues have helped in many ways. Jack Richards and Mike Long offered many suggestions and much encouragement in the long history of the project. I am also grateful to Diane Belcher, Brian Joseph, Carol Rosen, and Jacquelyn Schachter for their advice, and to members of the editorial staff at Cambridge University Press, especially Ellen Shaw and Mary Vaughn. Long before this project and during it, I have learned a great deal from two practitioners of pedagogical grammar who are not, unfortunately, represented in the volume: David Birdsong and Robbie Kantor. I also owe many thanks to Debbie Keene, Ivy Kupec, and Tom Wilk, my research assistants, who were a great help with some less exciting parts of the project. This work was supported by the Department of English, by the Department's Program in Rhetoric and Composition, and by the College of Humanities at the Ohio State University.

Terence Odlin

1 Introduction

Terence Odlin

What is pedagogical grammar?

Although it could cover more areas, the term *pedagogical grammar* usually denotes the types of grammatical analysis and instruction designed for the needs of second language students. The unique character of this analysis and instruction may be difficult to see without also seeing how pedagogical grammar is related to other conceptions of grammar. Numerous conceptions have been proposed, as the article by Westney in this volume shows. However, a fourfold distinction can illuminate contrasts especially important for an understanding of the place of pedagogical grammar: grammar as prescription, grammar as description, grammar as an internalized system, and grammar as an axiomatic system.

Grammar as prescription

To most people, the term *grammar* suggests dos and don'ts. "Make sure that your verbs agree with their subjects." "Never use *me* as the subject of a sentence." These and other rules codify many of the distinctions between standard and nonstandard varieties of a language, and such rules often influence people in choosing between "good" and "bad" grammatical forms. Much of the time, though not always, decisions about what is good and bad are essentially arbitrary and do not often reflect any crucial principle of language or thought. Some of the clearest evidence for such arbitrariness comes from the history of languages: When a language changes, rules that a prescriptivist sees as crucial often fall by the way. In English pronouns, for example, standard usage no longer distinguishes between second person singular and plural references. Sentences in isolation such as *You should be ready* are thus ambiguous since the addressee may be either one or more than one person. In contrast, the pronoun system of Old English distinguished singular and plural: The forms corresponding to modern *you* were reserved for plural reference while forms corresponding to *thou* were used for the singular. This system more or less continued into Middle English, albeit with some important sociolinguistic changes. By the period of Early

Modern English (1500–1700), *thou* was disappearing in standard speech, with *you* serving the functions it has today (cf. Baugh and Cable 1978; Leith 1983). This change did not sit well with some grammarians, however, as seen in the following denunciation from one George Fox:

> Do not they speak false English, false Latine, false Greek . . . and false to the other Tongues . . . that doth not speak *thou* to *one*, what ever he be, Father, Mother, King, or Judge; is he not a Novice and Unmannerly, and an Ideot and a Fool, that speaks *You* to *one*, which is not to be spoken to a *singular*, but to *many?*
>
> O Vulgar Professors and Teachers, that speaks Plural when they should Singular . . . Come you Priests and Professors, have you not learnt your Accidence? (Fox 1660/1968: 2–3)

The howl of indignation in this passage sounds remarkably like the strains of some latter-day prescriptivists (e.g., Newman 1976) who inveigh against other common practices such as the use of *data* as a singular noun.[1]

Yet even though many rules are arbitrary and liable to change, prescriptivism merits a more serious consideration than it has received from linguists, who have often depicted the history of prescriptivism as little more than an exercise in incompetence, oppression, or both (e.g., Leith 1983; Sledd 1988; Crowley 1989). Unquestionably, prescriptive tracts have often shown biased and amateurish views of language, and some tracts have been successful enough to engender superstitions (e.g., the taboo against split infinitives in English). Nevertheless, prescription makes possible the standardization of languages, which makes communication easier between highly different dialect regions, as some linguists have noted (e.g., Hughes and Trudgill 1987). Having a target language codified (even if imperfectly) simplifies both the teaching and learning of second languages. If there were no limit to the variation permissible, the speech (or writing) of learners would inevitably diverge much more from the target language. Constraining the divergence through prescription can help to make ways of speaking or writing mutually intelligible when learners modify their language toward a single standard, or at least toward a narrower range of standards (e.g., American, British).[2] While it is true that standard varieties are often associated with the richer and more powerful members of a society, education can – and should – make

---

1 Fox would no doubt feel discouraged to learn that *thou* has not been revived, though it is still used in a few nonstandard dialects in rural England. He would also be flustered to know that some of his capitalization, punctuation, spelling, and number agreement patterns would cause the red ink to flow from the pens of twentieth-century English teachers.

2 Space does not permit an extended discussion of the issue of how many "legitimate" varieties of English there are (cf. Kachru 1990; Quirk 1990). I will simply note here that most of the current pedagogical materials available now (and in the near future) are written in either British or American English.

the standard accessible to all. Pretending that language teaching does not entail prescription will hardly serve learners. One linguist well aware of the limitations of prescriptivism writes:

> If you want to create a truly elitist society, one in which a very few (a priest-hood, if you will) control everything, the best way to do so is to deny substantive education to the masses. Inevitably, however much we try to keep it from happening, there will be those intelligent enough to learn on their own, ambitious enough to do so, and ruthless enough to use what they know for their own advancement at the expense of the hapless, undereducated majority. Substantive education must include the development of knowledge about language and skill in using it, and there seems no way to do justice to these twin aims without prescriptivism of a sort. (Kac 1988: 84)

Grammar as description

Descriptive grammars provide a much more detailed look at languages than most prescriptive grammars do. For linguists, a "descriptive grammar of a language" consists of accounts of not only syntax and morphology but also phonetics and phonology, as well as semantics and/or lexis (i.e., vocabulary). Even when they restrict their descriptions to morphology and syntax, descriptive grammarians consider many structures that prescriptive grammarians either ignore or only briefly discuss: For example, Curme (1931) devotes almost ninety pages to adverbial clauses. Descriptive grammars sometimes provide a detailed look at both contemporary usage and earlier patterns in the language, as seen in Jespersen's seven-volume *Modern English Grammar on Historical Principles* (1922–42). In contrast to prescriptivists, descriptive grammarians often focus on nonstandard dialects. Thus Henry (1957) examines many patterns found in a dialect of Irish English, including patterns rarely if ever used elsewhere in the English-speaking world (e.g., the unusual construction involving a gerund in *I found it horrid sour in the drinkin' o'it* = I found it sour to drink).

For second language teachers, the boundary between prescription and description is not always so straightforward as it often seems for teachers working with native speakers of a language. A teacher in a composition class for native speakers of English would probably not spend much time on adverbial clauses apart from attention to a few matters such as dangling participles (e.g., *Bursting at the seams, the sailors repaired the hull*). The reason for only a cursory glance is clear: Native speakers have little difficulty in using most types of adverbial clauses in English. Teachers of English as a second language, on the other hand, cannot assume that their students are able to use a wide range.[3] Not surprisingly, textbooks

---

3 In the interest of brevity, I have chosen to use *ESL* as a cover term for both English as a second language and English as a foreign language. Distinguishing between the two in practice is often difficult.

and reference grammars for ESL students discuss many types of adverbial clauses, and examples they provide would often seem self-evident to native speakers (e.g., Leech and Svartvik 1975; Azar 1989). For example, native speakers have few problems in choosing the verb tense in an adverbial clause such as that seen in *Before Louis finishes work, he will give us a call.* In contrast, ESL textbook writers commonly inform students (with good reason) that present, not future, tense is normal in *Before Louis finishes work.* In effect, such descriptive information functions as a prescription to forestall deviations from the target such as **Before Louis will finish work, he will give us a call.*[4]

Grammar as internalized system

While descriptive grammars provide information about the wide range of structures in a language, they say little or nothing about the mind, which is the source of grammatical patterning. Views on the psychology of language have shifted drastically in the second half of the twentieth century, but scholars have long recognized that grammatical patterning reflects, however indirectly, a complex neurological system defined by the capacities and limitations of the human brain. The time still seems remote when neurolinguists might provide a convincing account of the physical correlates of such common grammatical properties as coordination and subordination. Nevertheless, there is little question that the capacity for language which any normal child possesses is an organized system that psychologists as well as linguists may profitably study.

What linguists find interesting about the relation between language and mind is not always the same as what psychologists find interesting. To some extent, the difference in interests is reflected in the frequently cited distinction of Chomsky (1965: 4) between *competence,* "the speaker-hearer's knowledge of his language," and *performance,* "the actual use of language in concrete situations." While psychologists tend to be more concerned with the performance mechanisms in speech production and comprehension, linguists tend to focus on the more abstract knowledge that makes production and comprehension possible. The competence that speakers have is evident in the grammatical patterning of any language, even though much of the patterning is not easily accessible to consciousness. For example, most speakers of English would be hard-pressed to see the similarities and differences in syntactic behavior in the following pairs of verbs: *want/need, avoid/imagine,* and *try/continue.* The following sentences show that each pair follows different rules for *complementation,*

4 The asterisk is a widely used convention to indicate ungrammatical sentences. I am aware of claims that English has no future tense; however, I find Comrie's analysis of tense (1985) to be sufficient theoretical grounds for viewing *will* as a future-tense marker in the sentences I have cited.

which here are restrictions on whether an infinitive or progressive verb form can follow the main verb:

Melissa wants to look for a job.
Melissa needs to look for a job.
* Melissa avoids to look for a job.
* Melissa imagines to look for a job.

Melissa avoids looking for a job.
Melissa imagines looking for a job.
* Melissa wants looking for a job.
* Melissa needs looking for a job.

Melissa tries to look for a job.
Melissa tries looking for a job.
Melissa continues to look for a job.
Melissa continues looking for a job.

In their everyday conversations, speakers demonstrate that they unconsciously distinguish between the three types of verbs, even though few could precisely characterize the distinctions. Although some psychologists have taken an interest in the distinctions above, far more linguists have studied the properties of complementation. The fact that speakers know different complementation patterns has many consequences for theories of syntactic structure, regardless of the psychological mechanisms that speakers rely on to make such distinctions (cf. Gregg 1989).

Children learning their native language usually come to make the same distinctions that adults do, and the competence they acquire can be viewed as an internalized system, that is, mental structures that guide everyday linguistic behavior. Although some linguists have (lately) avoided using terms such as *grammar* and *competence* in discussions of internalized systems, the notion of competence is still important in work on both first and second language acquisition. In studies of second language acquisition, Selinker's (1972) term *interlanguage* is frequently used to describe the developing competence of learners. Although interlanguage remains controversial in many ways, there is plenty of evidence that it is systematic, however much the system varies either from the developing competence in first language acquisition or from the competence of adult native speakers (cf. Bley-Vroman 1989).

Without some notion of competence, linguists would find it difficult to account for the systematicity of grammatical knowledge. Not everything that speakers say should be viewed as a part of the grammatical system. For example, adult native speakers have been known to use forms such as *specialating in* rather than *specializing in*. Although such a form could represent either an innovation or the competence of a language learner (child or adult), such forms also can crop up in the speech of adults who normally say *specializing in* (Clark and Clark

1977). The fact that adults will frequently correct their own speech errors is among the most important evidence that performance factors can affect what speakers actually do say. The notion of performance enables linguists to exclude *specialating in* from a descriptive grammar and to ignore other mishaps in speech production.

While the performance/competence distinction is useful, it can create misconceptions. One unwarranted assumption sometimes evident in work on syntax is that linguists interested in competence have direct access to it (e.g., Baker 1978). The most frequently used approach in modern syntactic research has been introspective; that is, linguists often use their own reactions to sentences to decide, for example, whether a sentence is grammatical or not, whether two sentences have the same meaning, and so forth. Although such research often succeeds in providing new insights, it sometimes leads to dubious judgments, as my article in this volume indicates. Judgments about grammaticality as well as other introspective methods are subject to many performance factors and thus are never "pure" competence data. Similarly, judgments elicited from second language learners can provide oblique indicators of developing interlanguage competence, but sorting out the performance factors that affect such judgments is not at all easy (Birdsong 1989; Ellis 1990a).

Performance and competence can interact in many ways, and some of these interactions have motivated a great deal of contemporary work on grammar which is often labeled *functionalist*. Functionalists see many "design features" in any language – and in human language generally – as reflections of performance factors. A simple example will show some common concerns in functionalist analyses. In English a conditional clause (often termed the *protasis*) can come either before or after the main clause (or *apodosis*), as in the following examples:

If we cross the river here, we may lose our food.
We may lose our food if we cross the river here.

Many languages do not allow such flexibility, however; in Turkish, for example, the protasis must always precede the apodosis (Comrie 1986). Conversely, no language appears to allow *only* the order apodosis-protasis (as in *We may lose our food if we cross the river here*). Thus there seems to be a widespread preference for the order protasis-apodosis, which Greenberg (1963: 84) claimed to be one of the universals of grammar: "In conditional statements, the conditional clause precedes the conclusion as the normal order in all languages." Even if this claim ever turns out to be too strong, Greenberg certainly noted a recurring regularity in human languages, one which may well have its roots in performance factors. The protasis-apodosis order often coincides with the order of events in the world. In such cases, the linguistic order complies with what Clark and Clark (1977) call the Order of Mention

Contract, which they see as a common heuristic in language comprehension. By this contract, the speaker agrees to mention "two events in the order in which they occurred" (1977: 129). Predictable speaker behavior will encourage listeners to develop a similar strategy: "Look for the first of two clauses to describe the first of two events, and the second clause the second event, unless they are marked otherwise" (1977: 78). Clark and Clark find considerable psycholinguistic evidence for such behavior by speakers and listeners, including evidence that the Order of Mention Contract facilitates child language acquisition. There is, moreover, evidence that the same principle has subtle effects in second language acquisition (Bardovi-Harlig 1992).

The "internalized system" in functionalist terms thus includes both competence and performance. This wider view of grammar and mind has benefited not only psycholinguistics but also other areas, including discourse analysis and historical linguistics (e.g., Tomlin 1987; Heine, Claudi, and Hünnemeyer 1991). Although these interdisciplinary connections may seem novel and even suspect in the eyes of some linguists, such investigations simply embody the spirit of linguistic inquiry advocated by Jespersen (1929: 3) in his *Philosophy of Grammar:*

> The essence of language is human activity – activity on the part of one individual to make himself understood, and activity on the part of that other to understand what was in the mind of the first. These two individuals, the producer and the recipient of language, or as we may more conveniently call them, the speaker and the hearer, should never be lost sight of if we want to understand the nature of language.

Grammar as an axiomatic system

The study of grammar has its roots in several traditions in the ancient world. One is the religious traditions of India, which encouraged the systematic study of Sanskrit, the sacred language of Hinduism (Deshpande 1986). Still another is the study of secular languages such as Greek: Dionysius Thrax of Alexandria compiled a pedagogical grammar that served as a model for subsequent grammars of Latin and, still later, the vernacular languages of Western Europe and other regions. The grammar of Dionysius Thrax is sometimes seen as the first codification of part-of-speech distinctions, but it benefited from a long tradition of study of logic and language by philosophers (Robins 1966). Although logic and grammar are now seen as different fields, philosophers have long been interested in both, and the development of symbolic logic in the nineteenth and twentieth centuries has led to a new conception of grammar, one that attempts to apply the rigor of mathematics to the peculiar regularities of human language.

Some characteristics of human language lend themselves readily to a highly formalized analysis. For example, prepositional phrases can be concatenated in English to produce unusual but quite possible sentences: for example, *We took a walk in the park on the edge of the new suburbs of one of the cities on our itinerary.* Editors or teachers might find such a chain of six prepositional phrases questionable for stylistic reasons, but a thorough descriptive grammar of English would surely have to include such sentences. Moreover, anyone trying to formulate a viable generalization about prepositional phrases in English could not easily specify the upper limit on such phrases. It would be risky to conclude that six or ten or even a hundred prepositional phrases constituted the limit on concatenations. Among other reasons, some poet or novelist might willfully write a sentence with seven, eleven, or a hundred and one prepositional phrases just to flaunt the artificial limit.[5] It appears that the only viable way to generalize about prepositional phrase chains in English is to allow for an indefinitely long chain, as the following rule does:

PP → P NP (PP)

This rule defines a prepositional phrase (PP) as a preposition (P) and noun phrase (NP), which may in turn be followed by another prepositional phrase (with the parentheses in the rule indicating that the enclosed phrase is optional). Any of the following concatenations are thus possible:

P NP
P NP P NP
P NP P NP P NP
P NP P NP P NP P NP
P NP P NP P NP P NP P NP
P NP P NP P NP P NP P NP P NP

The last chain corresponds to the concatenation in *We took a walk in the park on the edge of the new suburbs of one of the cities on our itinerary.* Moreover, the rule allows much longer concatenations:

P NP P NP P NP P NP P NP P NP
P NP P NP P NP P NP P NP P NP P NP
P NP P NP P NP P NP P NP P NP P NP P NP
etc.

In fact, the rule provides for an infinitely long chain of prepositional phrases. Obviously, the length of chains specified by this rule will often exceed what anyone could actually say. The rule nevertheless captures very concisely what seems to be an essential property of prepositional

5 Some readers will be aware of other types of structures used to illustrate recursivity. I have deliberately chosen prepositional phrases over, for example, self-embedded clauses because the former will probably seem less counterintuitive to readers unfamiliar with generative theories.

phrases in English, *recursivity*. Any recursive rule has the following abstract form:

A → B C (A)

That is, a recursive rule contains the same variable (here represented as A) on both sides of the arrow, which is simply a convention meaning that the rule constitutes a definition. The rule PP → P NP (PP) is thus just one instance of a recursive rule.

It has proved possible to use axioms and other conventions of symbolic logic to state in a most rigorous way the form of recursive rules along with other rules describing not only prepositional phrases but many other grammatical structures (cf. Wall 1972). Grammars are only one type of axiomatic system (many others being of interest only to mathematicians or logicians), and not all formal grammars are developed to study human language. A great deal of work in artificial intelligence involves formal systems which resemble the grammars of human languages but which serve the needs of computer scientists and philosophers concerned with diverse symbolic relations (e.g., Hofstadter 1979). Even so, the generative grammars developed to study human languages are one of the most important benefits of work on axiomatic systems.

At a minimum, generative grammars aim to achieve the comprehensiveness of an ideal descriptive grammar along with the systematicity of an axiomatic system. The challenges posed by English and by languages less studied are immense, and generative grammarians usually acknowledge that their best efforts have fallen short of the ideal. Nevertheless, generative work has encouraged more systematic approaches to the study of language as well as greater interest in language acquisition. Although not all generative grammarians agree with him, Chomsky believes that work in formal grammar has important consequences for understanding how children acquire language (cf. Chomsky 1972; Piattelli-Palmarini 1980). In the Chomskyan framework, Universal Grammar (UG) underlies the structural regularities found in all human languages, and UG principles can account for the wide variation in morphology and syntax in the languages of the world. While acquiring language, children putatively have unconscious access to UG, and this access guides them in the development of their internalized language systems. For Chomsky and other UG theorists, the access that children have is a biological inheritance. The specific linguistic competence that any child acquires (e.g., Japanese or Apache or English) results from an interaction of nature and nurture: that is, while children acquire different languages (and concomitant behaviors) through experience, their ability to acquire language is a natural inheritance reflecting (however indirectly) crucial adaptations of the human brain in evolutionary history (cf. Bickerton 1990). If Universal Grammar is accessible in first language acquisition, it may also be accessible to adult language learners. In fact a great deal of recent research has made just that argument (cf. Rutherford 1986, 1987; Rutherford and Sharwood Smith 1988).

Work in generative linguistics has thus greatly renewed interest in the relation between mind and language and in old philosophical questions such as the problem of innate ideas. Not all generative work, however, concurs with the philosophical agenda of Chomsky and others, nor does all of it concur with Chomskyan formulations of generative systems. Hubbard's article in this volume will present examples of work in some alternative approaches, including Generalized Phrase Structure Grammar, a generative system that diverges in many ways from the formalisms normally found in Chomskyan approaches. Yet along with controversies concerning the best formulation of a generative grammar, a crucial question for work in second language acquisition is the *psychological reality* of generative grammar. Here again, not all generative grammarians concur with Chomsky, as seen in the following observation:

We feel it is possible, and arguably proper, for a linguist (*qua* linguist) to ignore matters of psychology . . . it seems to us that virtually all the work needed to redeem the promissory notes linguistics has issued to psychology over the past 25 years remains to be done. If linguistics is truly a branch of psychology (or even biology), as is often unilaterally asserted by linguists, it is so far the branch with the greatest pretensions and the fewest reliable results. (Gazdar et al. 1985: 5)

Although the position taken by these and other grammarians probably reflects a minority viewpoint in generative grammar, the fact remains that it is possible to approach grammar as an axiomatic system yet not have much interest or confidence in the psychological or philosophical implications of Universal Grammar.

The hybrid nature of pedagogical grammar

Each of the four conceptions of grammar just discussed has implications for language teaching, and none of them alone satisfactorily covers the concerns of practitioners of pedagogical grammar (cf. Noblitt 1972). Without question, teaching grammar in a second language setting involves prescription, yet the range of structures important to consider resembles a descriptive grammar much more than a prescriptive grammar for native speakers. Moreover, teachers concerned about how their students succeed in learning any grammar will naturally be curious about the psychological constructs that underlie interlanguage competence and performance. Even though the extreme rigor of axiomatic systems is usually not found – or needed – in teaching materials in pedagogical grammar, the development of such materials has certainly profited from the discoveries made through formal analysis. Furthermore, the growing understanding of processes of second language acquisition stems in part from the formalisms and questions arising from research on Universal Grammar.

Pedagogical grammar is thus a practically oriented hybrid drawing on work in several fields. As with the fields that contribute to it, pedagogical grammar is not static: Many problems remain to be understood, and until they are, second language teaching will depend on guesswork (however inspired) more than is necessary (cf. Kelly 1969). Without question, excellent materials do exist. ESL teachers, for example, have a choice among several good grammars and dictionaries with grammatical information tailored for the needs of second language students (e.g., Hornby 1974; Collins COBUILD 1987); moreover, there is a growing body of literature on the special needs of students in particular fields (e.g., Swales 1990). Even so, there is certainly room for many more aids, especially since computers and other technologies have allowed for approaches to learning not so feasible before. This volume will, I hope, contribute to the development of new materials. Even more important, though, is the need it may help to meet in the professional development of second language teachers.

Motivations for pedagogical grammar

As a hybrid discipline, pedagogical grammar at its best requires careful and time-consuming interdisciplinary work. Accordingly, teachers and researchers should have clearly justifiable reasons for their efforts in this field. Four interrelated considerations seem especially crucial: instructional time, learner independence, fossilization of knowledge, and expert guidance.

Time

The time spent in language courses is only a fraction of what is needed to develop thoroughgoing proficiency in a second language. In many educational systems around the world, students do not begin to study a second language until secondary school. In about four years of instruction, one hour per day (in a five-day school week) might be devoted to second language instruction. In school systems with an academic year of about ten months (which is more rigorous than what is found in many systems), the maximum amount of classroom time spent on a second language in four years would be 800 hours (equals 5 hours × 4 weeks × 10 months × 4 years). For some languages, this amount of time might be sufficient to achieve a high level of proficiency. If a learner is a native speaker of English, the Germanic and Romance languages might be learnable in such a period, according to estimates cited in recent studies of language transfer (Ringbom 1987; Odlin 1989). Yet the same estimates suggest that 800 hours would be far too little for languages such as Russian, Arabic, and Japanese: The latter, according to the estimate cited by Ringbom, might require 1,440 hours. Such estimates also assume rather ideal conditions often missing in many educational systems such as long school years and small class sizes. Accordingly, it should come as no surprise that universities around the world frequently provide additional instruction in languages offered in secondary schools, if for no other reason than to attempt to complete the language-learning processes begun earlier.

Such attempts are often worthwhile, but they may never be completely successful: By its very nature, adult second language acquisition may not be a completable process. Work by Schachter (1990) and others suggests that such acquisition is inherently resistant to completion. Even if Schachter's conclusions are too pessimistic, one can certainly claim that people continue learning any language (as native or nonnative speakers) throughout their lives. In any case, becoming a proficient speaker or writer in a second language is an extremely lengthy process. Virtually every student will have much still to learn once the course (however advanced) is over.

Independence

Since instruction is so often incomplete, students will have to become independent analysts of the target language if they are to deal with all the problems that their instructors lack time to cover in much detail. Language teaching specialists have offered many reasons for eschewing pedagogies that make students extremely reliant on their teachers (e.g., Nunan 1988). Probably the most important reason of all is that time constraints make it virtually impossible for teachers to focus their students' attention on every aspect of grammar worth considering. Moreover, the ability to use some of the best instructional aids presupposes that learners have some grammatical sophistication. For example, Hornby's dictionary for learners of English (1974) provides detailed information about complementation patterns such as those discussed earlier in sentences such as *Melissa wants to look for a job* and *Melissa avoids looking for a job*. To be able to use that information on their own, students must have more than just a superficial acquaintance with grammar.

Fossilization

If students do not become capable analysts, their learning will probably fossilize; that is, their interlanguage competence will diverge in more or less permanent ways from the target language grammar (cf. Selinker and Lamendella 1981; Selinker 1992). Often the most salient evidence of fossilization comes from errors. Even though they do not constitute the only evidence, errors are the data that will most often create problems for students with teachers, employers, and others who can affect careers and lives. When students are able to analyze their own performance, they can be on guard for fossilized errors.

Even if the process of adult second language acquisition is inherently incomplete, as discussed earlier, adults can and sometimes do achieve an interlanguage competence which is virtually indistinguishable from that of native speakers. Recent work by Coppetiers (1987) and others shows that there are subtle differences between the intuitions of native and "near-native" speakers of French. However, Coppetiers managed to find several near-native speakers whose grammar in casual conversations was indistinguishable from that of native speakers. Some, moreover, had virtually no trace of foreign pronunciation. This research is a salutary reminder that second language acquisition need not show much fossilization.

Coppetiers' findings may be significant in two other ways. Most of the near-native speakers he found had lived in France for many years (the average being seventeen years), and most had had some formal study of French. The complexities of grammar in any language no doubt explain a lot about why grammatical fossilization is so common, and Coppetiers' findings suggest that most learners who are highly successful require considerable time to master the complexities. His findings also suggest that instructed adult second language acquisition will more often minimize fossilization in comparison with naturalistic (i.e., untutored) acquisition. Even though the naturalistic path can lead to the same ideal (or nearly ideal) goal, the path appears to be far steeper.

Guidance

Despite the skepticism about the efficacy of teaching sometimes found in the professional literature, some detailed evidence suggests that teachers can make a difference. Aside from the evidence in Coppetiers' study, there are other indications that formal study (including grammatical study) can increase a learner's chances of success. Ellis (1990b) reviews much of the research on this topic in the last twenty years and concludes that "Learners who receive formal instruction outperform those who do not; that is, they learn more rapidly and they reach higher levels of ultimate achievement" (1990b: 171). Formal instruction normally stresses conscious analysis of rules, but benefits may come simply from attempting to have learners focus on formal characteristics (Schmidt 1990). For example,

Hulstijn and Hulstijn (1984) studied word-order patterns used by adult learners of Dutch and found that the patterns were considerably easier for those who could actually formulate the rules (which, presumably, the learners had acquired through formal instruction). Yet even those who could not formulate a rule benefited from focusing their attention on word order. Such results support the view that "consciousness-raising" can succeed in changing interlanguage competence (cf. Sharwood Smith 1981).

Although the evidence increasingly suggests that formal instruction can succeed, caution is still necessary. It does not follow that grammar teaching will invariably succeed simply because some grammatical characteristics such as word order are amenable to instruction. Work by Pienemann (1984, 1989) and others on the acquisition of German indicates that some grammatical structures prove highly resistant to instruction, especially when teachers insist that learners try to use these structures before they are ready. Other work on German by Eubank (1987) indicates that formal learning can produce interlanguage structures that would not occur in naturalistic second language acquisition, and some classroom procedures may actually induce errors (Felix 1981).

Another reason for caution is that more research is necessary to determine the relative importance of communicative activities and formal analysis in language teaching. Spada (1986) compares the way three instructors balanced communicative activities with grammatical instruction and concludes that learners need practice in both formal analysis and functional (communicative) activities and that learning will suffer if either type of practice is neglected. As Spada observes, further research will have to be done to corroborate her findings. However, such findings concur with many language teachers' intuitions that although grammar instruction is a necessary condition for success in adult language learning, it alone is not a sufficient condition.

However effective grammar instruction may be and whatever methods may work best, the success – or failure – in such instruction hinges largely on teachers. Although students are capable of independent work, the complexity of the grammatical system of any language makes an expert guide highly desirable. The guidance that teachers provide will ideally include not only observations about *what* constitutes the grammatical system of the target language but also advice about *how* to explore the system independently. If teachers are to help students become independent analysts, they must be competent analysts themselves.

What this book will contribute

For pedagogical grammar to make a real difference, its practitioners must make informed choices in their teaching: Not all approaches to pedagogical grammar are equally effective. This volume provides new perspectives on some of the promising approaches. All of the articles address theoretical questions, and nearly all address practical questions as well.

Section I, "What Sort of Grammar?" focuses on issues of description and theory. Cook's article examines recent approaches to Universal Grammar and their implications for both second language acquisition and second language teaching. Characterizations of UG have changed considerably since the mid-1980s (cf. Cook 1988), and Cook discusses recent ideas on the importance of vocabulary in syntactic analysis as well as in language teaching. He also raises intriguing questions about whether the goal of language teaching should be the internalized competence of native speakers or a rule system encompassing not only competence but also performance capabilities often expected from fluent bilinguals. It remains unclear how the narrow conception of competence in generative grammar should be integrated into wider conceptions of communicative competence. Yet as Gregg (1989) and Celce-Murcia (1991) have argued, such attempts are necessary.

The next article in this section, by Hubbard, examines three alternatives to Universal Grammar: Relational Grammar, Lexical-Functional Grammar, and Generalized Phrase Structure Grammar. Although none of these approaches is well known either to second language researchers or to teachers, all three have attracted the attention of many linguists interested in formal grammar. As suggested earlier, teachers need not present grammar to their students in a rigorous axiomatic system, but theoretical work in the systems described by Hubbard has led to insights that practitioners of pedagogical grammar will find useful. For example, Hubbard notes that work in Relational Grammar led to detailed analyses of "unaccusative" verbs such as *exist* and *happen,* difficult verbs for ESL students, as seen in errors such as one noted by Zobl (1989): *The most memorable experience of my life was happened 15 years ago.* As Yip's paper in the second section shows, work in Universal Grammar and consciousness-raising has incorporated such insights into contemporary theory and practice, even though the analysis of unaccusatives originated in a rival approach to generative grammar. Clearly, the competition between approaches has led to some welcome cross-fertilization.

Although it addresses theoretical concerns in several ways, the third article, by Westney, does not consider at great length any particular formal approach to grammar but instead focuses on the concept of *rule,* a notion of obvious importance for any grammatical system. As Westney shows, there is much hidden behind the commonsense definition of a rule as an "observed regularity with predictive value." Using rules in pedagogical grammar entails three major problems: establishing the nature and the extent of the regularity or generalization; finding an appropriate formulation for the generalization; and finding a safe generalization. Westney cites a number of intriguing examples of how grammatical properties of English words often fly in the face of the "observed regularities" posited by ESL grammatical descriptions. For instance, the rule for indirect object pronouns in English is less than straightforward, as the following examples show:

I showed him the answer.
I told him the answer.
*I explained him the answer.

As Westney indicates, the ungrammaticality of the third sentence is not easy to account for, especially in view of the regularity of indirect object structures involving verbs such as *show* and *tell.* Knotty exceptions to the rule do not make attempts to formulate rules impossible, but they should induce teachers to consider carefully just what rules they present and just what the particular pedagogical circumstances may warrant.

Grammarians have long been aware of the connections of grammar with vocabulary and discourse. However, the interest in those connections has grown in recent years, and the four articles in the second section of this volume reflect that growing interest. Other articles in the volume address problems related to vocabulary, but those by Little and Yip consider the problems in the greatest detail. In one sense, Little's article comes the closest to presenting the perspective that many learners have when they confront grammar in actual communication: To them, the problem often appears to be how specific words relate to each other. As Little argues, much more could and should be done to combine the teaching of grammar and vocabulary in view of the fact that the semantic properties of words often have closely associated syntactic properties, a fact also noted by Hubbard and Yip (among others). Drawing his examples from the teaching of German, French, and English to nonnative speakers, Little provides examples of how innovative approaches to vocabulary teaching can also help with teaching difficult areas in grammar such as tense. Moreover, the approaches that he describes can aid learners in understanding the relations between sentence-level grammar and the structure of paragraphs and longer texts.

Yip's paper on ergative verbs explores the possibilities of consciousness-raising. After analyzing the semantics of ergatives, she considers the factors that so often lead students to produce errors such as in *The most memorable experience of my life was happened 15 years ago.* Theories of learnability in Universal Grammar provide the grounding for Yip's efforts in consciousness-raising with two groups of ESL students. The number of students in her study is small, but her results warrant the cautious conclusion she draws: When students were given guidance in attending to the differing syntactic and semantic characteristics of ergative and passive constructions, several of them showed improvement in distinguishing accurately between grammatical and ungrammatical uses.

Tomlin's paper considers functionalist theory and applies it to the problem of having students understand the use of subordinate clauses in discourse. Focusing on analyses of foreground and background in textual studies, Tomlin argues that these concepts, like much else in functionalism, have not been satisfactorily defined. He uses an experimental method to look at functionalist claims about correlations between foregrounding and two areas of grammatical structure, verb *aspect* and subordination. His experiment supports the claims made about subordination but not those about aspect. With this evidence Tomlin shows how teachers can effectively explain the functions of subordinate clauses in texts. Such explanations will no doubt help learners to understand the uses of such clauses and to write summaries and abstracts, two types of discourse crucial for university students.

In the next paper, Hasan and Perrett also take functionalism as their point of departure, but their concerns are quite different. Questioning the common identification of *function* with *use,* the authors argue that a broader conception of functionalism is needed to understand both the nature of language and specific problems of language teaching. Hasan and Perrett briefly describe "metafunctions" that have been identified in earlier functionalist work (e.g., Halliday and Hasan 1976) and focus on one of them, the "interpersonal." Contrasting the use of English in former colonies such as India with its use by immigrants in countries such as Australia, the authors see a need for learners and teachers in the latter context to be more concerned with shades of meaning that involve the interpersonal metafunction. Focusing on the concept of modality, Hasan and Perrett offer detailed contrasts between sentences such as *I insist that you wait, I want you to wait, You're required to wait,* and *You're supposed to wait.* As the authors argue, teaching a single pattern such as *You must wait* will not suffice for learners whose well-being depends very much on their ability to distinguish the levels of politeness in a wide range of structures involving modality. Hasan and Perrett thus explore in considerable depth the implications of Jespersen's exhortation that grammatical analysis should take into account the relations between speakers and hearers.

Aside from the problems of systems, rules, lexicon, and discourse addressed in the first two sections, there remain many other problems of theory and practice in pedagogical grammar, and several of these are addressed in the third section, "Putting Grammar to Work." The article by Master simultaneously addresses one of the key theoretical questions, whether difficult grammatical structures can be taught, and one of the most daunting areas in ESL grammar, the use of definite and indefinite articles. Using a classic pretest/posttest comparative method, Master shows that ESL students who received systematic instruction on article use outperformed students who did not have such instruction. Although his results are based on a discrete-point test and not on spontaneous usage, Master argues convincingly that students can profit from overt grammar instruction. His study and that of Yip concur not only with each other but also with several on teachability described by Ellis (1990b).

The next article, by Nunan, also concerns teachability, but it looks critically at some of Pienemann's claims discussed earlier. Nunan agrees with Pienemann that the readiness of learners is an important consideration in any teacher's decision about when to introduce particular grammatical structures. However, he sees reasons to introduce some of these structures to students even before they are ready to use them. For example, there are well-known difficulties in learning to use *wh*-questions such as *Where did you see the shark?*, and if cognitive considerations were the only relevant issue, such structures should not be presented until learners have received instruction on several other structures. Yet, as Nunan argues, *wh*-questions are so important for learners that teachers would err in delaying instruction in this area. Supporting his arguments with some detailed observations of actual teaching of *wh*-structures, his article offers further insights on the question also raised by Cook on the relation between grammatical and communicative competence.

My own article compares the intuitions of linguists, teachers, and learners. The intuitions of the three groups vary a great deal in their authority: Learners normally defer to the intuitions of teachers who may in turn feel a need to defer to the intuitions of grammarians. However, there are limitations on the ability of teachers and linguists to provide reliable judgments, as much of the evidence reviewed in the article suggests. The competence/performance distinction illuminates some of the most significant limitations. Moreover, this distinction is relevant to a crucial professional difference between linguists and teachers. While linguists are usually more concerned with questions of grammaticality, teachers have to be equally concerned with questions of grammaticality and acceptability, the latter being a wider and more challenging domain.

In the final article, Johns shows how a project using computers has succeeded in helping students to investigate various structures. Students have direct access to texts stored on a data base, and they can search for occurrences of particular structures (e.g., the modal *should*). As Johns observes, this project allows intuition (whether of student or teacher) to be tested in a very concrete way. Such testing will clearly help students to understand not only whether a structure is used but also under what conditions it may be used. Though it is not a panacea, computer-assisted learning can help students acquire the independence that is a crucial goal of effective pedagogical grammar.

References

Azar, Betty. 1989. *Understanding and Using English Grammar.* Englewood Cliffs, N.J.: Prentice Hall.

Baker, Carl. 1978. *Introduction to Generative-Transformational Syntax.* Englewood Cliffs, N.J.: Prentice Hall.

Bardovi-Harlig, Kathleen. 1992. The use of adverbials and natural order in the development of temporal expression. *IRAL* 30:299–320.

Baugh, Albert, and Thomas Cable. 1978. *A History of the English Language.* Englewood Cliffs, N.J.: Prentice Hall.

Bickerton, Derek. 1990. *Language and Species.* Chicago: University of Chicago Press.

Birdsong, David. 1989. *Metalinguistic Performance and Interlinguistic Competence.* New York: Springer Verlag.

Bley-Vroman, Robert, 1989. What is the logical problem of foreign language learning? In *Linguistic Perspectives on Second Language Acquisition,* ed. by Susan Gass and Jacquelyn Schachter. Cambridge: Cambridge University Press, 41–68.

Celce-Murcia, Marianne. 1991. Grammar pedagogy in second and foreign language teaching. *TESOL Quarterly* 25: 459–80.

Chomsky, Noam. 1965. *Aspects of the Theory of Syntax.* Cambridge, Mass.: MIT Press.

1972. *Language and Mind.* New York: Harcourt, Brace, Jovanovich.

Clark, Herbert, and Eve Clark. 1977. *Psychology and Language.* New York: Harcourt, Brace, Jovanovich.

Collins COBUILD. 1987. *English Language Dictionary.* London: Collins.

Comrie, Bernard. 1985. *Tense.* Cambridge: Cambridge University Press.

1986. Conditionals: A typology. In *On Conditionals,* ed. by Elizabeth Traugott, Alice ter Meulen, Judy Reilly, and Charles Ferguson. Cambridge: Cambridge University Press, 77–99.

Cook, Vivian. 1988. *Chomsky's Universal Grammar.* Oxford: Blackwell.

Coppetiers, René. 1987. Competence differences between native and non-native speakers. *Language* 63(3): 544–73.

Crowley, Tony. 1989. *Standard English and the Politics of Language.* Urbana: University of Illinois Press.

Curme, George. 1931. *Syntax.* Boston: D. C. Heath.

Deshpande, Madhav. 1986. Sanskrit grammarians on diglossia. In *South Asian Languages: Structure, Convergence, and Diglossia*, ed. by Bh. Krishnamurti. Delhi: Motilal Banarsidass, 312–21.

Ellis, Rod. 1990a. Grammaticality judgments and learner variability. In *Variability in Second Language Acquisition: Proceedings of the Tenth Meeting of the Second Language Research Forum*, vol. 1, ed. by Hartmut Burmeister and Patricia Rounds. Eugene, Oreg.: Department of Linguistics, University of Oregon, 25–60.

1990b. *Instructed Second Language Acquisition*. Oxford: Blackwell.

Eubank, Lynn. 1987. The acquisition of German negation by foreign language learners. In *Foreign Language Learning: A Research Perspective*, ed. by Bill Van Patten, Trisha Dvorak, and James Lee. Rowley, Mass.: Newbury House, 33–51.

Felix, Sascha. 1981. The effect of formal instruction on second language acquisition. *Language Learning* 31/1: 87–112.

Fox, George. 1660/1968. *A Battle-Door for Teachers & Professors to Learn Singular & Plural*. Menston, U.K.: Scolar Press.

Gazdar, Gerald, Ewan Klein, Geoffrey Pullum, and Ivan Sag. 1985. *Generalized Phrase Structure Grammar*. Cambridge, Mass.: Harvard University Press.

Greenberg, J. 1963. Some universals of grammar with particular reference to the order of meaningful elements. In *Universals of language*, ed. by Joseph Greenberg. Cambridge, Mass.: MIT Press.

Gregg, Kevin. 1989. Second language acquisition theory: A generativist perspective. In *Linguistic Perspectives on Second Language Acquisition*, ed. by Susan Gass and Jacquelyn Schachter. Cambridge: Cambridge University Press, 15–40.

Halliday, Michael, and Ruqaiya Hasan. 1976. *Cohesion in English*. London: Longman.

Heine, Bernd, Ulrike Claudi, and Friederike Hünnemeyer. 1991. *Grammaticalization: A Conceptualization*. Chicago: University of Chicago Press.

Henry, Patrick Leo. 1957. *An Anglo-Irish dialect of north Roscommon*. Dublin: University College, Department of English.

Hofstadter, Douglas. 1979. *Gödel, Escher, Bach: An Eternal Golden Braid*. New York: Random House.

Hornby, A. S. 1974. *Oxford Advanced Learner's Dictionary of Current English*. Oxford: Oxford University Press.

Hughes, Arthur, and Peter Trudgill. 1987. *English Accents and Dialects*. London: Arnold.

Hulstijn, Jan, and Wouter Hulstijn. 1984. Grammatical errors as a function of processing constraints and syntactic knowledge. *Language Learning* 34(1): 23–44.

Jespersen, Otto. 1922–42. *Modern English Grammar on Historical Principles*. London: Allen and Unwin.

1929. *Philosophy of Grammar*. London: Allen and Unwin.

Kac, Michael. 1988. Two cheers for prescriptivism. In *On Language: Rhetorica, Phonologica, Syntactica: A Festschrift for Robert P. Stockwell from His Friends and Colleagues*, ed. by Carol Duncan-Rose and Theo Vennemann. London: Routledge, 79–85.

Kachru, Braj. 1990. World Englishes and applied linguistics. In *Learning, Keeping, and Using Language*, vol. 2, ed. by M. A. K. Halliday, John Gibbons, and Howard Nicholas. Amsterdam: John Benjamins, 203–31.

Kelly, Louis. 1969. *25 Centuries of Language Teaching*. Rowley, Mass.: Newbury House.

Leech, Geoffrey, and Jan Svartvik. 1975. *A Communicative Grammar of English*. London: Longman.

Leith, Dick. 1983. *A Social History of English*. London: Routledge and Kegan Paul.

Newman, Edward. 1976. *A Civil Tongue*. New York: Bobbs-Merrill.

Noblitt, James. 1972. Pedagogical grammar: towards a theory of foreign language materials preparation. *IRAL* 10: 313–31.

Nunan, David. 1988. *The Learner-Centred Curriculum*. Cambridge: Cambridge University Press.

Odlin, Terence. 1989. *Language Transfer*. Cambridge: Cambridge University Press.

Piattelli-Palmarini, ed. 1980. *Language and Learning: The Debate between Jean Piaget and Noam Chomsky*. Cambridge, Mass.: Harvard University Press.

Pienemann, Manfred. 1984. Psychological constraints on the teachability of languages. *Studies in Second Language Acquisition* 6(2): 186–214.

———. 1989. Is language teachable? Psycholinguistic experiments and hypotheses. *Applied Linguistics* 10(1): 54–79.

Quirk, Randolph. 1990. Language varieties and standard language. *English Today* 6(1): 310.

Ringbom, Hakan. 1987. *The Role of the First Language in Foreign Language Learning*. Clevedon, U.K.: Multilingual Matters.

Robins, R. H. 1966. The development of the word class system of the European grammatical tradition. *Foundations of Language* 2(1): 3–19.

Rutherford, William. 1986. Grammatical theory and L2 acquisition: A brief overview. *Second Language Studies* 2(1): 1–15.

———. 1987. *Second Language Grammar: Learning and Teaching*. London: Longman.

Rutherford, William, and Michael Sharwood Smith, eds. 1988. *Grammar and Second Language Teaching: A Book of Readings*. New York: Newbury House.

Schachter, Jacquelyn. 1990. On the issue of completeness in second language acquisition. *Second Language Research* 6(2): 93–24.

Schmidt, Richard. 1990. The role of consciousness in second language learning. *Applied Linguistics* 11(2): 129–58.

Schumann, John. 1978. *The Pidginization Process*. Rowley, Mass.: Newbury House.

Selinker, Larry. 1972. Interlanguage. *IRAL* 10: 209–31.

———. 1992. *Rediscovering Interlanguage*. London: Longman.

Selinker, Larry, and John Lamendella. 1981. Updating the interlanguage hypothesis. *Studies in Second Language Acquisition* 3(2): 201–20.

Sharwood Smith, M. 1981. Consciousness-raising and the second language learner. *Applied Linguistics* 2: 2, 59–68.

Sledd, James. 1988. Product in process: From ambiguities of standard English to issues that divide us. *College English* 50(2): 168–76.

Spada, Nina. 1986. The interaction between type of contact and type of instruction. *Studies in Second Language Acquisition* 8(2): 181–200.

Swales, John. 1990. *Genre Analysis*. Cambridge: Cambridge University Press.

Thomas, Margaret. 1991. Universal Grammar and the interpretation of reflexives in a second language. *Language* 67(2): 211–39.

Tomlin, Russell, ed. 1987. *Coherence and Grounding in Discourse*. Amsterdam: John Benjamins.

Wall, Robert. 1972. *Introduction to Mathematical Linguistics*. Englewood Cliffs, N.J.: Prentice-Hall.

White, Lydia. 1989. *Universal Grammar in Second Language Acquisition*. Amsterdam: John Benjamins.

Zobl, Helmut. 1989. Canonical typological structures and ergativity in English L2 acquisition. In *Linguistics Perspectives on Second Language Acquisition*, ed. by Susan Gass and Jacquelyn Schachter. Cambridge: Cambridge University Press, 203–21.

SECTION I:
WHAT SORT OF GRAMMAR?

2 Universal Grammar and the learning and teaching of second languages

Vivian Cook

This chapter has the general aim of describing the possible relationships between Universal Grammar and language teaching. It first sketches an overview of the principles and parameters theory of syntax and shows how this relates to the Universal Grammar (UG) model of language acquisition; it then describes some of the issues in applying the UG model to second language learning; it concludes by drawing some implications for language teaching.

Principles and parameters grammar

The Chomskyan UG model of acquisition is based on the theory of syntax known variously as principles and parameters theory or Government/Binding (GB) Theory, named after Chomsky's book *Lectures on Government and Binding* (Chomsky 1981a). The basic concept is that language is knowledge stored in the mind. This knowledge consists of principles that do not vary from one person to another and parameter settings that vary according to the particular language that the person knows. Principles and parameters theory can be approached through an analogy to a video recorder. A recorder needs two elements in order to function: the unchanging equipment itself, which is the same in every set that is sold, and the variable tuning, which has to be set by the user to local circumstances. When a new recorder is switched on, everything may be in working order, but nothing appropriate will show on the screen until the channels have been tuned to the local TV stations. The combination of the two elements of permanent equipment and particular tuning allows the recorder to function in any situation.

The human mind similarly has built-in language 'principles' that are part of its knowledge of *any* language. But it also has 'parameters' within these principles whose values are set to the actual language it learns. The principles are the permanent equipment in all minds; the parameters tune the principles to a particular language or languages. A mind that knows English and one that knows French contain the same language principles; the main difference between them is the different settings for the language parameters.

These principles and parameters are highly abstract and they interact with each other in complex ways. The following discussion tries to illustrate these concepts without technical apparatus; however, behind these simplified descriptions stands a rigorous syntactic theory, outlined, for example, in Cook (1988) and Haegeman (1991), substantially different from theories current before the 1980s, even if it shares certain features with other syntactic theories of the 1980s such as Generalized Phrase Structure Grammar (GPSG) (Gazdar et al. 1985).

A much-discussed example of a principle is the principle of structure-dependency (e.g., Chomsky 1988). This states an obvious but curious fact: In many languages, the structure of questions depends on the structure of the sentence itself rather than on the sequence of words in it. The question:

Is Sam the cat that is black?

is linked to a similar structure to that seen in:

Sam is the cat that is black.

Forming a question involves knowing which of the two examples of *is* can be moved to the beginning of the sentence to get the grammatical sentence:

   Is Sam the cat that is black?

instead of:

* Is Sam is the cat that black?

The speaker of English knows that the *is* in the main clause must be moved rather than the *is* in the relative clause. The ability to form English questions therefore relies on the speaker's ability to tell the subordinate clause from the main clause. English questions always depend on knowledge of the structure of the sentence: They are structure-dependent.

Yet there is no real reason why questions should involve a knowledge of structure in this way. Many other ways of forming questions can be imagined which depend on the sheer sequence of words in the sentence rather than on its hierarchical structure – say, reversing the order of words or moving only the second word. Such alternatives are logically possible and are indeed carried out by computers with ease. But they do not occur in human languages. The mind knows that, in order to form a question by movement, it must rely on the *phrase structure* of the sentence instead of the sheer sequence of words. This applies not just to questions but to all other constructions in which movement occurs in the sentence, such as passives. All speakers of English know structure-dependency without having given it a moment's thought; they automatically reject *Is Sam is the the cat that black?* even if they have never encountered its like before. How do they have this instant response? They would accept many sentences that they have never previously encountered, so it is not just that they have never heard it before. Nor is structure-dependency transparent from the normal language they have encountered – only by concocting sentences that deliberately breach it can linguists show its very existence. Structure-dependency is, then, a principle of language knowledge built-in to the human mind. It becomes part of any language that is learnt, not just of English. Principles and parameters theory claims that an important component in the speaker's knowledge of any language such as English is made up of a handful of general language principles such as structure-dependency.

Let us now look at some parameters. In English, declarative sentences must have grammatical subjects, such as *he, it* and *there* in the following sentences:

He's going home.
It's raining.
There's a book on the table.

In Spanish, subjects are not needed in the equivalent sentences:

Va a casa.
Llueve.
Hay un libro en la mesa.

This difference is due to the 'pro-drop' parameter. Some languages, such as Spanish, Italian, Chinese and Arabic, permit sentences without subjects, and are called 'pro-drop' languages. Other languages, which include English, French and German, do not permit sentences without subjects, and are called 'non-pro-drop'. All languages fall into one or other of these groups. The pro-drop parameter therefore has two values or 'settings' – pro-drop or non-pro-drop. Any mind that knows a language has set the pro-drop parameter to one or other of these two values. A person who knows English knows the same principles and parameters as a person who knows Spanish but has set the value of the pro-drop parameter differently.

Another recently studied parameter distinguishes English from French. In English, it is possible to say:

John often drinks wine.

but not:

John drinks often wine.

However, in French the reverse is true in that it is possible to say:

Jean boit souvent du vin.

but not:

* Jean souvent boit du vin.

In other words, in English the adverb *often* precedes the verb; in French it follows it. English also permits:

John does not drink wine.

where the negative element *not* precedes the main verb *drink* rather than:

* John drinks not wine.

In French, however, it is correct to say:

Jean ne boit pas du vin.

The negative *pas* follows the main verb instead of preceding it; the other negative element *ne* indeed precedes the verb but is often left out in colloquial speech. Furthermore, English speakers say:

The workers all drink wine.

with the 'quantifier' *all* preceding the verb, but French speakers say:

Les ouvriers boivent tous du vin.

with *tous* following the verb.

These consistent differences over the elements that may follow or precede the verb can be accounted for by a further parameter called 'opacity' (Pollock 1989); in French certain grammatical elements must occur after the verb, in English before it. A French-speaking person has set the parameter so that these elements must *follow* the verb; an English-speaking person has set it so that these elements must *precede* the verb. They have tuned the parameter in different ways. The two languages differ in a single overall factor that affects all these constructions – the opacity parameter – rather than in terms of rules about the position of adverbs, negative elements and quantifiers like *all*.

The speaker, of course, knows many other aspects of language as well as principles and parameters. Knowledge of vocabulary is especially important to principles and parameters theory. A person who knows the verb *faint* knows not only its meaning but also how it is used in sentences: *Faint* usually has an animate subject in front of it but no grammatical object after it. So it is possible to find:

Peter fainted.

but not:

* The rock fainted.

where the subject is inanimate, or:

* Peter fainted Mary.

with a grammatical object. Knowledge of words is closely tied in to the syntax; the native speaker has learnt how words behave in sentences as well as what they mean. Many of the complexities of a language are now seen as having more to do with how particular words are used than with syntax. An extreme version of this position is Chomsky's controversial claim that syntax is innate but vocabulary is learnt: 'there is only one human language, apart from the lexicon, and language acquisition is in essence a matter of determining lexical idiosyncrasies' (1989: 44).

Grammar in the principles and parameters theory is concerned with the fundamental aspects of language knowledge – those aspects that are built-in to the mind and that vary within closely definable limits. This 'core' grammar is what distinguishes human language from animal or computer communication. Principles and parameters theory makes proposals chiefly about these 'core' areas; it has little or nothing to say about 'peripheral' areas outside their scope. Hence much of the everyday grammar speakers use and need is beneath its notice.

This chapter has outlined one principle and two parameters to give some idea of how the theory works. While there is considerably more to it than this, the complexity arises more from the way in which the various principles and parameters interact with each other than from their sheer number. The overview of the whole theory given in Cook (1988), for instance, makes use of about seven principles and five parameters.

The powerful type of description made available through principles and parameters theory has shed new light upon many aspects of grammar. The pro-drop or opacity parameters, for instance, are intriguing and novel ways of capturing the differences between English and Spanish, and French and English, or indeed many other pairs of languages. Actual syntactic descriptions in terms of principles and parameters have potential uses in syllabuses for language teaching and in teaching exercises. The syllabus for teaching French to English people can now include the crucial opacity difference between the two languages; teaching exercises could be devised that unify the teaching of such formerly disparate constructions as the positions of negation, adverbs, and quantifiers; students could be guided to understand such phenomena through 'language awareness' (Hawkins 1984) and 'sensitization' via the L1 (Riley 1985), or through 'consciousness-raising' in the L2 (Rutherford 1987).

Hence any teaching program that utilises syntax has a new and rich source of ideas to call upon. Syllabus design has by and large depended upon views of grammar no longer current in linguistics, primarily those of 'structuralist' grammar. Principles and parameters syntax is only one among the contemporary theories of syntax that are crying out to be applied; others are described in the later chapters of this volume and in Cook (1989). Syllabuses that fail to take on board current versions of syntax are ignoring information that may be extremely valuable. It would be a shame if language teaching is cut off from exciting developments in syntax because teachers see them as too difficult or too remote from their interest. As we have seen, at one level they can provide information about almost every sentence their students may want to say, whether concerning questions, the presence or absence of subjects, or the position of adverbs before or after the verb.

The Universal Grammar model of language acquisition

The principles and parameters theory may be utilised as a theory in its own right for the syntactic insights that it provides. However, its main function is within the Universal Grammar (UG) model of language acquisition. This claims that principles of language do not need to be learnt as they are already built into the mind. No child needs to learn structure-dependency because he or she already knows it in some sense; it is literally inconceivable for a human mind to know language in a structure-independent way. The same applies to all the other principles of language.

Naturally, the precise way in which principles apply depends upon the particular language involved. Japanese, for example, does not form questions by movement but uses question markers within the sentence. For instance in the sentence:

Kimi wa kono hon o yomimashito ka
you   this book   read (Have you read this book?)

the question marker *ka* at the end of the sentence signals that it is a question. So the arguments about structure-dependency employed so far do not apply to Japanese questions. However, the critical aspect for UG is that Japanese questions do not *break* this principle; they simply do not *need* it. To disprove structure-dependency would take a language that breaks the principle rather than ignores it. So far none has been found: All languages meet structure-dependency.

While the parameters themselves are also built into the mind, their values need to be set; the channels need to be tuned. Parameters are like electric switches that are moved to one position or the other. A child learning English needs to move the switches to non-pro-drop; a child learning Spanish to move the switch to pro-drop; a child learning French to move the opacity switch one way, a child learning English the other. Learning comes down to the setting of values for the parameters – to moving the switches. Learning English means setting all the values for UG parameters to those for English, learning French to those for French, and so on. This raises several issues:

What is the initial setting for a parameter?   In other words, what is the position of the switch to start with? It might be that a child starts from a neutral parameter setting and then adopts one or other of the possibilities – that the switch is initially in the middle instead of one way or the other.

neutral initial setting ⌐⟶ setting A (pro-drop)
                        └⟶ setting B (non-pro-drop)

A child learning English would start with a neutral setting for pro-drop and change it to non-pro-drop; a child learning Spanish would start from the same neutral setting and change it to pro-drop.

Or it might be that the switch starts in one or other of the two positions and has to be reset to the other position when necessary. In this case the parameter has a default value, called the *unmarked* setting, that children will retain unless something makes them change it to the nondefault value, or *marked* setting, of the parameter.

unmarked setting ⟶ marked setting (if necessary)

The unmarked setting therefore is used unless children encounter evidence to the contrary.

To settle this means investigating which is the first setting that children use. If children have a neutral setting to begin with, they will learn, say, English or Spanish with equal facility. If one or other of the two settings is an unmarked default setting, all children start with this, but some children, such as those learning English, will have to switch away from it. Hyams (1986) claims that young English children often produce sentences without subjects, such as *Want more bubbles* or *Now wash my hands,* and gradually learn that the subject is compulsory. They are initially treating English as if it were a pro-drop language like Spanish. So pro-drop seems to be the unmarked setting from which all children start, non-pro-drop the marked setting.

pro-drop setting (unmarked) ⟶ non-pro-drop setting (marked)

English children have to change the setting to non-pro-drop so that in due course they consistently produce sentences with subjects. Spanish children need to do nothing as the parameter is already set to the right value. There is, however, some controversy over Hyams' position; Hulk

(1987), for example, shows that French children do not have a pro-drop stage like the one found by Hyams in English children.

What changes the value for a parameter?   Children have to hear sentences that tell them which way to set a parameter; in other words they need some language evidence to find out the correct value. Often this evidence is fairly obvious; the child only needs a few sentences such as:

Mummy is phoning Daddy.

to know that English has Subject Verb Object order, a few sentences such as:

Hanako wa tegami o kaita
Hanako   letter   wrote (Hanako wrote a letter)

to know that Japanese has Subject Object Verb order.

Sometimes the vital clue may be more subtle. Hyams (1986) believes that the crucial evidence for setting the pro-drop parameter consists of sentences with 'dummy' subjects such as *it* and *there* as in

It's snowing.

or

There's a fly in my soup.

Such 'dummy' subjects are the giveaway that English is a non-pro-drop language as they are not found in pro-drop languages.

The evidence that the child encounters can be of two types: *positive* evidence of what actually occurs, and *negative* evidence of what does not occur (Chomsky 1981a). The dummy subject English sentences with *there* and *it* illustrate how the pro-drop parameter is set from positive evidence that the child actually hears. Negative evidence consists of two subtypes. One subtype is correction by people who tell the child what *not* to do:

No, we do not say 'is phoning', we say 'he is phoning'.

The other subtype is the *absence* of certain constructions from the input the child encounters; it might be that the fact the child never hears sentences without subjects in English tells him or her that English is non-pro-drop. To make an analogy, you could learn the rules of snooker simply by watching other people play – positive evidence – or you could learn by actually playing with someone and making mistakes that are corrected by other players – negative evidence.

Linguists have been reluctant to give negative evidence a large role in first language acquisition. On the one hand, parents hardly ever seem to make the right kinds of correction of their offspring; on the other, hearing what actually occurs is insufficient to tell them what can *not* occur,

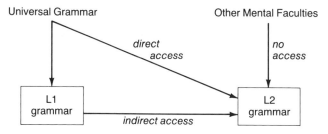

Figure 1   Access to UG in L2 learning.

as it does not distinguish between things which they have not heard because they are impossible and those they have not heard by sheer chance. Positive evidence of actual sentences the child hears has to suffice for language acquisition since it is the only type that can be guaranteed for any child in any situation.

Do the principles and parameters change as the child develops?   So far the child's mind has been described as if it were static and unchanging. But it might be that the child's mind develops over time; rather than all the principles and parameters being present from the beginning, they come into play at particular stages of development. The fact that English children initially produce sentences without subjects may not reflect their particular setting for the parameter, but indicate that the parameter itself has yet to develop in their minds. Various proposals have been put forward for 'growth models' of acquisition in which the UG properties themselves 'grow' in the mind over time (Borer and Wexler 1987). For instance, the lack of inflections such as possessive -*s* from early children's speech coupled with the lack of modal auxiliaries like *can,* tense forms like -*ed,* and other 'functional' parts of the sentence (Radford 1986, 1990) may show that certain types of phrase are not yet present in the children's minds; the reason for the comparatively crude structure of the child's sentences may be because part of the language faculty in the mind has not yet come into play.

Access to UG in second language learning

How can the UG model be related to the learning of languages other than the first? The usual demurral has to be made that, in L2 learning as in L1 acquisition, UG is only concerned with the central aspects of grammar. The main interest for L2 learning has been in the role that UG plays in L2 learning. This can be diagrammed as the three possible relationships given in Figure 1.

In a *no-access* model L2 learners acquire the L2 grammar without consulting the UG in their minds; the grammar is learnt through other mental faculties. In a *direct-access* model L2 learners acquire the L2 in exactly the same way as L1 learners by using UG; they set values for parameters according to the L2 evidence they encounter. In an *indirect-access* model L2 learners have access to UG through what they know of the L1, but they start with the parameters in their L1 setting instead of in their original state.

Controversy still reigns over the choice between these alternatives. Let us start with some of the general arguments for the no-access position, which claims that L2 learning makes use of other attributes of the mind than UG.

- While L2 learners show some effects of UG, they do not use it as consistently as L1 natives (Bley-Vroman, Felix and Ioup 1988); hence some other factor than UG must be involved.
- The knowledge of L2 learners is not as complete as that of L1 learners and they are not as successful (Schachter 1988; Bley-Vroman 1989), so UG is not centrally involved.
- Children manage to learn any L1 with equal ease; some languages are clearly much more difficult for L2 learners than others, for instance Chinese versus Italian for speakers of English (Schachter 1988); therefore UG is not available.
- L2 learners become 'fossilised' at some stage rather than progressing inevitably to full native competence, hence UG is not involved (Schachter 1988).

These arguments against UG involvement in L2 learning are valid insofar as they are based on evidence from areas that are the proper concern of the UG model. If the learner breaks principles of language or has impossible values for parameters, the UG position is discomfited. To make these arguments for no-access pertinent, it would have to be shown that these core areas were different in L2 learning. Yet, by and large, little of the evidence cited by these writers for these general arguments tackles principles and parameters issues. Claims that L2 learners know less of their L2 than their L1 are certainly true in a general sense, with some demurrals to be made later; but little of the research shows that learners know less of core UG grammar. If L2 learners knew principles partially, or if L2s differed in difficulty so far as central UG areas are concerned, or if principles and parameters were 'fossilised' in some way, the arguments would have some weight. So far, however, no clear evidence has been produced that L2 learners do not conform to a principles and parameters system; they are, for example, no more likely than children to use syntactic movement that does not depend on structure. L2 learners seem confined by the same UG as L1 learners; their grammars form 'normal' human languages.

More interesting are arguments that attack the availability of UG on its own ground, that is to say, by dealing with areas of core syntax. A further principle of grammar called subjacency needs to be introduced to illustrate this point. Sentences involving *wh*-words such as *who* and *what* are regarded as being derived from other structures via '*wh*-movement'. So:

Who did he say that John liked?

is based originally on an underlying structure similar to:

He said that John liked who?

But in English it is ungrammatical to say:

* *The task which I didn't know to whom they would entrust.*

although this sentence is derived from an underlying structure similar to that of the grammatical sentence:

I didn't know to whom they would entrust the task.

Why does *wh*-movement not work in this case? The reason is that the items must not be moved across too many 'barriers' in the sentence; the principle of subjacency says that an item can move across one such barrier but not across more.

Research with subjacency by Bley-Vroman, Felix and Ioup (1988) tested whether L2 learners who spoke an L1 that did not have subjacency showed signs of having acquired it in English; if they did, this would show that their UG was still available. While a group of Korean learners of English indeed turned out to recognise subjacency, they were not so successful as natives. So UG could be only partially available. Schachter (1989) performed an experiment with a similar logic on L2 learners of English with Chinese, Korean and Indonesian as L1s; she gave the learners both a syntax test to see if they knew the structure involved and a subjacency test. The aim was to see whether those who knew the syntax automatically knew subjacency as well. There are several problems with the methodology and statistics of this experiment. However, Schachter argues that UG is unavailable to L2 learners since they were not using the principle for structures they already knew, that is to say, those who passed the syntax test did not necessarily pass the subjacency test.

Both experiments come up against the problem of the psychological processing of a second language. L2 learners are known to have slower and less efficient cognitive functioning in the L2 than in the L1 in almost every respect, as reviewed for example in Cook (1991b). Such a 'cognitive deficit' in processing is one possible explanation for subjacency results such as those by Bley-Vroman, Felix and Ioup (1988); L2 learners are less than perfect because their processing in the L2 is less effective. Similarly Schachter (1989) compared sentence type X for the syntax task and sentence type X+movement for the subjacency test. The additional memory load that movement places on processing might easily provide a reason for the fall-off rather than subjacency itself. Several psychological and computer theories of syntactic parsing have indeed been developed to account for the memory load imposed on the comprehension processes by movement (Wanner and Maratsos 1978; Marcus 1980).

Another aspect of movement in the sentence has also been put forward as a proof of no-access. Clahsen and Muysken (1986) compared the learning of German word order by native children and foreign adults using many published studies. German has a Subject Object Verb (SOV) word order in subordinate clauses such as:

Ich sage, dass ich dich liebe. (I say that I you love.)

but a word order in the main clause in which the verb comes second, that is, an SVO order:

Ich liebe dich. (I love you.)

It is also possible to have OVS:

Dich liebe ich. (You love I.)

and Adverb VS:

Immer liebe ich dich. (Always love I you.)

Many linguists treat the SOV order as the norm, and derive the orders found in the main clause from it by moving the verb into second position. Clahsen and Muysken (1986) found that L1 children learning German first of all prefer to put verbs at the end of the sentence, although they have some in other positions; gradually they learn to move verbs with tense forms to second position; when subordinate clauses begin to appear in their speech, the verb comes in final position without any mistakes.

Adult L2 learners of German start with a fixed SVO order, then learn how to put Adverbials at the beginning of the sentence (i.e., Adverbial SV) before moving some particles to the end of the sentence and putting the verb second (i.e., Adverbial VS). Finally, they learn subordinate clauses with the correct SOV order. So, while L1 children start with SOV and gradually learn the verb second position (SVO), adults start with SVO and gradually learn when the verb is final (SOV). This leads Clahsen and Muysken (1986) to suggest that:

by fixing on an initial assumption of SVO order, and then elaborating a series of complicated rules to patch up this hypothesis when confronted with conflicting data, the L2 learners are not only creating a rule system which is far more complicated than the native system, but also one which is not definable in linguistic theory. (p. 116)

In later work Clahsen and Muysken (1989) suggest that L2 learners are still constrained by the principles of UG in some ways, but cannot set parameters as all the values have already been set for the L1; adult L2 acquisition is 'language acquisition without access to parameter setting'.

This claim for differences between L1 and L2 learners of German is scarcely by itself sufficient to disprove access to UG by all L2 learners for all aspects of syntax. Even accepting the Clahsen and Muysken stages as correct, other differences between the L1 children and the L2 adults may explain them. For instance, adult learners have a larger memory-processing capacity than children; for this reason children may start by not distinguishing subordinate from main clauses, and so use the verb-final forms interchangeably with the verb-second forms. Alternatively, adults may start by knowing from their L1 that subordinate clauses exist and have sufficient processing capacity to use them; the adult SVO starting point may be a handicap compared to the children's initial flexibility between verb-final and verb-second positions. The differences apparent between L1 children and L2 adults may not be caused by lack of access to UG by adults but by the fact that adults have already learnt one language and already possess mature cognitive systems; they necessarily have a different starting point for language acquisition, whatever the access to UG may be.

The principles and parameters theory is also changing rapidly in the areas of both subjacency and word order. For some time it has been claimed that subjacency includes a parameter which permits variation in the definition of the appropriate barriers to movement (Chomsky 1981b; Sportiche 1981; Rizzi 1982). The ungrammatical English phrase:

* The task which I didn't know to whom they would entrust.

is perfectly acceptable in Italian:

L'incarico che non sapevo a chi avrebbero affidato.

One barrier to movement that exists in English is not present in Italian. It is therefore hard to interpret research such as that of Schachter (1989) and Bley-Vroman, Felix and Ioup (1988) as their syntactic analysis allows for no variation between languages. White (1988, 1989) has carried out research with L2 learners with L1s that reflect this difference in parameter setting and has indeed found they have difficulties with subjacency in English.

The analysis of word order in German is also far from fixed in the form given by Clahsen and Muysken (1986). DuPlessis et al. (1987) provide an alternative analysis, based on current trends in the theory, which bases German word order on the interaction of three parameters; they argue that this accounts for the apparent peculiarity of the L2 learners' developmental order in German, and they produce supporting data from an experiment of their own. The case for no-access can be regarded at best as nonproven, at worst as irrelevant to the actual claims that the UG model is advancing.

UG and L2 acquisition

The choice is therefore between direct and indirect access to UG in L2 learning. The same questions that were outlined under L1 acquisition will be looked at with reference to L2 learning before developing a specific notion of L2 learning.

What are the initial L2 parameter settings?   This question has been the acid test between direct- and indirect-access models. If direct access is correct, L2 learners would start with the same values for parameters as L1 children and would set each parameter from scratch. If indirect access is correct, the starting point for L2 learners is the values of their first languages, which may or may not be the unmarked settings for L1 acquisition. They would have to reset those that were different in the L2, perhaps back to the unmarked value.

Evidence about initial settings for parameters is reviewed in White (1989). So far as pro-drop is concerned, French learners of English differ from Spanish learners in judgements about sentences without subjects (White 1986); the difficulty is that this does not apply to all the effects of the pro-drop parameter, an argument used by Bley-Vroman (1989) as support for the no-access model. Intermediate French learners accepted ungrammatical English sentences that go against the English setting for subjacency but that conform to the setting for French (White 1988), thus showing that the French setting was still present in their knowledge of English. Such results seem to exclude both the possibility that the initial L2 parameter setting is neutral and the possibility that there is a uniform initial setting. On this view L2 learning is unlike the acquisition of the first language because parameters already have a value – the switch is already in one position. To phrase this in terms of markedness, discussed earlier, this L1 value might be the same as the initial unmarked value (e.g., the pro-drop setting for Spanish children), or it might be the marked value learnt from positive evidence (e.g., the non-pro-drop setting for English children), depending on which L1 the learner speaks.

There may, however, be a problem of direction; a person going from an L1 that has the unmarked value, say the Spanish pro-drop value, to an L2 that has a marked value, say the English non-pro-drop value, may find it easier than someone going from marked to unmarked. An analogy can be made to cookery; once you've boiled an egg, it's too late to decide you wanted to have fried egg, as you can't return the egg to its original state. Revoking an initial parameter setting from marked to unmarked may involve similar problems. Nevertheless, Liceras (1989) found English and French L2 learners had little difficulty with subjectless Spanish sentences, despite the fact they were going from apparently marked to unmarked values of the pro-drop parameter.

What changes the L2 value for a parameter?   The issue of evidence is rather trickier for L2 learning than for L1 acquisition. In L1 acquisition the argument that only positive evidence is necessary is based eventually on the fact that all children learn language, but not all children get negative evidence; variation in the type of evidence cannot matter: The researcher looks for the lowest common denominator in the types of evidence available to the child. In L2 learning, very few learners master the L2 to the same extent that they master their L1. They also encounter a greater range of situations than the child does; in classroom situations, language itself will be the focus of the situation, which it seldom is in the L1.

The causes of this apparent deficiency have long been the subject of debate. One possibility is that the type of evidence is more crucial in L2 learning than in L1 acquisition; classrooms can be considered ways of optimising the evidence available to the learners; the varieties of evidence available to the L2 learner include many possibilities not available in the L1, whether habit-based structure drills, grammatical explanation, or controlled communication games. All or any of these may give the learner reasons for changing a parameter setting, which are unavailable in L1 learning. L2 learning research has to go beyond the logical problem of which types of evidence are available to the learner to the empirical question of which type is best for the learner.

The other possible cause of L2 deficiency is bound up with the concept of marked and unmarked parameter settings. Let us assume that L1 learners start from unmarked values which they reset, if necessary, from positive evidence. What happens in the L2 if they have to reset from a marked value to an unmarked value? According to a principle of learning known as the Subset Principle, often now used to complement the UG model, this is impossible from positive evidence (Wexler and Manzini 1987). Once learners have made too 'large' a guess, they cannot jump back to a 'smaller' guess as the positive evidence will never show this is necessary. If L2 learners are to be able to shift in this way, they will have to encounter evidence of different kinds that may be unnecessary in L1 learning.

Do the principles and parameters change as the L2 learner learns?   The access to UG might depend upon the learner's age. On the one hand, the development of the L2 in children might be in step with the development of the L1; accepting a growth model, if a principle or parameter has not become available to them in the first language, it is presumably not available to them in the second. Or there might be a delay between the UG property manifesting itself in the L1 and the L2. No evidence seems to be available on this issue.

On the other hand, the choice between the three models of access to UG might depend on the age of the learner. The Critical Period Hypothesis claimed that, for one reason or another, the ability to learn language in the normal fashion disappears after about the early teens (Lenneberg 1967). Again no real evidence on issues relevant to UG is available. In general the decline of L2 learning ability with age has been less well supported by researchers in recent years, often now turning into a contrast between short-term gains by adults and long-term gains by children (Long 1990), though there are certain methodological problems with the research base for this distinction (Cook 1986). The account of age effects by Singleton (1989: 266) sums this up in the statement:

> The one interpretation of the evidence which does not appear to run into contradictory data is that in naturalistic situations those whose exposure to a second language begins in childhood in general eventually surpass those whose exposure begins in adulthood, even though the latter usually show some initial advantage over the former.

Inasmuch as this is related to UG, it suggests that UG is more accessible in younger children. De Houwer (1990) indeed shows that a small girl in Belgium learnt both English and Dutch as if she were learning two languages independently.

Let us assume for present purposes that the L2 learner has finished developing and so possesses the mature adult grammar of the first language. The difference between growth and nongrowth theories does not apply to L2 learning as the learner already possesses UG in its entirety, whether present from birth or developed over time. The same is true for the distinction between acquisition and development. The learner's language will not be affected to the same degree by physical or cognitive development, for good or for ill, since this has already taken place.

Multicompetence

The last section represented a reasonably consensus view of L2 learning. The present section develops ideas of my own that take the L2 ideas in a particular direction (Cook 1991a, 1992). So far the starting point of the acquisition argument has been taken to be the acquisition of one language – the first; the point of UG is how a mind comes to acquire a grammar of *one* language in the form of the language principles and the values for parameters. But L2 learning is predicated on the fact that the mind can learn *two* grammars, both obeying the same principles but having different settings for parameters, even if the L2 grammars are rarely as 'full' as those of monolinguals. In terms of statistics, there are probably more minds in the world that contain more than one grammar than there are pure monolinguals. It has been argued that the choice of the monolingual's knowledge of language as the primary object of linguistic study is a justifiable idealisation:

> We exclude, for example, a speech community of uniform speakers, each of whom speaks a mixture of Russian and French (say, an idealized version of the nineteenth-century Russian aristocracy). The language of such a speech community would not be 'pure' in the relevant sense, because it would not represent a single set of choices among the options permitted by UG but rather would include 'contradictory' choices for certain of these options. (Chomsky 1986: 17)

However, this idealisation may state the problem of acquisition in the wrong terms. Putting acquisition in terms of how the mind comes to learn a grammar with particular parameter settings implies a fixedness and permanency about the settings: The output of language acquisition is the finished grammar with all its settings fixed. L2 learning is a matter of resetting these to produce a new grammar. If the mind is seen as potentially knowing more than one grammar from the outset, each parameter can have two settings; the mind switches from one to the other more or less from moment to moment. The foundation of the theory has to be this ability to know two settings simultaneously. Starting from the monolingual person commits the theory to a particular fixed architecture of the mind with the switches permanently set. The model has to recognise that minds with more than one setting for a parameter are the norm instead of the exception.

The state of the mind with two languages has been termed 'multicompetence', that is to say, 'the compound state of a mind with two grammars' (Cook 1991a). The mind of the person who knows two languages should be taken as a whole rather than as equivalent to two minds that know one language each. The problem of language acquisition is how one mind acquires one *or more* grammars from input. This can be seen either as *separatist* multicompetence, in which the two languages are effectively separate, or as *wholistic* multicompetence, in which they form a total system at one level or another. The evidence that the two languages can form a single system in the mind comes from many sources and is documented in Cook (1992): In terms of the lexicon, Beauvillain and Grainger (1987) showed that French/English bilinguals had access to both meanings of a word *coin* (English *piece of money* versus French *corner*); in terms of phonological processing, Altenberg and Cairns

(1983) found L2 users differed from monolinguals in their assessment of nonwords such as *gurch,* showing 'both sets of constraints are simultaneously available to the bilingual during processing'. Hence the argument for the no-access model that L2 learners have different grammars from L1 learners is beside the point; the total system of the L2 user is involved, and it is hardly surprising if that part of it dealing with the L2 is different from an L1 grammar known in isolation.

UG and language teaching

The usual qualifications on the scope of UG must be made when discussing language teaching. UG is concerned with knowledge of language in the human mind. It has nothing to say about how language is used and little to say about how it is processed. Language teachers must look elsewhere for ideas about communicative competence, pragmatic competence, or listening and speaking 'skills'. UG is concerned with core areas of language knowledge expressed as principles and parameters, not with numerous areas of syntax that teachers have to deal with every day. It is unlikely that any overall teaching methodology could be based on UG, if only for this reason.

UG is concerned by definition with 'obvious' things about language. Ideas like structure-dependency are built into the mind; they are not mentioned in typical grammar books for a language, because it can be taken for granted that all readers know them. They are not learnt, so do not need to be taught. Parameters too are so broad and 'obvious' that little is needed to set them off. As Chomsky has pointed out, a single sentence such as *John ate an apple* can set the values for the major word-order parameters in English (Chomsky 1988). It is not surprising that most principles and parameters are not mentioned in syllabuses for language teaching as there is no real need to state knowledge that is automatically part of the mind, if the no-access model is wrong.

Parameter setting in a second language may be a less simple matter than in a first, partly because of the already existing settings for the L1. In the indirect-access model the learner may be trying to go from a setting that is not a possible setting in the L1 and, like the old saying, *You can't get there from here,* the difficulty of resetting a parameter from some positions may be greater than from others. The learner may also be more restricted in processing capacity in the second language and so unable to cope adequately with demands of processing the L2. As we have seen, L1 learning is believed to need only positive evidence, while L2 learning may utilise a variety of other types of evidence.

One consequence for teaching is that concentrated examples of sentences showing the effects of a particular parameter could be helpful. In first language acquisition, for instance, Cromer (1987) showed that exposure to ten sentences with *easy/eager to please* constructions every three months was enough to teach children the difference between these two constructions. One perspective on language teaching is to see it as provision of concentrated language examples in this way and to deliberately provide evidence appropriate for setting particular parameters; English learners of French, for instance, might be given a range of sentences using the nonopaque position for negative *pas,* adverbial *souvent* and quantifier *tous.*

A further consequence for the language input provided to students for language teaching is the claim by Morgan (1986) that 'bracketing' is necessary for acquisition of some structures. Suppose a learner does not know whether a language is Subject Object Verb or Object Subject Verb; given sentences such as *The woman the man likes,* how does the learner discover that it means that the woman likes the man (SOV) rather than the man likes the woman (OSV)? Only, according to Morgan, if something in the input 'brackets' the structure of the sentence so that the learner effectively hears *The man [the woman likes]* with the Subject clearly separated from the Verb Phrase by some form of signal, shown here as square brackets. Morgan demonstrates that certain aspects of syntax may be unlearnable if the input does not have clear clues to its phrase structure. This may be done phonologically by the intonation pattern or by the length of vowel; the division of the sentence into two tone-groups separating Subject from the rest is one way of exploiting an existing resource in English to achieve this end. Again, L2 teaching could deliberately exploit this process by exaggerating such 'bracketting' intonation or increasing its frequency. If L2 learning needs different types of evidence, a systematic presentation of the evidence necessary for setting a parameter could be useful, whether in the form of concentrated doses of particular sentences or of amplified bracketting. Once the step has been taken to admit other forms of evidence in L2 learning, the door is open to facilitating the process via 'super-evidence'. In a parameter-setting model the chief role of teaching is to provide language evidence that can trigger the setting of parameters in the learners' minds, by whatever means.

The other main implication, curiously enough, concerns vocabulary. Current UG theory minimises the acquisition of syntax, maximises the acquisition of vocabulary items with lexical entries for their privileges of occurrence and so on. Teaching again may be most effective when it builds up this mental dictionary in the student's mind. L2 learners need to spend comparatively little effort on core grammatical structure of the type covered by UG, since it results from the setting of a handful of parameters. They do, however, need to acquire an immense amount of detail about how individual words are used in grammatical structures.

This represents vocabulary learning of a particular type, not only learning the dictionary meaning of words or pronunciation, but also learning how they behave in sentences. It is not just a matter of the L2 learner of English learning the syntax, function and meaning of *Cats like milk;* it is learning that in English the Verb *like* needs to be followed by a grammatical object and preceded by an animate subject – in other words, what can be called a syntactic view of vocabulary. Some idea of the scale and importance of this task can be found in work by Gross (1990), who found 12,000 'simple' verbs in French of which no two could be used in exactly the same way in sentences. Vocabulary may indeed be due for a revival in language teaching, not just through the traditional technique of frequency of usage, but through ideas of syntactic specification of lexical items inter alia.

Above all, the UG view is important for language teaching because of its view of language as knowledge in the mind. Cook (1990) drew some implications for the classroom of the distinction between I-language and E-language approaches to linguistics introduced by Chomsky (1986). External (E) language is concerned with language as a social reality – with people's relations with each other; the main function of language is communication; children learn language by working out the regularities in a sample of speech and by relating to other people. In this view, language teaching means providing sufficient data for students to work out regularities, and opportunities for them to relate to each other so that they will learn to communicate with other people. Internal (I) language is concerned with language as psychological reality in the mind of a single speaker. It stresses the many functions of language, both inside the mind and out; children acquire language by applying the internal structure of their minds to the speech they hear. In this view, language teaching is enabling the student to construct knowledge in his or her mind from language evidence, which can then be used for any purpose the learner likes. Recent developments in language teaching are beginning to balance the 'communicative' approaches concerned more with E-language with goals that are I-language in orientation; for example, the National Criteria for Modern Language Teaching in the UK include 'To develop an awareness of the nature of language and language learning' and 'To develop the pupils' understanding of themselves and their own culture'.

The concept of multicompetence also has consequences for teaching. At the level of goals, it suggests that teaching should not produce ersatz native speakers so much as people who can stand between two languages and interpret one to the other – what Byram (1990) calls 'intercultural communicative competence'. At the level of syllabus, it points up the fact that it is not enough to describe the target the learner is aiming at in terms of what native speakers do when talking to other native speakers; what is needed instead is the description of how fluent L2 users behave using both their L2 and their L1. Such a syllabus already exists for Languages for International Purposes designed by the Institute of Linguists (1988). A beginner's task may be reading an L2 travel brochure or listening to L2 answer-phone messages to get information that can be used in the L1. An advanced learner might have to research a topic through reading and conducting interviews in order to write an L1 report. In this international use, the L2 learner is always the mediator between two cultures, never operating solely in one language or the other, but balanced between the two.

Let us summarise some of the overall implications of the UG model for language teaching. UG is concerned with the core area of language acquisition; its very centrality means that it can be taken for granted and much of it does not need to be taken into account in language teaching, which has other more pressing concerns. Nevertheless, at the practical level, the UG model suggests that more attention is paid by teachers to the nature of the language input offered the students and to the teaching of specifically syntactic aspects of vocabulary acquisition. At a more general level, the UG model is a reminder of the cognitive nature of language: L2 learning is the creation of language knowledge in the mind as well as the creation of the ability to interact with other people.

Summary

The opening section sketches the principles and parameters model of Universal Grammar, otherwise known as Government/Binding theory, illustrating it from the syntactic examples of the two-valued parameter for the opacity of INFL that separates English from French (*John likes often whisky* and *John likes not whisky* are ungrammatical in English but not French) and the multivalued governing category parameter that decides whether noun phrases such as *John* and *himself* may corefer in sentences such as *John asked Peter to help himself* or *John reported Peter's criticisms of himself*. This model of syntax is then related to the parameter-setting model of Universal Grammar, considering in particular the evidence that is necessary for the learner to set parameters, illustrated from the Subset Principle applying to multivalued parameters.

The main body of the paper looks at the relationship of the model to L2 learning.

- *The syntactic basis.* Research into the acquisition of syntax needs a base in syntactic description. The GB theory at this level works as a syntactic model of an Internal-language type which can be used for studying L2 learning separately from the UG theory, as can be illustrated from recent L2 research.
- *The nature of the evidence available to the L2 learner.* A central argument for UG in L1 acquisition is the unavailability of types of negative evidence for the

child. In L2 learning, while the same argument applied logically, clearly the more valid question is not whether negative evidence occurs, but whether, if it occurred, it would be beneficial.

- *Access to UG.* A frequent topic in L2 discussion is what kind of access the learner has to UG. One possibility, advocated by Bley-Vroman and others, is that UG is no longer accessible; a second possibility is that UG is still directly accessible and hence L2 learning is just like L1 learning; the third, advocated by White inter alia, is that L2 learning is heavily influenced by the parameter values set in the L1.
- *The methodology of research.* UG, being an Internal-language theory of competence, relies for its support on the poverty-of-the-stimulus argument rather than on empirical data from language development. The search for valid types of data is tricky and full of pitfalls, whether observational studies, or grammaticality judgements or experiments.
- *Multicompetence.* A current position that is presented briefly is the version of UG termed 'multicompetence'. This claims that the normal state of the mind is to have more than one grammar and hence potentially more than one setting for each parameter.

The final section discusses the implications for second language and foreign language teaching, concentrating on:

- *Teaching as the provision of input.* The nature of the evidence that the learner receives is manipulable in L2 learning by the teacher in ways that it is not in L1 acquisition. UG theory emphasises the role of the teacher as provider of input.
- *The importance of vocabulary.* Current UG theory minimises the acquisition of syntax, maximises the acquisition of vocabulary items with lexical entries for their privileges of occurrence, etc. Teaching again may be seen as most effectively building up this mental lexicon in the student.
- *The role of 'core grammar'.* UG only operates within a carefully circumscribed domain of core syntax. Its claims are less and less relevant as idiosyncratic peripheral syntax is involved and as components of language are concerned outside syntax. Hence teachers must look elsewhere for ideas for teaching these.
- *Language as mental knowledge.* Teaching in the 1980s was primarily concerned with language as social behaviour. Whatever the goals of language teaching, it still has to aim to create the mental knowledge that underpins this behaviour.

References

Altenberg, E. P., and H. S. Cairns. 1983. The effects of phonotactic constraints on lexical processing in bilingual and monolingual subjects. *JVLVB* 22: 174–88.

Beauvillain, C., and J. Grainger. 1987. Accessing interlexical homographs: some limitations of a language-selective access. *J. Mem. & Lang.* 26: 658–72.

Bley-Vroman, R. W. 1989. The logical problem of second language learning. In *Linguistic Perspectives on Second Language Acquisition*, ed. by S. Gass and J. Schachter. Cambridge: Cambridge University Press, 41–68.

Bley-Vroman, R. W., S. Felix and G. L. Ioup. 1988. The accessibiiity of Universal Grammar in adult language learning. *Second Language Research* 4 (1): 1–32.

Borer, H., and K. Wexler. 1987. The maturation of syntax. In *Parameter Setting,* ed. by T. Roeper and E. Williams. Dordrecht: Reidel, 123–87.

Byram, M. 1990. Foreign language teaching and young people's perceptions of other cultures. *ELT Documents* 132: 76–87.

Chomsky, N. 1981a. *Lectures on Government and Binding.* Dordrecht: Foris.
1981b. Principles and parameters in syntactic theory. In *Explanations in Linguistics,* ed. by N. Hornstein and D. Lightfoot. Harlow: Longman.
1986. *Knowledge of Language: Its Nature, Origin and Use.* New York: Praeger.
1988. *Language and Problems of Knowledge: The Managua Lectures.* Cambridge, Mass.: MIT Press.
1989. Some notes on economy of derivation and representation. *MIT Working Papers in Linguistics* 10: 43–74.

Clahsen, H., and P. Muysken. 1986. The availability of universal grammar to adult and child learners – a study of the acquisition of German word order. *Second Language Research* 2(2): 93–119.
1989. The UG paradox in L2 acquisition. *Second Language Research* 5: 1–29.

Cook, V. J. 1986. Experimental approaches applied to two areas of second language learning research: age and listening-based teaching methods. In *Experimental Approaches to Second Language Learning,* ed. by V. J. Cook. Oxford: Pergamon.
1988. *Chomsky's Universal Grammar: An Introduction.* Oxford: Blackwell.
1989. The relevance of grammar to the applied linguistics of language teaching. *Trinity College Dublin Occasional Papers* 22.
1990. The I-language Approach and Classroom Observation. *English Language Teaching Documents* 133: 71–80.
1991a. The poverty-of-the-stimulus argument and multicompetence. *Second Language Research* 7(2): 103–17.
1991b. *Second Language Learning and Language Teaching.* Sevenoaks: Edward Arnold.
1992. Evidence for multicompetence. *Language Learning* 42(4): 557–591.

Cromer, R. F. 1987. Language growth with experience without feedback. *Journal of Psycholinguistic Research* 16(3): 223–31.

de Houwer, A. 1990. *The Acquisition of Two Languages from Birth: A Case Study.* Cambridge: Cambridge University Press.

DuPlessis, J., D. Solin, L. Travis and L. White. 1987. UG or not UG, that is the question: a reply to Clahsen and Muysken. *Second Language Research* 3(1): 56–75.

Gazdar, G., E. Klein, G. Pullum, and I. Sag. 1985. *Generalized Phrase Structure Grammar.* Cambridge, Mass.: Harvard University Press.

Gross M. 1990. Lexique – Grammaire LADL. Paper given at the AILA Congress, Thessaloniki. April.

Haegeman, L. 1991. *Introduction to Government and Binding Theory.* Oxford: Blackwell.

Hawkins, E. 1984. *Awareness of Language.* Cambridge: Cambridge University Press.

Hulk, A. 1987. L'acquisition du français et le paramètre pro-drop. In *Etudes de linguistique française offertes à Robert de Dardel,* ed. by B. Kampers-Manhe and Co Vet. Amsterdam: Editions Rodopi.

Hyams, N. 1986. *Language Acquisition and the Theory of Parameters*. Dordrecht: Reidel.

Institute of Linguists. 1988. *Examinations in Languages for International Communication*. London: Institute of Linguists.

Lenneberg, E. 1967. *Biological Foundations of Language*. New York: Wiley.

Liceras, J. M. 1989. On some properties of the 'pro-drop' parameter: looking for missing subjects in non-native Spanish. In *Linguistic Perspectives on Second Language Acquisition*, ed. by S. Gass and J. Schachter. Cambridge: Cambridge University Press, 109–33.

Long, M. H. 1990. Maturational constraints on language development. *Studies in Second Language Acquisition* 12(3): 251–85.

Marcus, M. P. 1980. *Theory of Syntactic Recognition for Natural Languages*. Cambridge, Mass.: MIT Press.

Morgan, J. L. 1986. *From Simple Input to Complex Grammar*. Cambridge, Mass.: MIT Press.

Pollock, J. 1989. Verb movement, UG, and the structure of IP. *Linguistic Inquiry* 20: 365–424.

Radford, A. 1986. Small children's small clauses. *Bangor Research Papers in Linguistics* 1: 1–38.

1990. *Syntactic Theory and the Acquisition of English Syntax*. Oxford: Blackwell.

Riley, P. 1985. Mud and stars: personal constructs, sensitization, and learning. In *Discourse and Learning*, ed. by P. Riley. Harlow: Longman.

Rizzi, L. 1982. *Issues in Italian Syntax*. Dordrecht: Foris.

Rutherford, W. E. 1987. *Second Language Grammar: Learning and Teaching*. Harlow: Longman.

Schachter, J. 1988. Second Language Acquisition and its relationship to Universal Grammar. *Applied Linguistics* 9(3): 219–35.

1989. Testing a proposed universal. In *Linguistic Perspectives on Second Language Acquisition*, ed. by S. Gass and J. Schachter. Cambridge: Cambridge University Press, 73–88.

Singleton, D. 1989. *Language Acquisition: The Age Factor*. Clevedon: Multilingual Matters.

Sportiche, D. 1981. Bounding nodes in French. *The Linguistic Review* 1: 219–46.

Wanner, E., and M. Maratsos. 1978. An ATN approach to comprehension. In *Linguistic Theory and Psychological Reality*, ed. by M. Halle, J. Bresnan and G. A. Miller. Cambridge, Mass.: MIT Press.

Wexler, K., and M. R. Manzini. 1987. Parameters and learnability. In *Parameters and Linguistic Theory*, ed. by T. Roeper and E. Williams. Dordrecht: Reidel.

White, L. 1986. Implications of parametric variation for adult second language acquisition: an investigation of the pro-drop parameter. In *Experimental Approaches to Second Language Acquisition*, ed. by V. J. Cook. Oxford: Pergamon, 55–72.

1988. Island effects in second language acquisition. In *Linguistic Theory in Second Language Acquisition*, ed. by S. Flynn and W. O'Neil. Norwell, MA: Kluwer Academic.

1989. *Universal Grammar and Second Language Acquisition*. Amsterdam: John Benjamins.

3 Non-transformational theories of grammar: Implications for language teaching

Philip L. Hubbard

Introduction

It is easy to be confused about the relationship between grammar theory and language teaching. Someone entering the language teaching profession at this time might reasonably expect that the results of decades of scientific study of language structure would have yielded some tangible results for teachers. Yet, if we look at the work of practicing teachers or read through the texts designed to teach language students something about the grammar of the language they are trying to learn, we find very little direct evidence of the influence of such theory. Contemporary texts teaching grammar, to the extent that they vary with traditional ones, have taken on instead notions from theories of acquisition and processing, focusing on the importance of meaningful and contextualized practice. The rules used to describe the language structures themselves, however, remain to a large degree unchanged from the form of traditional grammars, and where rules have been changed, the source of the change has often come from language teachers themselves rather than from theoretical linguists.

Linguistic theory has, of course, been directly applied in language teaching in the past. Audio-lingual texts and structural grammars attempted to take the sentence patterns from structural linguistic analyses and drill them into the students through pattern practice. Transformational grammar, too, was directly applied in the 1960s and early 1970s. The lack of success with these applications led to the idea that even if rule formulations from linguistic theory were not directly useful to the student, perhaps they were still useful to the teacher in writing grammar-based exercises, understanding and responding to student questions about structures, and dealing with learner errors. Celce-Murcia and Larsen-Freeman's *The Grammar Book* (1983) represents the most comprehensive realization of this position. Their text provides clear evidence that when linguistic theory is approached pedagogically, valuable insights can be gained by teachers and in some cases passed on to students.

The most interesting point about Celce-Murcia and Larsen-Freeman (1983) for the present discussion is the theory they used. Although occasionally making reference to other frameworks, in those places where they found syntactic theory relevant, they generally based their analyses on the transformational grammar model presented in Chomsky (1965), often referred to as the Standard Theory. This is the same theory that has been taught to most linguistically trained language teachers (in the United States, at least) for over twenty years, and it is probably still the theory of syntax most likely to be covered in an introductory linguistics course. However, many of its core assumptions, such as the linking of deep structure with semantic interpretation, were abandoned years ago. While its historic influence on contemporary linguistics is undeniable, it is, as a serious theory, obsolete.

For those teachers and teacher-training programs that have kept up with the field, recent years have seen the ascendancy of a new leader among theories of grammar, Chomsky's (1981) Government/Binding Theory. It is, in a strict sense, still a transformational grammar, though only a single transformation (Move-alpha, or "move anything anywhere") remains. Concepts from Government/Binding have been applied outside of theoretical linguistics in both first and second language acquisition studies (e.g., Hyams 1986; Flynn 1988) and pedagogical grammar (e.g., Rutherford and Sharwood Smith 1985). It is not, however, recognized among linguistic theoreticians in general as *the* theory, and this brings us to the two questions this paper addresses: What else is out there? And how can we use it in the teaching of grammar?

Larsen-Freeman (1990: 190), in an overview of the current state of pedagogical grammar, recognizes the problem and notes that

despite there being many linguistic frameworks from which to draw insights these days (e.g., Perlmutter's [1983] relational grammar; Bresnan's [1982] lexical-functional grammar; Gazdar et al.'s [1985] generalized phrase structure grammar), it is true that Chomsky's (1981) government-binding theory has received the most attention from second language acquisition [SLA] researchers and will thus likely have an increasing influence on pedagogical descriptions of grammar during the decade to come.

This chapter will look at the three alternatives to Chomsky's current theory specifically mentioned by Larsen-Freeman: Relational Grammar, Lexical-Functional Grammar, and Generalized Phrase Structure Grammar. All of these have made widely recognized contributions to linguistic research. They have in common the features of being non-transformational and being more or less ignored by language teachers. The purpose here is not to argue the superiority of one or another of these either as linguistic theories or as sources for pedagogical insights (although one may be more useful than the others in some particular domain). Rather, by providing language teachers with a more realistic view of the current state of linguistic theory and its relationship to pedagogy, this paper seeks to encourage the further exploration of these and other linguistic theories for insights of value to language teaching.

What kinds of insights might there be? It seems to me that theories of grammar and the analyses that follow from them are valuable to language teachers to the extent that they

- inform teachers about how language works according to our best models;
- highlight generalizations/regularities within a language that might otherwise be missed;
- identify certain cross-linguistic generalizations which might help predict areas of greater or lesser difficulty for learners;
- offer the basis for simpler (i.e., more learnable) ways of viewing complex phenomena;
- offer the basis for more accurate rule formulations;
- aid learners in identifying form-meaning relationships for syntactic structures and grammatical morphemes.

All but the first have some direct connection to pedagogical grammar, yet linguistics courses for teacher trainees often focus almost exclusively on that first one. It is the purpose of this paper to address some of the other points with respect to the three non-transformational theories under analysis.

We will take two passes through each of the three theories: a *top-down* pass and a *bottom-up* pass. The top-down pass will look at the theory's underlying assumptions and descriptive machinery, relate them to the language teaching situation, and discuss general implications for the teaching/learning process. The bottom-up pass will look at specific analyses, such as the way the theory describes a particular grammatical structure or hypothesizes generalizations accounting for links between superficially distinct grammatical processes. The description from the first pass will of necessity be superficial, and the examples of specific analyses based on the second pass will, of course, not be exhaustive of the potential for any particular theory. Together, however, they should provide an outline of what has occurred in linguistic theory in the past decade or so besides Chomsky's Government/Binding, along with some sense of its potential for impacting pedagogical grammar.

Before beginning the description of the three theories, it will be useful to take a top-down pass through the framework of Chomsky's (1965) theory. This will provide a foundation for comparison of the new theories in terms familiar to many readers.

A review of Standard Transformational Grammar

Chomsky's (1965) theory of transformational grammar (the Standard Theory) was a revision and expansion of his original (1957) theory. Following are some of the Standard Theory's key assumptions.

- A theory of grammar has as its goal the description of the linguistic competence of the idealized native speaker-hearer of a language. An adequate grammar must generate (or exhaustively describe) the set of all the possible grammatical sentences in that language while excluding all ungrammatical ones.

- A grammar consists of three basic components: syntax, semantics, and phonology. Syntax consists of two types of rules: phrase structure rules, which determine the deep structure of a sentence, and transformational rules, which change the deep structure through operations that insert, delete, replace, or move sentence constituents, eventually leading to the surface structure. Semantics is interpreted from the deep structure, while the surface structure provides the input to the phonological component for pronouncing the sentence.

- The lexical entries for words in a language include (besides phonological and semantic information) two elements. One is the strict subcategorization, which shows what other constituents can or must occur with the word (e.g., transitive verbs are subcategorized as requiring a following noun phrase). The other is selectional restrictions, which require a matching of semantic features between one word and another (e.g., *kill* requires a [+animate] object).

- Grammatical functions (subject, direct object, etc.) are structurally derived. For example, the subject can be defined as the noun phrase immediately dominated by the sentence and the direct object as the noun phrase immediately dominated by the verb phrase. Grammatical functions do not play any direct role in transformations, which are based exclusively on structural configurations.

The descriptive machinery of the theory includes basically the two types of rules noted above operating to define tree structures. The phrase structure rule S→NP+VP, for instance, defines a sentence as being comprised of a noun phrase and a following verb phrase. The transformational rule

NP AUX V NP   4 2 + be 3 + en by + 1
1   2   3 4

describes the transformation of a sentence from active (*Gremlins must have eaten the cake*) to passive (*The cake must have been eaten by gremlins*).

After undergoing several significant revisions in the 1970s, transformational grammar emerged as the version of the Revised Extended Standard Theory known as Government/Binding (Chomsky 1981). Although Government/Binding (often referred to as Universal Grammar) remains the most widely accepted replacement for Standard Theory, it is not covered in this paper. Studies such as those of Cook (this volume) and Rutherford and Sharwood Smith (1985) describe its relevance for pedagogical grammar, and theoretical overviews can be found in Sells (1985) and Horrocks (1987).

Relational Grammar

The first theory we will explore is Relational Grammar, developed initially by David Perlmutter and Paul Postal in the mid-1970s to account for certain types of cross-linguistic generalizations that transformational grammar and its offshoots at the time were unable to explain. Perlmutter and Postal (1977), which proposed a universal characterization of passive constructions, is regarded as the first major work in the new theory. The theory attracted the interest of a number of linguists during the decade that followed, and although no major breakthroughs have occurred in the past few years, many of the generalizations discovered by linguists working with Relational Grammar have influenced the development of other theories. Many of the most important papers in the development of the theory are found in Perlmutter (1983) and Perlmutter and Rosen (1984).

Theoretical assumptions and descriptive machinery for Relational Grammar

Like transformational grammar, Relational Grammar assumes syntax to be an independent component of linguistic structure, separate from phonology and semantics. However, it differs from transformational grammar in a number of its key assumptions.

- Grammatical relations (subject, predicate, direct object, etc.) are primitives. This means that they are a core part of the clause structure and not derived by structural description (e.g., the subject is the noun phrase immediately dominated by the sentence) as they were in transformational grammar.
- Linear order is a more or less independent aspect of clause structure. This allows a rule such as passive to be stated universally as the displacement of an underlying subject by a direct object, without respect to word order.
- Clause structure is not derivational (i.e., structure-changing rules do not apply in succession as in transformational grammar), but it is still multileveled. The representation of a passive sentence such as *Ken was shot by Barbie,* for example, contains the information that Ken was initially the direct object but is now the subject and that Barbie was initially the subject but is so no longer.
- Linguistic generalizations (rules for case marking and other inflectional morphology, word order, etc.) may make reference to any aspect of the clausal representation. The appearance of passive morphology in English, for instance (*be* plus the past participle ending), is allowed only in those clauses containing a direct object at the initial level which is also a subject at the final level, such as *Ken* in the preceding example.
- Possible representations of clause structure are limited by a set of universal constraints that set restrictions on the types of grammatical relation changes that can occur.

In the descriptive machinery of Relational Grammar, the most critical notion is that of the grammatical relation itself. The theory recognizes a number of relations divided into various classes. The most important ones include the following. Predicate is the central relation of a clause. It is normally carried by verbs, though adjectives may sometimes carry it as

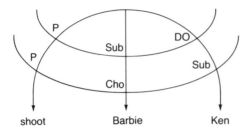

Figure 1   Stratal diagram for Ken was shot by Barbie.

well. The traditional Subject, Direct Object, and Indirect Object together form a class known as the *term* relations. These differ from other nominal relations in that they carry a range of semantic roles and act as a natural class with respect to certain grammatical processes. Other grammatical relations for nominals include the *oblique* relations (Benefactive, Locative, Instrumental, etc.), which in English are marked with prepositions, and a few others such as Possessor.

Although Relational Grammar deals centrally with the ways nominals and predicates can change their grammatical relations in a clause, it does not have relation-changing rules per se. The functional equivalent of such rules is captured by allowing the "derivation" of a sentence to be captured in a single multileveled structure (such as that in Figure 1). The basic goal of Relational Grammar as a universal grammar is to characterize the set of such possible structures in such a way that structures which do not occur in any language are blocked by universal principles. A grammar of a particular language, like English, would include additional restrictions that determine which subset of universally allowed structures could occur, along with statements of how (through word order, inflections, grammatical particles, etc.) the structural information would be indicated.

In place of the familiar tree structures of most generative grammars, the characterization of sentence structure in Relational Grammar is presented through a representational device called a *stratal diagram*. Figure 1 shows a stratal diagram for *Ken was shot by Barbie.* In this diagram, the arrows, called *relational arcs,* are labeled to show the grammatical relations that *Ken, shoot,* and *Barbie* carry, and the curved, latitudinal lines represent levels. The leftmost arc, with *shoot* at the end of it, carries the predicate (P) relation to the clause at both the initial (top) and final (bottom) levels. The next arc, with *Barbie* at the end, carries the subject (Sub) relation at the initial level and the chomeur (Cho) relation at the final level. *Chômeur,* from the French for "unemployed," is the label used in Relational Grammar to indicate that an item no longer has a central role to play in a clause. In the English passive, this means it will be marked with a *by*-phrase if it appears at all. The final arc, with *Ken* at the end, carries the direct object (DO) relation at the initial level and the Sub relation at the final level, indicating that *Ken* begins as the direct object but ends up as the subject. It should be noted that the network in Figure 1, while it captures the points deemed most significant by relational grammarians, is incomplete. Missing are indicators of word order (linear precedence relations) and tense, for instance, which would need to be specified in a full representation.

The preceding description of the assumptions and theoretical machinery provides only the barest sense of what Relational Grammar is really like, but even so, they suggest some interesting implications for language teaching. A few of the more pertinent ones include:

1. Grammatical relations are universally significant. There may be a payoff for teaching the notions of subject, direct object, indirect object, benefactive, instrumental, and so on, particularly if they can be linked to the corresponding concepts in the student's first language.
2. The predicate has a special role: It is the defining item for the clause, determining the number of noun arguments, the grammatical relations they will carry, and the semantic roles (agent, patient, etc.) that a particular grammatical relation will be linked with.
3. There is a distinction between subject, direct object, and indirect object (called the *term* relations) and all other grammatical relations. They are the ones not linked to a single semantic role, and they participate in most of the grammatical rule statements. Special attention should be given to them (though in English, the indirect object plays a less significant role than in many other languages).
4. There are universal characterizations of rules such as passive, indirect object movement, and so on. Thus, the concepts themselves do not need to be taught in many cases, only the English realizations of them.

A specific analysis: unaccusatives

Turning now to a bottom-up pass, we will look at a specific analysis, which has come from Relational Grammar, that has some relevance for pedagogical grammar. Consider the following examples produced by ESL learners:

This problem is existed for many years.
Something strange was happened before I could open the door.

Works dealing with error analysis, such as Richards (1973) and Burt and Kiparsky (1972), have considered these errors to result from an incomplete knowledge of the English tense/auxiliary system. If this were the case, we would expect all verbs to be equally susceptible to appearing with this incorrect morphology. It was reported in Hubbard (1983), however, that the overwhelming majority (more than 90 percent) of such

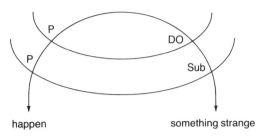

happen   something strange

Figure 2   Simplified stratal diagram for Something strange happened.

errors in a sample of compositions from eight different languages occurred with a specific class of intransitive verbs, verbs which in Relational Grammar have a special status and are called *unaccusative*. This
term was introduced by Perlmutter (1978), who hypothesized that these
intransitives have a direct object rather than a subject as their single
underlying argument. The class includes verbs of being or becoming,
verbs of happening, and in general any intransitive verb which indicates
something other than a conscious voluntary action. These verbs in many
languages are different in some way from other intransitives: One of the
more common ways is that they appear with the same morphology as
passives.

The unaccusative analysis suggests an explanation for why this particular pattern of errors may occur. Figure 2 shows a simplified stratal
diagram for *Something strange happened*. Under this analysis, the key to
the presence of passive morphology in sentences such as the two in the
preceding paragraph is the observation that verbs like *happen* have direct objects advancing to become surface subjects. Thus the production
of these sentences is not due to an incomplete knowledge of the tense/
auxiliary system, but rather to incorrectly assuming that English unaccusative verbs (or some subset of them) receive passive morphology. Hubbard and Hix (1988) classify these not as a general error in auxiliary
selection but as a form of lexical subcategorization error. Given the
existence of sentences such as *That store is located on Elm Street*, which
is arguably of the same form, it is not surprising that such errors would
occur with this class of verbs.

The insight provided by the unaccusative analysis has clear implications for pedagogical grammar. It suggests that grammar teachers (and
possibly textbook writers) need to be aware of the apparent source of
such problems and might want to mention it to students in advance,
perhaps at the same time passives are covered. More important, if such
errors occur in advanced student compositions, writing teachers should
point out that (with the possible exception of a handful of verbs like
locate) English only uses passive morphology if a corresponding active

transitive form, with an explicit agent indicated, is possible. An agent is clearly not possible in the examples in the preceding paragraph.

This is just one example of the possible bottom-up applications of Relational Grammar analyses. Other potential areas of interest to pedagogical grammar exist. One of these is *possessor ascension,* where a possessive relation is indicated at the surface level by an indirect object rather than with a possessive form internal to the noun phrase. Students coming from languages with possessor ascension might produce a sentence like *John stole the car to me* to mean "John stole my car," an error teachers would be likely to misinterpret as resulting from mixing *to* and *from.* Another is *inversion,* a common construction similar to passive where the initial subject appears as the indirect object and the initial direct object appears as the subject. A student coming from a language with inversion constructions might produce *They like to me* or *They are liked to me* for "I like them." These two constructions have been found to exist across a large number of languages (see Perlmutter [1983] and Perlmutter and Rosen [1984] for examples). When such structures are produced by ESL learners, the Relational Grammar analyses could provide information to the teacher regarding the source of the error as well as possibly suggest ways of explaining it to the student.

Lexical-Functional Grammar

Lexical-Functional Grammar represents an attempt to build a grammar that is consistent with research about human language processing. The cofounders of the theory are theoretical linguist Joan Bresnan, who in the late 1970s began arguing for a more psychologically real transformational grammar, and Ronald Kaplan, a psycholinguist. As the name of the theory suggests, the lexicon and language functions (roughly analogous to the grammatical relations of Relational Grammar) play a significant role in its language description. Bresnan (1982) includes papers covering various aspects of the theory. Sells (1985) and Horrocks (1987) provide more accessible overviews of it.

Theoretical assumptions and descriptive machinery for Lexical-Functional Grammar

The following are the key assumptions that underlie Lexical-Functional Grammar.

- A grammar should be psychologically real; that is, it should be a direct representation of the underlying linguistic competence of a speaker so that it can form the basis for a theory of language performance (both comprehension and production).

- The structure of a sentence has two forms: constituent structure, which is similar to the phrase structure trees of transformational grammar, and functional structure, which contains information about the relations of constituent elements to the clause (e.g., which NP is the subject).
- For a sentence to be grammatical, constituent and functional structure must each be well formed. Furthermore, the two must be mutually compatible.
- The lexicon plays a central role. Unlike in transformational grammar and its direct descendants, lexical entries subcategorize for functional as well as constituent structure.
- There are no transformations or movements of any kind, and the structure of a sentence is not "multileveled" as in Relational Grammar. Constituents that in other theories have been moved (such as *which* in *Which book did you read?* or *The car which I bought yesterday already has a flat tire* are generated in place and related by functional structure and/or lexical rules to the appropriate constituents.

The descriptive machinery of Lexical-Functional Grammar that will concern us here is of two types: that which describes constituent and functional structures and that which describes lexical relations.

Constituent structure in Lexical-Functional Grammar is like that of transformational theories in that it is generated by phrase structure rules of the type S→NP+VP (Sentence goes to Noun Phrase + Verb Phrase). It differs, however, in annotating this structure with the functional information necessary for linking it with the functional structure. Thus, in the tree structure generated by the preceding rule, the NP would be annotated with the feature (SUBJ), indicating that it is the subject of S.

Functional structure is quite different: It consists of *attributes* that are specified with particular *values*. A sentence like *The cat sleeps* would have the functional structure described in Figure 3. In this structure, the attribute SPEC carries the value THE, while the attribute SUBJ carries the value "the cat." The terms in single quotes (CAT and SLEEP) represent semantic values (roughly "words"), while items with primarily grammatical functions, such as THE, occur without quotes. The form <SUBJ> after *sleep* indicates that the value of SUBJ (*the cat* in this case) will carry the subject relation in the sentence. This functional structure thus includes the essential information necessary for assigning a semantic value to the sentence. It does not, however, specify linear order; this is the role of the annotated constituent structure.

The lexicon in Lexical-Functional Grammar has two interesting elements: the treatment of subcategorization and lexical rules. As with most recent generative grammars, the function of subcategorization is to determine what constituents can co-occur with a particular lexical item. The verbs *sleep* and *drink,* for instance, are subcategorized as intransitive (no NP after the verb) and transitive (an NP after the verb), respectively. Subcategorization in Lexical-Functional Grammar carries more information than in most other theories. Unlike transformational gram-

$$
\begin{array}{l}
\text{SUBJ} \quad \left[\begin{array}{l} \text{SPEC THE} \\[4pt] \text{NUM SG} \\[4pt] \text{PRED 'CAT'} \end{array} \right] \\[40pt]
\text{TENSE [PRES]} \\[6pt]
\text{PRED 'SLEEP} <(\text{SUBJ})>'
\end{array}
$$

(SUBJ = subject, SPEC = specifier, NUM = number,
SG = singular, PRED = predicate, PRES = present)

Figure 3   Functional structure for The cat sleeps.

mars, the subject is explicitly subcategorized for. Further, subcategorization is done in terms of function rather than structure; that is, *drink* is subcategorized to take an Object, not a Noun Phrase. The subcategorization entry also specifies the *thematic role* that a function is linked with. *Drink* would be specified as having a Subject-Agent and an Object-Theme (thematic roles are discussed later in this section).

Lexical rules in Lexical-Functional Grammar take a lexical item as input and return a related lexical item with a new subcategorization. That is, they account for the systematic relationships among the different forms of the same basic lexical item. They serve a function similar to that of transformations in Standard Theory. A lexical rule, for example, links the active and passive forms of a verb like *drink,* changing the base form to the participle *drunk* while changing the subcategorization so that the thematic roles shift along with the grammatical function. The resulting rule in simplified form is

(SUBJ) $\rightarrow \emptyset/(\text{OBL}_{AG})$
(OBJ) $\rightarrow$ (SUBJ)

where $\emptyset/(\text{OBL}_{AG})$ means that the original subject argument of a verb appearing as a passive is either not stated or appears as an oblique agent, which by other rules is required to occur as the object of the preposition *by.*

The underlying assumptions and descriptive machinery together suggest the following implications for language teaching:

1. Unlike transformational grammar and its direct descendants, grammatical functions are primitives. Thus, as with Relational Grammar, it is reasonable to state pedagogical rules using them.
2. The lexicon is a central part of the grammar, not just a dumping place for

exceptions to rules. Lexical rules relate verb forms of active and passive sentences to one another (rather than whole clausal structures, as in transformational grammar). This binds the learning of vocabulary and grammar more closely than is usually done in grammar texts, and certainly more so than in texts inspired by structural or earlier transformational approaches.

3. Similarly, in Lexical-Functional Grammar the content of a lexical entry is much more than a phonological form and one or more meanings: It includes all of the subcategorization information for constituent and functional structure. This suggests that the learning of vocabulary, particularly verbs, should include as much of this subcategorizational information as possible. For example, it is not enough for students to memorize lists of verbs taking infinitive versus gerund complements if other important aspects of subcategorization, such as whether or not the gerund or infinitive is preceded by an NP, are ignored.

A specific analysis: relation-changing rules

Levin (1988) presents an overview of lexically based relation-changing rules within the Lexical-Functional Grammar framework. Relation-changing rules include passive and others, such as indirect object movement (*I gave a book to John→I gave John a book*). Although aimed at theoretical issues, aspects of her analysis suggest some interesting consequences for how to teach certain English structures.

In Levin's analysis, a key to understanding how such rules operate is a recognition of the thematic relations entailed by the verbs involved in them. She uses the following definitions for the relations of theme, agent, goal, and patient:

Theme: something which is in some location or state, comes into or out of existence (at some location or state), or undergoes a change of location or state.
Agent: an entity which produces an effect on some other entity, causes another entity to be in some other location or state, causes another entity to come into/go out of existence, or causes another entity to undergo a change of location or state.
Goal: the endpoint of a change of location or state, the place or state in which a theme comes into existence, or an entity which comes to have possession of a theme.
Patient: a kind of goal. When an agent produces (brings into existence) an effect (theme) on an entity (goal), that entity is called a patient.

(Levin 1988: 11–12)

These concepts from lexical semantics can provide a more accurate account of the distribution of sentence types with specific classes of verbs. Only two examples will be presented here, though Levin offers several others.

First, there are a number of apparently transitive verbs which can occur as passives only if the agent is not stated in a *by*-phrase. For example, "The list includes some interesting items/Some interesting items are included (*by the list)." "The paper requires more work/More work is required (*by the paper) (Levin 1988: 26). A purely syntactic description of passives would incorrectly lead ESL students to assume that the asterisked versions of these (and a number of similar verbs such as *call, add, allow,* and *involve*) would be acceptable to native speakers. Using the Lexical-Functional Grammar framework, however, Levin isolates the problem. These sentences, she notes, are grammatical if the *by*-phrases are replaced by *in the list* and *on the paper.* Noting, further, that *in* and *on* are prepositions of location, she hypothesizes that there is a restriction on performing the SUBJ→OBL$_{AG}$ portion of the lexical passive rule; namely, that the change cannot occur if the original subject plays a location role.

Another process Levin argues to be semantically conditioned relates causative verbs in sentences like *The farmer grew the potatoes* to inchoative verbs in sentences like *The potatoes grew.* She shows that this Causative/Inchoative Rule works when the object of the causative verb is a theme, but not when it is a patient. That is, *The farmer kicked the potatoes* does not have a corresponding inchoative *The potatoes kicked* by this analysis because *kick* takes a patient rather than a theme as its object in the transitive form.

These are just two of several examples Levin presents of how thematic roles can be used to account for apparent exceptions to syntactic processes. While it is unlikely that such information would normally be included in a grammar text designed to introduce students to passive or causative/inchoative structures, Levin's Lexical-Functional Grammar analyses could prove helpful in explaining certain types of errors to more advanced students who produce them in their writing.

Generalized Phrase Structure Grammar

Generalized Phrase Structure Grammar is a theory developed by Gerald Gazdar, Ewan Klein, Geoffrey Pullum, and Ivan Sag to produce a grammar that provides in a single level of a single structure all the information necessary to derive a semantic form. Although, like Lexical-Functional Grammar and Relational Grammar, it does not use transformations, neither does it use the multiple-level approach of Relational Grammar or Lexical-Functional Grammar's combination of constituent and functional structure. It is truly a single-level theory of syntax: In Standard Theory terms, it has only a surface structure. The most comprehensive presentation of the theory is found in Gazdar et al. (1985). Overviews of the theory can be found in Sells (1985) and Horrocks (1987).

Theoretical assumptions and descriptive machinery for Generalized Phrase Structure Grammar

Generalized Phrase Structure Grammar represents a return to the interest in formal description that characterized transformational grammar in its early years. Here is a summary of the key assumptions:

- Explaining aspects of natural language requires a sufficiently complete and precise description of the relevant phenomena. This is in contrast to the approach taken by Chomsky and many other theorists who proclaim wideranging universals on the basis of relatively small chunks of data and who formalize only selected parts of the theoretical framework.
- A generative grammar should be constructed so that universals appear as *consequences* of the formal system rather than being merely expressible by it. For example, phrase structure rules utilizing X-bar syntax capture the generalization that a VP will have a verb head, an NP will have a noun head, and so on, without the need for a separate rule stating that a phrase must have a head of the same category.
- A syntactic structure needs only a single level of analysis. All of the information necessary for phonological and semantic interpretation can be presented in this single structure.
- Phrase structure rules are basically constraints on possible constituent structures. They do not specify linear order, only immediate dominance relations. For example, a noun phrase could be specified as including a determiner and a noun, but their relative order would be specified by a separate statement of linear precedence. This splitting of immediate dominance and linear precedence is also done in Relational Grammar, though through a quite different mechanism.
- The verb phrase has a special status among constituents: It is considered the head of the sentence in much the same way a noun is the head of a noun phrase or a verb is the head of a verb phrase.

The descriptive machinery of Generalized Phrase Structure Grammar includes a system of syntactic features, immediate dominance rules, and various restrictions, conventions, principles, and statements that combine to define the set of well-formed phrase structure trees for a given language. These trees represent all the structure necessary for both the semantic and phonological interpretation of a sentence.

Features of various types play an important role in Generalized Phrase Structure Grammar. Following a proposal of Chomsky's (1970), the major categories – noun, verb, adjective, and preposition – are represented in Generalized Phrase Structure Grammar by a combination of the two binary $(+/-)$ features N (nominal) and V (verbal). A noun in this system would be $[+N, -V]$, a verb $[-N, +V]$, an adjective $[+N, +V]$, and a preposition $[-N, -V]$. This is one of the more familiar uses of features and has been incorporated into several contemporary theories. Gazdar et al. (1985) present a list of thirty features of various types necessary for a grammar of English. Some, like N, V, PAST, and LOC (locative), are binary. Others, like CONJ (conjunction) and COMP (complementizer), have a list of linguistic items as their possible values (for COMP they are *for, that, whether, if,* and NIL). Still others, such as VFORM (verb form) have feature values denoting categories of lexical forms: BSE (base), FIN (finite), INF (infinitive), PAS (passive), PRP (present participle), and PSP (past participle). This rich feature system is critical in Generalized Phrase Structure Grammar both because of the necessity of including all the syntactic information in a single structure and because of its emphasis on comprehensiveness and explicitness. Although some other theories, Lexical-Functional Grammar in particular, make extensive use of features, "the theory of syntactic features in Generalized Phrase Structure Grammar has attained a level of development that far and away exceeds that attained in any other framework" (Horrocks 1987: 169).

The syntactic features appear on the nodes of tree structures whose specification begins with immediate dominance rules. Immediate dominance rules are of two basic types: lexical and nonlexical. Lexical immediate dominance rules specify the character of the hierarchical relationships that exist among items in constituents that include a lexical head, constituents such as noun phrases and verb phrases. Nonlexical rules specify other types of syntactic relationships. The subcategorization of verbs and other major lexical categories is crucially related to this division. The examples that follow should help clarify the difference.

VP→H[1] is the immediate dominance rule defining a verb phrase for a simple intransitive verb like *die*. The H here stands for Head. Head is a pivotal category in Generalized Phrase Structure Grammar and occurs on the right side of *all* immediate dominance rules. In lexical immediate dominance rules, a convention (the Head Feature Convention) requires that H always be the lexical category that matches the phrasal category on the left. An H after a VP, as in this example, must therefore be a verb, rather than, say, a noun or an adjective. (H varies in nonlexical rules in ways that need not concern us here.) Two other lexical immediate dominance rules are VP→H[2], NP and VP→H[3], NP, PP[*to*]. These two rules define simple transitive (e.g., *kiss Barbie*) and transitive with indirect object (e.g., *give a kiss to Barbie*) structures.

Nonlexical immediate dominance rules define the parts of a sentence not covered by the lexical ones. This distinction closely parallels the difference between subcategorizable and nonsubcategorizable structure recognized even in Standard Theory. A simple example will help show the difference. In the sentence *Ken kissed Barbie,* a nonlexical immediate dominance rule accounts for the structure NP VP. The lexical immediate dominance rule VP→H[2],NP accounts for the structure *kissed Barbie*. The distinction between the two rule types is also simple. The existence of a subject (*Ken* in this case) is a basic fact about English sentences. The existence of the direct object (*Barbie*) is a consequence of the subcategorization of the verb *kiss*.

Subcategorization, however, is not simply a lexical quality in Generalized Phrase Structure Grammar as it is in other generative grammars. The immediate dominance rules make direct reference to subcategorization classes. H[2] in the rule in the preceding paragraph, for instance, states that only a lexical head carrying the feature [SUBCAT, 2] can occur in that substructure: Simple transitives like *kiss* carry such a feature, while intransitives and other types of transitives (like *put*, which requires both a direct object and a locative phrase [Put the salt on the table]) carry other SUBCAT values linked to corresponding immediate dominance rules. Other parts of speech besides verbs have immediate dominance rules with head feature values linked to specific subcategorizations. For instance, the rule $A^1 \rightarrow H[24]$, PP[*about*] defines a structure for a particular kind of adjective phrase, one where the adjective occurs with a prepositional phrase headed by *about* (e.g., *Hal was angry about that*). Adjectives like *angry* and *happy* are then given lexical entries with the feature [SUBCAT, 24] so that they (but not, say, *likely* or *orange*) can appear as the head in the structure defined by that rule. Gazdar et al. (1985) list forty-five such rules, to be linked with the subcategorization classes of verbs, nouns, adjectives, and prepositions.

In a single-level grammar such as Generalized Phrase Structure Grammar, it is necessary to have some means other than relating one structure to another to capture relationships such as active-passive and statement-question. In the latter case, for instance, there are no movement rules such as subject-auxiliary inversion, yet the relationship is too systematic to be left unaccounted for. In place of transformations, Generalized Phrase Structure Grammar uses a set of *metarules*, that is, rules which operate on other rules to achieve further generalizations. The passive metarule states that for every immediate dominance rule for transitive verbs of the form VP→W, NP (where NP is the object), there is also a rule for passives of the form VP[PAS]→W, (PP[*by*]). The W in these rules stands for any material other than the NP that is specified by an immediate dominance rule, capturing the fact that transitive verbs in general can occur as passives without having to list separate rules for *kiss*-type, *give*-type, and *put*-type verbs, or in fact for each of the ten or more classes of transitives in English.

As noted earlier in this section, immediate dominance rules are only part of the Generalized Phrase Structure Grammar syntax. A set of linear precedence rules specifies word order. One particularly powerful generalization is provided by the rule [SUBCAT] < ~[SUBCAT]. This linear precedence rule states that items with the feature [SUBCAT] (that is, lexical items) will occur before those that do not have this feature. The verb in a transitive verb phrase, for instance (e.g., *kick the ball*), will always occur before the noun phrase because the verb carries the feature [SUBCAT], while the noun phrase, being a phrase rather than a lexical item, does not carry the feature [SUBCAT]. Gazdar et al. (1985: 50) claim:

From this single statement it follows that verbs will be VP-initial, that determiners are NP-initial, that English has prepositions rather than postpositions, that complementizers precede S[entence], that coordination words are conjunct-initial, that auxiliary verbs which are daughters of S are sentence-initial, that adjectives and nouns precede their complements, that comparative and equative particles are constituent-initial, etc.

With a handful of other linear precedence statements, it is possible to characterize the fixed word order portions of English grammar. In doing so, Generalized Phrase Structure Grammar claims to have achieved a higher level of generalization than is possible with phrase structure grammars that blend immediate dominance and linear precedence.

The remaining portions of Generalized Phrase Structure Grammar, stated in the form of restrictions and conventions, serve mainly to limit which features occur with which other features. The final form of a sentence in Generalized Phrase Structure Grammar is a labeled tree structure similar to those found in Lexical-Functional Grammar and Government/Binding. The underlying assumptions and descriptive machinery for Generalized Phrase Structure Grammar together suggest the following implications for grammar teaching:

1. Verbs are the key to the sentence. The VP is the head of a sentence and the verb is the head of the VP. By teaching verbs and the structures they directly govern, a significant portion of the grammar of a language is covered.
2. Subcategorization is a feature of all lexical items and directly determines which structures they may appear in. Teaching the form and meaning of a word without at the same time teaching its subcategorization will distance the student from critical information about how the word really operates in the language.
3. By the same token, much of the grammatical structure of English is directly linked to the logical structure of lexical items. This means that it may be more useful to think of introducing substructures through common words than as syntactic formulas with words as convenient placeholders. Doing so would yield a lexically driven grammar. This idea is explored in the next section.
4. Transformational exercises (e.g., change an active sentence into a passive) do not represent linguistically relevant stages in a derivation. Thus there is no theoretically justifiable reason for doing them (though there may be a pedagogical reason).

A specific analysis for Generalized Phrase Structure Grammar: the verb system

In the bottom-up analysis for Generalized Phrase Structure Grammar, we are going to concentrate on a larger chunk of the language than we have for the other two theories. We will also see it from the perspective of how a grammar text/course might be restructured rather than on how to anticipate or respond to a particular type of error. The area we will focus attention on here is the verb system, specifically the verbs in the VP and the constituents they subcategorize for.

As noted in the previous section, immediate dominance rules define the basic structural relations determined by particular lexical items. Thirty of the forty-nine lexical immediate dominance rules given in Gazdar et al. (1985) refer to the expansion of verb phrases, in each case explicitly (through the SUBCAT feature) linking a particular class of verbs with a particular structure. Given the acknowledged importance of the verb, this gives us the possibility of organizing grammar instruction to focus some attention on these structures. In the space available here it is not possible to cover all of the verb types these thirty rules refer to, and in fact there are many additional VP expansion rules which come about through the application of metarules to these basic immediate dominance rules (such as the rules generating passive structures). Consequently, only a few will be discussed.

The following versions of rules from Gazdar et al. (1985: 247) have been adjusted so as to incorporate linear precedence in the familiar phrase structure rule fashion and to indicate explicitly that the head is a verb. They have been numbered here for the purpose of exposition, and in each case they are followed by a sample verb and a sentence built on it. The underlined portion of each sentence is the part representing the constituents required by the rule.

1. VP→V[1]   *die* – "The cat died at midnight."
2. VP→V[2] NP   *kiss* – "Ken kissed Barbie softly."
3. VP→V[3] NP PP[*to*]   *give* – "Ken gave a ring to Barbie."
4. VP→V[5] NP NP   *give* – "Ken gave Barbie a ring."
5. VP→V[8] NP S[FIN]   *persuade* – "I persuaded Ken that I was too sick to work."
6. VP→V[11] (PP[*of*]) S[BSE]   *require* – "I require (of all my employees) that they be here on time."
7. VP→V[18] NP VP [INF,+NORM]   *persuade* – "I persuaded Ken to offer you the job last week."

Several points about English grammar can be introduced or clarified through these structures. First, by highlighting what is required, the essential versus nonessential information for particular verbs can be made clear. This also includes certain optional information that is part of the subcategorization: In Rule 6, for instance, the sentence is grammatical without the *of*-phrase, but the rule still specifies the preposition *of* to block sentences like *I require* to *all my employees* . . . A second generalization covered here concerns the nature of the relationship of verbs like *give* in Rules 3 and 4. In contrast to transformational grammar, no direct structural relationship is even implied in this analysis. At the syntactic level, it is simply a fact of English that there are verbs that take an object and a *to*-phrase and others that take a double object (e.g., *call* in *Barbie called Ken an idiot*). The systematic relationship between the two structures that *give* occurs in is handled in the lexical semantics. A similar observation can be made for Rules 5 and 7 for verbs like *persuade,* which can appear with both finite and infinitive complement structures. Finally, Rule 6 shows that the structure for verbs like *require,* where the verb in its complement clause occurs in the uninflected base form (BSE), is a natural part of the grammar, not some irregularity, as is often presented in grammar texts.

While no attempt will be made here to suggest how to integrate a verb subcategorization approach into grammar teaching, a few comments about the value of such an approach can be offered. First, if the verb classes can be set up and identified by prototypical exemplars (rather than numbers, as was done here), teachers and learners will have a convenient way of identifying and referring to these structures. Second, the more comprehensive learner dictionaries are set up to include this kind of information, yet without the grammar background to support it, students may not find it easy to make use of that information. Finally, there is the possibility that internalizing these structures as subcategorization frames will aid in the acquisition of new vocabulary. If, as Krashen (1989) hypothesizes, new vocabulary can be acquired most efficiently through reading, then it is important that not only the form and meaning of the new word but also its subcategorization information be acquired. Learners already sensitized to paying attention to accompanying elements – prepositional phrases and clausal complements, for instance – should be more likely to take note of them when new words are encountered. To the extent that these elements are semantically linked to the word in obvious ways (as in *send to* versus *receive from*), the information provided by accompanying elements may provide an additional aid to acquisition.

While it is not yet clear how to integrate lexical subcategorization and grammar teaching, it is clear that they need to be brought together to a greater degree than is commonly done. Hubbard and Hix (1988) claim that many of the errors ESL learners make can be traced to their incomplete knowledge of the subcategorization for a particular item. Generalized Phrase Structure Grammar offers a resource for pedagogical grammarians to tap in dealing with this situation.

Other non-transformational theories

Although the focus in this paper has been on Relational Grammar, Lexical-Functional Grammar, and Generalized Phrase Structure Grammar, this does not exhaust the supply of contemporary non-transformational theories. Besides Systemic Grammar (see Hasan and Perrett, this volume), two additional ones that seem particularly promising for their potential to influence pedagogical grammar are Head-Driven Phrase Structure Grammar (Pollard and Sag 1987) and Cognitive Grammar (Langacker 1987).

Head-Driven Phrase Structure Grammar is something of a descendant of Generalized Phrase Structure Grammar, though it draws on Government/Binding, Lexical-Functional Grammar, and other theories for its grammatical framework. More interestingly, it incorporates a semantic component to a greater degree than any of these previous theories. This component, based in part on Barwise and Perry's (1983) Situation Semantics, is linked to the syntax in such a way as to give an integrated theory of grammatical form and meaning. This link of form and meaning within a unified theory leads to an even stronger influence of the lexicon than in the theories previously discussed, and in doing so may lead to analyses that create more learnable generalizations for pedagogical grammar.

Cognitive Grammar is an extension of the Space Grammar framework of Langacker (1978). Unlike the other theories presented in this paper, it does not claim to be generative, nor to isolate language completely from other human faculties. Rather, it assumes that language is a part of overall cognitive organization and that "the grammar of a language is non-generative and non-constructive, for the expressions of a language do not constitute a well-defined, algorithmically computable set" (Langacker 1988: 4–5). Rather than trying to integrate independent syntactic, semantic, and phonological components, it claims that grammar is a system of symbolic units incorporating semantic and phonological structure "with lexicon, morphology, and syntax forming a continuum of symbolic structures" (Langacker 1988: 5). Thus the distinction between what we commonly call grammar and lexicon becomes blurred even further. A collection of papers on Cognitive Grammar appears in Rudzka-Ostyn (1988). Studies within this theory that have particular relevance to pedagogical grammar include Lindner's (1983) description of verb-particle constructions and Hawkins' (1985) study of spatial prepositions. Hubbard (1986) applies concepts from the theory in an analysis of modals specifically aimed at ESL teachers.

Conclusion

In reviewing the three non-transformational theories that represent the primary focus of this paper, along with Government/Binding, Head-Driven Phrase Structure Grammar, and Cognitive Grammar, some interesting trends in contemporary linguistics emerge, summarized as follows:

- Transformations can be significantly limited and probably eliminated altogether in the description of the structure of a sentence.
- Grammatical relations/functions, such as subject, direct object, and so on, are linguistically significant notions both within a language and across languages.
- Lexical subcategorization is closely linked to grammar, and thematic relations, such as Agent, Patient, and Goal, also play a role in determining which verbs can occur in which structures.
- The verb is the central component of a clause and determines a significant amount of the sentence structure. Sentence grammar is to a large degree *verb* grammar.
- Syntax and semantics are closely interrelated, and some of the most recent work seems to be drawing them even closer.

The most familiar version of transformational grammar, Chomsky's (1965) Standard Theory, has not for quite some time been considered an adequate characterization of the structure of human language, even by those (such as Chomsky) most closely associated with it. Other theories, however, such as Chomsky's Government/Binding Theory and those discussed in this paper, have emerged to supplant it because either their scope or their precision, or both, are greater than what they have replaced. Theoretical insights from one theory often influence a contemporaneous one, and the linguistic data from English and other languages brought to light within one descriptive framework may provide key information for the advancement – or even the abandonment – of another. The unaccusatives discussed in the section on Relational Grammar, for instance, have in some form been incorporated into several other theories, such as Lexical-Functional Grammar. It is thus a strength, not a weakness, of linguistic theory that alternatives exist, and anyone looking to linguistic theory for answers should be aware of these alternatives.

Those of us associated with language teaching have to be very cautious in dealing with theoretical linguistics. Theories of grammar and the analyses which follow from them should not be blindly embraced, as has sometimes happened in the past. Nor, however, should they be ignored. They should instead be carefully and systematically considered in light of the context – teaching language – in which we are seeking to apply them.

References

Barwise, John, and John Perry. 1983. *Situations and Attitudes*. Cambridge, Mass.: MIT Press.

Bresnan, Joan, ed. 1982. *The Mental Representation of Grammatical Relations*. Cambridge, Mass.: MIT Press.

Burt, Marina, and Carol Kiparsky. 1972. *The Gooficon: A Repair Manual for English*. Rowley, Mass.: Newbury House.

Celce-Murcia, Marianne, and Diane Larsen-Freeman. 1983. *The Grammar Book: An ESL/EFL Teacher's Course*. Rowley, Mass.: Newbury House.

Chomsky, Noam. 1957. *Syntactic Structures*. The Hague: Mouton.

1965. *Aspects of the Theory of Syntax*. Cambridge, Mass.: MIT Press.

1970. Remarks on nominalization. In *Readings in English Transformational Grammar*, ed. by Roderick Jacobs and Peter Rosenbaum. Waltham, Mass.: Ginn.

1981. *Lectures on Government and Binding*. Dordrecht: Foris.

Flynn, Suzanne. 1988. Second language acquisition and grammatical theory. In *Linguistics: The Cambridge Survey*, vol. 2, *Linguistic Theory: Extensions and Implications*, ed. by Frederick Newmeyer. Cambridge: Cambridge University Press.

Gazdar, Gerald, Ewan Klein, Geoffrey Pullum, and Ivan Sag. 1985. *Generalized Phrase Structure Grammar*. Cambridge, Mass.: Harvard University Press.

Hawkins, Bruce. 1985. *The Semantics of English Spatial Prepositions*. Trier: LAUT.

Horrocks, Geoffrey. 1987. *Generative Grammar*. London: Longman.

Hubbard, Philip. 1983. Relational grammar and language teaching. Paper presented at the Midwest Regional TESOL Meeting, Minneapolis, October 1983.

1986. Understanding English modals through space grammar. *Ohio University Working Papers in Linguistics and Language Teaching* 8: 34–47.

Hubbard, Philip, and Donna Hix. 1988. Where vocabulary meets grammar: verb subcategorization errors in ESL writers. *CATESOL Journal* 1: 89–100.

Hyams, Nina. 1986. *Language Acquisition and the Theory of Parameters*. Dordrecht: Reidel.

Krashen, Stephen. 1989. We acquire vocabulary and spelling by reading: additional evidence for the Input Hypothesis. *The Modern Language Journal* 73(4): 440–64.

Langacker, Ronald. 1978. The form and meaning of the English auxiliary. *Language* 54: 853–82.

1987. *Foundations of Cognitive Grammar*, vol. 1, *Theoretical Prerequisites*. Stanford, Calif.: Stanford University Press.

1988. An overview of Cognitive Grammar. In *Topics in Cognitive Linguistics*, ed. by Brygida Rudzka-Ostyn. Amsterdam: John Benjamins.

Larsen-Freeman, Diane. 1990. Pedagogical descriptions of language: grammar. *Annual Review of Applied Linguistics* 10: 187–95.

Levin, Lori. 1988. *Operations on Lexical Forms: Unaccusative Rules in Germanic Languages*. New York: Garland.

Lindner, Susan. 1983. *A Lexico-Semantic Analysis of English Verb-Particle Constructions with UP and OUT*. Trier: LAUT.

Perlmutter, David. 1978. Impersonal passives and the unaccusative hypothesis. In *Proceedings of the Fourth Annual Meeting of the Berkeley Linguistics Society*. Berkeley, Calif.: University of California Press.

ed. 1983. *Studies in Relational Grammar 1*. Chicago: University of Chicago Press.

Perlmutter, David, and Paul Postal. 1977. Toward a universal characterization of passivization. In *Proceedings of the Third Annual Meeting of the Berkeley Linguistics Society*. Berkeley, Calif.: University of California Press.

Perlmutter, David, and Carol Rosen, eds. 1984. *Studies in Relational Grammar 2*. Chicago: University of Chicago Press.

Pollard, Carl, and Ivan Sag. 1987. *Information-Based Syntax and Semantics*, vol. 1, *Fundamentals*. Stanford, Calif.: Stanford University Center for the Study of Language and Information.

Richards, Jack. 1973. A non-contrastive approach to error analysis. In *Focus on the Learner: Pragmatic Perspectives for the Language Teacher*, ed. by John Oller and Jack Richards. Rowley, Mass.: Newbury House.

Rudzka-Ostyn, Brygida, ed. 1988. *Topics in Cognitive Linguistics*. Amsterdam: John Benjamins.

Rutherford, William, and Michael Sharwood Smith. 1985. Consciousness-raising and Universal Grammar. *Applied Linguistics* 6(3): 274–82.

Sells, Peter. 1985. *Lectures on Contemporary Syntactic Theories: An Introduction to Government-Binding Theory, Generalized Phrase Structure Grammar, and Lexical-Functional Grammar*. Stanford, Calif.: Stanford University Center for the Study of Language and Information.

4 *Rules and pedagogical grammar*

Paul Westney

Introduction

One of the central tasks of pedagogical grammar is the formulation of rules, in the broad sense of the statement of language regularities. Yet the criteria for such rules are rarely discussed in any detail. According to one account, they should be: *concrete, simple, nontechnical, cumulative, close to popular/traditional notions* and *in rule-of-thumb form* (Hammerly 1982: 402); while in a recent critical overview, the following 'design criteria' are singled out: *truth, clarity, simplicity, predictive value* (i.e., precisely defining form-meaning relations), *conceptual parsimony* (i.e., being within the learner's current understanding) and *relevance* (i.e., taking account of L1–L2 contrasts and hypothesising interlanguage rules) (Swan 1992).

Such statements raise a number of complex practical issues, such as how a criterion like 'simplicity' is to be met, how rough, or vague, rules of thumb can be, and how systematically L1–L2 contrasts should be taken into account. There are also more basic speculative questions such as (a) what optimal ('true'?) language rules really look like, (b) what pedagogical rules represent, in linguistic or psychological terms, (c) how such rules are perceived by their users and (d) how they relate to acquisition. The last two questions are, in principle, capable of empirical investigation, problematic though that is (Ellis 1990: ch. 8); but, in general, such issues are wide open.

The purpose of this chapter is to attempt some clarification of the general notion of language rules as it relates to pedagogy. In particular, it will be claimed that since there is no way of establishing a 'best' rule for any particular set of language phenomena, and our understanding of linguistic structure and of psycholinguistic processes is not such as to influence the formulation of pedagogical rules other than indirectly,

I would like to thank the editor for numerous helpful comments on the draft version of this paper, and Michael Swan for letting me see his paper (Swan, forthcoming) prior to publication.

there are sound reasons, both practical and theoretical, for learners and teachers to assume a cautious, if not skeptical, attitude towards any pedagogical treatment of language regularities.

In the following sections, I will first justify taking rules as the focal point of interest and try to clarify how the term *rule* is used in contexts relevant to language teaching; this will involve a critical discussion of criteria for pedagogical rules such as were listed at the outset. Then I will consider the implications of a number of trends in current theory and practice that point to difficulties with the concept, or some concepts, of rules and rule systems. There will follow a detailed case study from a complex area of English syntax. In conclusion, I will suggest some of the implications of the discussion for both learners and teachers. I shall focus on issues that arise generally in English as a Second/Foreign Language, and ignore all issues concerning specific L1–L2 contrasts.

Grammars

The field of reference here is, in the first instance, pedagogical grammar; but the relationship between this and other types of grammar[1] – and, thus, of rule – must be made clear. A basic distinction between grammar as codified product and grammar as conscious or explicit knowledge can first be made. For grammars as *products,* a simple dichotomy between pedagogical and linguistic grammars and rules is often made; however, a three-way distinction of the kind Leech (1988) makes, with *descriptive* mediating between *theoretical* and *pedagogical* types, is both more realistic and more practical, and will be assumed here.[2] This model suggests that theory and pedagogical practice are each relatively self-contained, each with its own aims and criteria, whereas description tends naturally to be oriented towards one or the other – perhaps both.

As to *knowledge* of grammar, a three-way distinction has also been made (and this is partly relatable to the distinction of grammars as *products,* just outlined), with *academic* grammar (theoretical and descriptive: relevant to the needs of professional linguists and university students), grammar for *teachers,* and *pedagogical* grammar (for learners) (Leech 1991): In this analysis, teachers' knowledge of grammar is seen

1 The term grammar is, in one use, ambiguous between a narrower sense, denoting the morphology and syntax of a language, and a broader sense, also including its phonology and semantics, and extending in principle to any aspect that is capable of systematic description. This chapter assumes the broader sense, but is mainly concerned with the narrower area.

2 Grammar types can be finely subcategorised so as to include, for example, *pedagogical (learning), pedagogical (teaching), descriptive (linguistic),* and *descriptive (reference: user's) grammar* (Dirven 1990: 1). However, it is hard to find substantial evidence of such distinctions, or of their value, in practice.

both as mediating between the other two and as including specific requirements absent in the others, suggesting that teachers may need to 'know' more, or different, things than students, professional linguists or learners. This chapter is primarily concerned with the teacher in such a mediating role, with reference both to explicit knowledge and to possible formulations of that knowledge.

Rules

In talking about rules, I am simply focusing on what is standardly seen as distinguishing the information in grammars from that in dictionaries; more basically, I assume that the establishment of rules, of whatever kind, epitomises the function of a grammar, and hence of that aspect of organised language teaching that concentrates on grammar. Thus the discussion will centre on (but not be restricted to) questions of the formulation and use of languages rules.

A definition

An informal definition of a language rule might be *observed regularity with predictive value*. The first of the two requirements this embodies is that it correspond to publicly available facts and thus be descriptive: This may involve an appeal to generally accepted wisdom, whether codified in grammars or claimed by native speakers, but in principle should be capable of confirmation from a specific corpus, or a teacher's or learner's own observations. The second requirement is that it have predictive power, and this is typically expressed in statements to the effect that *x*, being an instance of *y*, will have a specific form, pronunciation, interpretation, etc., *z*. In a narrower sense, this is also applied to individual items, when some aspect of an item's behaviour is related to general concepts, as when *some,* as opposed to *any,* is termed assertive and for use in affirmative sentences, or verbs are said to have specific complementation options (e.g., whether they can – or must – take two objects). A rule may be said to be significant to the extent that the information it embodies has general applicability in the grammar; thus 'rule' is a gradable rather than an absolute concept.

In terming a rule 'pedagogical', or applying it in a pedagogical context, the further assumption is made that it is relevant to the needs of learners, according to criteria such as were set out in the introduction and will be illustrated in this section.

Rules of formation and rules of use

A distinction is often made between rules of *formation* and rules of *use,* the former concerning mechanical regularities in language and the latter matters of personal meaning and choice. The precise nature of this distinction is seen in various ways, but it is typically presented in terms of a contrast between (a) phonology, inflectional morphology and the basic principles of sentence structure – *low-level* rules, appropriate for rote learning, and (b) more complex syntax and semantics (not to mention pragmatics and discourse) – *higher-level,* meaningful use, more suitable for conscious, cognitive learning (e.g., Rivers 1968: ch. 3).

The ways in which such a dichotomy may work can be illustrated from two pedagogical works. Close (1981: 17), in an account of the 'constant grammatical problems' of English, makes a basic split between (a) a 'solid core of linguistic facts' (1981: 204), which is treated as learnable, whether consciously or not, and goes some way beyond morphology and low-level syntax, and (b) 'a more nebulous area' where complex choices are involved and mastery comes from exposure and practice. In this account, the 'solid core' is accounted for by simple (but not completely unproblematic) rules; however, the outer area cannot be handled by rules as such, but is determined to a major extent by the operation of conceptual 'primary distinctions', such as *general* versus *particular* or *restrictive* versus *nonrestrictive.* Close's account thus highlights and justifies a distinction between two language levels in terms of complexity, speaker's needs and learning problems.

Second, Sinclair (1990), a pedagogical reference grammar, makes a radical innovation in relegating all morphological, together with a few phonological, rules to an appendix, leaving the main text free for higher-level description; this work will be illustrated in detail in the section titled 'Language description'.

In general, low-level, as opposed to higher-level, rules are seen as uncontroversial: The language facts are 'well known', and exceptions listable. It is even doubtful how far they entail any pedagogical problems: Rutherford (1980: 63) claims that at least some low-level rules can safely be 'left to take care of themselves', since the real problem is to determine exactly what the higher-level ones are (and then what to do about them). Even so, the exact formulation of low-level rules may not be self-evident, as will be seen in the first illustration of problems of 'simplicity' below.

A dichotomy of the kind being discussed here, between well-defined areas of language and those where both the structure and its appropriate formulation may be far from obvious, is manifested in various other ways. For example, there is a parallel in the distinctions made in error analysis between 'overt', or 'local', and 'covert', or 'global', errors, respectively (cf. the overview by Lennon 1991): The former are relatively easy to identify and categorise, the latter not. The distinction also has some relation to the discussion by Tarone and Yule (1989: 13–17) of categorial (i.e., absolute) versus probabilistic (i.e., 'more often than not') rules, respectively, and the dangers of treating the latter as if they were like the former.

Uses and forms of rules

This discussion is neutral as to the possible pedagogical uses of rules, as it assumes that formulations of some kind need to be both available and usable in language teaching contexts, regardless of whether, in specific circumstances, (a) the method employed is inductive or deductive, (b) the teaching is concerned with language *knowledge,* in the sense of mastery of the system, or language *control,* in the sense of ability to use it for personal meanings (cf. Rivers 1990: 52–53) or (c) language descriptions are *product-* or *process*-oriented (cf. Widdowson 1979: 243–44; Rutherford 1987).

As to the *form* a rule may take, this can cover a wide variety of types, including 'formal rules, schemata, formulas, principles, conditions, constraints, postulates, hierarchies, maxims, and algorithms' (Rutherford and Sharwood Smith 1988: 3). For pedagogical purposes, there are specific requirements such as were referred to in the introduction to this chapter, and these will now be examined in some detail.

Some criteria

It is obviously essential that the content of a rule be (a) accurate and (b) expressed in natural language terms that can be understood and applied by its users. These two requirements are not ultimately separable, but for convenience will be discussed in turn as distinct issues; and they can be related to the two sets of criteria listed in the Introduction as follows. The issues involved in the quest for accuracy or truth include questions of acceptable generality and abstractness, and the discussion will take account of (a) Hammerly's criteria that rules be *cumulative* and *in rule-of-thumb form,* and (b) Swan's requirements for *truth* and the possession of *predictive value.* The need for simplicity will be treated as subsuming (a) Hammerly's requirement that rules be *concrete, simple* and *nontechnical,* and relating to his requirement that they conform to *popular/traditional notions,* and (b) Swan's criteria of *clarity, simplicity* and *conceptual parsimony.* Swan's remaining criterion – *relevance* – will not be taken into account here, as it involves L1–L2 contrasts.

TRUTH, 'GENERAL RULES' AND RULES OF THUMB

We are concerned here with the need for descriptive accuracy, and perhaps for linguistic 'truth', if that is accessible or relevant. Hammerly's requirements that rules be *cumulative* and in *rule-of-thumb form* can be included in conjunction here, since they together concern the need for rules to be (a) accurate, (b) usable and (c) capable of gradual integration into broader patterns which reveal more of the structure of the language – criteria that may easily conflict.

Here we encounter the well-known challenge of avoiding oversimplified 'basic' rules that inevitably prove inadequate, if not actually false, in subsequent learning, and have to be radically changed, hazards amply illustrated by Close (1981: 18–24). An explicit contrast between 'rules of thumb', in the sense of informal pedagogical formulations of limited validity and scope, and 'rules of grammar', in the sense of linguistically sound, highly abstract generalisations, is made by Berman (1979). Berman argues the need for both types in pedagogical grammar, with the former gradually leading to the latter. This process is, however, far from unproblematic, since it assumes that appropriate 'rules of grammar' are both available and able to assist the learner, neither of which assumptions can be taken as necessarily true, as the illustrations that follow in this section and the section titled 'Background' will suggest. Three distinct types of problem that can arise in the attempt to establish true, and usable, generalisations will now be illustrated.

Establishing the nature and extent of a generalisation. The first type concerns cases where the language facts that may be relevant appear well defined, and the problem is how an appropriately general formulation should best be presented for pedagogical purposes. *Some* and *any* provide a good illustration. Typically, these items are initially presented as alternating forms for use in affirmative and negative/interrogative sentences, respectively. Their complementary status can readily be shown by considering appropriate full answers to a question like *Have you got any money on you?* – i.e., *I've got some money* and *I haven't got any money.* Within a pedagogical context, a broader picture can gradually be developed, when other uses of these items, as in *Have you got some money on you?* and *Anyone can tell you that!*, as well as related items like *somebody/anybody*, are introduced. The aim in such a case is to ensure that such extensions – both in learning and in the relevant rule – are cumulatively effective.

Two formulations designed to cover the various uses of *some* and *any* will now be compared. First, Quirk et al. (1985: 782–84) present a list, presumably complete, of sets of related assertive/nonassertive/negative items, starting with *some/any/no,* and including, for example, *still/any/ no more* and *already/yet/*——. The essential contrast involved is summarized as follows:

The primary difference between *some* and *any* (and between the *some-* and *any*-compounds) is that *some* is specific, though unspecified, while *any* is nonspecific. That is, *some* implies an amount or number that is known to the speaker. This difference tends to correlate with the difference between positive and negative contexts.

This statement is not designed for pedagogical application, and this is evident in the language used: The *specific-nonspecific-unspecified* contrast and the reference to a tendency to correlate, for example, could be expected to be problematic for learners.

Second, Lewis (1986: 33–35), objecting to the standard association of *some* with positive and *any* with negative and interrogative contexts, on the ground that any viable *general rule* must cover *all*, and not just the main, uses of an item, proposes the following:

Some is used if the idea is *restricted* or *limited* in some way. *Any* is used if the idea is *unrestricted* or *unlimited*. *Any* applies to all or none; *some* applies to part.

This is designed for pedagogical use, and is simpler in language, and presumably more accessible to a learner, particularly with the visual supports provided. Further, some uses of the items seem to be more readily explained than is often the case; for example, the contrasting pair *Some help would be welcome* (the speaker hopes for a little help) versus *Any help would be welcome* (the speaker will gladly receive every kind of help).

However, there remains the wider question whether an optimal *cumulative* rule should include the broad framework of Quirk et al. (1985). If it does not, it fails to capture generalisations; while if it does, it will require sophisticated structuring if it is to cover both the range of uses of *some* and *any*, and the general marking of assertive/nonassertive/negative meaning across a wide set of determiners, pronouns and adverbs, as well as – as a basic grammatical principle in English – the opposition of assertiveness and nonassertiveness (Quirk et al. 1985: 83–85). There is clearly no easy answer here.

Finding an appropriate formulation for a generalisation.   In the second type, the descriptive 'facts' relating to, in this case, a grammatical category, are again well established, and there is often felt to be a basic semantic unity attaching to all the uses in question: The problem lies in subsuming this unity under a pedagogically effective formulation. The two illustrations involve tense and aspect.

I shall first take the simple past tense. Apart from past time reference, this tense has present and future time uses, as illustrated in *If they had the chance . . .* , *I wish I knew, It's high time we left*, and *I thought you might be interested*. Traditionally, some of these uses are treated as subjunctives, which happen to be homonymous with past tense forms (with the possible exception of the verb *be*). Attempts to deal with this more satisfactorily usually involve treating these nonpast cases as secondary uses derived from a basic temporal meaning, perhaps through notions like 'nonactuality' or 'factual remoteness'. Descriptive and pedagogical grammars do not normally aim at a general rule of use here: Past time reference is treated as dominant, and 'other uses' are simply appended (e.g., Quirk et al. 1985: 187–88). Here, again, Lewis (1986: 74) argues that a general statement is required, and proposes that the tense is essentially concerned with events that are *factual* but *remote,* with the variety of use resting in the nature of the 'remoteness'. The crucial problem, then, becomes how far the concept 'remoteness' is, or can be made, viable for learners.

The second case concerns the progressive aspect, specifically as shown in progressive-simple tense contrasts. Attempts to provide a general basis for this contrast, whether practically or theoretically oriented, predominantly focus on the *noncompleteness* versus *completeness* contrast.[3] This may perhaps be descriptively satisfactory, but it is, like *remoteness* in relation to the past tense, rather abstract, and there is no evidence of how pedagogically effective such terms are. One test of a viable statement for the uses of the progressive is how well it is felt by a user to explain cases like *I am continually encountering examples of this,* a use singled out as 'difficult' and 'unexpected' in one grammar for teachers (Celce-Murcia and Larsen-Freeman 1983: 72).[4]

In these two cases, a learner's – and perhaps also a teacher's – ability to conceptualise 'remoteness' or 'incompleteness' in the appropriate ways is crucial. The problem here, in other words, is at least partly metalingual; but it is also one capable of empirical investigation.

Finding a safe generalisation. The final type of problem with setting up generalisations concerns the pedagogical aspects of cases where the 'facts' themselves are not well established. The first example involves the English modal system, which, despite extensive investigation, remains highly resistant to tidy, systematic treatment; the second concerns a minor restriction of uncertain nature and scope.

The distinction in use between *must* and *have to,* which are sometimes taken as the paradigm case for the alternation of true and periphrastic modals, is peculiarly baffling. It is fairly common practice to

3 The problem here is well illustrated by the variety of names for the category itself – aside from *progressive,* there are also *continuous, durative* and *-ing form,* while meanings commonly found for the progressive include *duration, limited duration* and *temporariness.* The major difficulty with such labels is how the relevant concepts are to be related to each other.

4 There is a further problem here: Such uses are commonly said to have a negative or pejorative overtone – which is not necessarily true, and, arguably, a confusing complication (Westney 1977).

distinguish *must* and *have to*,[5] at least in their obligational uses, in terms of the speaker's role: *Must* is typically said to indicate the speaker's support for or involvement in an 'obligation', while *have to* is either neutral or involves outside initiation. Yet there is ample evidence that this is nothing like an adequate account. Thus, Palmer (1990: 115–16) easily shows from corpus data that there can be no general distinction of such a kind, while Celce-Murcia (1990: 247–48) cites corpus-based evidence of a highly complex pattern of use. There is, in fact, good reason to suspect that several factors may have some relevance here, including mode (speech/writing), level of formality, and variety (primarily, British/American English).

In this situation, descriptive and, above all, pedagogical, accounts have a particular responsibility to be cautious in their statements and generalisations, and proposals – of which there are many – for taking any distinction in meaning (such as the speaker's role mentioned earlier) as basic, or for generalising from the *must*/*have to* pair across a set of supposed modal/periphrastic pairs, should be viewed with suspicion.

The second example concerns the co-occurrence of multiple *-ing* forms, as in *He was just starting singing*. A restriction of some kind is often noted here, and pedagogical materials commonly warn against such combinations, sometimes for stylistic reasons. Descriptive and theoretical treatments range between taking the 'jingle' effect as basic, but allowing for multiple factors (e.g., Bolinger 1979), and arguing for a specific grammatical rule blocking certain combinations (e.g., most recently, Pullum and Zwicky 1991). For pedagogical purposes – assuming, crucially, (a) that one knows what *is* grammatical, and (b) that the issue is identified as serious – the question may boil down to whether the danger of 'allowing' or 'encouraging' such co-occurrences is outweighed by the danger of 'discouraging' learners by artificially defining a problem area.[6]

In cases such as these, the evidence available may simply not support any safe generalisation, and this can create a particular problem for both teachers and learners in situations where clear-cut rules and 'explanations' are over-valued.

SIMPLICITY

This term may, first, relate either to rules of formation (e.g., phonological or morphological) or to rules of use (e.g., semantic or pragmatic); and, second, it may be a linguistic, psycholinguistic or pedagogical

---

5 For the sake of simplicity, I am leaving out of account both the form *have got to* and the fact that *have to* sometimes seems to be a forced choice, as in *They may have to apply this year.*

6 This issue was highlighted in my experience by a highly proficient nonnative speaker who hesitated, in writing, over *I'm enjoying reading your latest poems,* and sought – in vain – a better formulation that would avoid the supposed anomaly.

concept – that is, it may reflect the perspectives of the descriptive linguist, the learner or the teacher, respectively. For the learner, whose
perspective must be primary, some factors may in a specific context have
overriding importance, such as whether, assuming that there is a natural
developmental sequence which is relatively fixed (cf. Ellis 1990: ch. 6),
they are 'ready' to acquire a particular structure or rule, and whether this
is, or can be, formulated in a 'user-friendly' way. Four different kinds of
problems that arise in the quest for 'simplicity' will now be illustrated.

Pedagogical versus linguistic analysis.   The first case concerns a familiar topic in English morphology and phonology, and will be set out in
detail. The {Z} and {D} morphemes each have three functions ({Z} marks
the plural, the third person singular, present tense, of the verb, and the
possessive case – as in the final sound in the words *dogs/dog's* in *three
dogs, that dogs her progress,* and *a dog's life;* while {D} marks the past
tense, the past participle, and *-ed* adjectives – as in the final sound in
earned in *she earned plenty there, he's earned respect over the years,* and
a well-earned rest); and each has three distinct phonological realisations
(/s/-/z/-/əz/, and /t/-/d/-/əd/). These 'facts' may seem straightforward, and
the way they should be presented self-evident; that is, two consecutive
two-way choices are involved in each case, based on the final sound in
the stem – for {Z}, (a) sibilant versus nonsibilant (and if sibilant, then
/əz/), and (b), for nonsibilants, voiced (then /z/) versus voiceless (then
/s/); and for {D}, (a) alveolar plosive versus nonalveolar plosive (and if
alveolar, then /əd/), and (b), for nonalveolars, voiced (then /d/) versus
voiceless (then /t/). For example, in forming plurals for the set *cat, dog*
and *horse, horse* is first distinguished as ending in a sibilant, and then the
absence or presence of final voicing distinguishes *cat* from *dog.*

This is the standard descriptive analysis, but Dickerson (1990) argues
that, for a learner at the early stage where these phenomena are encountered, such rules are both too complex and too difficult. Instead, he
suggests a different set of pedagogical rules, based on the spelling system
and reducing the importance attached to the voicing/nonvoicing choice.
In the case of {Z}, words like *miss, chance* and *fix* are to be singled out by
their spellings and assigned /əz/ for their plurals, and the rest left to take
/s/ or /z/ – a matter of phonetic detail for a later stage of learning. This
leaves a few exceptions, like *ache,* that simply have to be itemized for
individual learning.

In this case, data that might appear simple are found to be too complex for learners, and hence for teaching, resulting in a new analysis. In
other words, psycholinguistic criteria are used, and applied to pedagogical aims, producing an analysis that may well appear anomalous in
purely linguistic terms.

Formal versus semantic simplicity.   The next two examples, which will merely be mentioned here, illustrate formal simplicity combined with semantic complexity, and vice versa. The definite and indefinite articles form a system (or set of systems) that is formally – in its morphology and phonology – relatively simple, but in terms of its semantics notoriously complex (their forms and uses occupy one and twenty-three pages, respectively, in Quirk et al. 1985). By contrast, *wh*-question formation (as in the questions *Who went home?* and *Why did he go home?* in relation to the statement *He went home*) is formally highly complex, since it involves a number of syntactic operations, including word-order change and, in some cases, *do*-support, but is, arguably, semantically simple (cf. Krashen 1982: 17–18). These are descriptive observations, but must underlie any pedagogical approach to the areas in question.

Overt simplicity with covert complexity.   A quite different kind of example is provided by the general requirement that an English sentence have a preverbal subject: This can be stated in simple, unambiguous terms and is often felt to be so self-evident as to need no mention. However, it has wide and complex implications for the structure of the language, which means that it cannot properly be regarded as a 'simple' rule of either syntax or use. This can be illustrated by considering the function of the 'meaningless' but obligatory items *it* and *there* in *It's raining* and *There's a lot of noise outside,* and the preferred use of *there* in *There are several people waiting* (rather than *Several people are waiting*) when a new topic is being introduced. Existential *there* can, in fact, only be treated adequately in relation to discourse use and information structure. This is a complex area, and there is ample evidence that it is problematic for second language learners, especially with an L1 without the requirement for a preverbal subject (cf. Swan and Smith 1987).

Elusive simplicity.   The final example concerns the restriction that makes *I showed/told/etc. him the answer* possible, but not **I described/ explained/etc. him the answer.* This is a well-known learning problem (cf., most recently, Ellis 1991), and it is often assumed that there must be an explanation or rule to cover it. Most commonly, this is treated in terms of lexical restrictions: Verbs in the *show* group can dativise, while those in the *describe* group cannot, so that we have to say *I explained the answer to him,* and so on. It is sometimes noted that verbs that dativise tend to be native/Germanic and monosyllabic, and those that do not to be Latinate/Romance and polysyllabic, but this does not lead to a conventionally satisfactory rule, since it appeals to knowledge of etymology and still fails to account for several apparent exceptions, such as *say* and *offer.* It seems, in fact, that a fully adequate explanation of the data may have to take into account, in addition to the criteria already mentioned, stress placement, prefixation, and, above all, semantic subclassification (Pinker 1989: especially 119). While the restriction in question is (of course) psychologically real for native speakers, it is impossible to envisage a satisfactory pedagogical statement, since simplicity here would necessarily be at the expense of accuracy and lead straight to the popular stereotype of rules as always having exceptions.

CONCLUSION

The examples we have discussed illustrate a variety of practical problems that arise in attempts to deal with different aspects of English for pedagogical purposes, and cumulatively they suggest that it may often be misguided to look for clear-cut solutions, whether descriptive or pedagogical. To achieve optimal pedagogical rules (whatever they might be), it would be necessary to have access to (a) the best description of the language, (b) relevant psycholinguistic criteria that could determine how learners (whether considered collectively or individually) are best helped in acquisition and (c) a means of deriving appropriate pedagogical formulations from this information. The next section will discuss, from a number of different perspectives, general reasons why such information is simply not available.

Background

In this section the nature of the relation between theoretical and pedagogical formulations, and the possibility of equivalence between different types of rules or other constructs, will first be taken up. Then we will set out a number of current indications within linguistic theory, the description of English, acquisition research, and pedagogy that suggest problems with standard conceptions of rules.

Theory and practice: the question of equivalence

The first question, which is central within applied linguistics, involves the interface between theoretical concepts and practical applications. Quite different approaches are possible here. On the one hand, it may be claimed that since language is rule-governed, it is the business of linguistics to determine what the rules are; of descriptions to set them out systematically; of pedagogy to present them; of learners to internalize them, and so on, and it may be argued that the rules involved at each stage of this process are essentially the same, even if they are formulated differently. The alternative to such argumentation is quite simply to reject every such assumption of equivalence or even applicability.

Earlier statements of the relation involved here often argued that the contribution of theoretical linguistics to language pedagogy is to provide descriptions (e.g., Halliday, McIntosh and Strevens 1964: 167), or, more specifically, the means (rule systems) for producing these, and that these should be the best available (Saporta 1973: 271), and hence the newest (Corder 1973: 276). This approach is well illustrated in the *Edinburgh Course,* where the accounts of Pedagogical Grammar and Contrastive Analysis are exemplified by systems of generative rules (Allen 1974; van Buren 1974). The argument in such cases assumes a linguistic source with its own internal criteria, which provides the best product; this product – whether a generative description itself or the methodology for producing a description for particular purposes – is then available as a basis for pedagogical descriptions and teaching materials and practice.

These sources imply the existence of two rather different types of grammar and rule system, together with various possible forms of impact of the first on the second. Such an approach is illustrated in Berman's (1979) contrast of rules of grammar and rules of thumb (cf. the section titled 'Truth, "general rules" and rules of thumb'), and has been set out in various models of the operation of pedagogical grammar (e.g., Noblitt 1972). A corollary of this is that the rule systems involved are convertible, that is, that rules in one system can be directly related to those in another.

An extended demonstration of what convertibility, with the possibility of equivalence, means is provided by Krashen (1982: 92–94). Krashen's aim is to show how few of the rules of a language learners actually master, as opposed to what acquirers may internalise;[7] to illustrate his argument, he uses a set of seven concentric circles, in turn representing, from the outside to the core, the following:

(a) the totality of the rules of English,
(b) the subset of (a) that formal linguists have succeeded in describing,
(c) applied linguists' knowledge,
(d) the best teachers' knowledge,
(e) rules taught,
(f) rules actually learnt by the best students, and
(g) rules used in performance.

What concerns us here is not the issue of nonattainment, but the underlying assumption that the rules at each level *can* in principle be compared.

The thinking illustrated here is widely reflected, both informally (in any unqualified reference within a pedagogical context to explaining, learning, understanding or applying *the rules* for some phenomena), and

---

7 This involves a radical contrast between *learning* (conscious, typically in a formal setting) and *acquisition* (subconscious, typically in an informal setting).

formally, as in the sources cited earlier in this section (e.g., Saporta 1973). A further specific instance is shown in the kind of cognitive psychology presented by Anderson (1983), where the acquisition of a cognitive skill is described in terms of a progression from *declarative knowledge* (static and explicitly rule-based) to *procedural knowledge* (dynamic and relatively automatised). This model clearly requires that the totality of the rules in question be a unique set, whether they are consciously available or not; and when Anderson refers to FL learners as being aware of the rules of a language at the early stages, but eventually attaining a level at which they are often forgotten (1980: 224), the assumption of the equivalence or identity of the rules at different stages becomes explicit.

There are a number of questionable claims in such assumptions of rule equivalence, starting with the notion of a definable set of all the rules of a language, as in (a), and the implication that the definitive description of these is an ongoing process. However, the most important problem lies in the fact that the various rules in question are simply different kinds of entities. For example, (a) in the previous listing is the psychological property of an idealised speaker, (b) is the product of linguistic theory, (f) is crucially ambiguous between the external, explicit forms of pedagogical rules and what a learner may internalise, and (g) – to the extent that it *can* be described –is a psychological construct.[8] Whether or not one accepts that some linguistic concepts and rules have psychological reality, there is no sound basis for assuming the equivalence, or comparability, of this variety of linguistic and psycholinguistic rules.

This general case for nonequivalence is worth emphasising, since pedagogical rules have strictly practical functions, are severely constrained by the kinds of factors discussed earlier (e.g., that rules can be both accurate and simple) and as such are ad hoc entities for which no strong claims can be made. Apart from this, it should be noted that the standard argument within generative grammar (which in general makes the strongest claims for the validity of its constructs) has been that only 'the most elementary rudiments' of grammatical structure (i.e., low-level rules) can be taught since *explicit* knowledge of such structure is simply not available (Chomsky 1969: 68; cf. Cook 1988: 177).

A further, indirect kind of evidence for nonequivalence between rule types is to be found in their output. A recent comparative investigation into the descriptive output of generative and descriptive grammar in four complex areas of English syntax (Stuurman 1989)[9] comes to the conclusion that the two kinds of grammar are incompatible, with the former

8 The nonequivalence of explicit rules of the kinds in (b) and (f) is discussed by Odlin (1986: 125).
9 For descriptive grammar, Stuurman draws mainly on the traditional comprehensive grammarians such as Jespersen.

having no possible contribution to make to the latter. This non-equivalence may be seen in terms of the noncomparability of type (b) rules and type (c) rules, respectively.

Evidence of problems with rules

I will now move on to discuss a number of current trends within, in turn, linguistic theory, description, acquisition research and pedagogy that point to problems with rule formulation.

LINGUISTIC THEORY

To take linguistic theory first, recent developments within the dominant model of generative grammar have led to the consolidation of a theory where the focus is no longer on rule systems of the kind that characterised the *Aspects* model (Chomsky 1965), which was often found to be close enough to conventional ideas of syntactic rules to be readily applicable in descriptive and pedagogical contexts. Instead, the operation of abstract universal principles, with variable parameters, is assumed, with a heavy syntactic burden resting on individual lexical items. To take a simple example, a passive question (e.g., *Is that produced here?*, relatable to an active statement like *They produce that somewhere*) is now treated in terms not of PS rules together with passivisation and question formation transformations, but rather of the lexical properties of the specific verb, here *produce* (which state, for example, what kinds of noun phrase can, or must, occur with it), and of a number of parameterised principles (which help to determine, for example, where *is* and *that* can be moved). 'Rule', significantly, is treated as too vague a term to use for the operation of such principles (Chomsky 1986: 243–44). The possible relevance of this linguistic model to TESL/TEFL is a particularly challenging problem (cf. especially Cook 1988: ch. 7).

These comments strictly concern mainstream generative grammar. However, there are several other influential linguistic models, many of which focus on lexical meaning, and this entails a more radical reassessment of the nature and functions of syntactic rules (cf. Little, in this volume).

LANGUAGE DESCRIPTION

Two major points emerge from the vast amount of descriptive work done on English in recent years (and illustrated in various ways in the section titled 'Rules'). First, there is obviously no 'best' or final description of any area of language, and any account has to be seen in relation to its function or consumer. Second, even relatively 'basic', seemingly well-defined areas of the grammar can be shown to contain great complexity, which is complicated by inherent variability and vagueness of use. Passive participles provide a good example here (cf. Kilby 1984: ch. 5): There seems, for example, to be considerable uncertainty and variation in use about when such items can occur prenominally (e.g., *?an allowed example, ?the recognized outcome*), prenominally with adverbial modification (e.g., *?very disgusted look*), or predicatively after a verb like *appear* (e.g., *?it seemed recommended*). These points create obvious problems for clear-cut rule formation. As to alternative forms of description potentially more in accord with communicative methodology, the semantically/pragmatically based approach adopted by, especially, Leech and Svartvik (1975) has not been pursued significantly, and has been negatively assessed on the grounds that it simply lacks the generative potential of syntax (Brumfit 1980: 103–4).

A certain wariness about the exact nature of grammatical rules has become evident in reference grammars recently. In this connection, Sinclair (1990) represents a striking attempt to deal with the recognition that language is characterised by rules or regularities of rather varied kinds. In order to avoid the typical 'restrictive rules' that many pedagogical grammars concentrate on (1990: x), this grammar uses three types of regularity in its presentation: 'major statements' for the most general observations, corresponding closely to conventional rules; 'usage notes', where applicability is explicitly limited, for example, for ditransitive verbs where the indirect object normally comes first, as in *She allowed her son only two pounds a week* (1990: 161); and 'productive features', where the reader is told 'you can use the rules . . . in a creative and original manner, giving you greater freedom of expression in English' (1990: xvi), for example, for the addition of *-ful* to 'partitives' to give *armful, handful,* and so on (1990: 112).

Such descriptive mechanisms highlight the fact that regularities in language are of varied kinds and varying degrees of strictness, and, crucially, they confront the question of what the inherent creativity of language use might mean in practice for a learner. The 'productive features' are the most striking element and cover such varied phenomena as the combinatory possibilities of color terms, as in *greenish-white* or *blue-green* (1990: 68), and adjectival formation from nouns with *-less,* as in *heartless* (1990: 214). However, there are hazards in such a carte-blanche approach, as is evident, for example, in the case of the *-ing* forms of intransitive verbs used as attributive adjectives, on the lines of *falling employment* or *the governing authorities* (1990: 78), which naturally suggest the correctness of phrases like *the emptying hall* or *the leaving bus.*

A final indication of a move away from the dominance of syntactic structuring is shown in the recent trend for reference grammars to be designed on an alphabetical basis, so that grammatical topics or, in some cases, individual items can be found as in a dictionary (e.g., Swan 1980;

Leech 1989). This appears in its most extreme form in Chalker (1990), where the entire grammar is based lexically, so that, for example, tense usage is dealt with under the auxiliary involved (thus, the forms and uses of the progressive are dealt with under *be*).

SECOND LANGUAGE ACQUISITION RESEARCH

SLA research has tended to validate organised classroom instruction, and thus, by implication, rule-related learning (Long 1983; Ellis 1990: ch. 6). There is, on the other hand, striking evidence that the details of conscious rule-learning as such may have a minimal relation to either actual acquisition or performance (Seliger 1979); this further illustrates the problems of nonequivalence discussed earlier and suggests the possibility of noncorrespondence between the rules learners learn (in the strict sense of declarative knowledge) and those they have internalised. Such findings support the widely suspected lack of full equivalence between what is taught and what is learnt (or lack of fit between input and intake). Relevant experimentation (cf. also van Baalen 1983) has dealt with very 'simple' low-level rules; but it may be assumed that the situation described would be more marked at higher levels.

Another relevant SLA finding again concerns the relative weighting of syntax and lexis: Ard and Gass (1987), in an investigation of the acquisition of various areas of English structure, including dativisation, show that the semantic aspects of individual lexical items may become more significant at higher levels of performance, which suggests that successful learning may be associated with progressively reduced dependence on broad syntactic rules. There is some similarity here to the observation in first language acquisition that while low-level rules of morphology tend to be overgeneralized (as in *he goed* or *two sheeps*), higher-level rules of syntax are not applied indiscriminately, but require positive evidence, so that, for example, *They are probable to win,* on the analogy of *They are likely to win,* is not a normal first-language developmental error, despite the semantic closeness of *probable* and *likely* (Smith 1989: 194).

PEDAGOGY

Some traditional questions within TESL/TEFL as to whether, and how, rules (of whatever kind) should be used explicitly, with an accompanying vacillation between *inductivism* and *deductivism,* have been intensified by the rise of a general commitment to communicative methodology, with its ambivalent attitude towards the role of grammatical structuring. This has in turn contributed to the current revival of explicit interest in 'grammar'. One striking proposal for the place of grammar in such a methodology comes from Widdowson (1990: 95), where an approach is argued that reverses traditional practice and accords lexis a central and basic position: to 'begin with lexical items, and show how they need to be grammatically modified to be communicatively effective'. This clearly suggests a flexible, exploratory approach to grammatical rules.

Finally, the rationale behind the development of the lexical syllabus (Willis 1990) is highly relevant here, since its justification includes (a) the inherent inadequacy of any grammatical description or syllabus, and (b) the claim that learners in any case go beyond explicit grammatical instruction – i.e., in terms of the discussion in the section titled 'Theory and practice: the question of equivalence', they develop rules of type (g) – those used in actual performance – which cannot be related to those of type (e) – those explicitly taught.

Nonfinite complementation

A specific area of English syntax will now be investigated in detail in order to illustrate some of the main problems involved in rule determination for pedagogical purposes.

Verb complementation by infinitives (with or without *to*) and *-ing* forms, as in, respectively, *We asked to leave, They made him resign,* and *She regretted getting involved in politics,*[10] is pedagogically a well-known problem area and normally receives extensive treatment in reference grammars and practice material. At the same time, it is not obviously a self-contained area in theoretical or purely descriptive terms and involves particularly complex syntactic-semantic relations. Four possible, rather distinct, pedagogical approaches will be discussed here in turn.

A lexical approach

Within a strictly lexical approach, the syntax is simply treated as part of the properties of individual lexical items, so that, for example, it is a feature of *intend* that it can be followed by a *to*-infinitive or an *-ing* form, in each case with or without a preceding object; in this way, generalisations regarding complementation options become redundant. Such a solution is supported by the lack of evident semantic motivation for the wide variety of individual syntactic behaviour shown by complement-taking verbs, as seen in the chart on page 90, where some complement options are given for five verbs that might appear to be semantically close.

10 I am only concerned with a narrow range of verb + infinitive and verb + *-ing* structures and ignore the issue of whether, and when, *-ing* is a participle or gerund. To simplify matters, I leave *that*-clause complementation, as in *She regretted that she had got involved in politics,* out of account as far as possible.

| | Complement options | | | | |
	1	2	3	4	5
hope	+	−	−	−	+
intend	+	+	+	+	?
propose	+	−	+	?	+
want	+	+	−	+	−
wish	+	+	−	−	?

Complement options: (1) *to*-infinitive; (2) object + *to*-infinitive; (3) -*ing*; (4) object + -*ing*; (5) *that*-clause

That-clause complementation is included here for purposes of comparison.[11] In determining grammaticality, the sentences that derive from *I hope*, etc., with the complements (1) *to go*, (2) *them to go*, (3) *going*, (4) *them/their going*, and (5) *that I/they (will) go* are tested. Apart from evidence of this kind, there is considerable general variation in the use, or at least in descriptive treatments, of the syntax and semantics of complement-taking verbs: For example, do *attempt* and *plan* allow the -*ing* form, and, if so, is the meaning the same as with the *to*-infinitive?

In an approach which focuses on the syntactic features of individual items, dictionaries supply all the necessary information, and the job of a grammar is minimised. In this first case, from a theoretical perspective, the syntax has to allow all the complementation types (i.e., infinitive, -*ing* form, and *that*-clause), with one or more being selected lexically.

A semantic approach

Alternatively, a grammar can focus on such semantic factors as can be shown to be crucial to the syntactic choice and thus have some explanatory value, and cover as much as possible of the field systematically. An extended illustration of this is provided by Ungerer et al. (1984: ch. 8), where the subsections are largely given functional headings such as 'expressing one's occupation with something' (e.g., *practice, consider, try;* also *be busy, be engaged in*) or 'expressing an emotional reaction or attitude' (e.g., *enjoy, love, don't mind*), in all of which cases the verb or verbal unit, when used in the relevant sense, takes -*ing* complements. Obviously, such labels risk being opaque, and unclassifiable cases and exceptions remain; for example, *suggest* does not accept the infinitive, although apparently all other verbs of advising, allowing and forbidding do so when the reference is specific (thus, *I advised them to go later*, but only *I suggested [their] going later*).

11 There may be individual/dialectal variation here.

Compromise

Most commonly, a compromise solution is used: A system is presented, with certain semantic factors prominent, but, as is usual with language data, there are exceptions or odd cases that can only be 'explained' with difficulty. Close (1981: 139) illustrates this well: 'We can trace three differences in meaning between the infinitive and the *-ing*. They may help to explain why the infinitive has become adopted in one pattern, while the *-ing* is adopted in another; and they can help us to decide which form to use when there is a choice'. The author's wording is significant: He is only offering rough guidelines and concentrating on cases where there is a meaning-related choice.

Markedness

A quite different approach to the descriptive/pedagogical treatment of this area might be suggested by facts of the following kind: Complementation with the infinitive occurs much more frequently than with the *-ing* form (cf. data in Celce-Murcia and Larsen-Freeman 1983: 433); far more verbs take or allow infinitival than *-ing* complementation; the former appears earlier in first language acquisition (e.g., Brown 1973); and this is reflected in findings for second language acquisition (Mazurkewich 1988). Moreover, evidence from error analysis shows greater problems with *-ing* structures (this is apparent in Morrissey 1979); learner intuition testing very clearly suggests that the greatest problems in this area occur with cases where the *-ing* form is required grammatically, but the infinitive is strongly preferred.[12]

One explanation for evidence of these various kinds is in terms of *markedness:* that is, the infinitive structures are, or are perceived as, the norm, and the use of the *-ing* form is special, or exceptional, and thus requires special learning, just as exceptional verb morphology or spell-

---

12 In a survey, a group of eighteen students (with an average of nine to ten years of learning English, as well as an average of three months' residence in an English-speaking country) recorded their intuitions about the complementation options possible with a set of thirty predicates, indicating, for each of four possible structures (plain *-ing*, object + *-ing*, plain *to*-infinitive and object + *to*-infinitive), one of the four categories 'definitely OK', 'possibly OK', 'probably wrong' and 'definitely wrong'. To show the weight of intuitions for a particular option, these four values were counted as 4, 3, 2, and 1, respectively. This means that, for a group of eighteen, the maximum score possible for a specific item in a specific structure is 72 (meaning 'definitely OK' for all subjects), and the minimum 18 (meaning 'definitely wrong' for all subjects). The figures that stood out as the highest for wrong (ungrammatical) choices were 72 for *suggest,* 64 for *risk* and 59 for *avoid* and *imagine,* in each case for wrong complementation by plain *to*-infinitive as opposed to correct complementation by *-ing,* as in **Helen suggests to go . . .* as opposed to *Helen suggests going . . . .*

ings may require explicit learning, and hence may create greater learning problems. Pedagogically, this might suggest treating infinitive structures as the norm and focusing on *-ing* complementation as exceptional and requiring item learning.

At the same time, the fact that it is precisely verbs such as *suggest* (above all), *risk* and *avoid* that appear to present special learner problems points to some perceived anomaly. Thus, a typical statement of the difference in use between the infinitive and the *-ing* form, respectively, focuses on the following contrasts: (a) activity in general/act completed versus activity in progress, (b) new act versus activity in progress, (c) future activity versus previous activity (Close 1981: 139–41). The use of *-ing* complementation, and nonuse of the infinitive, with verbs such as these three seems to be strikingly at odds with these observations.[13] This might well suggest that it is preferable in such cases to offer no 'semantic explanation' at all.

Conclusion

This discussion points to various, rather distinct possible approaches to this area: Each has its advantages, but for pedagogical purposes there is no principled basis for opting for one over the others. The first, lexical approach makes the fewest claims, in that no generalisations are used; the others, in various ways, create complex conceptual systems that have to be justified and may prove pedagogical liabilities. Together, these approaches clearly illustrate the inevitable tension between the interests of generalisation and detail, or of simplicity and 'truth'.

Some conclusions

The salient points of this discussion can be summarised as follows: The nature of our knowledge of language and of language-learning processes is such that, beyond the low-level area, notions of optimally accurate and/or effective rules are neither realistic nor desirable in a learning/teaching situation.

More generally, it can be argued that an adequate model of language, for both the learner and the teacher, must allow for structure to be relatively obscure and only indirectly accessible to consciousness; and that any language user 'knows' that language is like this, or can have such knowledge brought to awareness, most obviously by considering aspects of his or her own language and its use. It could, in fact, be

---

13 It is, in any case, difficult to argue strongly for semantic values here when one considers, for example, that *suggest* formerly took infinitive complementation, at least in Shakespearean English, and the related noun *suggestion* still does so in some dialects.

claimed that, within pedagogical contexts, this knowledge is involved in awareness of language as 'rule-governed behaviour'.

From the *learner's* perspective, it is significant that the following are among the strategies that appear to lead to successful learning (cf. the overview of research in Rubin 1987): willingness to take risks, tolerance for ambiguity/vagueness, attention to linguistic form, and readiness to guess/inference. These factors suggest that the craving for 'explicit rules' that is sometimes observed in learners and used to justify formal instruction should not necessarily be viewed as a reflection of essential language learning processes themselves, but rather be seen as a manifestation both of a general problem-solving strategy in situations demanding the imposition of some order, and of a psychological need for security. Moreover, the use of simplified rules may be counterproductive, since the learner is encouraged to accept statements which conscious experience would (perhaps later, will) show to be in some sense inadequate or irrelevant; and this practice may be one reason for the mistrust of rules and 'grammar' that is often apparent in advanced learners.

For the *teacher,* this argumentation suggests that the roles of model, organizer and assessor are crucial: It is much more relevant to the learner's needs that a teacher can provide typical language data and monitor learner production effectively (whether for accuracy or for fluency) than that the most watertight, static formulations of language data be aimed at. This also means that an appropriate knowledge of the nature of language will entail an awareness of its complexity and its resistance to simple, clear-cut categorisation rather than an apparent, perhaps superficial, mastery of its supposed central rule systems.

References

Allen, J. P. B. 1974. Pedagogic grammar. In Allen and Corder (eds.), London: Oxford University Press, 59–92.

Allen, J. P. B., and S. Pit Corder (eds.). 1973. *The Edinburgh Course in Applied Linguistics,* vol. 1, *Readings for Applied Linguistics.* London: Oxford University Press.

1974. *The Edinburgh Course in Applied Linguistics,* vol. 3, *Techniques in Applied Linguistics.* London: Oxford University Press.

Anderson, John R. 1980. *Cognitive Psychology and its Implications.* San Francisco: Freeman.

1983. *The Architecture of Cognition.* Cambridge, Mass.: Harvard University Press.

Ard, Josh, and Susan M. Gass. 1987. Lexical constraints on syntactic acquisition. *Studies in Second Language Acquisition* 9: 233–52.

Berman, Ruth A. 1979. Rule of grammar or rule of thumb? *International Review of Applied Linguistics* 27: 279–302.

Bolinger, Dwight. 1979. The jingle theory of double -*ing*. In *Function and Context in Linguistic Analysis*, ed. by David J. Allerton, E. Carney and D. Holdcroft. Cambridge: Cambridge University Press, 41–56.

Brown, Roger. 1973. *A First Language: The Early Stages*. Cambridge, Mass: Harvard University Press.

Brumfit, Christopher J. 1980. Notional syllabuses: a reassessment. In *Problems and Principles in English Teaching*, ed. by C. J. Brumfit. Oxford: Pergamon, 98–106.

Celce-Murcia, Marianne. 1990. Data-based language analysis and TESL. In *Georgetown University Round Table on Language and Linguistics 1990*, ed. by James A. Alatis. Washington, D.C: Georgetown University Press, 245–59.

Celce-Murcia, Marianne, and Diane Larsen-Freeman. 1983. *The Grammar Book: An ESL/EFL Teacher's Course*. Rowley, Mass.: Newbury House.

Chalker, Sylvia. 1990. *English Grammar Word by Word*. Walton-on-Thames, U.K.: Nelson.

Chomsky, Noam. 1965. *Aspects of the Theory of Syntax*. Cambridge, Mass.: MIT Press.

1969. Linguistics and philosophy. In *Language and Philosophy: A Symposium*, ed. by S. Hook. New York: New York University Press, 51–94.

1986. *Knowledge of Language: Its Nature, Origin and Use*. New York: Praeger.

Close, Reginald A. 1981. *English as a Foreign Language* (3d ed.). London: Allen & Unwin.

Cook, Vivian J. 1988. *Chomsky's Universal Grammar: An Introduction*. Oxford: Blackwell.

Corder, S. Pit. 1973. Linguistics and the language teaching syllabus. In Allen and Corder (eds.), London: Oxford University Press, 275–84.

Dickerson, Wayne B. 1990. Morphology via orthography: a visual approach to oral decisions. *Applied Linguistics* 11: 238–52.

Dirven, Rene. 1990. Pedagogical grammar (state of the art article). *Language Teaching* 23: 1–18.

Ellis, Rod. 1990. *Instructed Second Language Acquisition: Learning in the Classroom*. Oxford: Blackwell.

1991. Grammaticality judgments and second language acquisition. *Studies in Second Language Acquisition* 13: 161–86.

Halliday, Michael A. K., Angus McIntosh and Peter Strevens. 1964. *The Linguistic Sciences and Language Teaching*. London: Longman.

Hammerly, Hector. 1982. *Synthesis in Second Language Teaching. An Introduction to Linguistics*. Blaine, Wash.: Second Language Publications.

Kilby, David. 1984. *Descriptive Syntax and the English Verb*. London: Croom Helm.

Krashen, Stephen. 1982. *Principles and Practice in Second Language Acquisition*. Oxford: Pergamon.

Leech, Geoffrey. 1988. Varieties of English grammar: the state of the art from the grammarian's point of view. In *Kernprobleme der englischen Grammatik: Sprachliche Fakten und ihre Vermittlung*, ed. by Wolf-Dietrich Bald. München: Langenscheidt-Longman, 5–17.

1991. Teachers' grammar – learners' grammar. In *Initial and In-Service Foreign Language Teacher Education (Bulletin, Greek Applied Linguistics Association* 4), 19–22.

Leech, Geoffrey (with Benita Cruikshank and Roz Ivanic). 1989. *An A–Z of English Grammar and Usage*. London: Arnold.

Leech, Geoffrey, and Jan Svartvik. 1975. *A Communicative Grammar of English*. London: Longman.

Lennon, Paul. 1991. Error: some problems of definition, identification, and distinction. *Applied Linguistics* 12: 180–96.

Lewis, Michael. 1986. *The English Verb – An Exploration of Structure and Meaning*. Hove, U.K.: Language Teaching Publications.

Long, Michael. 1983. Does second language instruction make a difference? A review of the research. *TESOL Quarterly* 17: 359–82.

Mazurkewich, Irene. 1988. The acquisition of infinitive and gerund complements by second language learners. In *Linguistic Theory in Second Language Acquisition*, ed. by Suzanne Flynn and Wayne O'Neil. Dordrecht: Kluwer, 127–43.

Morrissey, Michael D. 1979. A typology of errors in non-finite verb complementation. *Linguistische Berichte* 60: 91–101.

Noblitt, James S. 1972. Pedagogical grammar: towards a theory of foreign language materials preparation. *International Review of Applied Linguistics* 10: 313–31.

Odlin, Terence. 1986. On the nature and use of explicit knowledge. *International Review of Applied Linguistics* 24: 123–44.

Palmer, Frank R. 1990. *Modality and the English Modals* (2d ed.). London: Longman.

Pinker, Steven. 1989. *Learnability and Cognition: The Acquisition of Argument Structure*. Cambridge, Mass.: MIT Press.

Pullum, Geoffrey K., and Arnold M. Zwicky. 1991. Condition duplication, paradigm homonymy, and transconstructional constraints. *Proceedings of the 17th Annual Meeting of the Berkeley Linguistics Society*, 252–66.

Quirk, Randolph, Sidney Greenbaum, Geoffrey Leech, and Jan Svartvik. 1985. *A Comprehensive Grammar of the English Language*. London: Longman.

Rivers, Wilga M. 1968. *Teaching Foreign-Language Skills*. Chicago: Chicago University Press.

1990. Mental representations and language in action. In *Georgetown University Round Table on Language and Linguistics 1990*, ed. by James A. Alatis. Washington, D.C.: Georgetown University Press, 49–64.

Rubin, Joan. 1987. Learner strategies: theoretical assumptions, research history and typology. In *Learner Strategies in Language Learning*, ed. by Anita Wenden and Joan Rubin. Englewood Cliffs, N.J.: Prentice-Hall, 15–30.

Rutherford, William E. 1980. Aspects of pedagogical grammar. *Applied Linguistics* 1: 60–73.

1987. *Second Language Grammar: Learning and Teaching*. London: Longman.

Rutherford, William, and Michael Sharwood Smith (eds.). 1988. *Grammar and Second Language Teaching: A Book of Readings*. New York: Newbury House.

Saporta, Sol. 1973. Scientific grammars and pedagogical grammars. In Allen and Corder (eds.), London: Oxford University Press, 265–74.

Seliger, Herbert W. 1979. On the nature and function of language rules in language teaching. *TESOL Quarterly* 13: 359–69.

Sinclair, John (ed.-in-chief). 1990. *Collins COBUILD English Grammar*. London: Collins.

Smith, Neilson V. 1989. *The Twitter Machine: Reflections on Language*. Oxford: Blackwell.

Stuurman, Frans. 1989. Generative grammar and descriptive grammar: beyond juxtaposition? In *Reference Grammars and Modern Linguistic Theory*, ed. by Gottfried Graustein and Gerhard Leitner. Tübingen: Niemeyer, 229–54.

Swan, Michael. 1980. *Practical English Usage*. Oxford: Oxford University Press.

Forthcoming. Design criteria for pedagogic grammar rules. In *Grammar and the Second Language Classroom*, ed. by Martin Bygate, A. Tonkyn, and E. Williams. Englewood Cliffs, N.J.: Prentice-Hall.

Swan, Michael, and Bernard Smith (eds.). 1987. *Learner English: A Teacher's Guide to Interference and Other Problems*. Cambridge: Cambridge University Press.

Tarone, Elaine, and George Yule. 1989. *Focus on the Language Learner*. Oxford: Oxford University Press.

Ungerer, Friedrich, Gerhard E. H. Meier, Klaus Schäfer and Shirley B. Lechler. 1984. *A Grammar of Present-Day English*. Stuttgart: Klett.

van Baalen, Teus. 1983. Giving learners rules: a study into the effect of grammatical instruction with varying degrees of explicitness. *Interlanguage Studies Bulletin* 7: 71–100.

van Buren, Paul. 1974. Contrastive analysis. In Allen and Corder (eds.), London: Oxford University Press, 279–312.

Westney, Paul. 1977. Forever blowing bubbles: a consideration of the English habitual progressive. *English Language Teaching Journal* 32: 38–43.

Widdowson, Henry G. 1979. *Explorations in Applied Linguistics*. Oxford: Oxford University Press.

1990. *Aspects of Language Teaching*. Oxford: Oxford University Press.

Willis, Dave. 1990. *The Lexical Syllabus: A New Approach to Language Teaching*. London: Collins.

SECTION II:
GRAMMAR, LEXICON, AND DISCOURSE

5 Words and their properties: Arguments for a lexical approach to pedagogical grammar

David Little

Introduction

Pedagogical grammar is a slippery concept. The term is commonly used to denote (1) pedagogical process – the explicit treatment of elements of the target language system as (part of) language teaching methodology; (2) pedagogical content – reference sources of one kind or another that present information about the target language system; and (3) combinations of process and content. All three senses of the term will be addressed in this article.

Throughout the history of language teaching, the word *grammar* has usually meant sentence grammar and has been associated with a strong pedagogical emphasis on inflexional morphology and syntax. Recent formal concern with language in use offers to extend the scope of "grammar" to include, for example, discoursal and pragmatic dimensions. These will play an important role in the arguments that follow, though without dislodging sentence grammar from its central position.

If pedagogical grammar is simultaneously part of the process and part of the content of language learning, it also affects many decisions about what to teach in a language course. In other words, pedagogical grammar logically embraces all aspects of language teaching that in some way or other seek to systematize the target language for presentation to the learner. This includes the specification of learning objectives and the elaboration of the syllabus. The systematization on which learning objectives and the syllabus are founded may well (and appropriately) remain concealed from the language learner, but it should nevertheless be continuous with pedagogical grammar as part of the explicit process and content of teaching.

In the experience of language learners, pedagogical grammar is always likely to be a combination of content and process. However, it is impor-

I am grateful to the authorities of Trinity College, Dublin, for facilitating the preparation of this chapter by granting me leave of absence in Trinity term 1990; to the Arts and Social Sciences Benefactions Fund of Trinity College for financial support; and to David Singleton and Seán Devitt for much helpful discussion of the issues raised in the chapter.

tant to recognize that different kinds and combinations of content and process will be appropriate at different stages of second language development – may, indeed, be dictated by different levels of target language competence. For beginners, pedagogical grammar as content may be little more than a handful of general rules based on obvious contrasts with their first language, and pedagogical grammar as process may be difficult to disentangle from the other pedagogical measures that the teacher employs. On the other hand, for advanced learners, pedagogical grammar as content may be a detailed description of the target language prepared for native speakers, and pedagogical grammar as process may be easily distinguished from other language learning activities.

Because they are at the furthest remove from the native-speaker competence on which descriptions of the target language are based, beginners pose the greatest challenge to pedagogical grammar both as process and as content. How to teach beginners will always be one of language pedagogy's major preoccupations, partly because beginners will always be the most numerous category of learners, and partly because their early learning experience will inevitably influence their later learning behaviour – the greater the number of successful beginners, the greater the number of intermediate and advanced learners we shall have. While I believe that the arguments developed in this article are applicable to language learning at all levels, I also believe that they carry particularly urgent implications for the way we deal with pedagogical grammar in the earlier stages of learning.

The article draws directly on an experience of communicative language teaching in which authentic texts play a central role.[1] The first section explains briefly why pedagogical grammar has been thought important by theorists and practitioners of the communicative approach. The second section argues that the separation of form and meaning characteristic of traditional approaches to pedagogical grammar runs counter not only to the demands of communicative language teaching but to the realities of language acquisition and language processing. The third section reports on a pedagogical experiment that takes words as its starting point and explores the implications of the experiment for pedagogical grammar by analysing a French text produced by English-speaking learners and an English text produced by Danish-speaking

---

1 Specifically, the language learning materials produced by Authentik Language Learning Resources Ltd., a campus company of Trinity College, Dublin. Authentik publishes materials in four languages – English, French, German and Spanish – five times during the academic year. The materials consist of (1) a 24-page "newspaper" made up of articles selected from the target-language press; (2) a one-hour cassette of radio news, interviews and features, mostly related to material in the "newspaper"; and (3) a 16-page learner's supplement comprising a full transcript of the cassette and exercises and activities related to both the "newspaper" and the cassette.

learners. The fourth section offers some general proposals for a lexical approach to pedagogical grammar as process and content. Finally, the fifth section considers how such an approach might best be introduced to teachers in training.

Pedagogical grammar and the communicative approach to language teaching

It has often been assumed that the communicative approach to language teaching has no use for pedagogical grammar. This assumption has two principal sources. First, the communicative approach specifies its objectives in terms of the behavioural repertoire learners should achieve – what they should be able to do in the target language – rather than the features of the target language system they should master. This means that successful task completion is the chief criterion by which learners' performance is judged, and the importance attached to morphosyntactic accuracy varies according to the communicative task. For example, a relatively high degree of divergence from native-speaker norms may be tolerated in the performance of face-to-face oral tasks as long as the primary communicative purpose is achieved; on the other hand, the same degree of divergence is not acceptable in a business letter, where it may seriously impair communicative efficiency. The crucial difference here is that between reciprocal and nonreciprocal communication. In reciprocal communication, which is usually face-to-face, meaning is negotiated by the participants: Each contribution to the interaction is to some extent shaped by what has already been said and in turn helps to shape what will be said. Obscurities of all kinds, including those that arise from deficient linguistic resources, are routinely clarified as communication proceeds. In nonreciprocal communication, on the other hand, the message is elaborated by the sender without any immediate involvement on the part of the receiver. It can be much more difficult to clear up a misunderstanding when communication proceeds by exchange of letters and the two correspondents are, respectively, in Dublin and Chicago.

Of course, the interdependence of language skills is such that learners who have reached the stage of being able to compose an effective business letter in their target language are likely also to display a large measure of formal accuracy in conversational exchanges. Nevertheless, the communicative approach insists that at all levels of proficiency the purpose of communication is the negotiation of meaning rather than the elaboration of grammatical form. This has sometimes been taken to imply that "grammar doesn't matter". It is true that we can convey a limited range of meanings by single-word utterances – a refugee who knows few words of English needs only to say "Eat" in order to convey that he is hungry. But as soon as we attempt to move from atomistic to more complex meanings we are inevitably involved in grammatical relationships. The refugee who seeks to emphasize his hunger by saying "Eat me" is unlikely to be taken at his word; but successful communication cannot long survive if words are strung together without regard for grammatical convention. For this reason grammar is as important to the communicative as to any other approach to language teaching. Communicative learning targets are often specified in terms of the communicative functions, or purposes, learners should be able to fulfil and the notions, or meanings, they should be able to convey. But functional-notional categories assume the existence of grammatical categories, and the communicative competence that is the goal of communicative teaching can be developed only in proportion to the linguistic competence that underpins it.

The second source of the assumption that the communicative approach has no use for pedagogical grammar is its methodological tendency to teach language not only for but through communication (see Little, Devitt and Singleton 1989: 22ff.). This is partly a matter of common sense: Where the purpose of teaching is to develop learners' communicative competence, a strong methodological focus on communication seems both obvious and natural. But it is also based on a recognition that wherever language is learned without benefit of formal instruction, it is learned not through exposition and explanation but through communication. In other words, our inborn capacity for language acquisition is designed to feed off the raw linguistic data that social interaction provides for the nonexpert speaker. This explains why the communicative approach has given a central function to activities that involve reciprocal face-to-face communication. It also helps to explain why authentic texts in all media have assumed such importance as sources of target language input; for an authentic text is one that was produced to fulfil a communicative rather than a pedagogical purpose, and to grapple with it is to involve oneself in one of the target language community's modes of nonreciprocal communication.

The emphasis on learning through communication has led some proponents of the communicative approach to maintain the ban on explicit treatment of target language grammar that was imposed by audiolingual theory, though their reasons may be more closely related to the principles that underlay the Direct Method in the latter part of the nineteenth century (see Howatt 1984). The ban on explicit treatment of target language grammar has sometimes been justified by pointing to two central findings of empirical research into second language acquisition. The first of these is that language learning in formal educational contexts reveals the same developmental sequences as second language acquisition that proceeds "naturalistically", that is, without benefit of formal instruction. In other words, learners of all kinds pass through the same broad stages of development towards mastery of such target language features as negatives, interrogatives and the morphology of verbs (for a review and references, see Ellis 1985). The second finding is that developmental sequences cannot be changed in any serious way by pedagogical intervention (for a review of the evidence, see Long 1988). However, there is also strong empirical evidence that explicit treatment of target language grammar brings important benefits (again, see Long 1988 for a review); and in recent years a strong consensus has emerged in favour of a communicative version of pedagogical grammar. This consensus rests essentially on three arguments: that explicit knowledge of the target language can assist the development of the implicit knowledge on which spontaneous language use depends; that certain kinds of communicative activity are difficult to perform at all without explicit grammatical knowledge; and that explicit knowledge can help learners to overcome gaps in their implicit knowledge in certain communicative situations. I shall say a little about each of these arguments in turn.

Explicit knowledge of target language grammar is conscious knowledge of grammatical facts. It can be taught and learned in much the same way as any other kind of factual knowledge – mathematical theorems, historical dates, social statistics, biological taxonomies. Implicit grammatical knowledge, on the other hand, is unconscious knowledge of a much larger body of information that is the basis of automatic, spontaneous use of language. We acquire it by processes to which we have no direct access; it cannot be directly taught. The question of the relation between explicit and implicit knowledge has, of course, been one of the chief concerns of applied linguistics since the 1980s. Much of the debate has centred on Krashen's distinction between learning, which he associates with explicit knowledge, and acquisition, which he sees as the only route to implicit knowledge (see, e.g., Krashen 1981, 1982).

In the main, teachers have assumed that there is a fairly straightforward relation between explicit and implicit grammatical knowledge. For the past twenty years, the Irish language has been taught in Irish primary schools using a course designed according to strict audiolingual principles; but throughout that time classroom walls have continued to display tables summarizing the basic patterns of Irish grammar. Teachers simply refuse to abandon their common-sense belief that explicit treatment of Irish grammar will in some way support the processes by which learners develop their implicit knowledge of the language. In this they have the support of the majority of applied linguists. Although there is no general consensus on how the two kinds of knowledge are related, there is by now widespread acceptance that explicit knowledge can assist the development of implicit knowledge in a variety of ways (for a summary of the relevant arguments, see Little and Singleton 1988; see also Odlin 1986; Bourgignon and Candelier 1984, 1988). For example, learners confronted with a target language sentence they do not at first understand can use explicit knowledge of syntactic structure to locate the source of their difficulty, which they can then overcome, perhaps by referring to a dictionary. In this way explicit knowledge can be used to "pre-process" the data that feeds the development of implicit knowledge. What is more, explicit knowledge can help learners to reflect on the content and process of their learning in such a way as gradually to free them from the immediate context of learning. That is to say, it provides them with "frameworks" within which they can – to take two examples more or less at random – compare the dominant features of texts they have encountered or speculate on patterns of word formation in their target language. In this way explicit knowledge is a potentially important factor in establishing the autonomy on which successful target language use depends (for a fuller discussion of the concept of learner autonomy and an exploration of its implications, see Little 1991).

The second argument in favour of developing learners' explicit knowledge of target language grammar within the communicative paradigm has to do with the realities of language processing. As native speakers we are unlikely to draw much on explicit knowledge of our mother tongue grammar when we are involved in spontaneous face-to-face communication. On the other hand, we may frequently use such knowledge, whether we take it from memory or reference books, when we plan, monitor and edit more formal kinds of written and spoken discourse. This is partly because such knowledge provides part of the very basis for planning, monitoring and editing, and partly because the communicative effectiveness of planned discourse depends to a high degree on its formal correctness, and especially its syntactic transparency. In English, for example, ambiguity can easily arise if a prepositional phrase is clumsily deployed ("Joe looked at his brother with his new spectacles" – who had new spectacles?) or if a pronoun does not have a clear antecedent ("I saw Rachel and her mother yesterday. She was looking much better" – who had been ill?). These considerations apply equally to the production of planned discourse by second language learners. This argument is clearly related to Krashen's monitor theory (see, e.g., Krashen 1981), though it does not necessarily imply acceptance of other aspects of his position. It rests on a definition of pedagogical grammar that is not limited to the grammar of the sentence but embraces knowledge of discourse structure, common differences between spoken and written discourse, the functioning of reference and so on.

The third argument in favour of developing learners' explicit knowledge of target language grammar within the communicative paradigm is related to the second. Especially in situations where they have time to plan, learners may be able to use explicit knowledge to cope with gaps in their implicit knowledge. Thus, in some circumstances, knowledge of sentence structure may be used to compensate for a gap in lexical knowledge. For example, a learner of German who says, in response to a question that has to do with remembering, "Leider habe ich das . . ." (word for word: "Unfortunately have I that . . ."), will be readily understood as saying that she has forgotten. Other kinds of grammatical knowledge can be used to the same end. For example, if the same learner of German is aware of the grammatical category "verb", has a good knowledge of French and is aware that German verbs derived from French end in *-ieren*, she has a means of manufacturing "German" verbs when her mental lexicon fails her. Perhaps she will not often produce the verb a native speaker of German would use; but in many cases she will produce a form that a native speaker of German will readily understand.

Attempts to translate these arguments into pedagogical practice as part of a specifically communicative methodology have tended to follow the principle that formal features should always be treated in terms of the meaning they communicate. The aim has been to devise procedures in which form is explored as the servant of meaning, which entails deriving grammatical rules from specific instances of language in use, rather than presenting them as structural abstractions that may subsequently be clothed in words. This immediately raises questions concerning the appropriateness of traditional approaches to the process and content of pedagogical grammar, which I begin to explore in the next section.

Grammar in context: language as words

Traditional pedagogical grammars present paradigmatic rules of morphosyntax and sentence structure which have been derived from an analysis of the language produced by educated native speakers. Such grammars invite us to move from the abstract to the concrete, from the general rule to its specific realisation – which in many cases will turn out to be a partial exception to the general rule. Even when example sentences are provided to show rules in action, the overall effect of such grammars is to emphasize form to the virtual exclusion of meaning.

Although this separation of form and meaning poses a particularly acute challenge to the communicative approach, it should be noted that it has always created problems for language learners. For example, I well remember it as the single most frustrating thing about learning German via a grammar-translation method thirty years ago. As a relatively advanced learner I had little difficulty finding the words I needed, perhaps starting with an English-German dictionary, but always confirming my choice against a monolingual German dictionary. But if I had doubts about how those words behaved in relation to other words, I usually found that grammars provided insufficient lexical information and dictionaries insufficient grammatical information.

The communicative principle that form should always be subordinated to meaning and grammatical issues treated within a fully established context requires that learners derive their explicit knowledge of the target language system from analysis of particular instances of language in use. But when our starting point for grammatical exploration is an instance of language in use, what we have in front of us is not a structure but words, and our problem is not to associate those words with an abstract structure but to discover how precisely they are behaving in relation to one another.

Whether we are concerned with explicit or implicit grammatical knowledge, words inevitably come before structures. After all, explicit knowledge of grammatical rules is useless unless we know some of the words whose behaviour the rules describe; and implicit knowledge of grammatical rules can develop only in association with a developing mental lexicon. Communicative principles imply that pedagogical grammar should seek ways of responding to this priority of the word. The central importance attributed to the lexicon by recent work in formal linguistics and the central role of the word in language acquisition and language processing carry the same implication.

In his postscript to Sells's (1985) introduction to Government-Binding Theory, Generalized Phrase Structure Grammar, and Lexical Functional Grammar, Wasow observes that "contemporary syntactic theories seem to be converging on the idea that sentence structure is generally predictable from word meanings" (p. 204). The important word here is generally, for (again following Wasow) the particular achievement of these theories is to have identified the kinds of grammatical information that are not predictable from lexical semantics, and to have developed ways of expressing them economically. These formal theories are relevant to the concerns of this article to the extent that they make or imply claims about what is involved in learning a language. For example, Cook (1988: 57) writes of first language acquisition within the perspective of Chomsky's Universal Grammar: "While the acquisition of core grammar is a matter of setting a handful of switches, the child has the considerable burden of discovering the characteristics of thousands of words". This coincides with the layman's perception that learning words is the main part of language learning.

Through the successive stages of first language acquisition, beginning with single-word utterances and culminating in a fully developed syntactic range, children produce words: tokens which express with more or less precision the message that they want to convey. No doubt the gradual internalisation of a number of general rules is an essential part of the acquisition process; but as their metalinguistic awareness develops, they become conscious not of rules but of words. Throughout their lives they will be able to discuss words and how they should be used – grammatically, pragmatically, stylistically; unless they become linguists, however, they are unlikely ever to be able to say much to the point about general syntactic rules. Recent work by Radford (1990) serves to emphasize that children's capacity to convey meaning runs ahead of their capacity to produce fully formed syntactic structures. Working with a corpus of over 100,000 spontaneous utterances, Radford concludes that children's earliest structures are essentially lexical and thematic in nature: "Early child grammars of English are characterised by the acquisition of lexical category systems [nouns, verbs, adjectives, prepositions and their projections] and their associated grammatical properties, and by the nonacquisition of functional category systems [determiners, auxiliaries, complementizers and their projections] and their associated grammatical properties" (p. 243).

Words provide a central focus for psycholinguistics not least because they are what can be elicited from subjects in experimental and empirical research. Syntactic rules, by contrast, cannot be directly elicited; they can be investigated only indirectly, for example, by means of grammaticality judgements. The priority of the word in psycholinguistics suggests that there may be good reasons for placing the mental lexicon rather than abstract syntactic rules at the centre of linguistic competence. As Ard and Gass (1987: 250) point out, "The mere fact that learners are learning structures does not necessarily mean that they are learning them syntactically"; indeed, it seems possible that much of syntax is learned as a by-product of the semantic relations that underpin the meanings the learner needs to communicate. If we conceptualise linguistic competence as a mental lexicon and an associated "toolkit" of syntactic and lexical rules (Aitchison 1987), learning a second language becomes a matter of establishing an L2 mental lexicon and "toolkit". The lexicon inevitably plays a central role in research into communication and learning strategies that depend on word coinage, borrowings, idioms, prefabricated patterns and the like, but as Gass (1987: 129) notes, there have been relatively few studies devoted specifically to the area of the lexicon. In particular, study of the L2 mental lexicon is still very much in its infancy, and we have only provisional answers to basic questions. For example, when we learn a second language, do we add to our existing mental lexicon or establish a quite separate lexical store? The indications are that L2 lexical processing does not in essence differ from L1 lexical processing and that there is at least some degree of interconnection between L1 and L2 lexical storage and processing (Singleton and Little

1991). This certainly helps to make sense of many of the errors of transfer and interference to which L2 learners are subject. However extensively they are drilled in general syntactic rules, they continue to make mistakes that are essentially lexical in origin. For example, a German-speaking learner of English who says "It is told from Kaiser Wilhelm II that he was unbelievably arrogant" has not yet internalised the lack of total overlap in meaning between German *erzählen* and English *tell*, and in function between German *von* and English *from*. We may of course analyse examples of lexico-grammatical transfer and inter-ference in ways that lead us to draw general and abstract conclusions; but each individual instance is a matter first of words and only second of general rules.

A pedagogical experiment and its implications

It seems likely that grammar as a system of decontextualised general rules will remain obscure to learners until they have made substantial progress towards the native-speaker competence that the grammar itself describes. In the earlier stages of L2 learning they can neither fully understand the rules nor internalise them for subsequent use because their L2 mental lexicon has not yet developed the capacity to express the meanings whose full articulation depends on the rules. The communica-tive principle of dealing with the target language system in context, on the basis of concrete examples, raises the question whether there is an alternative approach to pedagogical grammar that might be more "learner-friendly". This in turn prompts a second question: whether learner-friendliness is likely to depend less on the "surface" organisation of the grammar than on the extent to which it can support unconscious acquisition processes by exploiting what we know about language acqui-sition and language processing. Some suggestive possibilities emerged almost by accident from a pedagogical experiment devised by Seán Devitt of Trinity College, Dublin.[2]

The purpose of Devitt's experiment was to persuade language teachers that authentic texts could play a much fuller role in language learning than has often been supposed, and especially that they could benefit beginners just as much as advanced learners. The experiment set out to exploit the fact that when we read any text we draw not only on linguistic knowledge, in the narrow lexico-grammatical sense, but also on our knowledge of discourse structures and our knowledge of the world. In principle, learn-ers' discourse and (especially) world knowledge should enable them to

---

2 The procedures were first developed for use in in-service teacher training courses run by Authentik.

compensate for deficiencies in their L2 linguistic knowledge when they are confronted with an L2 authentic text on a familiar topic.

Devitt assumed that knowledge is structured, stored and accessed in the kind of way implied by the theories of "frames" (Minsky 1977), "scripts" (Schank and Abelson 1977), "scenarios" (Sanford and Garrod 1981) and "schemata" (Anderson 1977). These theories are close relatives of Bartlett's (1932) argument that remembering is essentially a constructive process; that we do not store our memories in a fixed form but re-create them each time we respond to whatever it is that stimulates us to remember. Devitt hypothesised that learners would find it easier to read an authentic text in their target language if they first activated relevant discourse and world knowledge by constructing an appropriate "schema" in the target language. He recognised that, especially in the case of beginners, this discourse and world knowledge would be strongly associated with learners' L1.

The pedagogical procedures on which Devitt based his experiment can vary according to the particular learning purpose they embody (for a full discussion of the different possibilities, see Little, Devitt and Singleton 1989). They require learners to work in groups of three or four, partly in order to embed their learning in a framework of social interaction, and partly because in interaction their collective knowledge is likely to exceed the sum of its parts. When the purpose of the procedures is to give learners access to the meaning of an authentic text in their target language, they take the following form:

1. Learners are given a jumble of content words and phrases derived from the authentic text which is their goal (the words and phrases are chosen intuitively as belonging more to the centre than to the periphery of the text's concerns). The learners' first task is to identify any words and phrases they do not know. These are explained to them.
2. The learners' second task is to write each word or phrase on a separate Post-it (a small adhesive label that can be reused many times). This is intended to have the effect of fixing the meanings of the words and phrases in their collective awareness and beginning to activate their world knowledge.
3. Next the learners sort the words and phrases into overlapping categories of time, place, person and event by sticking the Post-its onto a large Venn diagram. This carries the process of knowledge activation a stage further by encouraging the learners to think about possible meaning relationships between the words and phrases.
4. The learners then devise a schema, or story outline, by arranging their Post-its in a linear sequence.
5. The learners expand this skeletal discourse into a text – a procedure that directly exploits the capacity of word meanings to generate sentence structures.
6. It is unlikely that the learners' text will have no point of contact with the authentic text from which the words and phrases have been derived. However, it is entirely possible that their story will differ in significant respects from the authentic text. Thus it is now necessary to provide them with a

bridge into the authentic text. This is done by giving them a jumble of sentences derived from a simplified version of the authentic text and inviting them to put the sentences into a plausible chronological order (there may be more than one possible solution).
7. Then the learners are given the simplified form of the authentic text and told to use it to check the order they have given to the jumble of sentences and to edit and improve/expand their own text.
8. Finally, the learners are given the authentic text and invited to compare it with their own text.

These procedures have proved a most effective means of giving learners access to texts which might otherwise remain opaque to them, and thus of involving them in authentic nonreciprocal communication in their target language. However telegraphic their own story may remain, it creates a frame of reference for their encounter with the authentic text and often enables them to focus on details of the authentic text that represent new knowledge for them. For example, on more than one occasion learners of German working towards a text reporting on the chance encounter of identical twin sisters many years after they had been separated reported that the German text first taught them that identical twins come from the same ovum.

But what is especially relevant to the concerns of this article is our recurrent experience that as learners move through the chain of activities, they tend to become increasingly preoccupied with issues of grammar (see Little and Singleton 1992 for a discussion of the procedures as a means of raising learners' language awareness). This suggests that Devitt's procedures may also be a good way of preparing learners to come to grips with the target language system in context. In particular, their own efforts to construct coherent meaning create a focus for the treatment of grammar by generating a lively sense of what specific grammar they need. We can explore this further by considering a French text produced by three English-speaking girls of thirteen in their second year of learning French,[3] and an English text produced by three Danish-speaking boys of fifteen in their fourth year of learning English. Both texts were produced at in-service days for language teachers. In both cases the succession of activities through which the learners were led was entirely new to them, and by their own account they had little previous experience of working together in small groups.

The authentic text in relation to which my French example was produced summarized the life and career of James Dean. It was published in the French magazine *Confidences* in October 1987, thirty-two years after Dean's death, and carried a photograph of Dean wearing a T-shirt, jeans and a denim jacket. The learners were given the photograph and the following fifty-eight items derived from the authentic text:

3 I am grateful to Seán Devitt for making this text available to me.

star   Salinas   célèbre   symbole   tuer   pur(e)   salles de cinéma   24 ans route   Porsche Spider   Géant   répugner   génération   se reconnaître   ligne jaune   visage   La Fureur de Vivre   Ford Modèle 50   révolte   représenter 1987   se presser   Bakersfield   écran   accident   choc   tanguer   septembre délavé(e)   franchir   A l'Est d'Eden   jeunesse   exalté(e)   mort   puissant(e) 1955   porter   sauveteurs   adopter   blue jeans   Brando   corps   porte-parole   volant   avoir mal   amas de ferraille   broyé(e)   uniforme   T-shirt les années 80   adolescents   Californie   défiguré(e)   adulte   32 ans choquer   inconnu(e)   James Dean

The learners were told to copy each item onto a Post-it and then to arrange their Post-its around the picture in such a way as to say as many things about James Dean as they could. This activity enabled them to generate a schema which they then expanded into the following text:

James Dean Septembre 1955: il habite en Bakersfield. Il aimé le cinema et à 24 ans il a allé en Californie et il entré le cinema. Il as très bien. Il ne porter pas uniforme, mais il preferè blue jeans et t-shirt. Les adolescents adorent James Dean et ses films, par example A l'Est d'Eden et Geant. Les années 80 le film "La Fureur de Vivre" très populaire. 1987 dans le Ford Modèle 50 il a eu accident et il mouri. Il a eu trente-deux ans. Aujourd-hui il a symbole et célèbre salles de cinema et les adolescents et les adultes moderne aiment James Dean.

Even a cursory reading of the text establishes that the learners are not closely familiar with James Dean, though they have worked out that he was a film star. They have taken the two dates provided, linked by "32 ans", as marking the beginning and end of his life, and used these as the chief supports for a biographical sketch. In other words, the schema they have activated is that of the biographical outline – birth, career, death. The ordering of the elements seems to have been arrived at by constructing common-sense answers to the question, "Then what?" Devising a coherent thematic structure is clearly not a problem for these learners. It is true that they do not use any lexical markers of intersentential cohesion, but the sentences follow one another in a perfectly acceptable sequence. Nothing in the text resists interpretation, though it is only in retrospect that the first sentence is confirmed as referring to Dean's birth (it is possible that its moodless form was a deliberate attempt to imitate an entry in a biographical dictionary).

The chief grammatical problems revealed by the text centre on the morphology of verbs. The present tense is well controlled: "il habite", "les adolescents adorent", "les adolescents et les adultes *moderne aiment"; and the learners clearly understand how the perfect tense is constructed: "il a eu", "il *a allé" (the asterisks indicate impossible or inappropriate forms). However, seriously deviant forms arise in contexts where it seems likely that the learners wanted to use the imperfect: "aimé", "*preferè" and "porter" may be graphic approximations to "aimait", "préférait" and "portait" ("entré" and "*mouri", by contrast, are probably flawed attempts to repeat the perfect tense already used earlier in the sentences in which they occur). Two deviant uses of *avoir* also deserve comment: "Il *as très bien" and "Aujourd-hui il *a symbole" suggest that these learners have confused forms of *avoir* with forms of *être*, perhaps because both verbs are used as auxiliaries in the perfect tense. It is worth pointing out that Irish learners of French taught in the traditional way encounter tenses in the order: present, perfect, imperfect. Learners in their second year of French would have spent much time on the present tense and would have been fairly thoroughly introduced to the perfect; but it is more than likely that when they produced this text they had not yet fully encountered the imperfect. By working on the verb forms in the text it would be possible to introduce learners to the imperfect tense not only as an aspect of the morphology of the verb but also as the carrier of a particular range of temporal meanings.

The authentic text in relation to which my English example was produced was published in *The Irish Independent* in October 1989 under the headline "Soviet UFO invader zaps little boy". The learners were presented with the following jumble of twenty-seven items:

at 6.30   REAPPEAR   alien   TAKE OFF   official news agency   LAND
boy   PLAY   gun   UFO   robot   Soviet scientists   CONFIRM   witnesses
sky   red ball   POINT   in Voronezh   SEE   park   SCREAM   evening
DISAPPEAR   spaceship   city   INFORM   world

Note that in this instance the verbs are printed in capitals. This makes them easy to identify and keep separate from other words (though it may be wise to explain that "UFO" is not a verb!). Experience has shown that a rapid identification of verbs tends to speed up the process of creating a story schema. The learners copied the items onto Post-its, sorted the Post-its into overlapping categories of time, place, person and event, constructed a story schema, and then elaborated the schema into the following text:

The evening news. At 6.30. The official news agency confirms, that witnesses have seen an Alien UFO coming from the sky, and landed in Voronezh Park. Suddenly the UFO disappeared and then it reappeared in the [added: same] city, on a parking lane. Soviet scientists informs the world, that the spaceship carrying a robot, pointed a gun at a boy, who was playing with a red ball. The boy began to scream, and then the spaceship made a take off [originally: took off].

In this case the learners have activated a basic UFO schema which begins with appearance and ends with disappearance. This has enabled them to produce an impressively coherent text in imitation of a radio news bulletin, where the first two sentences – "The evening news. At 6.30" – are intended as opening "titles". It is obvious that these learners have a much more fully developed L2 competence than the younger learners of French – indeed, perhaps the most obtrusive "foreign" feature of the text is their use of L1 punctuation conventions. Their control of the morphology of verbs is generally assured, the two exceptions being "landed" (presumably for "landing") and "Soviet scientists informs" (where the final -*s* on "inform" may arise from confusion between the plural forms of nouns and verbs). The two emendations to the original text are worth commenting on. The insertion of "same" came about as a result of discussion that focused explicitly on textual coherence; while "took off" was replaced by "made a take off" after one member of the group expressed doubt that "take off" was an English verb (despite the fact that, like all other verbs in the jumble of words and phrases, it was printed in capitals).

Although this text contains many fewer morphosyntactic errors than the French text, it is no less useful as a framework for the treatment of target language grammar. One might begin by identifying and correcting the learners' errors. Then the focus could shift to thematic and discourse structure – further details might be added to the story and alternative orderings of the material considered. In these and similar activities the newspaper report from which the word jumble was derived could be used as a source of lexical and structural information, thus sustaining the learners' involvement with authentic nonreciprocal communication in the target language.

In traditional approaches to language teaching, learners are first taught the elements of phrase and sentence structure and then required to combine sentences into paragraphs and longer texts. In Devitt's activity chain, by contrast, they move in the opposite direction. They begin by devising a thematic outline and then elaborate their own text by filling in as many of the "structural gaps" as their L2 linguistic competence allows. In this they are following the same order of things as naturalistic language learners, who (as we have seen) can learn only through communication and for whom therefore meaning inevitably comes before formal differentiation. Devitt's activity chain encourages learners to use all the knowledge sources available to them. Inevitably, in beginners this encourages the production of "pidginized" texts whose grammatical structure draws heavily on the learners' L1. But it is precisely because texts of this kind are genuine instances of L2 communication that they yield such an effective basis for the explicit treatment of target language grammar.

Modalities of a lexical approach to pedagogical grammar

The general approach to pedagogical grammar suggested by Devitt's activity chain is founded on the recognition that the largest part of language learning is the learning of words and their properties, and therefore that pedagogical grammar should be inseparable from vocabulary learning/teaching. But as it stands, Devitt's activity chain offers us no more than a pointer. It was devised, after all, for use with individual and more or less randomly selected authentic texts. The question is: Does it provide the basis for a fully developed pedagogical grammar – a pedagogical grammar that is fundamental to the process and content of language learning, centrally implicated in the design of the syllabus, and appropriate for learners at all levels? I believe the answer to this question is yes. In explaining the impact that a lexically oriented pedagogical grammar should have on syllabus, methodology and content, I shall continue to have in mind especially the early stages of learning, for the reasons indicated in my introduction. I shall also remain firmly within the communicative paradigm, which means that I shall assume (1) that the purpose of language teaching is to develop the learner's L2 communicative competence and (2) that communication itself is a principal vehicle of learning.

Following established communicative principles, our learners' syllabus needs to specify the behavioural repertoire they should attain. Skills in reciprocal oral communication are central to this repertoire, partly because they are fundamental to communicative competence, and partly because they are the indispensable tools of learning by communication, whether in the classroom or as a temporary member of the target language community. The core of this part of the learner's repertoire comprises those elements that facilitate participation in the interactive processes by which classroom activities are managed and classroom learning is mediated. Other elements will enable the learner to cope with a variety of everyday situations in the target language community. The functional-notional inventories pioneered by the Council of Europe (e.g., van Ek 1975; Coste, et al. 1976; Baldegger, et al. 1980) specify the speech acts that learners may need to be able to perform and offer examples of their linguistic exponents. But how does a lexical approach to pedagogical grammar imply that such a repertoire should be taught?

Traditionally, language teaching has not distinguished between spoken and written language; yet discourse analysis has made abundantly clear that there are major differences between the two varieties. In particular, it has shown that spontaneous conversation – where there is little time for planning, and speakers mostly grant one another only short turns – tends to use a limited range of lexis and thus generates a relatively limited range of structural patterns (see, e.g., Brown and Yule 1983: 14–19). This fact lends great plausibility to Nattinger and DeCarrico's (1989) proposal that learners should be taught to use "lexical phrases" as a means of realising speech acts in conversation. They define lexical phrases as "multi-word lexical phenomena that exist somewhere between the traditional poles of lexis and syntax" and divide them into six categories: polywords, phrasal constraints, deictic locutions, sentence builders, situational utterances and verbatim texts (pp. 118f.). They suggest that for pedagogical purposes, lexical phrases can be divided into three broad groups: "social interactions", "necessary topics" and "discourse devices" (pp. 120–25). The examples they give under each of these headings add up to a basic interactive repertoire that has much in common with a simple functional-notional specification. Encouraging learners to use lexical phrases as the blocks out of which they construct simple L2 conversations is very much in line with the approach adopted in Devitt's pedagogical experiment (see also Nattinger 1988). Again, learners' texts can provide the pretext and framework for the explicit treatment of target language grammar, though now their texts should take the form of audio or video recordings of their oral communication.

Of course, our learners' target repertoire should not be limited to spontaneous conversation. Where second language learning is part of formal education, it appropriately includes the development of listening, reading and writing skills that give learners access to the target language culture. In our syllabus these skills can be defined in terms of the nonreciprocal authentic texts – in print, audio and video – that learners need to be able to cope with and the nonreciprocal spoken and written tasks they need to be able to perform. After all, mass media provide an increasingly large part of speakers' L1 communicative experience, and authentic texts give native speakers as well as learners something to talk or write about.

Authentic texts that deal with everyday topics or events are likely to use a fairly predictable vocabulary, but we may still want our syllabus to specify the core vocabulary our learners should master. Once again, the functional-notional specifications sponsored by the Council of Europe offer a way forward, via the intuitively arrived at categories of specific notions. These allow us to establish for all areas of common experience a network of frequent words that can act as a web in which to catch whatever less frequent words learners come across and decide they need. An alternative approach is to exploit the findings of research into word frequencies. This is the basis of the Collins COBUILD English Course, designed according to data supplied by the COBUILD (Collins Birmingham University International Language Database) project. The principal focus for the three levels of the course was supplied by the following statistical considerations: "The 700 most frequent words of English account for around 70% of all English text. That is to say around 70% of the English we speak and hear, read and write is made up of the 700 commonest words in the language. The most frequent 1,500 words account for around 76% of text and the most frequent 2,500 for 80%" (Willis 1990: vi). Clearly, there is much to be said for teaching learners the language that they will be able to make most use of. On the other hand, claims based on frequency counts are not without their dangers. For example, it is important to be clear that the 700 most frequent words of English account for around 70 percent of text, not 70 percent of texts; even texts dealing with the commonest everyday topics often contain words of low frequency. Moreover, too rigid an adherence to words of high frequency may seriously frustrate individual learning. If we assume that an educated native speaker of English has an active vocabulary of at least 50,000 words (Aitchison 1987: 7), we must expect many of the words that define individual interests to fall some way outside the 3,500 most frequent. Beginning learners of English who spend much of their spare time making rugs will need the vocabulary of rug-making in order to talk about themselves in their L2.

As we have seen, the communicative approach to language teaching implies a methodology in which communication – reciprocal and non-reciprocal, oral and written – plays a central role. Within that methodology a lexical approach to pedagogical grammar employs techniques like those used in Devitt's pedagogical experiment both to prepare learners for communication and to analyse the products of their communicative effort. The central role played by writing in the educational processes of literate societies easily creates a bias against the spoken language, and this may be reinforced by the use of analytical activities whose very existence depends largely on the technology of writing. It is thus necessary to ensure that learners get plenty of practice in the oral manipulation of lexical tokens, for only in this way can they become familiar with and gradually internalise the phonological as well as the graphic shape of words and phrases.

Learners need to explore words in terms of the semantic links between them. Aitchison (1987: 74f.) suggests that in terms of the mental lexicon the four most important links are probably co-ordination (which refers to the way in which words cluster together at the same level of detail – e.g., *knife* and *fork; Monday, Tuesday, Wednesday*), collocation (which refers to the way in which words occur together in connected discourse – e.g., *sharp knife, happy day, shaggy dog*), superordination (where one word defines the class to which another word belongs – e.g., *animal* and *dog; month* and *January*), and synonymy (where two or more words have a closely similar meaning – e.g., *famished* and *starving, dog* and *canine*). These links can usefully be explored by using grids to analyse and categorise the semantic properties of words; Rudska, et al. (1981) show how this can be done for semantic fields and collocations. Such explorations lead easily into a focus on the detail of text production at sentence level using techniques such as Rutherford's (1987) "propositional clusters" – verbs and associated noun phrases, each of whose possible combinations will yield a different syntactic structure. Work on the syntactic properties of words will need to give particular attention to verbs and the verb phrase, for two reasons. First, the verb is the engine of syntactic structure – which helps to explain why early identification of the verbs in a word jumble speeds up the elaboration of a story schema. Second, it seems likely that in the mental lexicon the verb is particularly heavily loaded with syntactic information (Aitchison 1987: 101). On the one hand, there is evidence that the verb presents learners with their most persistent difficulties; on the other hand, when they are in control of the verb phrase, the rest of their morphosyntax usually falls into place (Harley 1986: 59f.).

In this account a lexical approach to pedagogical grammar turns out to be a general approach to language teaching that depends crucially on certain kinds of analytical activity; that is, it entails a certain kind of process. The raw materials for that process are provided partly by the lexical component of the syllabus and partly by the authentic texts which constitute a major part of the learners' input. But what about pedagogical grammar as content in the more conventional and limited sense of reference materials? Especially in the early stages, the most important kind of reference materials are arguably those that learners construct for themselves out of the analytical grids, charts and diagrams that their work with words generates. These will expand, changing their shape and emphasis, as learners' competence develops (for this reason loose-leaf binders may be preferable to bound notebooks).

Dictionaries and reference grammars obviously have a central role to play in support of learners' grammars, in the two senses of analytical notes and developing mental lexicon. Monolingual dictionaries have the advantage that they involve learners in significant L2 processing every time they use them. What is more, monolingual dictionaries that have been specially compiled for learners and nonnative speakers tend to carry much more grammatical information than dictionaries designed for native speakers (Carter and McCarthy 1988: 53). However, for languages that have no equivalent of the *Oxford Advanced Learner's Dictionary of Current English* (Hornby 1981), the *Longman Dictionary of Contemporary English* (Procter 1988), or the Collins COBUILD dictionaries (1987, 1988), learners may be better served by a good bilingual dictionary.

It is no doubt the case, as I have noted, that descriptive grammars of the target language can be used with ease only by learners who have made significant progress towards native speaker competence. But such grammars should be the teacher's constant standby, whatever the level of his or her learners. Two recent grammars of English are especially worth mentioning because they are centrally and explicitly concerned with grammar in use, as a tool of communication, rather than with the analytical description of grammatical structure for its own sake. Leech and Svartvik's *Communicative Grammar of English* (1975) is strongly influenced by Halliday's "functional" approach to language and the categories of sociosemantic analysis that underlie the Council of Europe's functional-notional specifications; while the *Collins COBUILD English Grammar* (1990) arose from the same corpus-based research that has produced the Collins COBUILD dictionaries. Even when grammars of this quality are inaccessible to learners, they remain a mine of information and implication for teachers, including teachers of other languages. For example, the general principles of organisation adopted in the *Collins COBUILD English Grammar* suggest a wealth of pedagogical procedures that can easily be translated into French or German, Italian or Spanish, and used to add further dimensions to the learners' own lexico-grammatical analysis.

A lexical approach to pedagogical grammar in teacher training

"There is nothing so practical as a good theory." And yet language teachers are notoriously hostile to theoretical discussion, apparently believing that it has nothing to offer the practitioner in the classroom. Many language teaching handbooks strengthen this prejudice by offering collections of practical hints without any kind of theoretical framework. But unless we have a theory, we have no means of moving from specific instances to general principles. This is not to say that language teachers need to be theoreticians themselves; but it is to say that they need to understand the principles on which their practice is based. Otherwise discussion of success and failure in the language classroom can never rise above the level of anecdote, assertion and counter-assertion.

Initial and in-service teacher training provides the obvious channel through which issues of theory and principle can best be explored with teachers. A minimal theoretical framework for first understanding and then implementing the approach to pedagogical grammar I have outlined in this article has three obligatory components. It must make clear the difference between explicit and implicit grammatical knowledge; it must explore the priority of words over structures in language acquisition and language use; and it must explicate the relation between form and meaning implied by the communicative approach to language course design. All of these issues can be investigated in workshop mode. For example, the task of writing a grammatical analysis of any simple sentence in their L1 should give teachers a fairly clear idea of the nature and extent of their explicit knowledge of the grammar of the L1; while an attempt to work out how a computer would have to be programmed in order to generate the same sentence should help them to understand that implicit grammatical knowledge is a matter not only of facts but of processes.

When this theoretical framework has been established, the principal task is to give teachers a first-hand interactive experience of the priority of words over structures from three points of view: that of the language learner, that of the native speaker and that of the teacher. This can be done by following closely the procedures used in Devitt's pedagogical experiment. Teachers can work in groups of three or four to generate a short text (1) in a language they have not encountered before, (2) in their L1 and (3) in the language they teach. Especially in exploring the learner's and teacher's perspectives, it is a good idea to work towards an audio as well as a printed text – for example, a radio and a newspaper report of the same event – because this helps to emphasise the problem of segmentation and the fact that we can segment only on the basis of our recognition of words.

In Devitt's experiment, the purpose of the activity sequence was to enable relatively inexperienced learners to understand an authentic newspaper text in their target language. Now, in exploring the learner's perspective, our aim is to arrive at a clear understanding of the grammatical problems raised by the attempt to generate a text in a largely unknown language, and the kinds of information needed to solve those problems. In particular, consideration can be given to the kinds of reference material most likely to be useful to beginners. Working groups should contain as wide a variety of linguistic backgrounds as possible, since this will generate the greatest variety of grammatical questions. For example, in an English-speaking group of teachers a Dutch text is likely to yield a wider range of insights if some, but not all, members of the group know German than if either all or no members of the group know German.

Having teachers generate a text in their L1 immediately after they have worked with a language they have not previously encountered has the advantage of emphasising the gulf between the beginner and the native speaker. This time, of course, we should expect the teachers to produce fully fluent texts. But now their task is not primarily to identify the grammatical problems that their developing schema needs to solve – as native speakers they are unlikely to hesitate over which verb form to use with a plural subject, or how to order direct and indirect objects. Rather, their task is to identify and analyse the grammatical knowledge they deployed in establishing links between the words they were given and to relate that knowledge to the information provided in a range of reference materials – grammars, dictionaries, thesauruses, style manuals, and so on.

In exploring the teacher's perspective, the analytical task is to predict the grammatical problems that learners at different stages will identify, and to propose ways of solving them. Solutions can then provide the basis for developing a battery of activities for a lexically focused treatment of target language grammar. Particular emphasis might appropriately be given to the elaboration of schematic techniques that learners can use to store and gradually enlarge the grammar that seems particularly important or useful to them. Vocabulary learning is greatly facilitated by arranging words in clusters according to meaning rather than listing them alphabetically or randomly. In the same way, learners can be helped to cope with the grammar of the verb by collecting semantically related verbs and using a grid to summarize the principal properties of each verb. If the language is German, these properties will include whether the verb is weak, strong or irregular, whether it forms the perfect tense with *haben* or *sein,* whether it takes an accusative or a dative object, and if it has a prefix, whether that prefix is separable or inseparable. Learners can also discover a great deal about the grammar of their target language by making their own concordances. For example, they can go through a text and copy out each instance of a particular preposition together with its immediate context – the three or four words that occur on either side of it. This can then serve as a reference source when they are composing in their target language. These are only two among many possibilities.

The procedures I have described in this section can be deployed with great flexibility, in proportion to the needs of a given teacher-training context. They can form the basis of a one-day seminar at one extreme, an extended course at the other. The lexical approach to pedagogical grammar I have outlined in this article can also be deployed with great flexibility, in proportion to what learners already know and what at any particular stage of learning they need to know. Because it depends, as process and as content, on the learners' own communicative activity, it cannot easily overwhelm them. Grammar has customarily been thought of as the most daunting and unpleasant part of language learning. In a lexical approach of the kind I have outlined, it quickly comes to seem the inevitable and indispensable centre of purposeful learning activity.

References

Aitchison, J. 1987. *Words in the Mind. An Introduction to the Mental Lexicon.* Oxford: Blackwell.

Anderson, R. C. 1977. The notion of schemata and the educational enterprise. In *Schooling and the Acquisition of Knowledge,* ed. by R. C. Anderson, R. J. Spiro and W. E. Montague. Hillsdale, N.J.: Lawrence Erlbaum.

Ard, J., and S. Gass. 1987. Lexical constraints on syntactic acquisition. *Studies in Second Language Acquisition* 9(2): 233–52.

Baldegger, M., M. Müller, G. Schneider and A. Näf. 1980. *Kontaktschwelle.* Strasbourg: Council of Europe.

Bartlett, F. C. 1932. *Remembering.* Cambridge: Cambridge University Press.

Bourgignon, C., and M. Candelier. 1984. Réflexion guidée sur la langue maternelle et apprentissage d'une langue étrangère. *Les Langues Modernes:* 147–61.

1988. La place de la langue maternelle dans la construction par l'élève des notions grammaticales requises pour l'apprentissage d'une langue étrangère. *Les Langues Modernes:* 19–34.

Brown, G., and G. Yule. 1983. *Discourse Analysis.* Cambridge: Cambridge University Press.

Carter, R., and M. McCarthy. 1988. *Vocabulary and Language Teaching.* London and New York: Longman.

Collins COBUILD. 1987. *English Language Dictionary.* London and Glasgow: Collins.

1988. *Essential English Dictionary.* London and Glasgow: Collins.

1990. *English Grammar.* London and Glasgow: Collins.

Cook, V. J. 1988. *Chomsky's Universal Grammar.* Oxford: Blackwell.

Coste, D., J. Courtillon, V. Ferenczi, M. Martins-Baltar and E. Papo. 1976. *Un Niveau Seuil.* Strasbourg: Council of Europe.

Ellis, R. 1985. *Understanding Second Language Acquisition.* Oxford: Oxford University Press.

Gass, S. 1987. Introduction to *Studies in Second Language Acquisition* 9(2), Special Issue, "The Use and Acquisition of the Second Language Lexicon".

Harley, B. 1986. *Age in Second Language Acquisition.* Clevedon, U.K.: Multilingual Matters.

Hornby, A. S. (with A. P. Cowie and A. C. Gimson). 1981. *Oxford Advanced Learner's Dictionary of Current English* (3d. ed., revised and reset). Oxford: Oxford University Press.

Howatt, A. P. R. 1984. *A History of English Language Teaching.* Oxford: Oxford University Press.

Krashen, S. D. 1981. *Second Language Acquisition and Second Language Learning.* Oxford: Pergamon.

1982. *Principles and Practice in Second Language Acquisition.* Oxford: Pergamon.

Leech, G., and J. Svartvik. 1975. *A Communicative Grammar of English.* London: Longman.

Little, D. 1991. *Learner Autonomy: 1. Definitions, Issues and Problems.* Dublin: Authentik.

Little, D., S. Devitt and D. Singleton. 1989. *Learning Foreign Languages from Authentic Texts.* Dublin: Authentik, in association with CILT, London.

Little, D. G., and D. M. Singleton. 1988. Authentic materials and the role of fixed support in language teaching: towards a manual for language learners. *CLCS Occasional Paper No. 20.* Dublin: Trinity College, Centre for Language and Communication Studies.

1992. Authentic texts, pedagogical grammar and Language Awareness in foreign language learning. In *Language Awareness in the Classroom,* ed. by C. James and P. Garrett. London: Longman, 123–32.

Long, M. H. 1988. Instructed interlanguage development. In *Issues in Second Language Acquisition,* ed. by Leslie M. Beebe. New York: Newbury House, 115–41.

Minsky, M. 1977. Frame-system theory. In *Thinking. Readings in Cognitive Science,* ed. by P. N. Johnson-Laird and P. C. Wason. Cambridge: Cambridge University Press, 355–76.

Nattinger, J. 1988. Some current trends in vocabulary teaching. In Carter and McCarthy: 62–82.

Nattinger, J., and J. DeCarrico. 1989. Lexical phrases, speech acts and teaching conversation. In *Vocabulary Acquisition. AILA Reiew 6,* ed. by P. Nation and R. Carter. Amsterdam: Free University Press, 118–39.

Odlin, T. 1986. On the nature and use of explicit knowledge. *IRAL* 24(2): 123–44.

Procter, P. (ed.). 1988. *Longman Dictionary of Contemporary English* (2d ed.). London: Longman.

Radford, A. 1990. *Syntactic Theory and the Acquisition of English Syntax.* Oxford: Blackwell.

Rudska, B., J. Channell, Y. Putseys and P. Ostyn. 1981. *The Words You Need.* London and Basingstoke: Macmillan.

Rutherford, W. E. 1987. *Second Language Grammar: Learning and Teaching.* London and New York: Longman.

Sanford, A. J., and S. C. Garrod. 1981. *Understanding Written Language.* Chichester: Wiley.

Schank, R. C., and R. Abelson. 1977. *Scripts, Plans, Goals and Understanding.* Hillsdale, N.J.: Lawrence Erlbaum.

Sells, P. 1985. *Lectures on Contemporary Syntactic Theories.* Stanford: Center for the Study of Language and Information.

Singleton, D., and D. Little. 1991. The second language lexicon: some evidence from university-level learners of French and German. *Second Language Research* 7(1): 61–81.

van Ek, J. 1975. *The Threshold Level.* Strasbourg: Council of Europe.

Willis, D. 1990. *The Lexical Syllabus.* London and Glasgow: Collins ELT.

6 Grammatical consciousness-raising and learnability

Virginia Yip

Introduction

Perhaps one of the questions most often raised by language teaching professionals is whether students should be taught grammar and if it really helps. It would be most welcome if there were a definite yes or no answer. If it were demonstrated that grammatical instruction does not help in any circumstances, we need not bother about it and could then turn to other ways of teaching methodology. If it could be shown conclusively to help, then we would need to know in what circumstances and how to go about it. Unfortunately, the question is not nearly so simple. The best answer we can currently offer is that it helps for certain learners at certain levels with certain aspects of grammar. If this is the case, the question is worth pursuing, and the research agenda is to spell out each of these conditions.

This paper focuses on the question of which aspects of grammar call for instruction and why. We investigate the role of grammatical consciousness-raising (C-R), a cognitive approach to grammatical instruction developed by Sharwood Smith (1981) and Rutherford (1987). The results of a classroom study on second language learners' acquisition of "ergative" verbs in English suggest that this approach is viable. We shall argue that in light of both empirical results and learnability considerations, certain areas of grammar call for some form of grammatical instruction, to which C-R can be an effective approach.

For and against grammatical instruction

Grammar instruction in general has been in and out of language methodologies following the pendulum swing from grammar-driven audio-

I would like to thank the instructors of the two ALI classes, John Hedgcock and Trevor Shanklin, and their students for allowing me to implement C-R during their class time, making this study possible. Many thanks also go to Stephen Matthews and Terry Odlin, whose comments have led to numerous improvements in the paper, and to Professor William Rutherford, who provided the inspiration for the study.

123

lingual methods to communicative approaches which consider grammar as something peripheral. At one extreme, grammatically structured syllabi still present explicit rules and paradigms with limited exposure to authentic input. Reacting to this approach, Krashen's (1985) Input Hypothesis claims that comprehensible input is both necessary and sufficient for successful second language acquisition (SLA), implying the insignificance of grammar instruction.

Sharwood Smith (1981) suggests that approaches to grammatical instruction can be considered and compared in terms of degrees of explicitness and of elaboration. C-R as described by Rutherford (1987) is something of a compromise: It focuses on aspects of grammar without necessarily using explicit rules or technical jargon. Instead of trying to impart rules and principles directly as in the traditional grammar lesson, it seeks to help learners discover them for themselves by focusing on aspects of the target structures. On the other hand, it differs from pure communicative approaches by telling learners which structures are ungrammatical and providing the grammatical counterparts.

In the following sections, we shall look at the motivation for this middle-ground position:

(a) empirical evidence that input alone is insufficient;
(b) theoretical reasons why grammar instruction may be necessary in principle.

Empirical motivation

Empirically, it is a very difficult task to single out effects of instruction. As Ellis (1984) has pointed out, not only focus on form, but also exposure to L2 data which comes with the instruction must be taken into account in evaluating the methodology. Nevertheless, several research findings cast doubt on the strong no-grammar position and lead to a reconsideration of the possible roles for grammar instruction. One notable study of the French immersion program by Harley and Swain (1984), called into question the adequacy of comprehensible input as the sole source of input to SLA. Despite the ample input provided by the immersion context, the students showed notable grammatical deficiencies: For example, the verbal system was restricted and lacked the full range of tense and modality. This finding is echoed in Schachter (1991), who identifies the verbal system as an area in which L2 competence typically remains incomplete. Two recent findings also support the usefulness of some kind of grammatical instruction: White (1991) found that French learners of English performed dramatically better on adverb placement given "form-focused" instruction; Carroll and Swain (1991) compared four levels of explicitness of feedback and found that explicit metalinguistic formulation was most effective in Spanish learners' acquisition of dative verbs.

These research findings suggest that comprehensible input is certainly necessary, but not sufficient to bring about successful acquisition. Harley and Swain point out that when accuracy is at issue, learners fall far short of nativelike proficiency. C-R is an attempt to bridge this gap in learners' competence. Clearly, there is a wide range of related variables that determine the usefulness of the particular type of C-R. Questions such as whether the individual learner is interested in grammar, concerned about form and accuracy, and willing to pay attention, and the nature of the structure in question should enter into our consideration of the role of C-R in SLA.

Theoretical motivation: learnability

The second strand of motivation for C-R is more theoretical. Recently, researchers have increasingly addressed the question of the "learnability" of a second language (Zobl 1988; Rutherford 1989; White 1989). Learnability involves the mechanism of progression from one state of knowledge to the next. One of the central questions is what kind of "evidence" triggers this progression. White (1988) and others have argued that input alone is insufficient, because it does not always provide the appropriate evidence. Specifically, when the learner's state of L2 knowledge leads her to overuse a rule, construction, and so on, there is nothing in the input to tell her not to use it. For example, consider a learner who invariably uses the Progressive form of the Present Tense, even in habitual contexts such as *I am often playing tennis.* The input will provide ample evidence that the Present does not always occur in the Progressive form; but it will not tell the learner that the Progressive is inappropriate in habitual contexts. What is needed is *negative evidence:* the information that a structure is ungrammatical or inappropriate.

White (1988), discussing the implications of learnability theories for SLA and teaching, suggests that a potential situation involving the relationship shown in Figure 1 on page 126 may be the appropriate context for C-R. X is the superset containing incorrect forms which have to be expunged from the learner's grammar. Y is the subset which contains the correct forms for the target language. According to White (1988: 3):

These are the situations which require negative evidence, that is, drawing the learner's attention to the fact that certain forms are non-occurring, or ungrammatical, in the target language. Such evidence would seem to be required when learners make certain kinds of overgeneralizations, i.e. arrive at grammars which are overinclusive.

The obvious solution to this problem is to resort to the traditional "red-pen" strategy of explicit correction. Well-known reservations about the negative psychological effects make this option unattractive. C-R is an

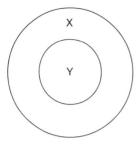

Figure 1

attempt to develop less drastic means to achieve the same goal without such side effects.

Considerations of learnability, then, provide a cogent theoretical argument in favor of some form of grammatical instruction, and for C-R in particular. Learnability theory also offers the means to identify which interlanguage phenomena call for attention to grammar.

Ergative verbs

It is only recently that discussion of "ergative" verbs has found its way into pedagogical grammars, for example, the Collins COBUILD grammar (1990), after a decade of theoretical discussion of their distinctive properties. It was Perlmutter (1978) who first discussed a class of "change-of-state" verbs, which he called "unaccusative," that denote processes that lack volitional control. They look like active intransitive verbs in that they subcategorize for a single Noun Phrase. He proposed the "unaccusative hypothesis," which makes a distinction between simple intransitive verbs, which imply volitional control, and unaccusative verbs, which do not. These have become known as ergative verbs, following Burzio (1981) and Keyser and Roeper (1984). Compare the transitive/intransitive pairs in (1) and (2):

1. a. The kids eat dinner early.   (transitive)
   b. The kids eat early.   (intransitive)

2. a. The burglar broke the window.   (transitive)
   b. The window broke.   (intransitive; ergative)

In the first case (1a–b), the subject *the kids* is the agent of the action in both the transitive and the intransitive structure. In the transitive use of the verb *break* (2a), *the burglar* is the agent and *the window* the patient. In the ergative construction (2b), the patient, *the window,* is now the subject.

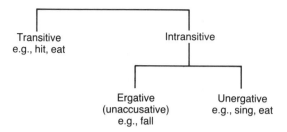

Figure 2

These differences suggest that the traditional transitive/intransitive dichotomy needs to be elaborated. Verbs can now be classified as shown in Figure 2. Simple intransitives (as in 1b) may be referred to as "unergative" for the sake of precision. A further distinction arises from the fact that some ergatives such as *break* also occur as transitive verbs, that is, they have two alternative subcategorization frames, while verbs such as *happen* can only occur as ergatives:

*ergatives **with** a transitive/causative counterpart*
3. a. The sun melted the ice.
   b. The ice melted.
4. a. The enemies sank the ship.
   b. The ship sank.

Other verbs that belong to this category include *boil, bounce, close, dry, fracture, hang, move, open, roll.*

*ergatives **without** a transitive counterpart*
5. Something happened.
6. The guests arrived.
7. The leaves fell.

These structures are parallel to (3b) and (4b) in that the subject of the sentence undergoes a change of state. Other examples include *appear, arise, disappear, emerge,* and *erupt.* The distinction between the two classes of ergative verbs proves to be important, in that the first type always allows the passive, whereas the second does not. We will see how these two types give rise to learnability problems of different kinds.

Previous studies have shown that the English ergative verbs pose an acquisition problem in SLA. Kellerman (1978) found that Dutch learners of English tended to reject and avoid typical "ergative" structures such as *The cup broke,* preferring the agentless passive, *The cup was broken.* Zobl (1989) discusses L2 production of passivized ergative constructions such as the following:

8. Most people *are fallen* in love and marry with somebody. (Japanese L1; high intermediate)

9. The most memorable experience of my life *was happened* 15 years ago.
(Arabic L1; advanced learner)

As Zobl shows, even very advanced learners have difficulty with these verbs, which involve certain fine and subtle semantic distinctions. This study selects ergative verbs as the focus of C-R and addresses the question whether C-R makes a difference in learning.

The tendency of second language learners to passivize ergative verbs can be traced back to their distinctive properties. Ergatives share close similarities with agentless passives: Both are intransitive, both lack an agent, while the patient appears in subject position. As the acquisition data show, learners seem to treat ergatives like passives. The tendency stems from the inherent similarities between the two structures.[1]

Background of the study

To investigate the difficulties posed by ergative verbs, we designed a judgment task consisting of ergatives and other related structures known to be problematic for second language learners. The questionnaire, reproduced in the appendix to this chapter, is contextualized in order to make the judgment task more naturalistic than in one consisting of isolated sentences. We shall focus only on the ergative structures here; the full results are reported in Yip (1989). Many students rejected ergative constructions such as the following as ungrammatical:

10. The mirror shattered during the last earthquake.
11. My car has broken down.

The judgments suggest that learners' grammar systematically undergenerates ergative constructions, as evidenced by their reluctance to accept good ergatives in the grammaticality judgment task. Even the most advanced learners are unable to accept all of the good ergatives, while performing like native speakers in other respects. At best, the highest scoring informant, a linguistics graduate student, judged the ergatives as

---

1 However, the two exhibit different syntactic behavior in that the passive allows a "by-phrase" (ia) and control into the purpose clause (iia) whereas the ergative does not (ib, iib):

(i)   a. The ship was sunk by the enemies.
      b. *The ship sank by the enemies.

(ii) a. The ship was sunk to collect insurance.
      b. *The ship sank to collect insurance.

As Jaeggli (1986) argues, when the "by-phrase" is present, it takes on the agent role, while in an agentless passive, the agent role remains as an "implicit argument," its presence implied by the passive morpheme: This explains why the passive allows control into the purpose clause (iia), since there is an implicit argument in the passive which is absent in the ergative structure.

probably grammatical. Most advanced learners reject good ergatives as *clearly* ungrammatical.

Subjects were also asked to make corrections if a given sentence was judged to be ungrammatical. Some of the corrections were quite revealing:

Judgment task	Corrections
12. The mirror shattered during the earthquake.	→ was shattered
13. My car has broken down.	→ has been broken/was broken down
14. What cooks most quickly?	→ can be cooked
15. We had some ice cream, but it has melted.	→ has been/was melted
16. What was happened here?	(accepted as clearly grammatical)

A clear pattern emerges: Learners tend to reject good ergatives and extend the passive rule to ergatives.

The fact that learners prefer the passive version suggests that they might be interpreting ergatives of both types as underlyingly transitive (since only transitive verbs allow passivization in English). Further evidence for this comes from the observation that they often turn ergative verbs into transitives/causatives. Some examples are cited in Rutherford (1987: 89):

17. The shortage of fuels *occurred* the need for economical engine.
18. This construction will *progress* my country.
19. Careless currency devaluation will *go back* us to old habits.

Why are ergatives so hard to acquire?

In this section we consider the question of where the difficulty posed by ergatives lies. Learners' treatment of ergatives as if they were passives may be seen as a reflection of the typological organization of English, in which grammatical relations are based on the nominative-accusative system. In this system, the semantic role of *agent* normally corresponds to the grammatical function *subject,* that of *theme* or *patient* to the grammatical function *object* (cf. Marantz 1984). Thus in a typical transitive sentence:

```
        subject    object
20. a. John kicked the ball.
       (agent)    (theme)
```

John is the "agent" responsible for the action, who provides the energy involved and willfully instigates it. *The ball* is the inert participant which undergoes a change of state (motion, in this case). This mapping of the *agent* role to the subject of a transitive verb is the most preferred and productive mapping in English. However, in a passive sentence, a *theme* surfaces in subject position, as in (20):

    subject
20. b. The ball was kicked (by John).
    (theme)   *(agent)*

In this case, *the ball* appears as subject but is not an agent, so the verb has special morphological marking to indicate the change. Fillmore, in an influential paper on the relation between semantic roles and grammatical relations, explains:

This "non-normal" subject choice is "registered" in the V. This "registering" of a "non-normal" subject takes place via the association of the feature [+passive] with the V. (Fillmore 1968: 37)

Despite the many similarities that ergatives share with passives, they differ in one crucial respect: Ergatives have no special morphological marking, but appear just like other simple intransitive verbs – a phenomenon which appears to be somewhat exceptional cross-linguistically.[2] Since passive is very productive in English, it is plausible for learners to adopt the working hypothesis: Whenever the *theme* is in subject position, mark the verb with passive morphology. However, the class of ergative verbs constitutes the exception to the rule. These verbs do not require any special marking to indicate the change in grammatical relation whereby the *theme* argument is not in its canonical object position. To master these verbs, the learner has to learn not to mark them, in contradiction to the typological organization of English grammar described earlier, whereby the subject of the sentence is assumed to be the agent of the action.

Moreover, there is a further factor that might contribute to the difficulty involved: Learners seem reluctant to believe that any change of state occurs spontaneously, without external causation.[3] One characteristic of ergative verbs is that the theme argument tends, by default, to be understood as the agent that causes the change of state; for exam-

---

2 Languages use various devices such as reflexive morphemes and vowel alternation to encode the transitive and ergative verbs differently, e.g.:

    French: *se briser* (erg.)   "break" – reflexive
                  briser (trans.)
    German: *sinken* (erg.)   "sink" – vowel alternation
                  senken (trans.)
    Japanese: *taoreru* (erg.) "fall"
                  taosu (trans.)   "fell"

3 This belief may have a deep-seated intuitive basis. Carey (1985) notes that laypeople – and even undergraduate physics students – have a firm but misguided intuition that no motion is possible without a force causing it. The preference of L2 learners for the passive over the ergative accords with this intuition by suggesting the presence of a missing agent.

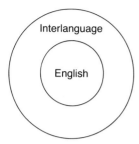

Figure 3

ple, *The ship sank* is interpreted as though the ship were sinking itself away. Indeed, many languages use reflexive forms to express such predicates (cf. footnote 2). Learners may be thinking: "There has to be a reason for everything." The logical gap can be filled by supplying the missing causal agent, which results in the creative causative/transitive use of ergatives as reflected in the passive. One example is learners' interpretation of *be happened* to mean "be caused/made to happen."

The learnability problem

The overgeneralization of passive to ergative verbs poses a challenging learnability problem of the kind discussed earlier. Recall that ergative verbs can be divided into two subgroups:

I. those that are always intransitive, such as *happen, appear;*
II. those that are both transitive and intransitive, such as *melt* and *break.*

The overgeneralization of passive to the first subgroup, at least, would create a situation corresponding to White's diagram in Figure 1. Learners' grammar generates a superset which includes both good passives and ill-formed passives such as *be happened, be fallen, be died* (Figure 3). The learnability question that arises is: How do learners cut back from the superset to the restricted subset which English allows? Put differently, how do the malformed passives drop out of the learner's grammar? There is no positive evidence in the English input for the nonoccurrence of these forms: They simply do not occur in the input. Hearing positive evidence exemplifying the ergative construction containing these verbs could not reliably lead the learner to the conclusion that they do not undergo passive. In fact, one subject in the study informed me that she thought *happen* allowed both the passive and active form. Hence, the active version (ergative construction) which she hears in the input would not serve as disconfirming evidence for the impossibility of the passive versions.[4]

This is where the question of grammatical instruction arises: The "negative evidence" which the situation seems to call for can be supplied in the classroom. Some form of C-R directing the learner's attention to the ill-formedness of the passive form of the first subgroup of ergative verbs may trigger the expunging of these forms. Instead of leaving it up to chance for the learner to notice the nonoccurrence of the deviant forms, C-R can alert the learner and thereby reduce the scope of passive so as not to include those ergative verbs in the first subgroup.

The second subgroup of ergatives, namely, those that *do* have a transitive counterpart, poses a different problem. Their transitive counterpart will always allow passivization:

21. a. The snow melted (in the heat).
    b. The snow was melted (by the heat).

The difficulty here lies in the distinction between the passive and the ergative construction: Learners do not seem to make a distinction between the passivized transitive verb and the ergative verb but instead collapse the two.[5]

In terms of learnability, the question here is not that the learner has to expunge the deviant form from the grammar; rather, what needs to be learned is the distinction between the passive and the ergative constructions. According to the Uniqueness Principle proposed by Pinker (1984), a learner assumes each meaning to be encoded by a single morphological form or syntactic structure, unless the language provides evidence to the contrary. Only when the learner perceives a difference in meaning will he or she mark a form distinctively. Given the subtle semantic distinctions between the two discussed earlier, what might motivate a learner to isolate the class of ergatives and encode them in a different way from the passive? Learners' intuitive logic seems to favor overwhelmingly the

4 One possibility is that the learner might notice the nonoccurrence of these forms. This would constitute what is known as "indirect negative evidence," believed to be a weak form of evidence.

5 Note that the difficulty cannot readily be attributed to transfer, at least in the case of Chinese L1 learners. First, the passive in Chinese is lexically and semantically restricted and not nearly as productive as in English: Many verbs which can be passivized in English cannot in Chinese. Thus, the passivization of ergatives is not likely to be based on the L1. Second, Chinese allows ergative constructions as in (i), corresponding to (21a):

   (i) Xue ronghua le.
       snow melt ASP
       "The snow melted."

   The presence of parallel structures in the L1 does not seem to help learners to produce them in the L2, suggesting that positive transfer fails here. One possibility is that transfer fails to occur when the structure in question is "marked" or exceptional cross-linguistically (cf. footnote 2).

passive interpretation involving a causal agent. In a situation like this, where logic may be misleading, collapsing two similar meanings into one single form, C-R may be useful in alerting learners to the alternative forms and the subtleties of meaning involved.

Methodology

The subjects in this pilot study were enrolled in two advanced ESL classes at the American Language Institute (ALI) at the University of Southern California. Five students in each class participated in the study. They were from a variety of L1 backgrounds: Spanish, Hebrew, Korean, Chinese, and Indonesian in the first class; German, Greek, Korean, Chinese, and Indonesian in the second class. First, they were given a pre-test in which subjects were asked to indicate whether a given sentence (contextualized: see the appendix) was clearly grammatical, probably grammatical, probably ungrammatical, or clearly ungrammatical. They were also asked to make corrections if they thought a particular sentence was grammatical. Immediately after the pre-test, the C-R sessions were held with the two classes. Two weeks after the C-R, a post-test was administered, using the same questionnaire, to the same subjects.

The C-R session in the first class lasted about forty-five minutes; that in the second class went on a little longer. The goal of C-R in general is to direct learners' attention to specific grammatical features. In this case, the target structure was the ergative construction, related structures such as passive, and the auxiliary system also being discussed. The topic was approached as a cognitive puzzle, and the presentation was couched in problem-solving terms; linguistic jargon was reduced to the minimum. I made up a number of examples similar to those in the questionnaire and explained to the learners how the passive form is used when an agent is intended, the ergative when it is not. I briefly alluded to the principles of typological organization and the gross grammatical characteristics of English without getting into the technicalities.

Results and discussion

The results of the pre-test and post-test are listed in Tables 1 and 2. The questionnaire is made up of thirty test sentences. They are categorized into ergatives and other categories which subsume pseudopassive, good passive, auxiliary, and distractor sentences. The percentage of errors is shown for ergatives, the structure under investigation in this paper, and all other categories, respectively, for the pre-test and the post-test.

The results of the subjects in the first class do not indicate any significant difference between the pre- and post-test scores. No subject did

TABLE I. RESULTS OF CLASS I PRE-TEST AND POST-TEST: % OF ERRORS

Subject L1	Ergatives total = 6 items		Other categories total = 24 items		Total 30	
	pre-	post-test	pre-	post-test	pre-	post-test
Spanish	17%	0%	4%	8%	6.5%	6.5%
Hebrew	17%	17%	12.5%	8%	13%	10%
Korean	33%	33%	21%	16.5%	23%	20%
Chinese	50%	33%	54%	54%	60%	50%
Indonesian	67%	50%	8%	0%	20%	10%

TABLE 2. RESULTS OF CLASS 2 PRE-TEST AND POST-TEST: % OF ERRORS

Subject L1	Ergatives total = 6 items		Other categories total = 24 items		Total 30	
	pre-	post-test	pre-	post-test	pre-	post-test
German	50%	33%	4%	4%	13%	10%
Greek	33%	33%	16.5%	21%	20%	23%
Indonesian	33%	17%	41.5%	37.5%	40%	33%
Korean	67%	17%	16.5%	8%	26.5%	10%
Chinese	83%	17%	54%	12.5%	60%	13.5%

worse in the post-test; all seemed to give similar judgments to the same sentences each time. It should be noted that with the first class, the actual answers to the questionnaire were not provided; only similar examples of each type of construction were discussed in the C-R session. This was intended to avoid handing grammatical information to subjects on a "pedagogical platter," the goal being to get subjects to work out for themselves the implications of the rules and generalizations and apply them creatively. On the other hand, one drawback is that the presentation suffered from lack of specificity and precision. In view of this problem, I decided to modify the procedure somewhat and include a review of the answers to the questionnaire.

The modification seems to have improved the total score of the subjects in the second class. However, it is hard to show that a causal relation between the two exists: It is not clear whether subjects memorized the answers or truly understood the structures. The disadvantage of using the same questionnaire in both the pre-test and the post-test is that there is no way to tap learners' creative use of the rules. To avoid this pitfall, a different but comparable questionnaire should be used instead. Judging from subjects' responses, however, especially those in the second class, it seems unlikely that what subjects did was rote learning, merely memorizing the answers without a genuine understanding of the constructions.

Next we consider the score in each category. First, subjects' judgment with respect to the ergative category either remained the same or improved. The verb *cook* seems recalcitrant and resists being treated as an ergative verb. Except for this verb, most subjects got the rest of the ergative verbs correct. One tentative explanation as to why the ergative use of *cook* is hard for the subjects is that it is simply infrequent in the input, thus inaccessible to them. In contrast, the transitive *cook* is much more frequent. Moreover, the semantic interpretation of the ergative *cook* is not so intuitively easy to construct: For example, *What cooks most quickly?* is interpreted as "What cooks itself most quickly?"

Two subjects in the second class incorrectly accepted *be happened* in the pre-test while correctly rejecting it in the post-test. In our earlier discussion of learnability problems posed by ergative verbs like *happen* which do not have a transitive counterpart, it was suggested that C-R may be useful in directing learners' attention to the nonoccurrence or ungrammaticality of the passive version of these forms. The result suggests that the subjects were sensitive to the ungrammaticality of *be happened* in the post-test.

Subjects' response to instruction

As might be expected, some subjects responded better than others. Certain individuals could be singled out as showing more interest in the topic of discussion. They were more willing to give answers when a question was asked and raise questions of their own. As a result, the animated discussion probably benefited the whole class, including those that did not show the same degree of involvement.

Overall, subjects in the second class were more active in their participation than those in the first class. The Chinese subject in particular showed an avid interest in the topic throughout the presentation and was somewhat shocked to find out about the ergative construction. Coming from a foreign language-learning background (Taiwan), he had never been taught the ergative construction by his teachers or textbooks. The rule he had was to form a passive whenever the object becomes the subject. This student did something further which I consider to be a hallmark of a good language learner: He consulted other ESL teachers and native speakers to verify what I had told him about the ergative structure. He was probably too overwhelmed initially, not quite ready to give up his long-held beliefs. It did not take too long to convince him about the difference between ergatives and passives. He seemed to be particularly impressed by this language learning experience.

The active participation of the Chinese and Korean subjects in the second class evidently paid off. In the ergative category, their pre-test error rates of 83 percent and 67 percent went down to 17 percent on the post-test, failing only on the ergative *cook,* which was hard for everyone. This dramatic improvement was especially encouraging and made the C-R worthwhile. These subjects represent the best case of C-R: the "eureka" effect of sudden enlightenment.

Conclusion

In this chapter, I have examined the rationale for C-R as an approach to grammatical instruction in terms of empirical findings and theoretical considerations of learnability. Several studies suggest that comprehensible input is necessary but not sufficient for acquisition of grammatical accuracy; learnability theory helps to identify situations that call for grammatical instruction. English ergative verbs are a case in point: They are known observationally to cause difficulty to learners of various L1 backgrounds and pose a logical problem of acquisition in that positive evidence (input) alone is in principle insufficient to resolve the difficulty.

The study reported here confirms the difficulty posed by ergative verbs and shows that C-R can be effective in such cases. A few subjects showed significant improvement in certain categories. Although the findings are not as dramatic as some, such as White's (1991) on adverb placement, the overall results as reflected by the post-test are encouraging. Because of the small number of subjects in the study, the results are at best suggestive; it is not clear how far one can generalize the findings. Another question yet to be addressed concerns the long-term effectiveness of C-R: whether the learner's grammar expunges the errors permanently or merely overrules them temporarily.

There was an obvious correlation between the degree of interest and participation shown by the subjects and their performance in the post-test. The more one is interested and concerned about the form in question, hence paying attention to what is presented, the more easily one can internalize the knowledge. The extent to which individual learners attend to linguistic forms is necessarily variable, given the wide range of inherent individual differences.

The question of the possible roles for C-R in language learning cannot be addressed meaningfully in isolation; a variety of factors necessarily enters into consideration. Not only learner-centered variables, but also the nature of the linguistic form and function, together with implications derived by theoretical research such as learnability and syntactic theory, should be brought to bear on this significant question. To sum up, I would like to quote from Rutherford (1988: 15–16):

A viable research program will of necessity establish itself by bringing into alignment the findings from several different sectors – namely, what we believe to be the fundamental principles of intrinsic language organization (a linguistic question), what we believe to be the way in which languages are learned (a question of psychology/second language acquisition), and what we believe to be the most effective kinds of teaching (an education question).

References

Burzio, Luigi. 1981. Intransitive verbs and Italian auxiliaries. Unpublished Ph.D. dissertation, Massachusetts Institute of Technology.

Carey, Susan. 1985. *Conceptual Change in Childhood*. Cambridge, Mass.: MIT Press.

Carroll, Susanne, and Merrill Swain. 1991. Negative evidence in second language learning. Presented at the Second Language Research Forum, University of Southern California.

Collins COBUILD. 1990. *English Grammar*. Collins, University of Birmingham.

Ellis, Rod. 1984. *Classroom Second Language Development*. Oxford: Pergamon Press.

Fillmore, Charles. 1968. The case for case. In *Universals in Linguistic Theory*, ed. by Emmon Bach and Robert Harms. New York: Holt, Rinehart, and Winston.

Harley, Birgit, and Merrill Swain. 1984. The interlanguage of immersion students and its implications for second language teaching. In *Interlanguage*, ed. by Allen Davies et al. Edinburgh University Press.

Jaeggli, Osvaldo. 1986. Passive. *Linguistic Inquiry* 15: 381–416.

Kellerman, Eric. 1978. Giving learners a break: native language intuition as a source of predictions about transferrability. *Working Papers in Bilingualism* 15: 59–92.

Keyser, Jay, and Thomas Roeper. 1984. On the middle and ergative constructions in English. *Linguistic Inquiry* 15: 381–416.

Krashen, Stephen. 1985. *The Input Hypothesis: Issues and Implications*. London: Longman.

Marantz, Alec. 1984. *On the Nature of Grammatical Relations*. Cambridge, Mass.: MIT Press.

Perlmutter, David. 1978. Impersonal passives and the unaccusative hypothesis. *Proceedings of the 4th Annual Meeting*, Berkeley Linguistics Society, 157–89.

Pinker, Stephen. 1984. *Language Learnability and Language Development*. Cambridge, Mass.: MIT Press.

Rutherford, William. 1987. *Second Language Grammar: Learning and Teaching*. London: Longman.

1988. Overview: formal consciousness-raising and the language learner's curriculum. Presented at TESOL, Chicago.

1989. Adult language learnability: subsets and semantics. Unpublished manuscript, University of Southern California.

Schachter, Jacquelyn. 1991. On the issue of completeness in second language acquisition. *Second Language Research* 6: 93–124.

Sharwood Smith, Michael. 1981. Consciousness-raising and the second language learner. *Applied Linguistics* 2: 159–68.

White, Lydia. 1988. Implications of learnability theories for second language learning and teaching. Presented at TESOL, Chicago.

1989. *Universal Grammar and Second Language Acquisition.* Amsterdam: John Benjamins.

1991. The verb-movement parameter in second language acquisition. *Language Acquisition* 1: 4, 337–60.

Yip, Virginia. 1989. Aspects of Chinese/English interlanguage: syntax, semantics and learnability. Unpublished Ph.D. dissertation, University of Southern California.

Zobl, Helmut. 1988. Configurationality and the subset principle: the acquisition of V' by Japanese learners of English. In *Learnability and Second Languages: A Book of Readings,* ed. by John Pankhurst, Michael Sharwood Smith, and Paul Van Buren. Dordrecht: Foris.

1989. Canonical typological structures and ergativity in English L2 acquisition. In *Linguistic Perspectives on Second Language Acquisition,* ed. by Susan Gass and Jacquelyn Schachter. New York: Cambridge University Press.

Appendix: Questionnaire on ergative constructions

Remember: a. Clearly good English (grammatical English)
   b. Probably good English
   c. Probably bad English
   d. Clearly bad English (ungrammatical English)

Scene: Study Room

Student A: Hi! How's it going?	
Student B: I have been working very hard.	(1)
A: Are your courses very tough?	(2)
B: My courses can classify into two types:	(3)
Some courses must study hard to get a passing grade,	(4)
some courses can pass without trying.	(5)
A: (*Amazed at how many books there are on the desk.*)	
All those books have read already, haven't you?	(6)
B. Two of them read last week.	(7)
The other ones have renewed already.	(8)
All these books should be returned in two weeks.	(9)
A: (*Pointing at the broken window.*)	
What was happened here?	(10)
B: The window was broken by the kids next door.	(11)
They should have punished.	(12)
A: What about the mirror?	
B: The mirror shattered during the last earthquake.	(13)
A: What are you doing tonight?	(14)
B: I have no idea. My car has broken down.	(15)
I don't know what went wrong.	(16)
The car just bought from the dealer last month.	(17)
It should be repaired soon.	(18)
A: I know there's a movie won some awards.	(19)
It was highly recommended.	(20)
They say it must see as soon as possible.	(21)
B: Good idea! But dinner should eat first.	(22)
Most of my food has eaten already.	(23)
What cooks most quickly?	(24)
A: Pizza can heat up in the oven to eat quickly.	(25)
B: Right! Maybe can find some dessert.	(26)
A: The fridge hasn't been working well.	(27)
Try these oranges. They were grown by my grandmother.	(28)
When they are ripe, they are fallen down everywhere.	(29)
B: She must be spent a lot of time in the garden.	(30)

7 Functional grammars, pedagogical grammars, and communicative language teaching

Russell S. Tomlin

Introduction

English language students commonly produce written paragraphs like the one in (1), and teachers just as commonly make suggestions to guide students toward revisions like those in (2).

(1) A student paragraph (as originally written)

> I came to America on June 11, 1989. **I came to Eugen by plane by myself.** The travel company made a complicated schedule for me. I stopped Osaka, Narita, Los Angeles, and San Francisco on the way to come to Eugene. **That was the first time for me to take a plane by myself, and I could speak English very well.** That was really scary for me. Even though the travel company gave me a lot of notes which showed me which way I should walk forward the gate in the each airports and *when I lost my way at the airport, how I asked people in English.*

(2) Some teacher suggestions for improvement

> I came to America on June 11, 1989, traveling to Eugene by plane alone. The travel company made a complicated schedule for me. I stopped in Osaka, Narita, Los Angeles, and San Francisco on the way to Eugene. Since it was the first time I took a plane by myself, it was really scary, even though I could speak English very well. Even though the travel company gave me a lot of notes which showed me the way I should walk in each airport, I lost my way and had to ask people for help in English.

At first glance the needed improvements seem both simple and transparent: The italicized dependent clauses read better when made independent, and the boldfaced independent clauses read better when subordinated. Why this is so may be less obvious because each individual sentence and clause is reasonably well formed, and one can derive successfully the critical meaning from the original paragraph. Still, whether the difference between (1) and (2) is viewed as a grammatical problem to be solved or simply as a matter of style, three critical questions remain:

1. What instruction[1] should the teacher[2] provide the student to correct or improve the writing in (1)?
2. From what source does the knowledge required for that instruction come?
3. On what principled basis is such knowledge derived?

The language teacher needs access to information about how different clause types – here, independent versus dependent clauses – are employed in written discourse. It is, of course, a pedagogical grammar which might well supply such information, detailing when and how various clause types are used in native speaker discourse. But the question of importance for this paper is the third one, for it asks how the information in a pedagogical grammar is developed, and it presupposes that the basis must be a principled one.

Developing a useful pedagogical grammar depends completely upon developing an adequate descriptive grammar of the target language. This paper examines the promise and limitations of functional grammars in providing the theoretical and descriptive foundations on which pedagogical grammars must rest. It argues, under the assumption of communicative language teaching theory, that development of L2 grammar arises from successful discourse *use* of the new language, that a pedagogical grammar must address how grammatical constructions are deployed in discourse, which is precisely what functional grammars do.

In addition to a critical review of functional approaches to syntax and discourse, we examine one specific functional problem – foregrounding and backgrounding in discourse and its relation to subordination and tense-aspect. We consider foregrounding both as a general functional problem and as an applied problem in pedagogical grammar.

Communicative language teaching theory: critical assumptions for pedagogical grammar

A pedagogical grammar depends on critical assumptions about the nature of language and its relationship to language learning. As others have documented (Howatt 1984), these assumptions change regularly in response to changes in both linguistic theory and language teaching theory. Communicative language teaching theory (Allen & Widdowson 1974; Widdowson 1978, 1979; Breen & Candlin 1980; Canale & Swain

---

1 We will ignore here all methodological questions regarding how grammatical knowledge is developed. We assume that whether grammar development or instruction is left implicit, as in much communicative teaching, or made explicit, as in grammar-translation, the problem of developing a principled basis for pedagogical grammars remains the same.
2 To avoid the stylistic awkwardness caused by the absence of a neutral gender in the English pronominal system for indefinite reference, I will, having made the assignment randomly, assign feminine form to an indefinite teacher and masculine form to an indefinite learner.

1980; Brumfit 1984) views language learning as a social and cognitive enterprise in which the learner entertains multiple hypotheses regarding the structure and function of target language constituents in natural discourse contexts until sufficient contextualized input is encountered to settle on and automate the learner's closest approximation of native speaker norms. This process of creative construction of an interlanguage grammar (Selinker 1972) is facilitated when linguistic input is comprehensible to the learner (Krashen 1977, 1982), when it is of sufficient quantity in a variety of discourse contexts, and when the affective environment does not constrain exploration and risk taking (Schumann 1978; Krashen 1982).

Language teaching represents the effort to set up these conditions for learning. With more or less finely grained teaching efforts, the teacher seeks to provide the learner with a sufficient quantity of comprehensible input drawn from a wide variety of genuine or authentic discourse contexts. Under the communicative approach, language is viewed as situated social activity, and learning as efforts of discourse production and comprehension, as *communication*. Thus, in communicative language teaching:

- Systematic attention is paid to functional as well as structural aspects of language (Littlewood 1984 :1).
- Classroom work is aimed at the situational and contextualized use of language (Piepho 1983).
- Teaching and learning are made observable and transparent through content which is made real to the learner through pictures, sketches, diagrams, and other representations (Piepho 1983).
- Attention is focused on the ability to understand and convey information, that is, on information transfer (Johnson 1982: 163–75).

These fundamental tenets of communicative language teaching theory very much guide how grammatical knowledge is viewed in language learning and consequently constrain the organization of a pedagogical grammar. Widdowson (1978, 1979) plainly describes the knowledge which the learner must acquire: (1) knowledge of grammatical structure – how syntactically well-formed utterances are composed – and (2) knowledge of grammatical use – how grammatical structures are employed in discourse. Some learners gain a high degree of facility in manipulating linguistic form in L2 but cannot determine when it is most appropriate to use one form over its alternatives. Since full communicative ability in L2 requires the learner to master use as well as form, one cannot be satisfied with a pedagogical grammar which does not address how grammatical forms are employed in discourse interaction. Any linguistic theory which restricts its descriptive and explanatory scope to syntactic form exclusively must, by its own definition, fail to provide the theoretical, descriptive, and explanatory bases on which a pedagogical grammar must be constructed.

The purpose of pedagogical grammars

Traditionally, pedagogical grammars are defined in taxonomic opposition to linguistic grammars. Linguistic grammars are descriptions of language forms, and in some cases functions, cast in a coherent, constrained, and self-contained metalanguage. A complete grammar includes descriptions of all major components of language – syntax, semantics, phonology, morphology, lexicon, and conditions on use. But such a grammar has never been written, and all linguistic theories are content to deal with relatively small subsets of the phenomena of interest, despite the intention and responsibility to deal with a wide range of matters.

Pedagogical grammars may well address several distinct audiences (Corder 1988). They may be used by language students to augment or clarify classroom activities. They may be used by prospective teachers and their professors to intensify their detailed knowledge of the workings of some target language. They may even be read by theoretical linguists at just the time when the theory being developed needs clarification from someone who actually understands the structure and workings of the actual language. But, all in all, the largest audience for pedagogical grammars is surely the language teacher, the individual engaged in the day-to-day practice of language instruction in the classroom.

For teachers, pedagogical grammars are ultimately translations of linguistic descriptions, translations which should help them enhance instructional efforts in two ways. One, they must provide explicit descriptions of grammatical structure and use in a simple and straightforward manner. Two, they should provide the basis, either explicitly or by example, for creating additions and amendments to pedagogical descriptions.

But by what principles are such translations to be formulated? It would seem that there is one requirement: A pedagogical description must provide the language teacher with information sufficient to construct learning activities targeting the selected grammatical problem. For instance, the teacher might wish to design learning activities which can help the learner formulate the right generalizations regarding English complementation, helping the learner distinguish and produce the grammatical examples in (3) while avoiding the ungrammatical ones:

(3)   Martha hoped to go to Japan.
   * Martha hoped going to Japan.
      Martha enjoyed going to Japan.
   * Martha enjoyed to go to Japan.
      Martha tried to go to Japan.
      Martha tried going to Japan.

The teacher might find adequate a clear description of the different forms of English complementation without regard for semantic differences among the complementation types. More likely, the teacher will find it useful, though she may not choose to deal with it through explicit instruction, to incorporate information on the semantics of English complementation (Quirk, Greenbaum, Leech and Svartvik 1985).

In the same way, the teacher dealing with the paragraph in (1) may well need advice on how independent and dependent clauses are structured. More likely, however, the teacher needs to know when a given proposition should be realized as an independent clause and when the same proposition should be realized as a dependent clause. Functional approaches to grammar deal directly with this second kind of question.

Functional grammars

In general, functional grammars embrace what we might call the "communicative imperative," the idea that linguistic form generally serves to code or signal linguistic function and that the shapes taken by linguistic form arise out of the demands of communicative interactions. Functional approaches embrace a number of central tenets which shape functional inquiry, but current research also suffers a number of serious limitations. We present these central tenets and consider the limitations in order to develop a balanced view of which functional approaches to grammar may offer pedagogical efforts.

An outline of functional approaches to grammar

Functional approaches to grammar share a number of essential goals and assumptions, as well as a number of serious problems. While it is beyond the scope of this article to detail the variety of functional approaches in the literature, there are several recent publications which do so. Hickmann (1987) and Dirven and Fried (1987) provide a general picture of functional linguistics. Pfaff (1987), Cooreman and Kilborn (1991), and Tomlin (1990) examine functional approaches within second language acquisition. Overall, functional work in linguistics falls into four broad divisions. First, there is Praguean functionalism, the historical precursor to contemporary efforts. Praguean work focuses on so-called *functional sentence perspective* (Daneš 1974b), which distinguishes a number of fundamental pragmatic statuses (*given-new, theme-rheme,* and so on) and describes their interactions with the syntax of word order, voice, and intonation (Daneš 1974a, 1987; Jones 1977). Second, there is the *Functional Grammar* of Simon Dik and associates

(Dik 1987), an approach dedicated to the formal specification of functional interactions. Third, there is the *Systemic Grammar* of Halliday and his associates (Davidse 1987; Halliday 1985), which is well described elsewhere in this volume.

Fourth, and finally, there is what one might call North American functionalism. While not a *school* of functionalism per se, the linguists within this group do share many of the fundamental tenets discussed below. Some of the key researchers in this tradition include Chafe (1971, 1980a, 1980b, 1987), Givón (1979a, 1979b, 1979c, 1983a, 1983b, 1984, 1988), Slobin (1973, 1982, 1985a, 1985b), Bates & MacWhinney (Bates & MacWhinney 1979, 1982, 1987, 1989; Bates, MacWhinney, Caselli, Devescovi, Natale & Venza 1984; Bates, MacWhinney & Smith 1983; Bates, McNew, MacWhinney, Devescovi & Smith 1982; MacWhinney, Bates & Kliegl 1984), and Hopper and Thompson (Hopper 1979; Hopper & Thompson 1980). There are certainly many others whose work fits well within this tradition (Tomlin 1990).

DESCRIPTIVE VERSUS EXPLANATORY EFFORTS

Like all other linguistic approaches, functional approaches pursue two related enterprises: description and explanation. Functional description centers on questions of form-function interaction. Functional analysis attempts to determine the semantic or pragmatic conditions which lead to the selection of alternative grammatical structures. For example, there is an extensive tradition of work in both linguistics and psycholinguistics which investigates the semantic and pragmatic factors involved in selecting active versus passive voice in English (Bates & Devescovi 1989; Chafe 1976; Kerr, Butler, Maykuth & Delis 1982; Tannenbaum & Williams 1968; Tomlin 1983, 1991; Turner & Rommetveit 1968). In general, the referent of a sentence which is more thematic[3] is assigned to syntactic subject. When the thematic referent is the agent, one observes an active clause; when the thematic referent is the patient, one observes a passive (Tomlin 1983, 1991). In this example, it is not the details of linguistic form that are of central interest, though one clearly must be able to state what the pertinent structural details of active or passives are. Rather, it is the interaction between linguistic form (subject assignment) and pragmatic conditions (thematic importance) that the descriptive enterprise accounts for.

Functional explanation considers a different kind of issue. Given a particular instance of functional interaction, like the interaction of the-

---

3 This idea of "thematic" is oversimplified here. There is, in fact, a great deal of research directed at what such a notion as "thematic" might represent (Tomlin 1991).

matic information and voice mentioned earlier, functional explanation provides the reason why the observed interaction could occur. Explanatory reasons might include appeals to historical change, communicative constraints, or cognitive constraints. So, thematic information may be assigned to syntactic subject in English because of a more general cognitive constraint that information provided first provides a cognitive frame for the hearer against which later information is integrated (Gernsbacher 1990). Such an explanation entails that this particular form-function interaction is not at all arbitrary but explainable in terms of more general cognitive considerations.

ESSENTIAL AND TYPICAL CHARACTERISTICS OF FUNCTIONAL GRAMMARS

A number of fundamental tenets distinguish functional approaches to language from their structuralist alternatives.

Linguistic form subserves communicative function.   This is *the* central tenet of functional linguistics. The basic idea is that language – its component systems and their systemic details – develops within human individuals and within human culture to ensure maximally successful communication. The goal of language learning is not to achieve competence only in the narrow sense of well-formed syntactic structures and propositional meanings but to achieve the facility to employ grammatical knowledge in pragmatically and socially successful ways, thereby achieving *communicative competence* (Hymes 1971).

Achievement of communicative competence requires success in a number of social and cognitive dimensions. Socially, for example, it involves a given speaker's knowing when and how to speak with individuals of differing social standing. But a great deal of functional research focuses on how differences between speaker and hearer – differences in what information is shared or emphasized or important at a given moment in time – are managed grammatically. Somehow the speaker can decide to put a given proposition into a dependent rather than an independent clause; somehow the speaker can decide to refer to a given entity using a pronominal NP (noun phrase) instead of a nominal one. To the functionalist, these decisions do not seem at all arbitrary, nor do they seem to fall outside the grammar the way that many social phenomena, like politeness, do. The ability to make such decisions, rapidly and consistently, forms part of linguistic competence just as certainly as does the ability to form complex relative clauses.

Competence and performance.   Within the classical generative tradition, the development of a theory of syntax is pursued from the point of view of an idealized model in which the speaker and hearer have the same fundamental knowledge of the world and are not impaired by limitations in memory or lexical knowledge and so on. This idealization makes good sense, as far as it goes, by restricting one's attention to the underlying competence any speaker possesses and not confusing that basic ability with the specific, flawed output characteristic of actual human performance.

The fundamental functionalist assumption that language is communication and that linguistic form serves communicative functions departs from that original assumption. It recognizes that human communication arises directly from the *mismatch* of knowledge and experience between speaker and hearer. Further, the human information processing system is one which exhibits limitations in memory and attention so that it is natural to expect linguistic systems to develop congruently with those cognitive capacities. Thus, the underlying competence acquired by the child for L1, and sought by the learner of L2, is at least partially constrained by the types of cognitive processing possible.

Two examples can help make this clearer. First, let us consider complementation again. The original classical assumption asks one to recognize that there is no logical limit to the number of finite clauses that can be embedded under verbs like *think* or *say*. The sentence in (4) is unusual, even peculiar, but it remains grammatical.

(4) Mary said that Tom thinks that Susan claimed that Barry believes that his sister hopes that everyone understands that no one really believes that anything is being said here.

It seems not merely reasonable but exactly correct to claim that the grammar of English includes a rule which permits the recursive generation of such sentences without regard for length. Cognitive constraints on memory may play some role in restricting the length of such sentences ordinarily to no more than three embeddings, but such constraints in this case seem not to be part of the grammar but constraints on the application of the grammar. This is the wisdom of the competence-performance distinction as originally articulated.

For the second example, let us consider voice. The structural details distinguishing active from passive voice in English are essentially clear: There is an alignment of active object and passive subject, of active subject and passive prepositional phrase with *by*, and of the two verb forms. But the conditions of use and how to account for them remain more problematic. The general wisdom has been that the difference between active and passive is largely a difference in *theme* or emphasis, the passive occurring when it is the patient which is more important than the agent. Psycholinguistic research (Bates & Devescovi 1989; Flores d'Arcais 1987; Goodenough 1983; Kerr et al 1982; Prentice 1967; Tannenbaum & Williams 1968; Tomlin 1991; Turner & Rommetveit 1968;

Turner & Rommetveit 1967) has investigated how perceptual factors and discourse factors conspire in the production and comprehension of active and passive clauses. Tomlin (1991) presents a cognitive model of sentence production in which subject assignment in English is tied directly to the locus of one's focal attention at the moment an utterance is formulated.[4] When showing subjects animations of one fish eating a second fish, directing the attention of the subject to the agent fish results always in an active. Directing attention to the patient fish results always in a passive clause. Simply put, there seems to be a rule in the grammar of English which assigns a focally attended referent to syntactic subject at the moment of formulating an utterance. Such a rule captures a pattern of linguistic competence no less invariable than one captures with, say, rules describing English relative clause formation.

If it is correct in this case to claim that there is a rule which links voice and syntactic subject to "thematic" information – that is, a focally attended reference – then we have an example of how the competence underlying the child's knowledge of English is tied to cognitive processes of information management. Cognitive constraints in this instance determine the linguistic forms selected during utterance formulation no less than grammatical gender determines the selection of pronominal form. In this second example, psychological considerations play a direct role in defining the grammar. It is precisely these sorts of considerations, differences between speaker and hearer and the apparent, rule-governed management of these differences, that underlie the functional assumption that linguistic form serves communicative function.[5]

Acquisition arises from use.   This second central tenet of functional linguistics deals with the problem of language acquisition in children. Children acquire language by interacting with adult speakers, who provide the critical social context for interaction and linguistic data congruent with those social interactions. There is a strong and a weak version of the nature and extent of grammar arising from discourse. The strong view is that all aspects of the grammar develop anew for each individual from the communicative environment. The child brings nothing specifically linguistic to the language learning enterprise but instead comes to it with a powerful set of general learning mechanisms, which are employed

4 In this model, the traditional notion of "theme" or "topic" is replaced by the cognitive notion of "focal attention," which is more amenable to empirical manipulation.
5 F. Newmeyer (personal communication) observes that the phenomena described in this example could as well be construed as exemplifying language and grammar linked simply to information processing rather than to communication. Communication may represent the adaptation of information processing constraints to communicative interaction. This seems to me to be an intriguing alternative to the ordinary assumption of communication. Note, however, that this assumption is also a functionalist one, in that linguistic form is still linked to larger, language external considerations.

to bootstrap a grammar from the rich data of human discourse interactions. The weak view is that there may be some aspects of language knowledge which are available from the outset, but that the language-specific manifestations of such knowledge must arise from a principled interaction of the learner with the discourse environment.

The same premise underlies communicative models of second language acquisition and teaching. Models of input and interaction argue that SLA is facilitated when L2 input is provided in an environment rich in subject matter information and social interaction. Learner and teacher cooperate to restrict the interpretation of L2 input to be congruent with the meaning intended by the teacher. Use and interaction thus form a central research core in SLA research, a research core completely aligned with functional approaches to language.

Discourse basis for form selection.   Functional efforts direct their greatest attention to the role of syntax in discourse. Both in the theoretical and applied literature, numerous analyses are devoted to puzzling out how contextual features of a text correlate with specific grammatical forms. At a descriptive level, the research focuses on identifying discourse functions and arguing that certain syntactic forms correlate with those functions. Among the functions that have been examined are: *old* versus *new* information (also called *given, known, shared*), *theme* versus *rheme* (also called *topic-comment*), *foreground* versus *background* information, *contrastive* information, *newsworthiness, focus, topic continuity, identifiability* and *referentiality*, and *evidentiality*, to name several. These functional parameters have been linked to a number of grammatical construction types: pronominalization, voice, constituent order, intonation, subordination, tense-aspect, and modality, again to name a few.[6]

At an explanatory level, functional research argues that the interaction of form and function at the descriptive level is neither arbitrary nor accidental. Instead, such research often proposes that specific form-function interactions occur precisely to make discourses either easier to comprehend or to produce. For example, the hypothesis that the English active-passive alternation is tied to the assignment of a focally attended referent to syntactic subject might be explained as an English-specific instance of a more general cognitive strategy that places important elements first in linear arrays. Such a putative explanation links principles external to language to facilitating discourse comprehension or production.[7]

6 It is beyond the scope of this chapter to provide detailed bibliographic sources for each of these areas.
7 I should note that no substantive empirical or theoretical work has been done which argues convincingly for such an explanation. It is offered here merely as an example of how a discourse-based functional explanation might be formulated.

Limitations of functional grammars

A number of problems limit the development and usefulness of functional linguistics. None of the problems, however, challenge the logic of functional analysis. The major problems facing functional research are problems either in formulating claims and hypotheses or in carrying out functional analysis. In principle, each can be managed, even if none can be managed easily.

THE DEFINITION AND IDENTIFICATION OF LINGUISTIC FUNCTIONS

Since considerable energy is devoted to examining the interaction of grammatical form with pragmatic functions in discourse, it is essential that so-called pragmatic functions receive clear and explicit definition and that suitable methods be employed to identify instances of such functions in linguistic data. Yet most linguistic functions, particularly pragmatic functions like *old* information or *topic* or *focus,* lack either theoretically satisfying definitions or reliable means of identification.

For example, most functionalists would probably agree that "thematic information" comes earlier in the sentence than does nonthematic information. Despite widespread agreement on the general idea, there is no theoretical treatment of *theme* with sufficient specificity to command systematic use among functional efforts. Even worse, there is no reliable *and* demonstrably valid operational means of identifying themes in discourse data. Other basic pragmatic notions reveal similar problems.

The efforts by Givón and others (1983a) to develop a set of simply applied text-counting measures for examining topic continuity represent one major and systematic effort to deal with these issues. The experimental approaches of Bates & MacWhinney also minimize this problem. Experimental efforts in discourse production studies (Tomlin, 1985, 1987a, 1991) also attempt to escape these dilemmas by manipulating text-independent psychological correlates to pragmatic functional notions.

ESCHEWING THEORY AND THE REJECTION OF FORMALISM

Many functional linguists deliberately reject the prospect of developing a formal theory of functional interactions. The reasons for this are admirable in some ways. Functional efforts generally require careful attention to empirical data, in particular to the discourse productions of real speakers. Functionalists often see theory development as premature unless considerable energy has been invested in describing linguistic facts. The data are seen to speak for themselves, with theory arising inductively from empirical data.

Yet the concern for empirical rigor becomes a limiting preoccupation with data when theory is ignored. It is very difficult to consider the merits of specific proposals and hypotheses when their place in an over-all system is unclear. There are two good examples of areas in which greater attention to the formulation of theory might well help functional efforts to advance: (1) We need a theory that distinguishes the kinds of functional interactions that one might see in linguistic data – the prob-lem of *coding* (Tomlin 1987b). One might well see all sorts of correla-tions and associations in empirical data, but it is not clear which sorts of relationships should be taken as significant ones. (2) We need a theory that constrains the kinds of functions permitted, not to limit inquiry but to guide it so that new functions essential to the understanding of lan-guage are added to a theory when needed instead of multiplying func-tions for the convenience of the analyst. For example, how many kinds of "old" information does a theory need: one (*old-new*), two (*old-new, know-unknown*), three (*active, semiactive, inactive*), or more (*evoked situationally, evoked textually, noncontaining inferrable, containing in-ferable, unanchored brand-new, anchored brand-new, unused*)? Con-straints on functional theory do not limit inquiry; they discipline it.

THE CONFLATION OF STRUCTURE AND FUNCTION

Surprisingly, functionalism routinely conflates syntactic matters with their semantic or pragmatic correlates, often incorporating semantic or pragmatic information into fundamental definitions. This trend began most noticeably with the work of Keenan (1976) on the notion of sub-ject. Keenan proposed a universal definition of subject in which a subject was defined as that NP class in which inhered a preponderance of a set of identifying features. These features included syntactic features (subject-verb agreement), semantic features (agent), and pragmatic features (old information). Subject is the class of NPs in which most of these variables coalesce. A similar approach has been used to examine foreground-background information (Hopper 1979; Hopper & Thompson 1980) and to examine the notion of topic. In each of these cases a new, hybrid category is created, neither a syntactic category nor a semantic or prag-matic function, but something intermediate.

This strategy creates two problems for functional analysis. First, by blurring the boundaries between linguistic form and linguistic function, it makes it particularly difficult to be clear about what constitutes func-tional interaction. Second, by combining both formal and functional facts in defining linguistic categories, it in effect presupposes functional interactions which may not hold up when different languages or differ-ent groups of speakers are considered.

CONSTRAINING THE TYPES OF FUNCTIONS

The term "function" is used rather freely to describe a number of rela-tively distinct kinds of information or behavior. Sometimes a function is a semantic or pragmatic category, a component part of a proposition. For example, the case role of agent or experiencer or the semantic aspect of perfective represent such functions. At the other extreme, rhetorical actions or speech acts are considered functions. So, for example, many language textbooks count "requesting" or "disagreeing" as linguistic functions. Similarly, editorial motivations or planning are sometimes counted as functions. Thus, one of the functions associated with English passive is "avoiding assigning responsibility" to an agent. It is necessary to constrain the types of function in functional theory in order to understand how low-level functions, like agent or topic, relate to "higher-level" functions, like speech acts or general planning strategies.

PREMATURE EXPLANATIONS

This problem involves the mixing of functional description with functional explanation. One kind of difficulty occurs when very general explanatory principles are invoked to explain language-particular or individual-particular behavior. For example, typological generalizations, which represent empirical observations about sets of languages, have been used to provide explanations of some second language acquisition behavior (Fuller & Gundel 1987; Rutherford 1983). To the extent that such efforts really import typological generalizations to SLA directly, their logic is flawed, because the individual language learner has no access to such generalizations. To the extent that such efforts represent a shorthand means of expressing more individual-specific cognitive or linguistic principles, then appropriate clarification is needed to articulate what those individual-specific general linguistic principles must be.

The logic and practice of functional analysis

The logic and practice of functional analysis can be articulated clearly, but its implementation is often difficult to carry out. There are five components: (1) problem formulation, (2) articulation of a theoretical framework, (3) operational or empirical definition, (4) data collection, and (5) data analysis/hypothesis testing. In general, functional analysis seeks to identify interactions between linguistic form and linguistic functions, separating true interactions from spurious correlations.

PROBLEM FORMULATION

There are two ways of formulating a functional problem. One can begin with a syntactic alternation, for example, active and passive clause structures or nominal versus pronominal NPs, and try to determine what semantic or pragmatic parameters condition or determine the selection among the alternatives. Alternatively, one can begin with a particular semantic or pragmatic function, for example, clause level theme or contrastive information, and examine which linguistic forms, if any, are employed to signal the given function in linguistic behavior.

We will examine later on the problem of foregrounding in English discourse. It has been claimed that the selection of sentence type – independent versus dependent clauses – is determined by whether a given sentence is foregrounded or not. It has been claimed that the selection of verbal aspect – imperfective (realized by progressive in English) and perfective – is also determined by foregrounded status.

THEORETICAL FRAMEWORK

Since there is no comprehensive theory of functional interaction, it is generally important to present the theoretical framework in which the analysis is conducted. This requires at least three distinct efforts. First, one must carefully and explicitly define the semantic or pragmatic function of interest. Such definitions must be made without reference to grammatical form, either explicitly or implicitly, in order to avoid circularity in arguing for form-function interaction. Along with clear theoretical definition comes the problem of providing some way of identifying instances of the pertinent function in linguistic data.

Second, one must be clear about the syntactic form(s) one is concerned with. Linguistic forms, like functions, must be defined explicitly and without reliance on semantic or pragmatic information, again to avoid circularity. Some functional analysis has not been careful in separating syntactic from semantic or pragmatic function – for example, in some relatively early work on the notion of *subject* in which semantic and pragmatic information is incorporated into the basic definition of the category (Keenan 1976). Syntactic forms should be *defined* without reference to semantic or pragmatic functions, and they should be *identified* without reference to them as well.

Third, one must be explicit regarding the kind of functional interaction one is describing. There are four possibilities. It is possible that there is *no relationship* between the form and function. This is the null hypothesis against which all other kinds of interaction must compete.

It is possible that the linguistic form does interact with semantic or pragmatic function, either to *syntactically code* the function or *pragmatically signal* it. A syntactic form syntactically codes a given function if, and only if, the presence of the function in the message requires the speaker automatically and invariably to use the specific syntactic form, and the hearer, upon hearing the specific linguistic form, automatically and invariably recovers the associated function. A syntactic form pragmatically signals a function if the presence of the form permits the hearer to infer a particular function in a given context, but there is no automatic production requirement on the speaker.

Finally, it is possible that the syntactic form correlates highly with

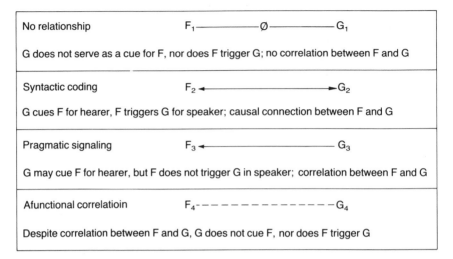

Figure 1   Four types of functional interaction.

some function but still does not interact with it systematically. Such an *afunctional correlation* occurs when an additional semantic or pragmatic function intervenes between the examined form and function, unnoticed or not analyzed by the linguist.

The four possibilities are illustrated in Figure 1.

The principal difficulties facing functional analysis center on determining whether linguistic data reveal a significant correlation between form and function and, if there is one, whether the correlation is one exploited by speaker and hearer during discourse interactions.

OPERATIONAL OR EMPIRICAL DEFINITIONS

Once the theoretical framework has been set, one must specify how instances of form and instances of function are to be identified in linguistic data. It is inadequate, as has been the case with most functional analyses, to rely on introspective application of theoretical definitions. For example, the notion of clause level *theme* has received reasonable theoretical definition under a number of frameworks. Virtually all of these frameworks treat theme as the "starting point" of an utterance (Daneš 1974a) or as "that which is being talked about" (Halliday 1967, 1976, 1985). Yet none of these treatments indicates any way to identify instances of theme in linguistic data. Without some operational means of doing this, one relies on introspection, and there is no way to know that introspection does not covertly employ linguistic form in reaching its conclusions, rendering the functional analysis hopelessly circular.

For example, let us suppose two things. First, let us suppose that we employ the definition of theme articulated by Halliday ("that which is being talked about") and that we use our best judgment for each clause in some pertinent data to determine what the clause level theme is, given the theoretical definition. Second, let us suppose that the hypothesis we wish to test is that theme is coded by syntactic subject in English and, importantly, that this hypothesis in fact is true. We proceed through the text data clause by clause, underlining the theme in each one. At the end we consider whether our hypothesis has been fairly tested and conclude that we have done well since every subject is also the clause level theme. But how does one know that it is not the implicit knowledge of English, in this case that subject codes theme, that has covertly helped us identify the themes in each clause? As long as we depend on introspection, we cannot rule out such a possibility. Thus, one must find some operational means, not dependent on linguistic structure, to identify instances of the targeted pragmatic or semantic functions in linguistic data.

DATA COLLECTION

Most functional analysis deals with the use and distribution of grammatical forms in discourse and consequently requires collecting good samples of discourse data in which can be found tokens of the grammatical forms under examination. Good discourse samples meet a number of criteria. Discourse data should be authentic performance data and not data created by the analyst. The data should represent natural speech. The data, at least in the long run, should cover a range of genres (narrative, expository, descriptive, etc.) and types (planned, unplanned, etc.). Importantly, data should be drawn from multiple speakers performing the same discourse task.

There are three basic methods one can employ to gather discourse data: convenience samples, controlled elicitations, and experimental elicitations. Convenience samples are gathered by selecting or collecting, with more or less care, oral or written discourse in uncontrolled settings. For example, one might select a few pages from a popular novel or technical writing, or one might set up an audiorecorder during a dinner conversation. The advantages of convenience samples are their relative ease of collection and their authenticity. The disadvantages include problems in comparing data from multiple subjects or across languages and in puzzling out the details of the contextual setting the data were produced in. Still, such data are immensely useful for initial exploratory study.

Controlled elicitations are presently the most common means of collecting discourse data. In a controlled elicitation, the linguist sets a given task before subjects and records their performances. Great care is taken in the design of the tasks to ensure that contextual variables are as well controlled as can be managed. The best-known controlled elicitation format is probably Chafe's "pear film" (Chafe 1980b). Chafe produced a short film depicting in narrative style the adventures of several children as they interacted with each other and with a man picking pears. This film was shown to speakers of many languages, and protocols were collected of their attempts to relate the events witnessed in the film. Other sorts of controlled elicitations include Linde and Labov's apartment description protocol (Linde & Labov 1975).

Experimental elicitations of discourse are quite similar to controlled except for one principal attribute. In experimental elicitations, the linguist systematically varies some component of the elicitation setting or stimulus and then examines how that manipulation affects the language produced. For example, in investigating when individuals use nominal versus pronominal NPs in narrative production, Tomlin (1987a; Tomlin & Pu 1991) elicits spontaneous narratives by showing subjects a sequence of still pictures depicting one animal meeting, chasing, and eating another. The same set of pictures is presented in three different ways in order to manipulate how a given character is represented in memory during the narrative task. The expectation is that the choice of noun versus pronoun is determined by whether a given referent is memorially activated or not (Chafe 1987), so by manipulating memorial activation with the same set of pictures, one hopes to elicit nominal NPs under one condition and pronominal NPs under another. Experimental manipulations thus differ from controlled elicitations (which are not experiments) in their planned manipulation of the factors the experimenter believes determines selection between alternative grammatical forms.

DATA ANALYSIS AND HYPOTHESIS TESTING

Collected data must be coded and analyzed. Adequate coding requires the use of operational definitions or procedures to identify instances of both linguistic form and linguistic function, and each must be identified independently of the other. When this is done, the result is the creation of contingency tables – cross-tabulations of instances of success and failure of one's expectations about form-function interaction. For instance, in examining the hypothesis that foreground information is coded by independent clauses and background information by dependent clauses, properly coded data will distribute into contingency tables like the one in Figure 2.

The data in the upper-left and lower-right cells represent the data congruent with the hypotheses. The data in the remaining cells represent data which are exceptions to the hypotheses. These exceptions, which one can call the *residue,* and their contribution to the overall pattern of the data ultimately make or break the functional analysis. The analytical problem is to determine whether the pattern revealed in the data is an accidental one or not. So one needs to estimate what the probability is

	Ind	Dep
Foreground	71	4
Background	13	45

Clause type

Figure 2   Contingency table for functional analysis (fictional data).

that the pattern of results found in the contingency table might be due to simple chance.[8] Data analysis seeks to do just this.

The most basic kind of data analysis, and one this author finds acceptable only for initial exploration of ideas, is analysis and arguments of congruence. In such arguments, the linguist proposes a certain form-function interaction and proceeds to offer example after example of data congruent with that hypothesis. When a substantial number of examples is presented, the analysis is concluded with the assertion that the hypothesis has been validated. Such analysis effectively ignores the residue and embraces the fallacy of "confirming the consequent," and certainly should be avoided.

A second type of analysis is analysis of simple statistical frequency. In this approach, contingency tables are produced similar to the one in Figure 2. The analyst then compares the frequency of occurrence in the upper-left cell with the frequency of occurrence in the lower-right cell. If both numbers appear to be large ones, generally revealed by a report of the proportion of congruent cases in each cell, it is asserted that form and function do interact. For example, one might report that contrasting information occurs preverbally in 85 percent of one's observed data and that noncontrastive information occurs postverbally in 90 percent of one's observed data. Does this mean that contrastive-noncontrastive

8   One helpful way to think about this is to think about flipping a coin. If the coin is fair, one expects half of the flips to be heads and the other half tails. Thus, if one flips the coin 1,000 times, one expects to see 500 heads and 500 tails. Suppose one ends up with 510 heads and 490 tails. What is the chance that what one observed (510-490) departs from what one expected (500-500)? Intuitively, and mathematically, the chances are pretty small that one would observe 510-490 if the coin were *not* fair.

In the same vein, suppose one observed 1,000 heads and 0 tails. Does this mean the coin is not fair? It probably does because the chances of getting 1,000 heads and 0 tails in 1,000 flips of the coin are exceedingly small, though not 0. Note that in both cases (510-490 and 1,000-0) one is estimating the odds that what one has observed departs from the expectations one has of what ought to occur.

information is coded by pre- and postverbal order? It might be true, but it also might well not be true. For example, 85 percent of 6 observations is just 5 positive cases and 1 exception; what is the probability of chance occurrence of 5 versus 1 in such a small body of data? On the other hand, suppose one had 1,000 observations, yielding 850 congruent cases. Should one then ignore the 150 exceptions? Simple reports of statistical frequency ignore the residue, too.

A third type of analysis takes the residue into account, but it is seldom performed. This third type is statistical inference. It takes the contingency table in Figure 2 and determines the probability that the overall pattern is due to chance. It takes into account the contribution of both the congruent and exceptional cases to the hypothesis one is testing. While it is beyond the scope of this paper to discuss how statistical inference is conducted, Woods, Fletcher, and Hughes (1986) provide a good introduction for linguists, as do Hatch and Farhady (1982) for applied linguists.

Finally, it is important to understand what to make of the residue. The residue derives from three possible sources. First, the residue may be due to errors in coding of data by the linguist. One might have incorrectly marked a clause as subordinate when it was independent, for example. Such errors are to be expected, but should constitute only a very few cases.

Second, it may be due to a performance error on the part of the individual generating the data. For example, suppose a speaker is asked to describe events seen in a film but instead at some point comments on the quality of the film's animation. The resulting utterance would not conform to the task the data-collection technique was aiming at and might, because of this, show up as an exception in the data table (Tomlin 1985).

Third, the residue may well be due to a problem in the theory or model or hypothesis one is investigating. In fact, a good way to argue within functional analysis is to show that one's hypothesis better accounts for certain data (that is, reduces the residue) than its best competitor.[9] One way to visualize this is to compare two "theories," as presented in Figure 3. Notice that both theory A and theory B, which differ only in the nature of the "function" each theory proposes, account well for the data since each has only a small residue. But theory B seems to do a somewhat better job than does theory A; that is, the residue is smaller. Thus, even though theory A provides a good account of the interaction between grammatical form and linguistic function, theory B provides a more complete account (reduces the residue) and thus should be preferred.

9 It is a wise strategy to seek out these "competing" hypotheses, both by reviewing carefully the critical literature and by exploring the "logic" of one's problem.

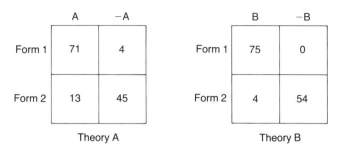

Figure 3 *Comparing two competing treatments of a functional interaction.*

Foregrounding and backgrounding in discourse

Perhaps the best way of revealing the inherent strengths and limitations of functional linguistics for pedagogical grammars is to examine one problem in more detail. We will examine the problem of foregrounding and backgrounding in English and its relation to the selection of independent and dependent clauses and to tense-aspect selection.

The basic idea in foregrounding is that the clauses which make up a text can be divided into two classes. There are clauses which convey the most central or important ideas in text, those propositions which should be remembered. And there are clauses which, in one way or another, elaborate on the important ideas, adding specificity or contextual information to help in the interpretation of the central ideas. The clauses which convey the most central or important information are called *foregrounded* clauses, and their propositional content is *foreground* information. The clauses which elaborate the central propositions are called *backgrounded* clauses, and their propositional content is *background* information. So, for example, the boldfaced clause in the text fragment below conveys **foreground** information while the italicized clauses convey *background*.

(5) A text fragment: written edited 010:32

The smaller fish is now in an air bubble
spinning
and turning
and making its way upward

This fragment was produced by an individual recalling action she witnessed in a brief animated film (Tomlin 1985). Clause 1 conveys foreground information because it relates the critical proposition for the discourse at this point: the location of the "smaller fish." The state of the air bubble and its motion are less central to that description, so that the other clauses seem merely to elaborate or develop a part of the proposition contained in clause 1.

The central questions for a functional theory involve formalizing this informal characterization of foreground and background information, finding ways to identify foreground versus background propositions in data, and examining how syntactic structures are used (if at all) to signal that some information is more or less important.

The earliest work on foregrounding (Longacre 1968, 1976; Grimes 1975) distinguished *backbone* information from *background* information and employed this distinction to account for syntactic alternations in a number of languages. Longacre (1976), for example, examined the use of the *waw*-predicate construction in biblical Hebrew. On the surface, there seems to be no semantic difference between clauses with the *waw*-predicate construction and those without. However, in looking at their distribution in text data, in particular the flood narrative in the Old Testament, Longacre observed that the subset of clauses with the *waw*-predicate construction formed a coherent abstract of the overall narrative while the remaining clauses did not. Thus, it appeared that the *waw*-predicate construction was used to signal the importance of the clauses forming the backbone of the narrative.

Later work by Hopper (1979) developed the original ideas of Longacre and Grimes. For Hopper, information could be characterized either as *foreground* or *background*. Foreground information in narrative discourse includes "the parts of the narrative belonging to the skeletal structure of the discourse" (1979: 213). Background information is "the language of supportive material which does not itself relate the main events" (1979: 213). Hopper examines the distribution of foreground and background information in a number of languages. He claims that foreground clauses correlate with both independent clauses and perfective aspect.

Hopper linked foreground information with the event line of narrative discourse. The clauses which relate events falling on the main event line are foreground clauses, while those which do not fall on the main event line are the background ones. As an operational treatment of foregrounding, the appeal to event line makes good sense. The purpose of narration is to relate a sequence of events, so it is not surprising that the events themselves represent the most important information to be conveyed in narrative. There may well be clauses not relating events which are thematically important, and there may be clauses relating events which are not particularly important thematically, but these sets will be small in narrative discourse, and one seems not to lose too much, practically speaking, by ignoring them.

However, even if this residue could be ignored, narrative is not the only kind of discourse one's treatment of foregrounding ultimately must deal with. Expository discourse in particular requires a treatment of foregrounding which is not dependent on the notion of event line for its theoretical definition. Tomlin (1984, 1985, 1986) offers a treatment of foregrounding which alleviates the dependence on event line for both theoretical and empirical purposes. This approach was used to examine the two hypotheses Hopper proposes for the syntactic management of foreground and background information:

Hypothesis 1: Foreground propositions are signaled by independent clauses.
Background propositions are signaled by dependent clauses.

Hypothesis 2: Foreground propositions are signaled by perfective aspect.
Background propositions are signaled by imperfective aspect.

In this treatment, foregrounding is viewed as a thematic matter. The centrality of any given proposition in discourse arises from the intersection of the theme of the discourse at that point – the subject-matter content being developed – and the rhetorical goal of the discourse, whether that goal is to narrate, or describe, or evaluate, and so on.

Recalling the logic of functional analysis, there are four matters this analysis must attend to:

- Definition of foreground and background which does not use structural information
- Means of identifying and coding foreground/background in collected data
- A source of data permitting comparison among a number of speakers
- Data analysis that permits inference of one of the specific functional interactions described in Figure 1.

Foreground information is divided into two subcategories: pivotal and foreground information. Following the lead of Jones and Jones (1979), pivotal information was defined as the most general proposition describing a significant event. Foreground information was defined as those propositions which develop or describe any other event. Background information elaborates either pivotal or foreground information.

These definitions are tied in with the means developed to identify the information types which, in turn, is connected to the data collection technique. Four groups of subjects were shown an animated film of 108 seconds' duration depicting the rather frantic interaction of a cartoon goldfish, a crab, and a large pike. There is a great deal of frenetic action in this little film as the little goldfish tries to avoid capture and consumption by the other two.

The subjects in each group were asked to describe the events they witnessed in the film in slightly different ways. One group of subjects was asked to produce on-line oral protocols in which the speaker produced an oral description of the unfolding action concurrently with the film. These protocols resemble the play-by-play reporting of sports announcers. A second group of subjects watched the film and produced an oral description of what they remembered immediately after seeing it. These protocols are called oral immediate recall protocols. A third group also produced immediate recall protocols, but instead of speaking, they wrote what they had seen. These were the written immediate recall protocols. Finally, the fourth group was permitted to see the film four times, and even to take notes, for their task was to produce a written version of the film with as much editing as they chose over a two-day period. These were the written edited protocols. By having different sorts of speaker performances, one could examine whether there might be a difference in the use of independent and dependent clauses or tense-aspect in different task or genre settings.

The text fragment in (6) illustrates the kind of data this elicitation procedure produces.

(6) Data from unplanned, unedited, written recall protocol by subject #11

The fish then tried to hide from the crab
by disguising itself as a snail,
moving along the ocean floor under a snail shell at a slow pace.
The shell was dislodged from the fish's back by a twig,
and the crab then realized that the "snail" was actually the fish he was
    pursuing.
The crab moved over next to the fish
and tipped his shell,
as a man would his hat,
startling the fish.
The fish hurriedly swam off,
after the snapping sequence was repeated.

Using films permitted a text- and structure-independent way of identifying pivotal, foreground, and background information. If one could identify the events in the film and determine their significance, one could then identify the thematic significance of the propositions speakers produced by aligning those propositions with the events they described.

Drawing on research in social psychology on event perception (Newtson 1973; Newtson & Engquist 1976; Newtson, Engquist & Bois 1977) and on the literature on film editing (Reisz 1976; Monaco 1981), operational definitions were developed to identify events and episodes within the animated film. An *event* was defined as the action occurring between two *breakpoints*. A breakpoint was operationally defined as the introduction or exit of a character or as a video cut, the splicing of quite distinct video frames next to one another. The breakpoints so identified permitted one to identify a total of 36 events in the film.

Only some of these events are significant ones, events that stand out as particularly important to the developing story. The best way to determine which events were the significant ones was to have an independent group of 15 subjects view the film and signal when they witnessed something they took to be important. An event was then defined as significant if at least 12 of the subjects identified that event as significant. This effort permitted one to identify 14 events as significant and 22 events as nonsignificant.

Armed with this nonlinguistic analysis of the film, one has a way of identifying pivotal, foreground, and background information without resorting to any structural information in the texts the subjects produced. One can determine which event a given clause describes with relative ease. If the clause describes a significant event and it is the most general proposition doing so for that event, the clause is counted as pivotal information. If the clause is the most general proposition describing any other event, the clause is counted as foreground information. All other propositions are counted as background information.

With these analytical procedures in place, one can determine the events described by each individual and which clauses convey pivotal, foreground, or background information. The data in (7) display the same text data as (6), but now coded for the event reported (significant events are boldfaced) and the status of the information in each clause (Pivotal, Foreground, Background).

(7) Events and information status for the data in (6)

Event	Info	Text
4	P	The fish then tried to hide from the crab
4	B	by disguising itself as a snail,
4	B	moving along the ocean floor under a snail shell at a slow pace.
10	P	The shell was dislodged from the fish's back by a twig,
12	F	and the crab then realized that the "snail" was actually the fish he was pursuing.
14	P	The crab moved over next to the fish
14	P	and tipped his shell,
14	B	as a man would his hat,
14	B	startling the fish.
15	F	The fish hurriedly swam off,
15	B	after the snapping sequence was repeated.

One must also identify the grammatical forms one wishes to correlate with foregrounding, in this case independent and dependent clauses and perfective versus imperfective aspect. The details of how clause type is managed are found in Tomlin (1984, 1985). To keep matters simple, we will simplify the aspectual matters by stating that imperfective aligns with progressive verbal forms and perfective with nonprogressive. Thus, the data analysis can now add information on both clause type and tense-aspect. Note that this analysis has no logical or empirical connection to the prior analysis of information structure.

(8) Events and information for the data in (7)

Event	Info	Clause	Asp	Text
4	P	Ind	Perf	The fish then tried to hide from the crab
4	B	Dep	Imp	by disguising itself as a snail,
4	B	Dep	Imp	moving along the ocean floor under a snail shell at a slow pace.
10	P	Ind	Perf	The shell was dislodged from the fish's back by a twig,
12	F	Ind	Perf	and the crab then realized that the "snail" was actually the fish he was pursuing.
14	P	Ind	Perf	The crab moved over next to the fish
14	P	Ind	Perf	and tipped his shell,
14	B	Dep	Perf	as a man would his hat,
14	B	Dep	Imp	startling the fish.
15	F	Ind	Perf	The fish hurriedly swam off,
15	B	Dep	Perf	after the snapping sequence was repeated.

Having completed the coding of the collected data, one can then build contingency tables. These are displayed for this data in Figure 4. Please keep in mind that these data are only part of the data produced by subject #11, so the tables are illustrative only. Such tables can be formed for both hypotheses for each of the subjects in each of the four elicitation types. The final stage of analysis involves determining which of the four types of interaction (Ø, syntactic coding, pragmatic signaling, or afunctional correlation) best describes the interaction seen across all of the data. We need to determine whether information type is linked significantly to clause type and to tense-aspect. If the interaction is in some way part of the grammar, one would expect it to hold up no matter which individual subject was considered in order to rule out stylistic variation as a reason for the patterns of data observed. Similarly, one would expect the interaction to hold up across the four elicitation types in order to show that the observed patterns were not due to the kind of discourse individuals produced.

Ultimately, one must perform some sort of statistical analysis of the data to examine whether there are real interactions between form and function or merely the appearance of interaction. The method employed in these studies is called log linear analysis.[10] Log linear analysis permits one to consider how well the data one has collected and coded fit various logical models of how in principle the variables the data represent could interact. For either the study of foregrounding and clause type or the

10 At first glance, a formal statistical analysis of such data may seem daunting. Two comments are in order. First, learning to perform such statistical analyses can be well managed by most individuals at the graduate level. Second, even if it were difficult, there is no real choice if an empirical approach is embraced.

	Ind	Dep
Pivotal	4	0
Foreground	2	0
Background	0	4

Clause type

	Perf	Imp
Pivotal	4	0
Foreground	2	0
Background	2	3

Tense-aspect

Figure 4   Contingency tables for illustrative data.

study of the foregrounding and tense-aspect, there are three main variables: linguistic function (pivotal-foreground-background), grammatical form (either independent-dependent clause *or* perfective-imperfective), and subject (person 1-person 2, etc.). Treating subject as a variable is the way one manages stylistic variation. If the interaction one sees between form and function changes depending on who is speaking, then the variable of subject will not prove independent of the form-function interaction. If the interaction one sees remains essentially constant, no matter who the speaker is, then the interaction would hold independently of the speaker and thus be a candidate for a general functional rule within the grammar.

Logically speaking, there are eight possible patterns of interaction or lack of interaction one could see among three variables. At one extreme, speaker or subject, linguistic function, and grammatical form might be totally independent of each other. This would mean that linguistic function did not at all correlate with or predict grammatical form; both form and function varied more or less freely among the subjects in the elicitation. We could symbolize this complete absence of interaction as in (9a).

At the other extreme, one could see the ideal pattern of interaction. Form and function would be linked, but that association would be independent of the various speakers. This can be symbolized as in (9b).

Six other patterns of interaction are logically possible. These are also represented in (9). The actual log linear procedure and its interpretation permit one to evaluate which of the competing models is best fit by the observed data.

(9) The possible models of interaction among linguistic function (F), grammatical form (G), and subject (S).

    a. S, G, F
    b. S, GF
    c. G, SF
    d. F, SG

    e. SG, SF
    f. GS, GF
    g. SF, GF
    h. SF, SG, GF

For Hopper's Hypothesis 1 (that foreground-background information is coded or signaled by clause type) log linear analysis reveals the best-fitting model to be GF, SF. Further, the data fit this model significantly better than chance alone would predict. What this model says is that there is an interaction between foregrounding and clause type as well as an interaction between foregrounding and subject. How should this be interpeted? The first part, that foregrounding and clause type are associated, means that foreground information (either pivotal or foreground) shows up as independent clauses, and background information shows up as dependent clauses more frequently than chance alone would predict.

The second part, that foregrounding is associated with subject, means that there were differences among the subjects in the *amount* of foreground or background information produced. For example, some subjects provided a lot more elaboration of the events they described than others – but they still used dependent clauses to do the job. Other subjects described more events than others, which means that those speakers would have more foreground propositions, but these speakers still put foreground material into independent clauses.

The overall pattern of data, then, reveals that foregrounding and clause type do interact as Hopper hypothesized. However, one cannot tell with log linear analysis whether the pattern one sees is an instance of syntactic coding or merely of pragmatic signaling. This weakness cannot at this time be overcome by statistical means. Still, the finding that clause type and foregrounding interact does have worthwhile implications for pedagogical purposes.

For Hypothesis 2 – that foreground-background information is coded or signaled by the use of perfective and imperfective aspect – log linear analysis reveals the best-fitting model to be S, GF. However, the association is an exceedingly weak one, certainly not better than one could predict might occur by chance. Thus, one cannot conclude that foreground information is coded or signaled by perfective aspect, or that background information is coded or signaled by imperfective aspect. That is, one must reject as unproven that tense-aspect has anything to do with foregrounding in English.

In summary, a careful empirical analysis of the interaction between foregrounding and grammatical form reveals that foregrounding is managed by the grammar through the selection of independent and dependent clauses, but it is not managed through the use of tense-aspect. The analysis described in this section meets well the logical and empirical requirements of functional analysis. It is analysis of this sort, or at least the best approximation of the ideal we can achieve, that must form the descriptive basis for pedagogical grammars. Such analysis can permit one to distinguish form-function interactions which appear significant but which are not from those which are genuine and merit inclusion in pedagogical practice.

Pedagogical grammar and functional analysis

In the previous sections we have done two things. First, we have described the general nature of North American functional linguistics, focusing on its general principles and problems and articulating the ideals of its logic and practice. Second, we have considered the problem of foregrounding as an instance of functional research that illustrates reasonably well the strengths and some of the limitations of functional analysis of discourse and syntax. In this final section, we examine the problem of foregrounding as an applied pedagogical problem.

Subordination and foregrounding in technical writing

THE LEARNER'S PROBLEM

Students of English as a second language (ESL), or more narrowly of English for science and technology (EST), often well know how to construct various kinds of subordinate clauses. But knowledge of how to construct such clauses in no way represents knowledge of when to construct them, either during drafting or during editing of technical writing.

CONVENTIONAL ADVICE

Examination of a large number of writing guides, textbooks, and technical manuals reveals a common recommendation for selection between independent and dependent clauses:

- Put important ideas into independent clauses; put less important or supporting information into dependent clauses.

For example, Glorfeld, Lauerman, and Stageberg (1977) observe:

Subordination is a matter of writing style about which there are no absolute rights or wrongs. The general principle is this: Put the important part of your message in an independent clause and the supporting or collateral parts in subordinate elements. (p. 107)

Shurter and Williamson (1964) observe:

An important element of clarity is proper emphasis. This means simply that important ideas should be emphasized, less important ones subordinated. . . .

The general rule is that the important point should be in the main, or independent clause. (pp. 19–20)

Similar statements can be found in a wide range of publications: Ulman 1952; Crouch & Zetler 1954; Mills & Walter 1954; Emberger & Hall 1955; Marder 1960; Shurter & Williamson 1964; Mitchell 1967; Reisman 1967; Mitchell 1968; Glorfeld, Lauerman & Stageberg 1977.

Despite this general, and correct, consensus, there are three critical problems with such recommendations. First, there is an epistemological problem – such recommendations are virtually without substantive empirical grounding, and one cannot determine their truth merely from their assertion. Second, there is a definitional problem – nowhere is it ever specified precisely what *important* means. Third, there is a practical problem – identifying instances of importance on a clause-by-clause basis. Despite the epistemological and definitional problems, of scant significance in most settings which call for pedagogical grammar support, conventional treatments do not help the learner figure out what the important clauses are, nor do they offer exercises or activities to develop an intuitive sense of "importance."

Identifying foreground and background propositions

Given the research described in the section titled "Foregrounding and backgrounding in discourse," we can take as a given for this pedagogical problem that foreground propositions are signaled by independent clauses and background propositions by dependent clauses. We have seen rejected the other hypothesis regarding foregrounding and tense-aspect. These hypotheses were tested through a reasonably rigorous empirical procedure, involving a great deal of energy to set up and carry out. Such methods, while critical for establishing the foundational functional analysis, are simply impractical for any pedagogical setting. So the question remains, How can we employ the insight from the theoretical work in this applied domain?

One direction to consider is developing practical procedures for heuristic purposes. Such procedures may not be adequate to "prove" that foreground information and independent clauses are related, but with appropriate foundational functional analysis this question is rendered moot. Instead, one can focus on utility in devising practical procedures for identifying foreground and background information. For narrative discourse, for instance, one might exploit the event-line method of Hopper and others. In narrative discourse, propositions dealing with events on the main event line are foreground information not because narrative events are inherently foreground information. Rather, they represent foreground information because the rhetorical goal of narration (relating a history of happenings) and the subject matter for narration (a discrete sequence of events) conspire to elevate the importance of propositions describing primary events above those doing other jobs. The event-line method is inadequate from a theoretical point of view, but it is perfectly suitable as a method for identifying foregrounding in narrative discourse for pedagogical reasons.

In other types of discourse, where the subject matter and the rhetorical goals are different, there is every reason to expect that the foreground and background information will be different. The differences arise not because of inherent differences in foreground and background proposition types in each genre; they arise out of differences in the rhetorical goals and subject matters dealt with. So, for example, consider the following paragraph from a technical article:

(10) Technical writing sample

    1 To the uranium search Exxon brings not only obviously solid financing but also an array of sophisticated tools,
    2 including some adapted from oil exploration.
    3 One such tool is the gamma ray log.
    4 Lowered into a drilled hole on the end of an electric cable,
    5 the device records the level of radioactivity in relation to depth,
    6 and indirectly indicates the amount of radioactive material that may be present.
    7 By drilling and logging a series of test holes,
    8 a geologist can determine the size and grade of uranium accumulation.

This expository paragraph tells the reader about a specific tool, the gamma ray log; that is, the rhetorical purpose of the paragraph is to describe something and the subject matter is the gamma ray log. Propositions which deal with the description of the gamma ray log will be the foreground information, while those which do not will convey background information. Those which seem clearly to be foreground include 3, 5, 6, and 8; 3 introduces the tool, 5 and 6 describe what it does, and 8 relates its value. Clauses 2 and 7 elaborate how the gamma ray log is manipulated and seem comparatively less central to the description of the tool than the others.

The relatively greater importance of clauses 3, 5, 6, and 8 was determined in this instance by introspection and intuition – precisely what we have done as teachers routinely, and precisely what motivates the conventional pedagogical suggestions. Still, it would be even more helpful if one could devise a specific method for identifying which clauses in expository text convey foregrounded propositions and which convey backgrounded propositions.

ABSTRACTING METHOD (JONES AND JONES 1979)

Jones and Jones (1979) propose a method based on abstracting for identifying foregrounded and backgrounded propositions in narrative. Those propositions, which form the "backbone" of a narrative, will, when taken together, form a reasonable summary of the overall narrative. Conversely, those propositions which constitute the background will not form a coherent summary when taken together.

One can extend this method to expository discourse quite easily. The set of foregrounded propositions will form a coherent abstract, while the set of background propositions will not.

(11) Since automatic monitoring is not presently required for brass and bronze plants, record keeping on a routine basis becomes extremely important to provide a method for the air pollution control officer to determine that operating and maintenance practices are consistent with reasonable air pollution control needs. Records should be kept on production processes, on control equipment, and on emissions. Each of these parameters is described separately, although obviously there are interrelationships.

Independent clauses	Dependent clauses
. . . record keeping on a routine basis becomes extremely important . . .	Since automatic monitoring is not presently required for brass and bronze plants, . . .
Records should be kept on production processes, on control equipment, and on emissions.	. . . to provide a method for the air pollution control officer to determine that operating and maintenance practices are consistent with reasonable air pollution control needs . . .
Each of these parameters is described separately . . .	. . . although obviously there are interrelationships.

The three independent clauses in this example do form a coherent abstract, one which conveys the central theme of the paragraph – record keeping. The four dependent clauses do not form a coherent abstract; they do not permit any sort of thematic integration and require additional information for a proper interpretation.

The example in (12) illustrates the method in another subject matter domain.

(12) This kind of practical focus is consistent with the teaching philosophy shared by the authors. As applied especially to the learning of relatively complex material, our philosophy boils down to one of *clarification* and *simplification*. Throughout the text, we attempt to translate otherwise esoteric statistical methods into a form that can be easily introduced by potential consumers of these methods in the social sciences. To this end, we offer numerous verbal and pictorial examples, analogies, and simplifications. By presenting the material in a comparatively simple, and often

intuitive, form, we hope to introduce multivariate techniques to students and researchers who might otherwise have consciously avoided them.

Independent clauses	*Dependent clauses*
This kind of practical focus is consistent with the teaching philosophy shared by the authors.	As applied especially to the learning of relatively complex material,
. . . our philosophy boils down to one of *clarification* and *simplification*.	. . . that can be easily introduced by potential consumers of these methods in the social sciences,
Throughout the text, we attempt to translate otherwise esoteric statistical methods into a form . . .	By presenting the material in a comparatively simple, and often intuitive, form . . .
To this end, we offer numerous verbal and pictorial examples, analogies, and simplifications.	. . . who might otherwise have consciously avoided them.
. . . we hope to introduce multivariate techniques to students and researchers . . .	

Again, the clauses in the left column form a coherent abstract of the paragraph. While they are not adequate alone to convey the full meaning the authors intend, they do convey the authors' teaching orientation. The clauses in the right-hand column in no way form any sort of coherent whole. They look precisely like elaborative material without linkage to the main ideas.

TEACHING APPLICATIONS

The abstracting technique can be employed in composition teaching in at least three ways. First, the teacher can help the student see the connection between foregrounding and clause type by presenting expository paragraphs utilizing the abstracting technique. The notion of the "importance" of a sentence can be tied to the overall development of the paragraph, and the contribution of individual sentences to that overall development and to other sentences can be examined and discussed.

Second, the teacher can present a paragraph in which the sentences have been rewritten as independent clauses. Students are asked to identify the important information, the information to be foregrounded, by forming a reasonable abstract from the given set. The paragraph can then be rewritten, subordinating the less central, supporting propositions to the foregrounded set. The examples in (13)–(15) illustrate a possible application.

(13) Unorganized sentences

The fact is an ugly one.
Computer viruses are something we have to live with.
The great majority of viruses are more annoying than deadly.

Protecting your floppy disks and hard drives is important.
You frequently exchange floppies with other Macintosh users.
SAM was one of the first commercial products to fight viruses.
Rival is one of the new contenders.
Both products do the job.
They take different paths.

(14) One reasonable abstract with resulting **foregrounded** and *backgrounded*
clauses

The fact is an ugly one.
Computer viruses are something we have to live with.
The great majority of viruses are more annoying than deadly.
Protecting your floppy disks and hard drives is important.
You frequently exchange floppies with other Macintosh users.
SAM was one of the first commercial products to fight viruses.
Rival is one of the new contenders.
Both products do the job.
They take different paths.

(15) Paragraph rewritten taking (14) into account

Though the fact is an ugly one,
computer viruses are something we have to live with.
While the great majority of viruses are more annoying than deadly,
protecting your floppy disks and hard drives is important,
if you frequently exchange floppies with other Macintosh users.
SAM was one of the first commercial products to fight viruses,
and Rival is one of the new contenders.
While both products do the job,
they take different paths.

This technique can help the student develop sensitivity to the problem of
foregrounding and can be used to connect the selection of sentence type
with foregrounding.

The third technique is simply to use the abstracting method with
student-produced paragraphs. The teacher can have the student edit his
own writing or another's efforts. The teacher can prepare overheads of
student paragraphs to consider. Or the teacher can replace the clauses in
a student paragraph with independent clauses and conduct the kind of
sort and rewrite activity described. Thus, the paragraph in (1) could be
presented as in (16), and subsequent sorting and rewriting might very
well generate the kind of final paragraph we saw in (2).

(16) Paragraph (1) transformed into independent clauses and sorted into a
reasonable abstract (bold)

I came to America on June 11, 1989.
I came to Eugen by plane by myself.
The travel company made a complicated schedule for me.
I stopped Osaka, Narita, Los Angeles, and San Francisco on the way to
come to Eugene.

That was the first time for me to take a plane by myself.
I could speak English very well.
That was really scary for me.
The travel company gave me a lot of notes.
The notes showed me which way I should walk forward the gate in the each airports.
I lost my way at the airport.
I asked people in English.

(2) Rewritten paragraph

I came to America on June 11, 1989, traveling to Eugene by plane alone. The travel company made a complicated schedule for me. I stopped in Osaka, Narita, Los Angeles, and San Francisco on the way to Eugene. Since it was the first time I took a plane by myself, it was really scary, even though I could speak English very well. Even though the travel company gave me a lot of notes which showed me the way I should walk in each airport, I lost my way and had to ask people for help in English.

Conclusion

Whenever a teacher tries to help a student select among grammatical alternatives, she must access knowledge about the conditions which call for the use of one form rather than another. In many cases the teacher can depend on her intuition and experience as a writer and teacher to do this, but two kinds of problems ultimately persist: (1) the teacher may not be able to be certain that her intuitions are correct and thus may want or need academic support for those beliefs; (2) some teachers, in particular nonnative speakers, may not have reliable intuitions about use, making more explicit descriptions necessary.

Functional approaches to syntax and discourse provide the descriptive basis for examining how grammatical forms are employed in discourse. In this paper we have examined both the promise and limitations of current functional research in providing the theoretical and empirical foundations on which pedagogical grammars and their applications must rest. And we have articulated the ideal logic and method of functional analysis.

The problem of foregrounding illustrates well both the promise of functional analysis and some of the limitations. Careful theoretical and empirical study does show that foregrounding is linked to clause type in English (but not to tense-aspect). Still, the precise nature of this linkage remains unclear, principally because the statistical tools needed to determine that relationship more precisely do not presently exist. Nonetheless, the resulting functional description remains the best one presently available, and it is certainly a better basis for pedagogical purposes than mere intuition.

While I have tried to show some of the present weaknesses in functional work, it is nevertheless the case that the underlying assumptions of functional grammar – the communicative imperative, the connection of acquisition with use, and the discourse basis for much grammatical selection – are entirely congruent with current insights in both SLA and second language teaching. Greater attention to the basic problems articulated here, coupled with greater specificity and detail in particular analyses, will result in functional work which warrants careful attention by those designing pedagogical grammars.

References

Allen, J. P. B., & H. G. Widdowson (1974). Teaching the communicative use of English. *IRAL* 12, 1–21.

Bates, E. & A. Devescovi (1989). Crosslinguistic studies of sentence production. In B. MacWhinney & E. Bates (eds.), *The Crosslinguistic Study of Sentence Processing* (pp. 225–56). Cambridge: Cambridge University Press.

Bates, E. & B. MacWhinney (1979). A functionalist approach to the acquisition of grammar. In E. Ochs & B. Schieffelin (eds.), *Developmental Pragmatics* (pp. 167–211). New York: Academic Press.

(1982). Functionalist approaches to grammar. In E. Wanner & L. Gleitman (eds.), *Language Acquisition: The State of the Art* (pp. 173–218). Cambridge: Cambridge University Press.

(1987). Competition, variation, and language learning. In B. MacWhinney (ed.), *Mechanisms of Language Acquisition* (pp. 157–93). Hillsdale, N.J.: Lawrence Erlbaum.

(1989). *Functionalism and the competition model.* (ms), UCSD & Carnegie-Mellon.

Bates, E., B. MacWhinney, C. Caselli, A. Devescovi, F. Natale, & V. Venza (1984). A cross-linguistic study of the development of sentence interpretation strategies. *Child Development* 55, 341–54.

Bates, E., B. MacWhinney, & S. Smith (1983). Pragmatics and syntax in psycholinguistic research. In S. Felix & H. Wode (eds.), *Language Development at the Crossroads* (pp. 11–30). Tübingen: Gunter Narr.

Bates, E., S. McNew, B. MacWhinney, A. Devescovi, & S. Smith (1982). Functional constraints on sentence processing: a cross-linguistic study. *Cognition* 11, 245–99.

Breen, M. P., & C. N. Candlin (1980). The essentials of a communicative curriculum in language teaching. *Applied Linguistics* 1(2), 89–112.

Brumfit, C. (1984). *Communicative Methodology in Language Teaching.* Cambridge: Cambridge University Press.

Canale, M., & M. Swain (1980). Theoretical bases of communicative approaches to second language teaching and testing. *Applied Linguistics* 1(1), 1–47.

Chafe, W. (1971). *Meaning and the Structure of Language.* Chicago: University of Chicago Press.

(1976). Givenness, contrastiveness, definiteness, subjects, topics, and points of view. In C. N. Li (ed.), *Subject and Topic* (pp. 25–56). New York: Academic Press.

(1980a). The deployment of consciousness in the production of narrative. In W. Chafe (ed.), *The Pear Stories: Cognitive, Cultural, and Linguistic Aspects of Narrative Production* (pp. 9–50). Norwood, N.J.: Ablex.

(1980b). *The Pear Stories: Cognitive, Cultural, and Linguistic Aspects of Narrative Production.* Norwood, N.J.: Ablex.

(1987). Cognitive constraints on information flow. In R. Tomlin (ed.), *Coherence and Grounding in Discourse* (pp. 21–52). Amsterdam: John Benjamins.

Cooreman, A., & K. Kilborn (1991). Functionalist linguistics: (we've got to start meeting like this). In T. Huebner & C. A. Ferguson (ed.), *Cross-Currents in Second Language Acquisition and Linguistic Theories* (pp. 195–224) Amsterdam: John Benjamins.

Corder, S. P. (1988). Pedagogic grammars. In W. Rutherford & M. S. Smith (eds.), *Grammar and Second Language Teaching* (pp. 123–45). New York: Newbury House.

Crouch, W. G. & R. L. Zetler (1954). *A Guide to Technical Writing* (2d ed.). New York: Ronald Press.

Daneš, F. (1974a). Functional sentence perspective and the organization of the text. In F. Daneš (ed.), *Papers on Functional Sentence Perspective* (pp. 106–28). The Hague: Mouton.

(ed.). (1974b). *Papers on Functional Sentence Perspective.* The Hague: Mouton.

Daneš, F. (1987). On Prague school functionalism in linguistics. In R. Dirven & V. Fried (eds.), *Functionalism in Linguistics* (pp. 3–37). Amsterdam: John Benjamins.

Davidse, K. (1987). M. A. K. Halliday's functional grammar and the Prague school. In R. Dirven & V. Fried (eds.), *Functionalism in Linguistics.* (pp. 39–79). Amsterdam: John Benjamins.

Dik, S. C. (1987). Some principles of functional grammar. In R. Dirven & V. Fried (eds.), *Functionalism in Linguistics* (pp. 101–34). Amsterdam: John Benjamins.

Dirven, R., & V. Fried (eds.). (1987). *Functionalism in Linguistics.* Amsterdam: John Benjamins.

Emberger, M. R. & M. R. Hall (1955). *Scientific Writing.* New York: Harcourt, Brace & Company.

Flores d'Arcais, G. B. (1987). Perceptual factors and word order in event descriptions. In G. Kempen (ed.), *Natural Language Generation: New Results in Artificial Intelligence, Psychology, and Linguistics.* Dordrecht: Martinus Nijhoff.

Fuller, J. & J. K. Gundel (1987). Topic prominence in interlanguage. *Language Learning* 37, 1–18.

Gernsbacher, M. A. (1990). *Language Comprehension as Structure Building.* Hillsdale, N.J.: Lawrence Erlbaum.

Givón, T. (ed.). (1979a). *Discourse and Syntax.* New York: Academic Press.

(1979b). From discourse to syntax: grammar as a processing strategy. In T. Givön (ed.), *Discourse and Syntax* (pp. 81–112). New York: Academic Press.

(1979c). Methodology: on the crypto-structuralist nature of transformational grammar. In *On Understanding Grammar.* New York: Academic Press.

(ed.). (1983a). *Topic Continuity in Discourse: Quantitative Cross-Language Studies.* Amsterdam: John Benjamins.

(1983b). Topic continuity in spoken English. In T. Givón (ed.), *Topic Continuity Discourse: Quantitative Cross-language Studies* (pp. 343–63). Amsterdam: John Benjamins.

(1984). Universals of discourse structure and second language acquisition. In W. Rutherford (ed.), *Language Universals and Second Language Acquisition* (pp. 109–36). Amsterdam: John Benjamins.

(1988). The pragmatics of word order: predictability, importance, and attention. In M. T. Hammond, E. A. Moravcsik & J. R. Wirth (eds.), *Studies in Syntactic Typology* (pp. 243–84). Amsterdam: John Benjamins.

Glorfeld, L. E., D. Lauerman & N. C. Stageberg (1977). *A Concise Guide for Writers* (4th ed.). New York: Holt, Rinehart & Winston.

Goodenough, C. (1983). *A Psycholinguistic Investigation of Theme and Information Focus*. Unpublished Ph.D. dissertation, University of Toronto.

Grimes, J. (1975). *The Thread of Discourse*. The Hague: Mouton.

Halliday, M. A. K. (1967). Notes on transitivity and theme in English (part 2). *Journal of Linguistics* 3, 199–244.

(1976). Theme and information in the English clause. In G. Kress (ed.), *Halliday: system and function in language* (pp. 174–88). London: Oxford University Press.

(1985). *An Introduction to Functional Grammar*. London: Edward Arnold.

Hatch, E. M. & H. Farhady (1982) *Research Design and Statistics for Applied Linguistics*. Rowley, Mass.: Newbury House.

Hickman, M. (ed.). (1987). *Social and Functional Approaches to Language and Thought*. New York: Academic Press.

Hopper, P. (1979). Aspect and foregrounding in discourse. In T. Givón (ed.), *Discourse and Syntax* (pp. 213–41). New York: Academic Press.

Hopper, P. J. & S. A. Thompson (1980). Transitivity in grammar and discourse. *Language, 56*, 251–99.

Howatt, A. (1984). *A History of English Language Teaching*. Oxford: Oxford University Press.

Hymes, D. (1971). *On Communicative Competence*. Philadelphia: University of Pennsylvania Press.

Johnson, Keith (1982). *Communicative Syllabus Design and Methodology*. Oxford: Pergamon Press.

Jones, L. B. & L. K. Jones (1979). Multiple levels of information in discourse. In L. Jones & L. Jones (eds.), *Discourse Studies in Mesoamerican Languages: Discussion* (pp. 3–28). Arlington, Tex.: Summer Institute of Linguistics.

Jones, L. K. (1977). *Theme in Expository English*. Lake Bluff, Ill.: Jupiter Press.

Keenan, E. L. (1976). Towards a universal definition of "subject." In C. N. Li (ed.), *Subject and Topic*. New York: Academic Press.

Kerr, N. H., S. F. Butler, P. L. Maykuth & D. Delis (1982). The effects of thematic context and presentation mode on memory for sentence voice. *Journal of Psycholinguistic Research* 11, 247–64.

Krashen, S. (1977). *Second Language Acquisition and Second Language Learning*. Oxford: Pergamon Press.

(1982). *Principles and Practice in Second Language Acquisition*. Oxford: Pergamon Press.

Linde, C. & W. Labov (1975). Spatial networks as a site for the study of language and thought. *Language* 51, 924–40.

Littlewood, W. (1984). *Foreign and Second Language Learning*. Cambridge: Cambridge University Press.

Longacre, R. L. (1968). *Discourse, Paragraph, and Sentence Structure in selected Philippine Languages.* Santa Ana: Summer Institute of Linguistics.
(1976). The discourse structure of the flood narrative. In G. Macrae (ed.), *Society of Biblical Literature: 1976 Seminar Papers* (pp. 235–62). Missoula, Mont.: Scholars Press.

MacWhinney, B., E. Bates, and R. Kliegl (1984). Cue validity on sentence interpretation in English, German, and Italian. *Journal of Verbal Learning and Verbal Behavior* 23, 127–50.

Marder, D. (1960). *The Craft of Technical Writing.* New York: Macmillan.

Mills, G. H. & S. A. Walter (1954). *Technical Writing.* New York: Rinehart and Company.

Mitchell, J. (1967). *A First Course in Technical Writing.* Condon: Chapman and Hall.

Mitchell, J. H. (1968). *Writing for Professional and Technical Journals.* New York: John Wiley & Sons.

Monaco, J. (1981). *How to Read a Film.* Oxford: Oxford University Press.

Newtson, D. (1973). Attribution and the unit of perception of ongoing behavior. *Journal of Personality and Social Psychology* 28, 28–38.

Newtson, D. & G. Engquist (1976). The perceptual organization of ongoing behavior. *Journal of Experimental Social Psychology* 12, 436–50.

Newtson, D., G. Engquist & J. Bois (1977). The objective basis of behavior units. *Journal of Personality and Social Psychology* 35, 847–62.

Pfaff, C. W. (1987). Functional approaches to interlanguage. In C. W. Pfaff (ed.), *First and Second Language Acquisition Processes* (pp. 81–102). Cambridge: Newbury House.

Piepho, H. (1983). Establishing objectives in the teaching of English. In C. N. Candlin (ed.), *The Communicative Teaching of English* (pp. 8 – 23). Essex, England: Longman.

Prentice, J. L. (1967). Effects of cuing actor vs. cuing object on word order in sentence production. *Psychonomic Science* 8, 163–64.

Quirk, R., S. Greenbaum, G. Leech, & J. Svartvik (1985). *A Comprehensive Grammar of the English Language.* London: Longman.

Reisman, S. J. (ed.). (1967). *A Style Manual for Technical Writers and Editors.* New York: Macmillan.

Reisz, K. (1976). *The Technique of Film Editing* (2d ed.). New York: Hastings House.

Rutherford, W. E. (1983). Language typology and language transfer. In S. M. Gass & L. Selinker (eds.), *Language Transfer in Language Learning* (pp. 358–70). Rowley, Mass.: Newbury House.

Schumann, J. H. (1978). Social and psychological factors in second language acquisition. In J. C. Richards (ed.), *Understanding Second and Foreign Language Learning: Issues and Approaches* (pp. 163–78). Rowley, Mass.: Newbury House.

Selinker, L. (1972). Interlanguage. *IRAL* 10, 209–31.

Shurter, R. L. & J. P. Williamson (1964). *Written Communication in Business.* New York: McGraw-Hill.

Slobin, D. I. (1973). Cognitive prerequisites for the development of grammar. In C. A. Ferguson & D. I. Slobin (eds.), *Studies of Child Language Development* (pp. 175–208). New York: Holt, Rinehart & Winston.
(1982). Universal and particular in the acquisition of language. In E. Wanner

& L. Gleitman (eds.), *Language Acquisition: The State of the Art* (pp. 128–70). Cambridge: Cambridge University Press.

(ed.). (1985a). *The Cross-Cultural Study of Language Acquisition*. Hillsdale, N.J.: Lawrence Erlbaum.

(1985b). Crosslinguistic evidence for the language-making capacity. In D. I. Slobin (ed.), *The Crosslinguistic Study of Language Acquisition* (pp. 1157–249). Hillsdale, N.J.: Lawrence Erlbaum.

Tannenbaum P. H. & F. Williams (1968). Generation of active and passive sentences as a function of subject and object focus. *Journal of Verbal Learning and Verbal Behavior* 7, 246–50.

Tomlin, R. S. (1983). On the interaction of syntactic subject, thematic information, and agent in English. *Journal of Pragmatics* 7, 411–32.

(1984). The treatment of foreground-background information in the on-line descriptive discourse of second language learners. *Studies in Second Language Acquisition* 6, 115–42.

(1985). Foreground-background information and the syntax of subordination. *Text* 5, 85–122.

(1986). The identification of foreground-background information in on-line descriptive discourse. *Papers in Linguistics* 19, 465–94.

(1987a). Linguistic reflections on cognitive events. In R. Tomlin (ed.), *Coherence and Grounding in Discourse* (pp. 455–80). Amsterdam: John Benjamins.

(1987b). *The problem of coding in functional grammars*. Paper presented at the University of California Davis Conference on the Interaction of Form and Function in Language, Davis, California, January 1987.

(1990). Functionalism in second language acquisition. *Studies in Second Language Acquisition* 12, 155–77.

(1991). *Focal attention, voice, and word order: an experimental, crosslinguistic study* (Technical report no. 91-10). Institute for Cognitive and Decision Sciences, University of Oregon.

Tomlin, R. S. & M. M. Pu (1991). The management of reference in Mandarin discourse. *Cognitive Linguistics* 2, 65–93.

Turner, E. & R. Rommetveit (1968). Focus of attention in recall of active and passive sentences. *Journal of Verbal Learning and Verbal Behavior* 7, 543–48.

Turner, E. A. & R. Rommetveit (1967). The acquisition of sentence voice and reversability. *Journal of Verbal Learning and Verbal Behavior* 7, 246–50.

Ulman, J. N. J. (1952). *Technical Reporting*. New York: Henry Holt and Company.

Widdowson, H. G. (1978). *Teaching Language as Communication*. Oxford: Oxford University Press.

(1979). *Explorations in Applied Linguistics*. Oxford: Oxford University Press.

Woods, A., P. Fletcher & A. Hughes (1986). *Statistics in Language Studies*. Cambridge: Cambridge University Press.

8 Learning to function with the other tongue: A systemic functional perspective on second language teaching

Ruqaiya Hasan and Gillian Perrett

Introduction

As a domain of academic enterprise, applied linguistics has had more than its fair share of "approaches". Each new approach is presented as "the" solution to some major problem encountered in its practice; each approach promises to shore up its theoretical foundations. But the remark that Harold E. Palmer, one of the earliest pioneers in the field, made nearly a century ago still appears apposite: "Evidence of various kinds shows that this subject has not attained the scientific stage, but is so far in the experimental or empirical stage" (Palmer 1917: 1). To remedy the situation, he recommended greater focus on language, believing that inquiry into its nature "must necessarily be of interest to method-writers, to teachers, and to students" (Palmer 1917: 3); and a countless number of applied linguists have rightly embraced this view – we say "rightly" because it seems reasonable to hope that an understanding of what language is like would help in deciding what to do about teaching it efficiently. We grant also that when Palmer was expressing these views, our understanding of the true nature of language was not very deep. But if the strident claims made by today's dominant paradigms of linguistics are to be believed, by now the many marvellous "revolutions" in linguistics ought to have remedied this situation: We ought to have "the" true insights into the nature of language. Clearly this has not happened, for applied linguistics still continues in ferment. It is still in search of that which it is supposed to be already applying, and there seems to be a constant uncertainty about what constitutes its centre of gravity.

To us it seems that the fundamental issues of applied linguistics have remained problematic because linguistic revolutions have not delivered what they promised. The conception of language which has emerged from these revolutions and which applied linguistics has typically

Our thanks are due to Kristin Davidse (Catholic University, Leuven) and to Jane Torr (Macquarie University, Sydney) for help in the earlier stages of this paper. We thank Bev Deriwianka, Michael Halliday, Graham Lock, Terence Odlin, David Nunan, and also the anonymous readers for their helpful comments and constructive critique. The responsibility for the views expressed is entirely ours.

chosen to work with calls for revision because it fails to do justice to the complex issues that have to be addressed in doing applied linguistics. Consider, for example, three concepts crucial to the field – teaching, learning, and language – each of which is highly complex, and this complexity is even further compounded by the complicity of these concepts: One cannot teach or learn without (some sort of) language since *semiosis* – that is, making and exchanging meaning through symbolic mediation – is an essential ingredient in all acts of teaching and learning; nor can one *language* without teaching and learning: Semiosis – the exchange of meaning – logically entails both teaching and learning. To hold this view is to claim that not all teaching and learning is necessarily intentional, deliberate, and self-conscious. But the deliberate pedagogy of the classroom and the un-self-conscious instructions of life situations must confront each other at some point in the history of the same individual, and the two need not be in agreement; they could, in fact, run counter to each other. So it could come about that what one might learn from participating in a pedagogic speech event is not necessarily what someone consciously set out to teach; otherwise the system of education would not be so haunted by failures. When we add to this already complex situation the necessity of having to language in order to teach someone how to language with "the other tongue", we meet a situation the complexity of which is not paralleled by any other academic enterprise (Halliday 1991: 22).

Assuming that these complex factors influence the practices of applied linguistics, what the field needs as its foundation is not a model of language as an autonomous system which is taken to evolve in isolation from human interaction. Nor can it thrive on a physicalistic theory of mental development where cognition is equated simply with some human biological equipment whose growth follows a preordained path laid out once for all by nature (Piaget 1960, 1973; Brown 1973; Krashen 1987), as if the individual's interactive history played no part in the process. (For a critique of the Piagetian approach, see Vygotsky 1962; Donaldson 1978; Doise and Mugny 1984.) Such models of language and human cognition fail to accommodate the complex relations between teaching, learning, and language, since the origin of this complexity is social rather than biological. We, therefore, agree with Candlin (1991: vi) that what applied linguistics needs is a thoroughgoing "social theoretical basis for its principles and its activities". But it needs to be recognised also that this "social theoretical basis" is not an optional extra to be added to "linguistics proper". Rather, it is an essential requirement for a competent model of language that it should successfully model the genuinely many-faceted character of language, which is at once physical, biological, social, and semiotic (Halliday, in press). However, over the years, linguists have shown considerable disdain for the social basis of language, excluding it from their models of language, though it is without doubt integral to language. Certainly an understanding of the social aspect of language is essential to the understanding of what language is and how it does what it does for its speakers.

It is the basic concern of this paper to develop these claims. Accordingly, we shall need to show what language as a system looks like when it is given a *social* theoretical basis. This is the question we address in the next section ("Functionalism: the social theoretical basis of language"). By way of answer, we shall highlight certain characteristics of the systemic functional (henceforth, SF) model as an example of a theory which adopts precisely this perspective. The SF model claims that to treat the social aspect as integral to language is to accept *functionalism* as the underlying principle of the system of language. The terms *functionalism, functional,* and the like are used differently in different models. We shall clarify how this term is conceptualised in the SF model. The section is thus concerned with two closely related problems: First, what is linguistic functionalism? And second, what does the language system look like when seen from a functional perspective? The consideration of these issues allows us to ask how an understanding of language as a functional system might furnish a viable social theoretical basis for the principles and practices of applied linguistics. Obviously this is a large question, and we shall limit its scope by focusing on certain aspects of teaching and learning another tongue. Taking ESL as an example, the third section of the paper ("Contexts of learning in a functional perspective") will be concerned with some *macro issues,* which place ESL in the wider context of the living of life, exploring questions of wider relevance: How is the activity of teaching and learning ESL valued in a given cultural system? Who are the learners of ESL, and how are they socially positioned by engaging in its practices? In general, applied linguistics has treated ESL pedagogic practices as if they occur in contexts that are sociopolitically neutral. Using the insights of a socially informed theory of language, we will argue that ESL has an essentially politico-economic nature, and like all pedagogic activities, its decisions participate in the politico-economic history of the community in question (Phillipson 1990; Tollefson 1991).

In the fourth section ("Grammar as meaningful choice in context"), we shall turn to a *micro issue* which will be concerned with a question relevant to the narrower context of the ESL classroom: What insights into the lexicogrammatical description of language could a socially based model, such as SF, provide to the ESL teacher? Using the SF description of a small fragment of English grammar, we hope to show how this model treats wording as a resource for meaning. The paper will close with a brief general review of the importance of a discussion of this type in the context of comparative perspectives on pedagogic grammars.

Functionalism: The social theoretical basis of language

Let us begin by considering the SF claim that "to treat the social aspect as integral to language is to accept functionalism as the underlying principle of the system of language". We need to clarify what such a claim means, and the first step in this clarification is to explain what we mean by functionalism.

In one sense of the term *functional,* scarcely any one would deny the functional nature of language: This is the sense "which defines language as a form of communication" (Leech 1983: 48), seeing it simply as a "useful" tool for bringing about speakers' purposes. This view makes the expression *functions of language* synonymous with *uses of language.* The usefulness of language is certainly an element of functionalism, but a simple affirmation of this kind is not to be confused with a functional theory. In fact, no theory is needed for such an affirmation, which could be based on empirical observations alone: The ability to make this claim does not depend on an explicit understanding of the *internal* nature of language. So it follows that where functionalism consists *simply* in claiming the usefulness of language and/or in identifying the uses of language, it will fail to explain many important facts about the system of language. To take a simple example, this approach to functionalism has no way of determining what, if any, functions are universal to human language, and why. It is just possible that an observation of "ways of speaking" prevalent in a community (Hymes 1986: 58) might enable one to draw an inventory of that community's typical language functions, specifying "who says what to whom and when" (with apologies to Fishman 1972: 244). *Language functions* in this sense of the term are known as *registers* in the SF model (Halliday et al. 1964; Halliday 1974, 1977, 1991; Halliday and Hasan 1989; Hasan 1973, in press), and it is a well-known fact that register repertoires are not identical across communities (Hymes 1968; Gumperz 1971; Fishman 1972; Frake 1986).

Moreover, in principle, these repertoires are open-ended, since there is no natural necessity governing the array of the uses of language. It follows that old uses can discontinue, and new uses can be added (Halliday 1973, 1974). Obviously, variant inventories of this kind show that functions of languages, in this sense of the term, are *not* universal. Consider another problem in this view of functionalism: Granted that language is useful, as the view claims, what accounts for the fact that it is able to meet speakers' needs for bringing about their myriad purposes? That language actually does so is, clearly, a fact of a different order from the fact that it has the *potential* for doing so. And it is valid to ask: How do we explain the fact that human language universally enjoys this potential, even though the register repertoire of languages is not identical? Linguistic functionalism interpreted as simply the usefulness of language is unable to answer these and other important questions because it is not a theory of language: It has nothing to say about language as a system. It bows to the empirically validated existence of *parole* – the social use of language – but has no way of relating it to the theoretical entity *langue*. It fails to provide the social theoretical basis for the description of language.

We are suggesting that where a theory treats the social aspect as integral to language, it would not be limited to just pointing out the social uses of language; it would also be committed to showing how the social uses of language relate to the internal system of language. Such a functional theory will aim to describe how *parole* permeates *langue*, and how *langue* enables *parole* – in short, how the two co-exist in a dialectic relation, both being maintained and altered by the mutually responsive workings of each other. For a theory to be functional in this sense, the concept of *function* needs to be more abstract than function equated with specific language use. It is only when functions are identified at a high level of abstraction that they can be recognised as essential to *all* uses of language, and it is only when they are recognised as essential to *all* uses of language, becoming a property of the entire linguistic social process as such, that they can be viewed as integral to the system of language, serving to explain the nature of its internal structure by relation to its social uses. Because the term *function* has been used in different senses (see discussion in Leech 1983; also Dirven and Fried 1987), to avoid confusion we shall use the term *metafunction* to refer to the more abstract functions as postulated in the SF theory.

In the SF model, three metafunctions are considered necessary for an adequate description of language: (1) *interpersonal,* (2) *textual,* and (3) *ideational.* Since detailed discussions of these are available (e.g., see Halliday 1970a, 1973, 1975, 1977, 1979b; Martin 1984, 1991, 1992; Matthiessen 1990, 1992), only a brief account of each is provided here. Take first the INTERPERSONAL METAFUNCTION: Language acts as a potential for the expression of speakers' subjectivity – their assessment of probability, obligation, and commitment; their attitudes and evaluations. Further, engaging in *any* use of language implies that speakers must assume some speech roles, thus by implication, allocating speech roles to their addressees. For example, by asking a question, a speaker places the addressee in the position of one who is to respond. This is not to claim that the addressee is *forced* to respond; simply that given this situation whatever the addressee does thereafter, its interpretation will be coloured by the fact that the addressee had been positioned as a respondent. To say that speakers are able to do these "things with words" (Austin 1962) is to say that language has an interpersonal metafunction. This metafunction in the SF model subsumes what Bühler referred to as *expressive* and *conative* functions of speech, but (contra Leech 1983) it goes beyond primitive notions of exclaiming and signalling, as it also goes beyond the speech act theorist's concept of illocutionary force.

Turn now to the TEXTUAL METAFUNCTION of language. In *any* social use of language, interactants indicate what can be taken as given, what is new, what is the speaker's point of departure, whether further verbal action is anticipated, how the various parts of the discourse relate to each other, what degree of specificity is needed to get the message across (e.g., whether one can get by with "don't leave them there" or needs to say something like "John, when you bring back my books, don't leave them in my mail-box"), whether information is presented as retrievable from what has already been "said" (e.g., the expression "such relevancies" and "such meanings" as used in the next sentence), whether more information is to be presented in the on-going discourse (as indicated by the use of "first" in "take first the interpersonal metafunction"), and so on. Language is a resource for creating such relevancies, and the potential of language that enables the speakers to mean such meanings is the basis for recognising the textual metafunction of language.

The third metafunction of language – the IDEATIONAL – is said to have two components: the *experiential* and the *logical*. The EXPERIENTIAL METAFUNCTION of language is the resource speakers draw on to construe their experience of the world – both the outside world of physical phenomena and the inside world of feelings, beliefs and reflection. Human language acts as a resource for the construal of classes of things (e.g., "magnolia, linguistics, time"), qualities (e.g., "pretty, pink, good"), and quantities (e.g., "some, many, two, four"), and also of events, happenings and goings-on (e.g., "doing, happening, being, saying, thinking," and so on) which imply certain participants and circumstances. But in such construals of experience, speakers do not simply focus on things and events as isolated phenomena; they use the resources of their language to create complex categories such as "three dark purple magnolias", where a complex class characterised by certain qualities and quantity is "created"; similarly, the single events and happenings combine to produce complex events, happenings, and so on, as in "it rains whenever I decide to go out for a long walk". The LOGICAL METAFUNCTION "is" the potential of language concerned with the construal of such complex things and events. It is a resource for creating such relations as those of subclassification ("an A *sort of* B"; or "a B that *has an* A"), addition ("A *and* B"), variation ("X *or* Y"), concurrence ("M *while* N"), condition ("*if* P [*then*] Q"), report ("say that X"), idea ("think that X"), and so on.

It is clear from this account that *metafunctions* are abstract properties of language which cannot be confused with functions in the sense of social uses. The concept of metafunctions in the SF model is more abstract than the functions of language in pragmatic functionalism (such as in Leech 1983), or even in Prague School linguistics (Davidse 1987). And they are certainly far more abstract than are functions in the proposals of Wilkins (1976) or in the Council of Europe's concept of the functional-notional syllabus (van Ek 1976), all of which are based on an interpretation of function as language use. The difference in the conceptualisation of *function* and *metafunction* has certain logical consequences. Consider how functions in the sense of uses have to be mutually exclusive. If we say, for example, that a speaker is using language to give a sports commentary, we cannot say, without self-contradiction, that at the same time the same speaker is using language to give a sermon: The speaker typically engages in this use *or* that, not both. This kind of mutual exclusion is impossible in the abstract interpretation of the term: No matter who says what to whom and when, speakers cannot just use the ideational metafunction on one occasion, the interpersonal the next time, and the textual metafunction in yet another use. Quite obviously, adoption and allocation of speech roles is not limited to any *one specific* speech variety; equally, no matter what the social use of language, speakers will need to invoke categories of their experience – they will need to refer to things and events and so on; and in all communication, they will attempt to maintain discoursal relevancies. This is the reasoning that lies behind the SF claims (1) that all metafunctions have to be operative simultaneously on all occasions of language use; (2) that each is needed for explaining the properties of language use and language system; and (3) that although linguists have typically prioritised the ideational metafunction, all three are equally integral to language. But if metafunctions are not to be interpreted as social uses of language, then how do they relate to the social basis of the system of language? We shall answer this question in two parts: First, what is the social basis of metafunctions? And second, what are the grounds for claiming that the social basis is integral to the system of language?

In a very real sense, the metafunctions are abstractions based on an analysis of the social situation within which language use is embedded. We will refer to the social occasion of talk by the technical term CONTEXT OF SITUATION. Context of situation is not the same thing as MATERIAL SITUATIONAL SETTING (Hasan 1973); the latter refers to all of what surrounds the speakers, including both external phenomena and the speakers' internal states, here and now, in the moment of speaking. Instead, context of situation is that part of the speakers' environment – both external and internal – which is *invariably* illuminated by the language in use. In other words, cases of language in use will always bear testimony to the nature of context of situation. As participants in a speech event on any one occasion of talk, we are aware of many factors that exercise pressure on our acts of communication, and no two occasions of talk can be said to be identical at this degree of detail. If we are to create a framework for the analysis of the social occasion of talk, it is necessary to invoke categories rather than to focus on the actually occurring factors that instantiate the categories. The notion *context of situation* is concerned with identifying precisely such general categories which are *always active* in exercising pressures on our acts of communication, shaping every discourse in any speech variety whatever. According to the SF model, no matter what speech variety/register is considered, the aspects of the social environment invariably highlighted by the language of the discourse can be assigned to one or the other of the following categories: (1) the *social relations* between the participants of the discourse; (2) the nature of the *social process,* that is, what is being achieved in and by the discourse; and (3) the *semiotic management of the interaction* as a social event (e.g., whether the activity is achieved by persuading, coercing, or by instructing). These three categories have been traditionally referred to in the SF model as *tenor, field,* and *mode of discourse,* respectively (Halliday, McIntosh and Strevens 1964; Halliday 1974; Hasan 1973), and together they constitute the schematic construct known as *context of situation.* We are claiming, then, that these three sorts of pressures are always active in the production and comprehension of any discourse; and in support of this claim we are citing the fact that it is factors of these three categories that are always "illuminated by language in use". In other words, what creates our concept of the context of situation is the *ongoing evidence from language in use:* It is in the nature of language to construe context, and it is in the nature of social contexts that they are knowable only through semiosis.

This is where the metafunctions enter into the picture: The SF model claims (Halliday 1977; Martin 1991; Halliday and Hasan 1989; Hasan in press) that language as a resource is metafunctionally specialised with respect to the three contextual categories. There is a division of labour, so that typically, one distinct metafunction serves to express one distinct contextual parameter. The pairing of the linguistic metafunctions and the parameters of context is as shown in Figure 1. The SF model claims that there is a logical basis for the "hook-up" between a specific metafunction and a particular contextual parameter. Taking the metafunctions to refer to aspects of language as a potential for meaning, the claim is that each metafunction "is" an aspect of language as meaning potential which is particularly relevant to the construal of a specific contextual category. Take, for example, tenor and the interpersonal metafunction. Tenor is concerned with social relations between participants. The interpersonal metafunction "is" the potential of language to enable speakers to choose meanings which are concerned with speech role allocation, with the speaker's judgements of possibility, and obligation, with her evaluations of phenomena, and so on. It is meanings of this kind that construe the situational parameter we have called tenor,

Semiotic structure of situation		Functional components of language
field (type of social action)	associated with	ideational metafunction
tenor (social relations)	" "	interpersonal metafunction
mode (verbal action and contact)	" "	textual metafunction

Figure 1   Context and linguistic metafunctions: realizational tendencies (after Halliday 1977).

but this is not the entire story. The relationship between this metafunction and tenor has to be viewed from two complementary perspectives. To take the first perspective: From the listener's point of view, when a speaker means a certain set of interpersonal meanings, this choice of meanings will construe for the listener a certain social relation between the participants. For example, on hearing A give a direct command to B, a listener will construe their relation as A most probably having greater discretion than B unless there is *good reason* (see Halliday 1976: 216) for construing the relation in another way. The second perspective relates to the speaker: It is *his* perception of a certain social relation with his addressee that activates a certain set of interpersonal meanings. For example, wanting to get his boss to do something for him, A as the speaker will most probably not give a direct command to B, his boss; his perception of his social relation with B will incline him to choose some other indirect mode of command. The two perspectives of construal-activation are described here in terms of specific speech events, but of course they apply longitudinally as well. For example, human social relationships are (typically, if not always) the artefact of interaction: Even the mother-child relation, cited often as the most "instinctive", requires *mothering* as an essential condition for its creation. Human social relations are cumulatively created, maintained, and changed through semiotic interacts, particularly through the interpersonal meanings of linguistic semiosis. At the same time, even the most elementary social interact in any community has a history of assumptions and expectations which plays a part in activating the choice of meanings in social interaction. In view of these observations, it seems reasonable to suggest that the relationship between the tenor of discourse and the interpersonal metafunction is a *natural* one: The two co-evolve; social relationships do not pre-exist acts of meaning, and acts of meaning presuppose social relationships. Similar arguments have been made with regard to the pairing of the ideational metafunction to field and of the textual metafunction to mode. Rather than detailing these here, let us look into the significance of these claims.

First, the construal-activation relation between the metafunctions and contextual parameters explains the social basis of the metafunctions. Language has just these three metafunctions because these alone are necessary and sufficient for construing the categories of context, which are themselves criterial in activating the meaning choices in a speaker's use of language. Each aspect of the potential of language has evolved in response to speakers' needs to express certain sorts of meaning whenever language is being used, and language has the potential to meet the needs of its speakers for any language use whatever because it is through the communicative pressures of language in use that the system has evolved as it has: This is how *parole* permeates *langue*. Language use and language system co-evolve; they are in a dialectic relation. Second, if each of the metafunctions is specialised vis-à-vis some particular contextual parameter, *and* if the contextual parameters identified here are necessary and sufficient for the description of the social environment of all speech communities, then it would follow unavoidably that the three metafunctions proposed in the SF model are universal to human language. This is entailed by the logical basis for the hook-up between context and linguistic metafunctions. Third, because of this logical relation between context and metafunctions, an adequate model of language is forced to treat language not as an autonomous system but as one that is relevant to the human social context. Accordingly, context has to be integral to any functional model for the description of language. In the SF model it is treated as an essential component of the theory. The technical term for components of the linguistic theory is *strata*, and *context* is the highest stratum in the theory of language description. The logical relation of construal-activation which links the stratum of context to language is known as *realization*.

Let us turn now to the second question: What are the grounds for claiming that the social basis is integral to the system of language? Given the arguments for the social basis of the metafunctions, a cryptic answer to this question would be that the system of language is itself metafunctionally organised. The reasoning underlying this answer is not difficult to follow: If the metafunctions have a social basis, then the language itself has a social basis *provided* it is true that language is metafunctionally organised. The remainder of this section is concerned with spelling out the more specific details of this claim by examining the organisation of the strata internal to the system of language. The SF model recognises three strata internal to language: (1) SEMANTICS, that is, systems of meaning, where the term "meaning" is to be interpreted not simply as *cognitive/ referential* meaning, as in formal linguistics, but all kinds of meanings already discussed; (2) LEXICOGRAMMAR, that is, systems of wording, in-

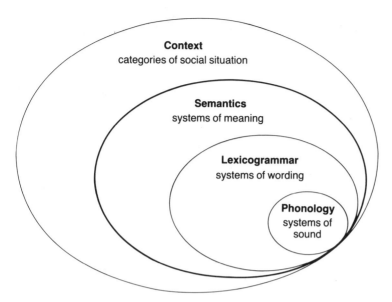

Figure 2   The four strata of the SF model.

cluding both grammar and lexicon; and (3) PHONOLOGY, that is, systems of sound, both segmental and suprasegmental. When the stratum of context is taken into account, this produces a stratal theory of linguistic description consisting of four strata, although for the purposes of this discussion the last mentioned, *phonology,* will be ignored. The remaining three strata – *context, semantics,* and *lexicogrammar* – are linked to each other by the logical relation of realisation, that is, construal-activation. The four strata of the model are as shown in Figure 2, where the darker boundary line separates the language-external stratum of context from the three language-internal ones.

In discussing the social basis of language, we have already drawn attention to the metafunctional specialisation of language. To claim that the strata of semantics and lexicogrammar are metafunctionally organised is to say that the facts of these strata are best described by using the metafunctions as a grid for their organisation. If this claim is substantiated, then it would be viable to treat the notion of metafunctions as an explanatory principle underlying the internal organisation of the system, which, in turn, would imply that the social basis is integral to the system of language. In the following paragraph, we introduce the notions necessary for describing stratal organisation, before attempting to substantiate the claim that the language-internal strata are metafunctionally organised.

The crucial concept for the organization of the internal strata of language is that of SYSTEMIC CHOICE. *Choice* does not refer here to deliberate acts of choosing; it simply refers to the fact that speakers are never constrained to do just one thing; whatever the environment, there always exist alternatives to choose from. In this sense, the idea of choice is fundamental to the conception of language as a potential. A potential must offer choices. If by way of demanding service one always *had to* produce a direct command, then no specific significance could be attached to this form of demanding service, and language would have to be seen simply as a set of mandatory rules which must be followed mechanically. The possibility of choice removes this mechanical determinacy from language, and imbues the alternatives – the terms of the system – with value. Simplifying the crucial notions, a system consists of some environment that acts as the *entry condition* to a *set of options*, such that if the entry condition is satisfied, then one, and only one, option must be chosen. The value of any one option in the system is determined by its relation to the other options that were "available" in the system at that point. Take an example from semantics (see Hasan 1989, 1992): If the entry condition *message demanding service* is satisfied, then one system with the following three choices becomes available: (1) the demand may "be" *exhortative* (e.g., "tidy up your room"); or (2) it may "be" *assertive* (e.g., "you have to tidy up your room"); or (3) it may "be" *consultative* (e.g., "could you tidy up your room?"). These three options constitute one system where the value of each term is its relation to the other terms; and the system represents what speakers of English *can mean* in the environment of demanding service up to a certain point in *delicacy*. The term *delicacy* refers to the degree of detail in description. This degree of detail in description increases as each option of a system in its turn acts as an entry condition for some other set of options. To continue with the same example (and again simplifying the picture), if the option *assertive* is chosen, then it becomes an entry condition to the systemic choice between the options *desiderative* (e.g., "I'd like you to tidy up your room") or *mandatory* (e.g., "you must tidy up your room"). Here the systemic choice between *desiderative* or *mandatory* is said to *depend on* the option *assertive*. A single entry condition can permit entry into more than one system of choices. So, given the entry condition *message demanding service*, not only do we have a system – call it system A – with the options *exhortative* or *assertive* or *consultative* (introduced above), but *at the same time* there exists at least one other system – call it system B – with the option *suggestive* or *nonsuggestive*. Here systems A and B are said to be *simultaneous*. Each of the three options in system A *must* combine with one option in system B, thus giving us finer distinctions of choices in meaning. For example, "could you tidy up your room?" combines the option *consultative* from system A with the option *nonsuggestive* from system B, while "how about tidying up your room?" combines *consultative* with *suggestive*. When systems of options interlock by virtue of relations of the kinds exemplified here – that is, *dependency* and *simultaneity* – then together they constitute a *system network*. (For two examples of system networks from the lexicogrammatical stratum, see Figures 4 and 5 in the section titled "Grammar as meaningful choice in context".) Systems of options that make up one system network show "a high degree of internal constraint: that is, of interdependence among the various options involved. The selections made by the speaker at one point tend to determine, and be determined by, the selections he makes at another" (Halliday 1979a: 61). An example of such "interdependence" was presented in describing systems A and B, which must form part of the same system network. (See the iconic representation of such interdependencies in Figures 4 and 5, on pages 208 and 211, respectively.) By contrast, between *distinct* system networks "there is very little constraint of this kind: little restriction on the options available and little effect on their interpretation" (Halliday 1979a: 61).

This discussion is useful for exploring the question at hand. We have established that a system network is an identifiable entity. If the organisation of the internal strata is effected through such entities, then an examination of their underlying principle can determine whether or not the organisation of the internal strata of language is metafunctional. For example, if at the semantic stratum we find one system network of options (in meaning) which construe the social factors relevant to tenor, another that represents meaning options that construe factors relevant to field, and a third system whose choices construe the mode of discourse, this could be treated as evidence that the organisation of the semantic stratum is metafunctional: Its nature can be explained by reference to the realisational relation that logically links the system networks of meanings to the contextual categories. But is it true that the internal strata of language are metafunctionally organised?

When the set of semantic choices available to speakers of English are represented as system networks (Halliday 1973; Hasan 1989, 1991, 1992; Hasan and Cloran 1990), it appears that the options at the semantic stratum can be represented as four system networks, and each of these networks does represent the options relevant to one specific metafunction: One network represents choices in meaning pertaining to the interpersonal metafunction; a second represents those pertaining to the experiential one; a third, to the logical; and a fourth represents the textual choices in meaning. *Within* each system network there is a "high degree of internal constraint", whereas *between* the system networks "there is very little constraint". So choices from the interpersonal system network – for example, those which pertain to taking up and allocating speech roles (e.g. *demanding* or *giving*) – "show a high degree of internal constraint": From the system of speech function, it is not possible to choose both *give* and *demand*, and both *information* and *goods/services* at one and the same time; only one term from each pair can combine.

This is because all four terms form part of the same network, and their choice is internally constrained. However, any one of these terms can combine freely with any term of the experiential system. This is because the experiential system network is a different entity, and across system networks the constraint is minimal. So the choice of process can vary independently of the choices made from the interpersonal system network. For example, any giving or demanding of information can combine with almost any process type, whether it is material action as in 1a and 1b, or mental cognition as in 2a and 2b, or attribution as in 3a and 3b, respectively:

1a: I have left him in there.   1b: Shall I leave him in there?
2a: I realised my mistake.   2b: Why didn't I realise my mistake?
3a: I was a baby then.   3b: Was I a baby then?

The organisation of the semantic stratum reveals, then, that each metafunction has a system network "dedicated to it". These distinct system networks are *not alternatives;* making choices from one system network does not preclude making choices from the others. On the contrary, it is *impossible* to describe the semantic properties – the meaning structure – of a message completely without considering the message as the *instantiation* of choices from all system networks. This is in keeping with the view that, unlike functions in the sense of register/language use, metafunctions are not mutually exclusive: Speakers do not choose from among the various metafunctions; and (contra Leech 1983) there is no support in the stratal organisation of semantics for treating the ideational metafunction as more integral to the language system than either the interpersonal or the textual. This examination of system networks at the semantic stratum suggests that the metafunctional hypothesis will serve as a viable explanation for its internal organisation.

But, of course, the organisation of semantics cannot be seen in dissociation from what speakers do with linguistic meanings or from how linguistic meanings relate to the lexicogrammar. Semantics is an interface between context and lexicogrammar. We have already discussed the construal-activation relation between the strata of context and semantics. A similar realisational relation links the internal strata of semantics and lexicogrammar. In the SF model, linguistic meanings are treated as the artefact of lexicogrammar: If a meaning cannot be construed by the lexicogrammar of a language, then it is not a *linguistic* meaning in that language. The realisational relation between meanings and forms implies the double perspective we have mentioned before: Listeners are able to construe the speakers' linguistic meanings on the basis of their lexicogrammatical choices, while the speakers' lexicogrammatical choice is activated by their choice of (context-construing) linguistic meanings. So linguistic meaning is not something that simply "mirrors" reality, whatever the term might mean; rather, linguistic meanings are an "interface" between the extralinguistic world and the linguistic form. If the stratum of linguistic meanings is functionally organised, as we have argued, then because of the realisational relation between the strata there exists a strong possibility that a similar organisation will be found also at the lexicogrammatical stratum.

Halliday (1970a) claims that he arrived at the metafunctional hypothesis, in the first place, from a consideration of the internal organisation of the lexicogrammatical stratum. When the lexicogrammar of a language is paradigmatically represented as systems of options, this reveals a pattern reminiscent of the semantic stratum. Thus, restricting ourselves to the *clause* as an entry condition, we would find system networks whose underlying basis is metafunctional, so that each system network is specialised with respect to some metafunction. The *transitivity system network* specifies the options of processes, participants, and circumstances. The choices from this system network construe that set of meanings which together make up our sense of what is going on, what kind of event is being referred to. Technically, transitivity options construe *states of affairs* or *goings-on* (some of these have been touched upon in the preceding discussion of examples 1a–3b on page 192; further examples will be found in the next paragraph). The system network of *mood* and *modality* construes interpersonal meanings, realising the rhetorical strategies for stating, questioning, ordering, and so on, and the speakers' assessment of probability, usuality, and their judgement about obligation, inclination, and the like (see the discussion in the section titled "Grammar as meaningful choice in context"). The system networks of *expansion* and *projection* realise logical meanings, such as "and", "or", "then" and "if", as well as metatextual relations, such as "say that", "ask if", "tell someone to", "think that", "wonder if", and so on. The system networks of *theme* and *information focus* realise textual meanings. Examples of each are presented in the next paragraph, and despite this condensed account, it seems obvious that the internal organisation of the lexicogrammar is best seen as having a metafunctional basis. (For details of the metafunctional organisation of lexicogrammar, see Halliday 1985; Halliday and Hasan 1989; Matthiessen 1990; Martin 1991, 1992.)

At the lexicogrammatical stratum, two kinds of theoretical statements have to be made: first, the paradigmatic representation of the form as a resource for making meanings, and second, the structures that instantiate the choices. "The grammatical system has ... a functional input and a structural output; it provides the mechanism for different functions to be combined in one utterance" (Halliday 1973: 36). Each clause has a structural description in respect of the system networks named. It is not simply that the systems at the lexicogrammatical stratum are metafunctionally organised; the metafunctional organisation also characterises the structures found at this stratum. When these structures are examined in abstract terms, a different *type* of structure is found to be associated with each distinct metafunction. The system of transitivity realising the experiential metafunction "has" syntagmatic structures that are *segmental* – consisting of elements "each of which has a special and distinct significance with respect to the whole" (Halliday 1979a: 63). For example, in a clause such as "My mother gave my sister a new car on her birthday", the significance of each element with respect to the whole is distinct: "my mother" is *Actor* of a *Process: dispositive* "gave", with "a new car" functioning as *Goal*, "my sister" as *Beneficiary*, and "on her birthday" as *Temporal Circumstance*. The systems of expansion and projection realising the logical metafunction "have" syntagmatic structures that are *iterative*, as in "I went to Felicity's because she needed help because her baby was unwell". Representing this string schematically as "state of affairs A *because* state of affairs B *because* state of affairs C", we note that the relation of interdependency holds between the elements A, B, and C, such that each has a similar significance with respect to the other two. Another example would be: "Did you know that they told Mabel that they are leaving?", which may be schematically represented as A *that* B *that* C. This differs markedly from the segmental structure, where each element has a different significance vis-à-vis the others. The systems of mood and modality realising the interpersonal metafunction generate structures that are *prosodic;* so in "Could we perhaps do it tomorrow?", "could" and "perhaps" together express the choice of modality; each does not have a distinct significance with respect to the whole. Further details of modality will be discussed in the section titled "Grammar as meaningful choice in context". The systems of theme and information focus realising the textual metafunction generate structures which are *periodic;* like waves, they have peaks of prominence. Textual metafunction concerns relevancies between textual units. Since periodicity cannot be the feature of just one unit, all single-clause exemplification of theme or information focus is a contradiction in terms. Adequate natural examples tend to demand much time and space. Consider an example from a familiar text:

Jack and Jill went up the hill	**Jack and Jill** went up the hill
Jack fell down	**down** fell Jack
and (**Jack**) broke his crown	and **his crown** broke
and **Jill** came tumbling after	and **tumbling after,** came Jill

The original nursery rhyme stanza in the left column shows a consistency in the thematic peaks represented in its various clauses; this consistency is absent from the version on the right. Since the grammar of the clauses in the two columns does not vary in any other respect, it is fair to assume that what makes a difference to their status as (part of) texts is the fact that, unlike the stanza in the right column, the one in the left has a "well-formed" periodic structure in terms of theme selection. This is why it strikes one as textually better organised, while the transformed version is "all over the place", as teachers of composition would put it. There are other methods than that of simple repetition of content in theme for creating consistency of thematic peaks. (For details, see Fries 1983; Jones et al. 1989; Matthiessen 1990.) The relevant point is that the selection of theme, realising the periodic structure, is not random.

This closes our discussion of what it means to give linguistics a social theoretical basis. We have argued that this calls for an abstract concept of (meta)functions. In fact, metafunctions are not some *thing* that can be found at some specific point in language: When we say that language is metafunctional, we mean that the underlying principle of language is functionality. This is what explains the patterns of organisation at the strata of context, meaning and wording. Figure 3 presents a picture of the metafunctional specialisation of these strata in summary form. It shows that linguistic metafunctions are not restricted to any one stratum of the model: They "resonate" throughout the system and process of language, acting as the underlying principle for its organisation.

Figure 3 shows that the metafunctional principle "orders" the facts of speakers' social environment for linguistic interaction as well as those of the strata of semantics and lexicogrammar. The latter two strata constitute the "intelligible" plane of language and the relationship between them is *not arbitrary:* It is *natural*. This is in contrast to the *arbitrary* relation of phonology to lexicogrammar and meaning, which has been referred to as *conventional:* Phonology does not *define* the nature of a unit at the level of form or meaning. By contrast, the value of a semantic unit *is* defined by the grammar that construes it, while its signification is defined by relation to context. These three strata – context, meaning, and wording – are really three perspectives on the phenomenon of human semiosis; none of the three perspectives can be ignored without distorting the description of language.

Contexts of learning in a functional perspective

If our arguments in the preceding section are accepted, then it must be conceded also that language is a *relevant,* not an *autonomous,* system. In the final analysis, we know absolutely no natural language which is not responsive to the sociality of its speakers. In this section we explore the macro issue concerning the nature of ESL as a social activity when it is considered in its wider social context. We expect such an examination to

Metafunction	Contextual variable	Meaning system	Wording system	Wording structure
interpersonal	social relation (= *tenor*)	role exchange; assessment of probability, obligation	mood system (e.g., declarative v. interrogative...); system of modality, modulation	prosodic
experiential	social action (= *field*)	states of affairs; classification of phenomena	transitivity system (e.g., material v. verbal...); lexical systems...	segmental
logical		relations of states of affairs; relations of phenomena	expansion, projection systems; modification...	iterative
textual	semiotic management (= *mode*)	point of departure; news focus; points of identity, similarity	thematic, information systems; cohesive connections	periodic

Figure 3   The metafunctional specialisation of the strata of context, meaning and wording.

reveal some facts that will be relevant both to the social activity of ESL and to the ESL learner's social positioning.

In considering ESL as a social activity, the first logical question is: What is a second language? Indeed, what is a first language, what is a foreign language? The difference between first and second language has been characterised as resting either on which language was learnt first (Stern 1983: 12), or on which language is "best developed" (Stern 1983: 13). The difference between second and foreign language is generally characterised in terms of a second language being learnt where it is used in some "indigenous" context(s), while a foreign language is said to be learnt where it does not form part of the community's register repertoire. These distinctions fail to do justice to the complex situations that arise from the phenomenon that Phillipson (1990: 4) describes as "English rules the waves". Thus the distinctions ignore the constantly increasing availability of international education as evidenced by the growing number of non-English-speaking–background students from "emergent" countries seeking higher education in "developed" English-speaking countries – a phenomenon that is itself motivated by politico-economic considerations. These criteria ignore also the related fact that English as the major language of international communication is increasingly employed in the management of the international politico-economic order. One result is that the contexts, and indeed the sequences, of learning language are becoming more complex and diverse.

When the activity of learning another tongue is placed in the wider social context, the critical question is not *when* or *where,* but *why* and *how:* Why is this activity to be performed at all? How do learners engage with the various languages that they learn? In the context of this discussion, a consideration of mother-tongue learning is not irrelevant. Consider its significance in the learner's life. The learning subject's self is created in the learning of a first language (Mead 1934; Wittgenstein 1953; Vygotsky 1962; Bernstein 1971; Bateson 1972; Halliday 1975). Her concepts of reality, her workaday knowledge of the world, her sense of the normal are all created as the child re-creates her mother tongue with those who form her "meaning group" (Halliday 1975; 1979b: 180). These important aspects of first language development have dropped out of sight because of a disproportionate emphasis on "untutored acquisition" and because of a narrow interpretation of what it means to learn a mother tongue. If, however, the first language development is thought of as "learning how to mean" (Halliday 1975), then the process of learning language cannot be dissociated from learning *through* language. We argued (in the section titled "Functionalism: the social theoretical basis of language") that language construes speakers' sense of their social universe; this implies that as the structure of language is internalised, the knowledge of the world is also internalised. Both internalisations share an important characteristic: Both are *unanalysed.* So the world and the language both appear entirely "natural": It is as difficult to question the represented world as it is to question the way one's first language represents this world. Both are aspects of a subject's *primary socialization.* We would draw attention to an important consequence that follows from these observations: The contexts of learning a first language are typically supportive in the sense that there is no other "natural" reality, and the infant identifies with the speakers whose language she is now re-creating for herself (Halliday 1975; Newson 1978; Painter 1984; Oldenburg 1986). How does this compare with the learning of another tongue?

Taking the wider social contexts and their implications for the learner into account, the *first language* appears to be a language for the creation of self in society; it creates the learner's primary world of reference for understanding reality. The extreme opposing case to this is a foreign language. A *foreign language* is foreign to the interests of the learner-speaker; it does not impinge directly on the daily living of life. This is not to say that a foreign language would be necessarily irrelevant to either the community's wider politico-economic interests or to the learner-speaker's personal advancement, simply that the processes in which the learner needs to engage in everyday living *need not call* for the use of a foreign language. There is, of course, a third, intermediate case, in which a language other than the first is used to construe at least some crucial processes of the social context, such that the processes necessarily impinge on the daily living of life for all subjects in the community, irrespective of what first language they might have learnt. Here, certain politico-economic activities which are essential to the survival of the community are symbolically construed and organised by using another tongue. We suggest that this other tongue in question holds the status of a *second language.* By characterising the first language as the creator of self and reality, we are not implying that the second language is passive or irrelevant in the learners' definition of self or their construction of reality. On the contrary, our account suggests that it must have these uses; to participate in the critical social processes for the maintenance of a full social life, the second language speaker requires a systematic use of two (or more) distinct language systems, which is tantamount to saying that part of the second language learner's universe is created by the second language. But these processes are not criterial to the *primary socialisation* of the speaker. Typically, the knowledge created in the process of learning a second language is *uncommonsense knowledge* – it is knowledge which does not have a "natural", "self-evident" character, forming part of the process of *secondary socialisation*. It is also necessary to point out that, as the terms primary and secondary socialisation imply, the creation and definition of self is a continuing process which covers a relatively longer period of life than is popularly imagined; similarly, first language development extends over a longer period of the child's life than formalist accounts of first language acquisition might lead one to believe. So, depending on changes in the speaker's social context, one and the same language may, within certain limits, have a different status at different times.

In defining the second language thus, we do not wish to reject out of hand the popular view that the learning of other languages apart from the mother tongue is a positive asset as a form of knowledge. But it would be politically naive to pretend that for a migrant in Australia the learning of an aboriginal language is just as positive an asset as the learning of Australian English! Second languages are not learned simply for love of knowledge (Tollefson 1991), even though it may be ideologically prudent to persist in this view. In fact, by its very nature, a second language is an instrument of power, because it has jurisdiction over some part of the learner-speaker's social context, and because access to a second language is seldom a natural consequence of simply living in a community. Stern appears to recognise the political power of a second language when he suggests (1983: 16) that a second language is a non-mother tongue with an "official status or a recognised function". Because of the official status and function of the second language, its learners do not *really* have a "free choice": To function as reasonably effective members of the community they *must* learn this language. We can, if we wish, describe the learner's refusal or agreement to learn a second language as an act of free consent, but, as Tollefson (1991: 11) points out, the desire to engage in this activity is described more accurately as "manufactured consent", and the forces which "manufacture" this consent are also the ones that diminish the possibility of abstaining. It is not surprising that typically the development of a second language has to be assisted by institutional management: A large part of the dominion of applied linguistics is founded on this need for the institutional management of ESL. Our discussion suggests that ESL pedagogy cannot afford to ignore these considerations, since they must play some part in shaping the learner's motivation.

This socially based definition of second language allows us to probe more deeply into what ESL might mean in different social contexts. The more specific "meaning" of ESL as a social activity is likely to differ from one context of culture to another, since this meaning is itself defined by the relation of ESL to other activities in the cultural system. To elaborate this point, let us examine two specific cultural contexts for ESL. First, there is ESL for the colonised – for example, the India of the first half of this century – and second, there is ESL for the migrant – for example, Australia in the second half of this century. Referring to these as CESL (colonised learning ESL) and MESL (migrants learning ESL), respectively, we will attempt to highlight some of the ways in which these two cases of ESL will differ systematically from each other because colonisation and migration "create" different contexts of culture for the learners. We are not implying that CESL and MESL will each take the same form wherever they occur. The forms would respond to other elements in the wider context, but one thing is certain: A consideration of the wider cultural context will have repercussions on nearly every aspect of the ESL pedagogic situation.

In colonised India, English was the instrument of power: All functions of the state, except the very lowest, and therefore only the local ones, were typically carried out in the language of the ruling community. Superficially, the situation for the migrant in Australia seems to be the same, but there are important differences. It is true that in India English had a hold on the production and distribution of material wealth, and so in time it also encroached on the intellectual capital of the country, making certain forms of knowledge, reasoning, and thinking obsolete; nonetheless, there still remained significant social processes to which English stayed foreign in India. With the migrant in Australia, the hold of English is supreme, and typically all except the most intimate processes of human social relations require the use of English. Where the migrant family has young children, the "appropriate social adjustment" of these young persons to their new country can impinge even on this intimate process within the family. There is a significant difference between CESL and MESL in this respect: Colonisation – unless it is highly repressive, such as that of the Australian Aborigines – does not threaten the validity or the possibility of retaining one's sense of the normal. Migration, by definition, is an abandonment of the normal for the strange. And the more different the original culture of the migrant is from that of the adopted community, the truer this observation is. Thus the migrant in Australia, particularly if he is from the so-called third world, is in a situation where most things do not readily "make sense", are not self-evidently so. The learning of a non-native tongue is one among these many strange experiences. From this point of view, the significant difference between monolinguals such as the majority of English-speaking Australians and the second language speakers in Australia is that in the case of the latter, the social universe is cleaved into two, revealing that neither is necessarily ordained by nature. For the monolingual, the universe tends to retain its self-evident naturalness, and, for reasons we have already indicated, virtually the same is true for the colonised Indian, particularly at the early stages: In the CESL context, ESL itself is integrated into the scheme of things as a part of the same wider context, gaining a degree of normalcy by contact with the indigenous social processes. ESL was simply one of those peculiar things one did in places of learning. So, compared with the CESL situation of the Indian, the MESL situation is one of a much wider destabilisation:

Here, ESL is part of the story of encountering and trying to make sense of the strange.

But how does this impinge on ESL pedagogic activities as such? We suggest two ways in which this may happen: first, through the psychological consequences for the learner, and second, through implications for what ESL teaching is to achieve. Taking the first, both MESL and CESL situations are in striking contrast to the situation in first language development, where the environment is typically supportive, especially within the learner's *meaning group;* the world being construed by the language system is as normal as the language itself, and neither is challenged by alternative conceptions. If an intelligible world creates a supportive environment, which in turn acts as an important positive force in successful engagement in social activities, then obviously the absence of the sense of normalcy in MESL learning contexts must have some negative consequences; at the least, it would create stress of the type that the colonised Indians would not have become aware of until they arrived in the U.K. for higher education. Applied linguistics has shown little interest in factors of this kind, which must affect the quality of the learner's engagement with the learning tasks. This is not because it is unconcerned with the cognitive aspects of learning: Applied linguistics does engage with concepts such as "developmental stages", "reading readiness", "learning sequence", and so on, which appear to involve consideration of cognition. However, in the theory underlying these concepts, cognition, intelligence and ability to learn are thought of as properties of individuals which are entirely biological, having no social basis. And so, instead of attempting to understand how, because of factors of the kind we have discussed, the MESL learner's social environment might impinge on the success of ESL teaching, applied linguistics has concentrated on "ensuring" that the teaching materials are right, that the methodology of teaching is perfect, and that ever more sensitive instruments for evaluating language proficiency are invented, as if these were the only and all-important considerations worthy of attention. Naturally, we are not suggesting that these considerations are irrelevant, or even less important; we are arguing simply that this unconcern with the learner's social environment as a factor relevant to second language learning leaves something to be desired.

The second important reason for attempting to understand the different contexts of ESL is quite obviously its relevance to the goals of ESL teaching. This has to be based on some understanding of what the learners might be expected to achieve by using their second language. A long tradition in applied linguistics has advocated the conscious modelling of "second language acquisition" on the first. How do the two compare when the wider social context is considered? We agree with Rutherford (1987: 5) that a first language is not learnt through "acquiring" "accumulated entities" one by one as isolated units of linguistic form. It is quite obvious that the first language learner learns her mother tongue in using it: The process of learning how to mean is also the process of knowing who says what to whom and when. If the second language learner is to use his language effectively, then as an important part of his language learning he too needs to know what to "say" to whom and when. Since the notion of *register/genre* is critical in *all* language learning, it is important to understand the genesis of registers/genre learning. The first language learner's initial familiarity with (parts of) the register repertoire of her community is a natural outcome of her participation in certain social activities. In this respect, the colonised Indian's situation is not very different from the first language learner's. In the CESL context, so long as English was being used to construe essentially indigenous contexts, the world was in its proper place; the social situations made sense; the registers, particularly of everyday contact, were familiar – as they should be in one's own culture. This is in fact what underlies the impetus for the Indianization of English (Kachru 1983). Using ESL in his own culture, the Indian learner kept using his second language to construe the culturally legitimised contexts for meaning. Under the contextual pressures that impinged on the CESL learner's language use, the system of English brought in by the rulers was *resemanticised:* English English evolved into Indian English. This is not how things are in the case of the migrant. Depending upon where he comes from, what might be a social situation of one sort for the MESL learner could well be a social situation of another kind for the native English-speaking Australian; the MESL learner's participation in even everyday social processes in and by the use of English could become problematic. The cultural confrontation that the Indian learner was able to at least postpone, if not altogether avoid, is thrust upon the migrant from the very start. This mismatch between conceptions of how things are done in the two cultures is an important factor in cultural stereotyping: The differences are interpreted as aggression, pomposity, verbosity, lack of politeness, intelligence, and so on. This highlights yet again the problematic nature of the migrant's position in the adopted country, and brings to attention a practical issue in MESL pedagogy: The desirable goal for the MESL social context demands a "genre-based" language pedagogy (for discussions of genre-based pedagogy in the SF framework, see Jones et al. 1989; Martin 1989; Rothery 1989; Christie 1992). To adjust in the adopted culture, to learn to be effective with its language, the MESL learner *needs* to feel comfortable with the adopted community's register repertoire almost from day one. This need leads us to consider another issue.

The question of model(s) is relevant to all language teaching and learning, but both "which model" and "how this model is to be accessed" are particularly crucial questions in a second language teaching learning context. And it is important to keep in mind both kinds of teaching and learning – that which is institutionally organised, and that to which we referred as the "unselfconscious instructions of life situations". The models for the two are not necessarily the same; compare, for example, the "official" pedagogic model of English in Singapore with the "actual" model(s) from everyday life situations. Interesting differences between CESL and MESL emerge when we consider them from this point of view. The colonised Indian lived and acted in a community comprised largely of non-native speakers of English. Whatever the "official" model, the "actual" model of English accessible to the majority was one "created" within India. The position for the migrant in Australia is again different: Despite the fact that a large proportion of Australians are native speakers of some language other than English, it is Australian English that is overwhelmingly the language of daily contact, particularly outside the home and outside "ethnic" community contexts. So the model to which the MESL learner is more often "exposed" is an "authentic" model, perhaps much closer to the "official" pedagogic one; this was neither true of the colonised Indian nor of the present-day Singaporean. But there is another aspect to be considered: A passive "exposure" to language may be more relevant to the learning of phonological patterns than it would be for learning the patterns of wording and meaning. For the latter, active participation in social processes is necessary. This follows from our claim that a first language is learnt through active participation in social processes. It is salutary to ask: What are the social processes in which a MESL learner will "naturally" participate in Australia? Clearly, the answer to this depends on the politico-economic "meaning" of one's migrant status.

In this section, we have probed the nature of second language teaching and learning in relation to its wider social context. We have argued that the "value" of ESL is not absolute; it must differ by reference to the other terms in the cultural system. A comparison of CESL and MESL suggests that, given the typical politico-economic "meaning" of migration, MESL contexts are likely to be more stressful, both in the degree of destabilisation which follows from "choosing" to abandon the "normal" in favour of the "strange", and in the demands on the learner *if* the learner is to act as a "full" citizen. We have suggested that the stress to which migrant learners are exposed must bear some relevance to their learning activities. Conventionally, such concerns have been "defined out" of the discipline of applied linguistics not because *objectively* they are irrelevant but because our ideology makes them appear irrelevant. The goals and practices of ESL are predicated by the demands made on the learner. We have claimed that as with the first language, the learning of a second language too is best interpreted as learning the ability to exchange meanings in social contexts, which, given the goals of ESL, suggests genre-based pedagogy as crucially relevant. Obvious as this conclusion may be, its implications for applied linguistics need to be spelt out. A pedagogy that calls for an understanding of what is meant by register and genre must take the social basis of language seriously. It could not continue with a descriptive model in which the language system is "a-social", which somehow permits the possibility of language use in social contexts. So applied linguistics will need to theorise the relation between society, forms of talk, and the language system as a resource for bringing about those forms of talk in social contexts. This in turn means a reconceptualisation of the "subject matter" of ESL teaching and learning. From this point of view, success in attaining the pedagogic goals of ESL is not ensured *either* by just finding the "best" pedagogic grammar *or* by just focusing attention on meaning. It is not a choice between *either* grammar *or* meaning; *both* are equally necessary. The idea of linguistic meaning as divorced from linguistic form is problematic. In the final analysis, "a preoccupation with meaning and an effort to cope with communication" (Prabhu 1987: 17) cannot be dissociated from how anyone knows what meanings a speaker is preoccupied with, and what it is that permits the interactants to cope with communication. If linguistic form is not just a set of labels which *name* pre-existing elements of reality; if, instead, it is what *creates* our representation of reality, then "preoccupation with meaning" logically implies a preoccupation with linguistic form seen in relation to its use in social contexts. In making these claims, we are not implying that linguistic form must necessarily be taught overtly. This is an issue which cannot be resolved once for all.

Finally, to return to the question of models for ESL: The aim of bringing about in the ESL classroom a preoccupation with meaning so as to assist the pupil in coping with communication necessarily requires the "creation" of conditions in the pedagogic context which simulate the "natural" environment for talk. Disregarding the difficulties in successful simulation, consider two other problems. First, since not *all* social occasions of talk can be simulated in the classroom, which ones should be selected, and why? Clearly, the ESL learner's place in the wider social context will be relevant in arriving at an answer to these questions. Second, the simulation of meaning exchange cannot be dissociated from encouraging the pupils to talk English the way that "people normally talk English". This raises the question of who the people are, and what is meant by "normal". The answers cannot be the same for all wider social contexts. The Task-Based Approach in CESL and MESL may have the same abstract aim of focusing on meaning, but in order to be effective teaching strategies, the tasks themselves will need to be different for the different ESL situations. The CESL contexts are contexts natural to the learner; the MESL contexts need not be. And that in turn leads us to ask:

What is likely to be a successful teaching strategy in the MESL context? Are there arguments for introducing contexts that are normal to the MESL learner's original culture rather than simulating those which are typical of the adopted one? In ESL, as in any pedagogic activity, the situation is highly complex. So, making absolute rules is fraught with difficulty, and the enunciation of absolute rules for classroom practices should be ruled out! It is in this spirit that we turn now to a brief discussion of grammar as a resource for meaning.

Grammar as meaningful choice in context

In this section we discuss the narrower question of lexicogrammatical description for ESL pedagogy. In a functional model the lexicogrammar is only one of the three perspectives necessary for describing language as a resource for meaning. Therefore it cannot be considered in isolation from the descriptions of context and meaning without causing distortion. The *ideational, textual* and *interpersonal* metafunctions serve to explain the internal organisation of social context, meaning and lexicogrammar. The contextual factors of *field, mode* and *tenor* are linked realisationally with the systemic organisation of meaning and form, as depicted in Figure 3. These facts are relevant if we recognise that the enterprise of teaching any language implies the need for a linguistic model which shows how the features of the social context articulate with meaning and form in language. The teacher's task is to sensitise students to the lexicogrammar as the resource for meaning, and meaning as the artefact of lexicogrammatical choice in social contexts. In order to be effective, a pedagogic grammar must break the bonds of "form" to reach out into concerns of meaning and social context on a systematic rather than an ad hoc basis. These observations suggest two related conclusions:

1. Teachers need to be sensitive to linguistic functionality as interpreted in this paper; they need to be able to relate saying to meaning and meaning to the perception and creation of social contexts.
2. Students' learning of any element is likely to be facilitated and made more effective if the same three foci are kept in view: the properties of a formal pattern – both paradigmatic and syntagmatic ones; the semantic value(s) of that formal pattern; the context(s) in which the choice of the pattern is possible.

Applied linguistics has certainly been concerned with context of situation, with meaning, and with form, but without making explicit the ways in which these three aspects of language description are inherently related and interdependent. This indifference to theorising the relations of context, meaning and form has led to an underestimation of the power of language as a meaning-making system. For example, examination of the contexts of situation in which MESL occurs is common in TESOL pedagogy, and it is not confined to the functionally oriented applied linguist. However, even though much has been written on the inappropriateness of Western pedagogy to Eastern or developing countries (for example, Sarwar, Shamim & Kazi 1985; Burnaby and Sun 1989; Tickoo 1990), the arguments in these critiques have tended to focus as much on the cultural contexts of learning as on the contexts of the language being taught. An examination of recent TESOL literature on methodology will reveal the reason why this critique is couched in terms of methodology rather than language content. Situational language methodology has tended to present basic structures in situations which were contrived to make propositional meanings clear without using translation; its activities had not called for social authenticity of language and were not based in the social context or the development of the text (see the description of situational language teaching in Richards and Rodgers 1986: 38). Some changes have occurred in this approach in the last twenty-five years, whose justification is to be found in the models of communicative competence, which include sociolinguistic, discourse, and strategic competencies (Canale and Swain 1980; Bachman 1990). While these advances have helped to counteract the limitations of the concept of linguistic competence, the models of language used in such approaches have not been functional in the sense in which the term has been used in this paper. As a result, teachers still lack explanations of how language actually functions in social context. In our view, this reduces the effectiveness of their teaching strategies, since too often communicative competence is reinterpreted as mere communicative fluency. The focus on communicative fluency has been encouraged to a certain extent by the argument that natural language acquisition finds its own routes without overt instruction or intervention from the teacher (see Dulay and Burt 1973, who ask "Should we teach children syntax?"; consider also the "natural approach" developed by Krashen and Terrell 1983). Not surprisingly, this has sometimes encouraged teachers to virtually ignore lexicogrammar in favour of trying to devise methods for encouraging fluency – a concept which remains ill-defined. By these steps, some teaching practices have come to diverge widely from the stated aim of the communicative method of teaching, according to which "a basic principle underlying all communicative approaches is that learners must learn not only to make grammatically correct, propositional statements about the experiential world, but must also develop the ability to use language to get things done" (Nunan 1988: 25).

Communicative language teaching has appealed to views of learning which emphasise the necessity for the learner to be actively involved in what she is learning. Task-based learning shares this impetus; and in the hands of a competent practitioner it can yield impressive results. However, tasks are often only a means of making communicative methodology more goal-centred; they do not intrinsically do anything to link language use systematically to its context. Notwithstanding the recommendation by Long and Crookes to develop pedagogic tasks which are "systematically related to real world tasks" (quoted in Nunan 1988: 86), task-based pedagogy tends to encourage the "assumption that the specific nature of the task and the content on which it is based are unimportant, [and] that, as long as learners are productively engaged in a task, they will be acquiring the target language" (Nunan 1988:85). Simply because pedagogy is task based, an understanding of language is not automatically created. In task-based pedagogy, it has not been considered necessary to theorise the concept of context as an essential part of a linguistic model; so the teacher might have very little idea of the significance of what went on during a particular activity, what was learned, how, and what might be done for its development. This is not calculated to facilitate teaching how to mean. As Palmer claimed (1917), an essential requirement for successful language teaching is for the teacher to know the nature of that which she is professing to teach; she should be able to understand and explain in viable terms, at least to herself, what is going on, linguistically speaking, at any one moment in her classroom. This is an exacting requirement but entirely realistic in terms of pedagogic needs. Whether or not lexicogrammar should be taught overtly is still an open issue. What is not an open issue is the need for the teacher to understand how language works – how linguistic form acts as a resource for meaning.

In Figure 4 we first provide a very small portion of the SF lexicogrammar as an illustration of what a functional description of form looks like. This will be followed by a general discussion of a functional grammar for language pedagogy. The fragment of lexicogrammar selected for presentation here is known as MODALITY, which pertains to the interpersonal metafunction. As pointed out in the section titled "Functionalism: the social theoretical basis of language", this is the metafunction of language for construing the speaker's intersubjectivity, whereby social relations are created, maintained, and, in time, changed. The environment, par excellence, for the workings of modality is the dialogic one. By construing the speaker's opinions and judgements, the lexicogrammar of modality can become one delicate indicator of interlocutor relationships. It is an aspect of language that could be particularly relevant to teaching workplace communication in the MESL contexts. Figure 4 represents the set of choices up to a particular degree of delicacy in the modality system of English.

Following the principles of linguistic functionality, the terms in the system in Figure 4 are realisationally related to the stratum of semantics

208

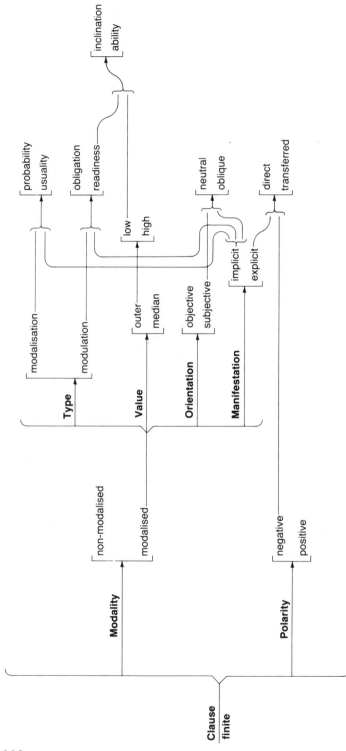

Figure 4   A simplified system network of modality in English.

on the one hand, and to that of phonology/graphology on the other. Each option in the network has a consequence for meaning, and configurations of these systemic choices together characterise a lexicogrammatical entity whose "output" is some phonological/graphological structure. We shall not be concerned with the details of the latter, but will focus on the grammatical choices and their semantic value. Although the English language has only a handful of *items* that are conventionally thought of as modal auxiliaries, the system in Figure 4 gives some idea of the finer distinctions of meaning construed by the configuration of the options in the system. Each such configuration identifies a lexicogrammatical *entity* whose meaning differs from all the others in some specific way. Part of the complexity of the grammar of modals lies in the *one-to-many* relation of what is popularly known as "a" modal auxiliary – for example, *may* (considered as a single phonological/graphological item) – to the diverse grammatical entities it expresses and to the multiple meanings which are "associated" with the item. Each modal item such as *must, can, may* does duty for the expression of related but distinct meanings, and each represents more than one lexicogrammatical entity. For example, consider the modal item *must* as used in two examples by Halliday: "she must be very careful" (where "must" is a modal with features *high obligation*) and "she must be very careless" (where "must" is a modal with features *high probability*). Obviously, it is not feasible within the scope of this paper to discuss the full set of options, their configurations, and realisations which yield well over a hundred fine distinctions of meaning. A fuller account of modality will be found in Halliday (1970b, 1982, 1985: 85–89, 332–41). Figure 4 was produced here to give an idea of the richness that is characteristic of *all languages*. This does not mean that exactly the same lexicogrammatical and/or semantic choices are universally present in all languages – simply that the potential for meaning and wording is much richer than is indicated by the set of orthographic or phonological items. We will abstract a set of contrasting features from Figure 4 to discuss in some detail; but first, a few introductory comments about modality.

Modality options construe "the area of meaning that lies between yes and no – the intermediate ground between positive and negative polarity" (Halliday 1985: 335). What this means in specific terms is explained by reference to message function, which also is an aspect of interpersonal meaning. In the environment of a PROPOSITION – that is, where the speaker is concerned with giving or demanding information (asserting or asking) – the area between "yes" and "no" specifies degrees of *probability* or *usuality* (e.g., as an example of probability, consider "must" in "Ask Mary. She must know the answer", where "must know" approximates "is sure to know", while in "Ask Mary. She'll know the answer", the group of words "to know" approximates "is likely to know"). The systemic options construing this area of probability-usuality are the set of choices in the modality system which is referred to as *modalisation,* or using the philosopher's term, these "are" EPISTEMIC modals. In the environment of a PROPOSAL – that is, where the speaker is giving or demanding goods and services (making offers or issuing orders) – the area between "yes" and "no" specifies degrees of *obligation* or *readiness* (e.g., as an example of obligation, consider "must" in "Mary must sign the register on arrival", where "must sign" approximates "is required to sign", while in "Mary can leave earlier on Friday", "can leave" approximates "is permitted to leave"). The systemic choices here are concerned with *modulation,* or in the terminology of the philosopher, they identify what is known as DEONTIC modals. This semantic characterisation of modality is based on the lexicogrammatical behaviour of the modal items in distinct formal environments. Figure 5 abstracts from Figure 4 the options that are relevant to *modulation* (as opposed to *modalisation*). The possible configurations of the options from Figure 5, together with their realisations, are listed in Table 1.

The entry condition for the modality choices is the formal unit FINITE CLAUSE. In the semantic characterisation of modality in the last paragraph, we have drawn attention to its relation to POLARITY. Figure 5 shows that modality and polarity are simultaneous systems. This means that the *positive* versus *negative* distinction applies to the options *modal* versus *non-modal.* We shall return to POLARITY later. We ignore *non-modal,* as in this discussion we are concerned only with some systemic options that depend on the option *modal.* Figure 5 shows that four simultaneous systems of choices depend on this option, all of which are labelled for ease of reference. The system of choices called TYPE displays the first choice between *modalisation* and *modulation,* which has already been introduced in the last paragraph. The option *modulation* itself leads to a choice between *obligation* or *readiness.* In Figure 5, the term *readiness* is followed by an asterisk; this is to show that the choices applicable to this term will not be discussed in this paper. In effect, the discussion is limited to the systemic options that can be co-selected with the option *obligation.*

Since *obligation* is a term in a system which is concurrent with three other systems of choices, the option *obligation* may combine freely with any of the choices of these systems. So to turn to VALUE, *obligation* may combine with the option *high* (e.g., "you **must** wait"), or *low* (e.g., "you **can** wait"), or *median* (e.g., "you **had better** wait"). The choices from VALUE construe the degree of obligation. The *median* value is somewhat advisory in meaning, and at this degree of detail in the description "had better" could be a near-paraphrase of "should". When the speaker's assessment of obligation is *high,* this imposes a strong requirement on the addressee; where this assessment is *low,* this leaves the addressee

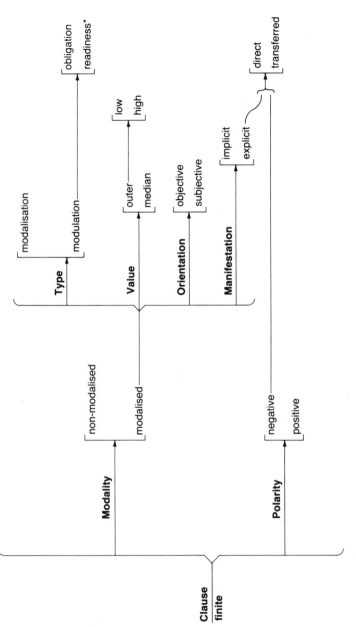

Figure 5   A fragment of modality system network in English.

211

TABLE I SOME SELECTED OPTIONS FROM FIGURE 5 AND THEIR LEXICOGRAMMATICAL EXPRESSIONS

| | Systemic options in type of modulation: obligation | | | Lexicogrammatical expressions | |
Polarity	Value	Orientation	Manifestation	Expression	Clausal example
1. positive	outer :high	subjective	implicit	must/have to	you *must* leave today
2. —ᵃ	:—	—	explicit	I insist (that you)	I insist (that) you leave today
3. —	:—	objective	implicit	required to	you're required to leave today
4. —	:—	—	explicit	it's necessary that	it's necessary that you leave today
5. —	:low	subjective	implicit	can/may	you can leave today
6. —	:—	—	explicit	I permit you to	I permit you to leave today
7. —	:—	objective	implicit	permitted to	you're permitted to leave today
8. —	:—	—	explicit	it's permissible	it's permissible (for you) to leave today
9. —	median	subjective	implicit	should/had better	you should leave today
10. —	—	—	explicit	I want you to	I want you to leave today
11. —	—	objective	implicit	supposed to	you're supposed to leave today
12. —	—	—	explicit	it's desirable	it's desirable (for you) to leave today
13. negative	outer :high	subjective	implicit	must not	you must not leave today
14. —	:—	—	explicit :direct[b]	I insist . . . don't	I insist (that) you don't leave today
15. —	:—	—	:transfrd	I don't permit	I don't permit you to leave today
16. —	:—	objective	implicit	required not to	you're required not to leave today
17. —	:—	—	explicit :direct	it's necessary . . . don't	it's necessary that you don't leave today
18. —	:—	—	:transfrd	it's not permissible	it's not permissible for you to leave today
19. —	:low	subjective	implicit	can not	you can (if you wish) *not* leave today
20. —	:—	—	explicit :direct	I permit you not to	I permit you not to leave today
21. —	:—	—	:transfrd	I don't insist	I don't insist that you leave today

No.					Expression	
22.	–	–	objective	implicit	permitted not to	*you're permitted not to leave today*
23.	–	–	–	explicit:direct	it's permissible . . . not	*it's permissible for you not to leave today*
24.	–	–	–	:transfrd	it's not necessary	*it's not necessary for you to leave today*
25.	–	median	subjective	implicit	should not	*you should not leave today*
26.	–	–	–	explicit:direct	I want you not to	*I want you not to leave today*
27.	–	–	–	:transfrd	I don't want you to	*I don't want you to leave today*
28.	–	–	objective	implicit	supposed not to	*you're supposed not to leave today*
29.	–	–	–	explicit:direct	it's desirable . . . not	*it's desirable for you not to leave today*
30.	–	–	–	:transfrd	it's not desirable	*it's not desirable for you to leave today*

[a] A dash in a column indicates the same option as the one in the line above in that same column. Thus in line 2, in the first column the dash means positive; in the second column, the dashes mean outer:high, and in the third, the dash stands for the option subjective. Only the differing choice, viz. explicit, is entered in the final column for systemic options. In the column labelled "Expression", at least in some cases, other items than simply those shown here can function as "expression" of the set of selected options in question. For example, in line 2, besides "I insist", there are other expressions such as "I demand, I require". These alternatives are not shown for lack of space.

[b] The networks in Figures 4 and 5 have been simplified in many ways. For example, access to the systemic choice between direct and transferred depends, in fact, only on the option negative, not on the conjunction of negative and explicit, as shown in the two networks. Constraining the availability of choice naturally reduces the "output". Without such simplifications (and omission), Table 1 would have been much longer. Note that examples of implicit are provided as if the options direct negative have been chosen. A transferred negative equivalent of 16 "you are required not to leave today" (direct) would be "you're not permitted to leave today" (transferred).

[c] Note how with transferred negative polarity, the values of high and low terms are reversed. For example, the equivalent of "I insist that you don't" (direct) is "I don't permit you to" (transferred): "Insisting that not x" is approximately the same as "not permitting that x". The regularity of this reversal of values can be derived from a comparison of the examples of direct and transferred in the context of median (examples 29–30; 26–27) vis-à-vis those in the context of high (examples 14–15; 17–18) and of low (examples 20–21; 23–24). No reversal occurs in the context of median, which is the fulcrum of the modality system.

discretion (cf. "you can wait", which means neither "you have to go" nor "you have to stay"). Conventionally, "you can wait" has been described as the granting of permission; allowing discretion is, clearly, an important aspect of the meaning of permission. Such discretion is not found with high obligation. This difference between low and high obligation explains why it is odd to say "you must wait, if you like" while "you can wait, if you like" is unremarkable. With high obligation the meaning is that of strong requirement, the source of which is external to the addressee; it is therefore contradictory to make the desired action conditional on the addressee's preference by adding "if you like". The configuration of VALUE and TYPE options refines the distinctions in the meanings of obligation.

The primary choices in the system labelled MANIFESTATION are *implicit* or *explicit*. When a speaker says "you must wait", it is clear that the assessment of the addressee's obligation is high, but it is not *stated* what the source of this obligation is, that is, where it derives from. However, the speaker might indicate the same high degree of obligation *and* also a source of the obligation. Thus compare "you must wait" (obligation; high; *implicit*) with "I insist (that) you wait" (obligation; high; *explicit*). In both cases the assessment of the obligation would be ascribed to the speaker; but it is only in the second case – "I insist that you wait" – that the responsibility for the imposition of the high obligation is clearly construed to lie with the speaker: The option *explicit* is realised by "I insist". As Table 1 shows, any VALUE of *obligation* can combine with any MANIFESTATION of *obligation*.

In choosing *obligation*, there also exists a choice in the ORIENTATION of the speaker's message; this may be *subjective* or *objective*. These options are significant for the construal of a meaning which is perhaps central to the interpersonal metafunction: This is the notion of responsibility. In the two examples "you must wait" and "I insist (that) you wait", the ORIENTATION was *subjective:* That is to say, whether it was explicitly stated or not, in both cases the speaker is construed as the source of the judgement. She may, however, choose to give an *objective* ORIENTATION: That is, she may give the judgement of obligation *an appearance of being imposed from outside*. This could be *explicit* as in "it is necessary for you to wait" (high; obligation; *explicit*; *objective*) or it may be left *implicit* as in "you are required to wait"; both signal that there is some external pressure. The choice of the option *objective* thus construes the meaning that the assessment of obligation has an "impersonal" character. Holding constant the options *obligation* and *high*, Table 2 gives the four possibilities from the intersection of the last two systems. Table 2 highlights an interesting fact. In most formal models, modality is something that only modal auxiliaries express. As the approach begins with words (or lexemes) themselves, so the question is:

TABLE 2. HIGH OBLIGATION

	Implicit manifestation	*Explicit manifestation*
Subjective	you must wait	I insist that you wait
Objective	you're required to wait	it is necessary that you wait

What classes do these words belong to, and what words do they combine with? In Table 2, the modal auxiliary occurs only in one clause, "you must wait"; in all other cases, the options of the system are realised by predication, either in the verb (e.g., *insist, required*) or in an adjective as complement to the verb *be* (e.g., *necessary*). A criticism often voiced against a grammar of this kind is that it is "not formal", implying that therefore it is less valid. But the criticism itself is valid only under a certain conception of what the "form of language" consists in. If form is interpreted as consisting only in the behaviour of items that can be identified purely on the phonological and/or morphological basis, clearly the description above is not formal: No similarity exists between modal auxiliaries and adjectives or predicates or projection of one clause by another. But if the form of language is thought of in more abstract terms, consisting in possible systems of relations, then other criteria become relevant (e.g., what relations a unit can enter into). It is interesting to note here that all four examples in Table 2 are subject to the same condition which applies to the clause with "must". We cannot sensically say: "you must wait, if you like"; nor can we say sensically "if you like" with any of the other three clauses in Table 2. The reason in *all* cases is the same: The clauses "have" in them the grammatical features *high obligation*. Figure 5 represents a grammar concerned with relations which do not *depend* on whether or not each of these is expressed by exactly the same "form" in the limited sense of the term "form".

Let us turn now to the system of choices called POLARITY. As a term in a system that ultimately depends on *modal,* the option *obligation* may combine with *positive* or *negative* POLARITY. In simple formal terms, this means nothing more than that the modal auxiliaries may or may not be followed by negation. But when negation is examined in relation to other systemic choices, an interesting difference emerges. *Negative* polarity functions differently in the environments of *high* as opposed to *median* VALUE of *modulation*. This is illustrated by the examples in Table 3: The table is divided into two blocks, **A** and **B,** and two columns. Block (**A**) exemplifies the option *subjective,* and block (**B**), *objective.* The left column presents examples of *high modulation*, the right, of *median.*

Note that in the left column, where *modulation* is *high,* the meaning of negative (1) differs significantly from that of negative (2). If the choice is *direct negative* – i.e., negative (2) in Table 3 – the *obligation*

TABLE 3. NEGATION AND MODAL VALUE

	High explicit modulation	*Median explicit modulation*
	(A)	
Positive	I insist that you wait	I want you to wait
Negative (1)	I don't insist that you wait	I don't want you to wait
Negative (2)	I insist that you don't wait	I want you not to wait
	(B)	
Positive	you're required to wait	you're supposed to wait
Negative (1)	you're not required to wait	you're not supposed to wait
Negative (2)	you're required not to wait	you're supposed not to wait

remains *high:* "I insist that you don't wait" and "you're required not to wait"; the requirement is negative, but strong. By contrast, if the choice is *transferred negative* – i.e., negative (1) in Table 3 – the *obligation* "switches" to *low:* "I don't insist that you wait" and "you're not required to wait" give discretion – you may or may not wait; you may use your personal discretion. A comparison with the right column shows that with the *median* option it makes no difference whether the *negative* is *transferred* – negative (1) in Table 3 – or *direct* – negative (2). Although Table 3 does not contain any examples of *modalisation*, exactly the same situation obtains there as well: With *high modalisation* the choice of *transferred negative* "switches" to *low;* with *median* it makes no difference.

The account provided here does not exhaust the details of the modality system, but it is sufficient to indicate how the grammar of a language is described in the SF model. It may be useful here to draw attention to three features of a functional grammar. First, when in a stratal model, the lexicogrammatical form of a language is represented as a set of systems of choices; these systems "look" in three different directions via the relation of realisation. They "look upward" to the levels of semantics and context to determine what meanings are construed by a certain (configuration of) option(s), and what contexts are construed by those. The systems "look downward" to the levels of phonology to determine how a (configuration of) grammatical choice(s) may be expressed as some phonological structure. Finally, the systems "look alongside" the same stratum to see how a (configuration of) choice(s) is actualised as a (syntagmatic) structure. In other words, the grammatical description is validated not by a single reference point – morphological and/or phonological – but by reference to multiple criteria including meaning, form, and phonology. Second, a grammar conceptualised as choice in some environment brings the various options in relation to each other in a systematic way. Thus the nature of "modals" is explained by seeing them in relation to choices of mood and polarity. Note that all three pertain to the same metafunction. Third, the concept of choice emphasises the idea of language as a resource – what speakers have the potential of doing. To link the system networks at the various strata by the underlying metafunctional principle is to ensure that the description of the system of language is not divorced from the description of how it can be used for the living of life. A model which sees the lexicogrammar as a means of creating meanings, and maintains simultaneous focus on meanings and wordings, can become a powerful tool for helping the student in coping with communication, and in making explicit the basis on which one might ascribe to a speaker a preoccupation with some meaning.

We have argued that learning language is learning how to mean and that *linguistic* meaning is meant by lexicogrammatical patterns. If this is so, then enabling the student to perceive what meanings are typically exchanged in what context would have to be an essential goal of any responsible pedagogy, but for reasons to which attention has been drawn, this need is even more pressing in the MESL context than elsewhere. Teaching the orthographically identified items of modal auxiliary or their morphological variants is not going to do much for a MESL learner in enabling her to see the finer shades of meaning differences that are presented in Table 3. However, for the true development of language proficiency, the MESL learner does need precisely these "shades of meaning"; this is the type of detailed semantico-grammatical insight which will enable her to be "on the wavelength" (see the discussion by Gibbons and Markwick-Smith 1992). Nowhere is the influence of tenor more apparent than in the expressions that involve modulation: Power is closely linked to the right to tell others what they must do and what they can do. The MESL learner will need to be alerted to the various ways in which different shades of meaning can be construed, and this will require going beyond modal auxiliaries as items whose identification is based on purely morphological and/or phonological criteria.

We claimed (in the section titled "Functionalism: The social theoretical basis of language") that wording and meanings do not just reflect the relationships in a pre-existing context of situation; they are actually involved in the on-going negotiation of the context as a step toward its validation. It follows that in an interactional situation, speakers can effect changes in the defining parameters of their on-going context; for example, by varying the choice of certain features from the system of modality, one might indicate a shift in power relation. To exercise some degree of control over one's interactive context without in the process alienating others is clearly important for successful negotiations. And an insight into how "modal auxiliaries" help or hinder these processes is clearly relevant. All this suggests that lexicogrammar is far too important to be ignored by teachers, and that functional explanations are clearly so necessary that they cannot be avoided. Whether the teaching of grammar should under all conditions and for all students remain unconscious – or covert – is a separate issue. We have argued that the ESL teaching context is not the same everywhere: The length of the program, the age of the learner, her needs, her cultural and educational background, and other such issues are important (see the discussion of individual differences in Long and Larsen-Freeman 1991: 153–219).

One source of difficulty the teacher may encounter in teaching modulation in the MESL context needs to be mentioned. Here, the grammar of modality could be "taught" at first as formulae in social contexts which can be put to immediate use. Establishing a firm context for the presentation of the meanings of modality will avoid the need to present overt explanations. However, as our presentation shows, the choices of modality express the speaker's attitude either to her interlocutor or to the propositional content of her message. This makes the use of such teaching strategies a little problematic, and in this respect modulation may be more problematic than other aspects of grammar. New linguistic items are frequently presented in ESL contexts in a text, so that students can first listen or read, and then learn. If the context of situation and the co-text are carefully chosen and appropriate explanations are given, students can be expected to understand the different meanings of the wordings. Beyond this presentation stage, students generally become involved in communicative activities or tasks which are devised to give them practice with the "target" structures or meanings. For example, a class might be given a moral or practical problem or game in which they have to devise possible courses of action and offer possible solutions within the "context" which the teacher has set up. Such a teaching situation is fine for assessing and correcting many of the students' linguistic practices, but the teacher often has real difficulty when it comes to the expression of modality. Difficulties with syntagm formation can be easily identified, but it may be impossible for the teacher to know whether, in choosing a particular form of expression, the student has got across her intended viewpoint. The solution of directing students to assume roles and telling them what their attitudes "must" be is not a happy one, if the teacher's aim is to promote an increased ability to express their own ideas, even though this may be a necessary stage on the route to autonomous expression.

An emphasis on receptive activities can assist in this interference with authenticity. Students could listen to dialogues and identify the relevant features of the context of situation; they could be asked to compare similar texts produced on different occasions where the language of the texts has construed field, mode, and tenor which are similar in some respects but different in others. Advanced students could be asked what choices of wording and meaning construe what aspects of the context; they could be asked to make changes to the lexicogrammar to correspond with certain specified changes in field, tenor and mode. At an advanced stage, when students' ability to mean is relatively developed, they could be introduced to choices from the system in such a way as to make them aware of the differences in meaning that correspond with differences in wording. Self-critique of produced material could be an alternative activity. However, one point that needs to be made clear is that we do not suggest using system networks themselves in the classroom for the direct presentation of points of lexicogrammar. The systems are a useful source of information for the teachers, and only at the most advanced levels might some selected meaning contrasts be discussed when learning *about* language might appear a useful activity. In the course of discussing the system network, we have pointed out that systems can be drawn to different degrees of delicacy, depending upon the detail of description required for the purpose in hand. For example, Figure 4 is more delicate than Figure 5. This means that teachers can choose to "read" a system network at different degrees of delicacy. For example, they could simply draw attention to the manner in which *modulation* ("you must be very careful") contrasts with *modalisation* ("you must be very careless"), without going into any of the other details discussed earlier, or they can choose to build in even finer details than have been presented here. This decision about how much to teach will be made not on the basis of what there is in the system of language but on what the learners need or what their proficiency level is.

Concluding remarks

This chapter has traversed a large area. Perhaps less than one-fourth of it would be popularly seen as "belonging" in a volume concerned with pedagogic grammars. So in the closing move of this discourse, it seems appropriate to say a few words about what place we imagine a chapter such as this to have in a volume such as this. Why talk about the social basis of linguistic theory, when the brief is to talk about pedagogical grammar? Perhaps we owe an explanation to our readers.

In choosing the design and content of our chapter, we deliberately set out to distance ourselves from certain views about the nature of human language, about what it means to "do grammar", and what the place of grammar is in language pedagogy. The central concern of this volume, if we are not mistaken, is with ways of doing grammar in the context of language pedagogy. It is commonly assumed that grammar is one area of language study that can be discussed in convenient isolation from everything else. And of course, in practical terms, we can pull out even a minute segment of grammar itself to speak about – as we ourselves have done with modality. But doing grammar brings with it a set of underlying assumptions about the nature of language, as it did in our description of modality. In some cases – for example, in our description here – these assumptions are clearly articulated; in others, they remain invisible. Certainly, every language "has" grammar, but the grammars that linguists do – what Halliday (1984) has referred to as *grammatics* – should not be confused with "the" grammar of some language. The grammar that scholars do – i.e., any instance of *grammatics* – is simply an attempt to represent someone's idea of what the grammar of the language being described is like. The excellence, authenticity, and so on, of the grammatics of a language cannot be determined by checking how well it corresponds to the grammar that inheres in that language, since this question cannot be answered with any greater validity than the question about which language corresponds best to the "real" universe. So a criterion for judging a scholar's grammar is by reference to the underlying principles that govern his or her representation of a language's grammar, and this cannot be separated from the scholar's views on the nature of language. When we are planning to "simply" use a grammar – say, for pedagogical purposes – we imagine that it is possible to "pull out" the grammatical description on its own; nothing else need be assumed. By the design and content of our chapter, we have implied that this is a misconception: A grammar is only as usable/useful as the view of language that underlies it. These views cannot be sealed off; they spill over when the grammar is put to use. This is one argument why grammars have to be seen as part of an overall framework. It seems unrealistic to imagine that the issue of pedagogical grammars can be discussed without relating the grammar to the theory of language description.

The second reason why we cannot talk about grammar in isolation arises from a consideration of the basis for our interest in it in this volume. The choice of a grammar that might be used for teaching someone "to function with the other tongue" can hardly be dissociated from what it is that a teacher needs in order to be able to "facilitate a learner's second language development". But the teacher's "needs" in teaching cannot be independent of the learner's "needs" in learning. If the choice of a pedagogic grammar is related to teachers' needs, then it is ultimately related to the place of second language learning within the society, since learners' needs do not arise in a vacuum. So when it comes to the choice of a pedagogic grammar, from this point of view we need to ask two sets of questions: (1) What sort of grammar is needed for learning a language? What does it mean to say that someone has learnt a language?; (2) Who is the second language learner? Why is the second language being learnt? Does grammar play any part in language learning/teaching? Does the grammar of a language play any part in the creation, perception, maintenance, and change of the speakers' social environment? Clearly, if any grammar is at all relevant, it has to be one which forms part of a theoretical framework that coherently and systematically spans this vast area from the nature of language to how language is related to its speakers' conceptions of social reality. Once again, grammar needs to be seen in relation to "non-grammar": The validity and value of a pedagogic grammar are not likely to be determined by examining the grammar alone.

In our paper we have traversed the area from social context to lexicogrammar. In doing this we are not implying that context, meaning, or form are new concepts for applied linguistics; applied linguistics has been familiar with these terms for as long as it has existed. For example, speaking broadly, there has been interest in the "language and culture" issue. But the accounts have lacked theoretical depth; "the connections between the language of a culture and the culture itself have . . . frequently been reduced to lexification of curious objects or behaviours, or the providing of inventories of appropriate phrases whose reasons for appropriateness, sources and constitutive sociologies have remained quite opaque" (Candlin 1989: 1). It is this lack of theorisation whereby context is treated as a thing apart – a scenario – within which speaking happens; speaking itself becomes a series of words and structures, and the role of lexicogrammar in the creation of meaning is attenuated. This leaves gaps between; and the gaps are filled by such notions as knowledge of the world, speakers' intentionality, beliefs, and cultural conventions, leaving us wondering how the knowledge of the world comes about, how cultures come into being, and how the speakers' private intentionalities, desires and beliefs attain intersubjective objectivity so that the conversational "other" is able to "read them off" from the words and structures and/or the context. Bringing the discussion down to a practical level, task-based approaches, situational pedagogy, the learner-centred approach all call for a theory of language description that models the close relation between context, meaning, and linguistic form. If context is defined by the meanings at risk in it, if form is seen as a resource for meaning, this permits a language-based understanding of which tasks, which situations, which texts are alike, which different in what way, and how they can be used profitably with what kind of learner.

The teaching and learning of language cannot be equated with simply acquiring control over items. The mechanical operation of "converting" this structure into that, of providing lexical equivalents, is, within reason, easy to teach; this teaching leads nowhere. Speaking meaningfully is not simply producing a structure or a set of words; it is using wording for meaning within a social context for the living of life. The choice of a pedagogic grammar has to engage with the issue of whether or not grammar is relevant to successful communication. If the answer is yes, this argues very strongly for a grammar that can be used to explain the nature of text – how and why a saying comes to mean what it does. Applied linguistics has bowed to the notion of social context, to the importance of culture, to the supremacy of discourse, to a recognition of the importance of learner's culture: These "fashions of speaking" have risen into prominence, one at a time, and then subsided, not because the problems associated with these concepts ceased to exist but because fashions in academia changed. Forever in search of its centre of gravity, applied linguistics has focused on whatever might be the new bright idea of the decade, forever failing to grasp the complexities inherent in its enterprises. As Stern points out, "language teaching has suffered from an overemphasis on single aspects, and . . . language teaching is multi-faceted. . . . the different facets should be consistent with each other" (1984: 11). The search for a pedagogic grammar is in the last resort a search for a consistent theory of language which will permit applied linguistics to address the complex issues.

References

Austin, J. L. 1962. *How to Do Things with Words,* ed. by J. O. Urmson and Marina Sbisa. Oxford: Oxford University Press.

Bachman, L. F. 1990. *Fundamental Considerations in Language Testing.* Oxford: Oxford University Press.

Bateson, G. 1972. *Steps to an Ecology of Mind.* New York: Ballantine.

Bernstein, Basil B. 1971. A sociolinguistic approach to socialization: with some reference to educability. In *Directions in Sociolinguistics: The Ethnography of Communication,* ed. by John J. Gumperz & Dell Hymes. New York: Holt, Rinehart & Winston.

Brown, R. 1973. *A First Language.* Cambridge: Harvard University Press.

Burnaby, B. & Y. Sun. 1989. Chinese teachers' view of Western language teaching: context informs paradigms. *TESOL Quarterly* 23(2): 219–38.

Canale, M. & M. Swain. 1980. Theoretical bases of communicative approaches to second language teaching and testing. *Applied Linguistics* 1(1): 1–47.

Candlin, C. N. 1989. Language, culture and curriculum. In *Language, Learning and Community,* ed. by C. N. Candlin & T. F. McNamara. Macquarie University: NCELTR.

1991. Introduction to *Planning Language, Planning Inequality: Language Policy in the Community* by James W. Tollefson. In *Language in Social Life Series,* ed. by C. N. Candlin. London: Longman.

Christie, Frances (ed.). 1992. *Literacy in Social Processes: Papers from the Inaugural Australian Systemic Linguistics Conference,* Deakin University, 1990. Darwin: Centre for Studies of Language in Education, Northern Territory University.

Davidse, Kristin. 1987. M. A. K. Halliday's Functional Grammar and the Prague School. In *Functionalism in Linguistics,* ed. by René Dirven and Vilem Fried. Amsterdam: John Benjamins.

Dirven, R. & V. Fried (eds.). 1987. *Functionalism in Linguistics: LLSEE 20.* Amsterdam: John Benjamins.

Doise, W. & G. Mugny. 1984. *The Social Development of the Intellect*. Oxford: Pergamon Press.

Donaldson, M. 1978. *Children's Minds*. Glasgow: Fontana/Collins.

Dulay, H. & M. Burt. 1973. Should we teach children syntax? *Language Learning* 24: 245–58.

van Ek, J. A. 1976. *The Threshold Level for Modern Language Learning in Schools*. London: Longman.

Fishman, J. A. 1972. *Language in Sociocultural Change*, selected and introduced by Anwar S. Dil. Stanford: Stanford University Press.

Frake, C. O. 1986. "Struck by speech": the Yakan concept of litigation. In *Directions in Sociolinguistics: The Ethnography of Communication*, ed. by J. J. Gumperz & D. Hymes. London: Basil Blackwell.

Fries, Peter H. 1983. On the status of theme in English: arguments from discourse. In *Micro and Macro Connexity of Texts: Papers in Textlinguistics*, vol. 45, ed. by Janos S. Petofi & Emel Sozer. Hamburg: Helmut Buske.

Gibbons, John & Mary Markwick-Smith. 1992. Exploring the use of a systemic semantic description. *IJAL*, vol. 2, no. 1: 36–50.

Gumperz, John J. 1971. *Language in Social Groups: Essays by John J. Gumperz*, ed. by Anwar S. Dil. Stanford: Stanford University Press.

Halliday M. A. K. 1970a. Language structure and language function. In *New Horizons in Linguistics*, ed. by John Lyons. Harmondsworth: Penguin.

1970b. Language structure and language function as seen from a consideration of modality and mood in English. *Foundations of Language* 6(3): 322–61.

1973. Towards a sociological semantics. In *Explorations in the Functions of Language*. London: Edward Arnold.

1974. *Language and Social Man*. School Council Programme in Linguistics and English Teaching: Papers, series 2, vol. 3. London: Longman.

1975. *Learning How to Mean: Explorations in the Development of Language*. London: Edward Arnold.

1976. *System and Function in Language*, ed. by Gunther Kress. Oxford: Oxford University Press.

1977. Text as semantic choice in social contexts. In *Grammars and Descriptions: RTT 1*, ed. by Teun A. van Dijk & Janos S. Petofi. Berlin: de Gruyter.

1979a. Modes of meaning and modes of expression: types of grammatical structure, and their determination by different semantic functions. In *Functions and Context in Linguistic Analysis: A Festschrift for William Haas*, ed. by D. J. Allerton, Edward Carney & David Holdcroft. Cambridge: Cambridge University Press.

1979b. One child's protolanguage. In *Before Speech: The Beginning of Interpersonal Communication*, ed. by M. Bullowa. Cambridge: Cambridge University Press.

1982. The de-automatization of grammar: from Priestley's "An Inspector Calls". In *Language Form and Linguistic Variation: Papers Dedicated to Angus McIntosh*, ed. by J. M. Anderson. Amsterdam: John Benjamins.

1984. On the ineffability of grammatical categories. In *The Tenth LACUS Forum 1983*, ed. by Allan Manning, Pierre Martin, & Kim McCalla. Columbia, S.C.: Hornbeam Press, 3–18.

1985. *Introduction to Functional Grammar*. London: Edward Arnold.

1991. The notion of context in language education. In *Language Education:*

Interaction & Development. Proceedings of the International Conference, Vietnam 1991, ed. by Thao Le & Mike McCausland. Launceston: University of Tasmania.

1992. How do you mean? In *Recent Advances in Systemic Linguistics*, ed. by Martin Davis & Louise Ravelli. London: Frances Pinter.

in press. The act of meaning. In *Language, Communication, and Social Meaning: Georgetown University Round Table on Language and Linguistics*, ed. by James E. Alatis. Washington, D.C.: Georgetown University Press.

Halliday, M. A. K. & Ruqaiya Hasan. 1989. *Language, Context, and Text: Aspects of Language in a Social-Semiotic Perspective.* London: Oxford University Press.

Halliday, M. A. K., A. McIntosh & P. Strevens. 1964. *The Linguistic Sciences and Language Teaching.* London: Longman.

Hasan, Ruqaiya. 1973. Code, register, and social dialect. In *Class, Codes, and Control*, vol. 2: *Applied Studies Towards a Sociology of Language*, ed. by Basil Bernstein. London: Routledge & Kegan Paul.

1989. Semantic variation and sociolinguistics. *Australian Journal of Linguistics* 9(2): 221–75.

1991. Questions as a mode of learning in everyday dialogue. In *Language Education: Interaction & Development. Proceedings of the International Conference, Vietnam 1991*, ed. by Thao Le & Mike McCausland. Launceston: University of Tasmania.

1992. Meaning in sociolinguistic theory. In *Sociolinguistics Today: International Perspectives*, ed. by Kingsley Bolton and Helen Kwok. London: Routledge.

in press. The conception of context in text. In *Discourse and Meaning in Society*, ed. by Peter Fries and Michael Gregory. Norwood, N.J.: Ablex.

Hasan, Ruqaiya & Carmel Cloran. 1990. A sociolinguistic interpretation of mother child talk. In *Learning, Keeping and Using Language: Selected Papers from the 8th World Congress of Applied Linguistics*, vol. 1, ed. by M. A. K. Halliday, John Gibbons & Howard Nicholas. Amsterdam: John Benjamins.

Hymes, Dell H. 1968. The ethnography of speaking. In *Readings in the Sociology of Language*, ed. by Joshua A Fishman. The Hague: Mouton.

1986. Models of the interaction of language and social life. In *Directions in Sociolinguistics: The Ethnography of Communication*, ed. by John J. Gumperz & Dell Hymes. London: Blackwell (first edition: 1972, New York: Holt, Rinehart & Winston).

Jones, J., S. Gollin, H. Drury & D. Economou. 1989. Systemic functional linguistics and its application to the TESOL curriculum. In *Language Development: Learning Language, Learning Culture. Meaning and Choice in Language: Studies for Michael Halliday*, ed. by Ruqaiya Hasan & J. R. Martin. Norwood, N.J: Ablex.

Kachru, Braj B. 1983. *The Indianization of English: The English Language in India.* Delhi: Oxford University Press.

Krashen, S. D. 1987. *Principles and Practice in Second Language Acquisition.* Englewood Cliffs, N.J.: Prentice-Hall International.

Krashen, S. D. & T. D. Terrell. 1983. *The Natural Approach: Language Acquisition in the Classroom.* Oxford: Pergamon Press.

Leech, Geoffrey N. 1983. *Principles of Pragmatics.* London: Longman.

Long, M. H. & D. Larsen-Freeman. 1991. *An Introduction to the Second Language Acquisition Research.* London: Longman.

Martin, J. R. 1984. Functional components in a grammar: a review of deployable recognition criteria. *Nottingham Linguistic Circular* 13: 35–70. Nottingham University: Department of English Studies.

1989. *Factual Writing: Exploring and Challenging Social Reality.* London: Oxford University Press.

1991. Intrinsic functionality: implications for contextual theory. *Social Semiotic,* vol. 1, no. 1: 99–162.

1992. *English Text: System and Structure.* Amsterdam: John Benjamins.

Matthiessen, Christian. 1990. *Metafunctional Complementarity and Resonance in Syntagmatic Organization.* Sydney University: Department of Linguistics.

1992. Interpreting the textual metafunction. In *Recent Advances in Systemic Linguistics,* ed. by Martin Davis & Louise Ravelli. London: Frances Pinter.

Mead, George Herbert. 1934. *Mind, Self, and Society,* ed. by C. W. Morris. Chicago: University of Chicago Press.

Newson, J. 1978. Dialogue and development. In *Action, Gesture, and Symbol: The Emergence of Language,* ed. by A. Lock. New York: Academic Press.

Nunan, D. 1988. *The Learner-Centred Curriculum.* Cambridge: Cambridge University Press.

Oldenburg, Jane. 1986. The transitional stage of a second child – 18 months to 2 years. *Australian Review of Applied Linguistics* 9(1): 123–35.

Painter, Clare. 1984. *Into the Mother Tongue: A Case Study in Early Language Development.* London: Frances Pinter.

Palmer, Harold E. 1917. *The Scientific Study and Teaching of Languages.* George G. Harrap & Co. (republished 1968. Vol. 18 in series Language and Language Learning: The Scientific Study and Teaching of Languages. David Harper [series ed]. London: Oxford University Press).

Phillipson, Robert. 1990. *English Language Teaching and Imperialism.* Tronninge: Transcultura.

Piaget, Jean. 1960. *Language and Thought of the Child.* London: Routledge & Kegan Paul.

1973. *The Child's Conception of the World.* Translated by Joan and Andrew Tomlinson. London: Paladin.

Prabhu, N. S. 1987. *Second Language Pedagogy.* Oxford: Oxford University Press.

Richards, J. C. & T. S. Rodgers. 1986. *Approaches and Methods in Language Teaching.* Cambridge: Cambridge University Press.

Rothery, Joan. 1989. Learning about language. In *Language Development: Learning Language, Learning Culture. Meaning and Choice in Language: Studies for Michael Halliday,* ed. by R. Hasan & J. R. Martin. Norwood, N.J.: Ablex.

Rutherford, William E. 1987. *Second Language Grammar: Learning and Teaching.* London: Longman.

Sarwar, Z., F. Shamim & A. M. Kazi. 1985. *A Think-Out on Oxford English for Colleges.* Karachi: Kifayat Academy Educational Publishers.

Stern, H. H. 1983. *Fundamental Concepts of Language Teaching.* Oxford: Oxford University Press.

1984. Review and discussion. In *General English Syllabus Design: Curriculum and Syllabus for the General English Classroom.* Oxford: Pergamon.

Tickoo, M. L. 1990. Towards an alternative curriculum for acquisition-poor environments. In *Learning, Keeping and Using Language: Selected Papers from the 8th World Congress of Applied Linguistics,* vol. 1, ed. by M. A. K. Halliday, John Gibbons & Howard Nicholas. Amsterdam: John Benjamins.

Tollefson, James W. 1991. Planning language, planning inequality: language policy in the community. In *Language in Social Life Series,* ed. by C. N. Candlin. London: Longman.

Vygotsky, Lev Semenovich. 1962. *Thought and Language,* translated by Eugenia Hanfmann and Gertrude Vakar. Cambridge, Mass.: MIT Press.

Wilkins, D. A. 1976. *Notional Syllabuses.* Oxford: Oxford University Press.

Wittgenstein, L. 1953. *Philosophical Investigations,* translated by G. E. M. Anscombe. Oxford: Blackwell.

SECTION III:
PUTTING GRAMMAR TO WORK

9 The effect of systematic instruction on learning the English article system

Peter Master

The English article system consists of four items: *a, an* (a **phonetic variant**), *the,* and Ø (the **zero article**).[1] The simplicity of the words that make up the system masks the complexity of the rules for nativelike usage. For this reason, several researchers consider the article system to be unlearnable and therefore unteachable, that it can only be acquired through natural exposure to the language (e.g., Dulay, Burt, and Krashen 1982). For many language learners, especially those at the intermediate level and beyond, this is an unacceptable explanation. They usually have only a limited amount of time to spend in language courses, and they naturally expect to learn the language faster than they would by mere exposure. The present study describes a systematic program of instruction for teaching the article system to learners at this level and measures the effect of this program in a controlled quasi-experimental design.

In the early 1980s, **communicative competence** became the primary object of second language instruction, while grammatical instruction fell into disfavor because it was thought to influence the learner's **monitor,** or linguistic editor, but not to aid acquisition (Krashen 1981). The belief was that **comprehensible** (spoken) **input** provided by the instructor in a low-risk environment was sufficient for the learner to acquire grammatical competence. The pedagogical framework that embodies this belief is called the **Natural Approach** (Krashen and Terrell 1983) because it is meant to parallel first language acquisition. Even though Krashen's theories have since been challenged, many aspects of the Natural Approach are appropriate for the beginning levels of language instruction.

Unfortunately, aspects of syntax that contribute little to communicative effectiveness, such as the articles *a* and *the,* which are almost always unstressed, are very difficult to hear. They are also accorded little impor-

I would like to thank Marianne Celce-Murcia for early comments, Grant Henning and Brian Lynch for their assistance in the statistical aspects of this study, and Terry Odlin, Shigeko Okamoto, and Melinda Johnson for comments on the final draft.

1 Although many researchers include unstressed *some* (sometimes denoted *s'm*) as a member of the article system (e.g., McEldowney 1977; Celce-Murcia and Larsen-Freeman 1983), I have restricted the members to these four so as not to have to consider other mutually exclusive members of the class of central determiners.

tance in the learner's spoken competence because communication is rarely hindered by their misuse. In fact, a person may communicate effectively in spoken English even when article use is entirely erroneous. For example, a waitress in a Los Angeles cafeteria was observed to instruct the cook to heat the piece of apple pie she handed him with the words "Make a pie hot!" The cook immediately understood what was required even though, if he had not seen the pie, he could have understood her to mean that she needed another piece of pie to be heated up (She should have said, "Make *the* pie hot."). The result is that the articles are often either ignored or used in an entirely random fashion.

In fact, accurate article use does not really become important until the learner begins to write. Since a writer is normally separated from the reader in space and time, the writer cannot depend on extralinguistic cues such as pointing and gesturing to aid the reader. For this reason, the writer is forced to be precise with article use. The difficulty of attaining such precision is well known to ESL students, whose corrected compositions are commonly strewn with crossed-out *the*'s and missing *a*'s, and they naturally ask for and are entitled to an explanation that will help them to avoid these errors. This would seem to be sufficient justification for some kind of grammatical instruction. The question is whether instruction will really help the learner and, if so, what form that instruction should take.

The question of the efficacy of grammatical instruction (i.e., focus on form) has since received increasing attention. One reason for this is evidence that instruction whose only goal is communicative competence with no focus on form, such as the Natural Approach, may be insufficient for acquisition. Schmidt (1983) showed that uninstructed learners can become communicatively effective without developing high levels of linguistic accuracy, while Higgs and Clifford (1982) suggested that grammarless instruction could lead to **fossilization**. This directly challenged Krashen and Terrell's (1983) claim that comprehensible input in a low-risk environment was a sufficient condition for language acquisition.

Researchers also began to investigate the specific effect of form-focused instruction. Hulstijn and Hulstijn (1984) found in a study of the learning of two Dutch word-order rules that "even L2 learners with only an implicit knowledge of the rules were able to boost the correctness of their performance significantly when asked to pay attention to form" (p. 41). Spada (1986) found that form-focused instruction was a more powerful predictor of success on grammar and writing tests than contact with native speakers, but that contact in conjunction with instruction produced better results than either contact or instruction alone. In formulating his **"teachability hypothesis,"** Pienemann (1988) studied the effect of instruction on German word-order rules and provided preliminary evidence that any effort to alter the process (e.g., the order) of natural acquisition would not succeed. Nevertheless, he noted that "instruction can improve acquisition with respect to the speed of acquisition, the frequency of rule application, and the different contexts in which the rule has to be applied, *if* the interlanguage development fulfills the requirements [i.e., if the learner is ready] for such an influence" (p. 99). In summarizing the results of several studies, Ellis (1990) and Larsen-Freeman and Long (1991) found that, in general, Pienemann's findings were supported. Instructed second language acquisition does not seem to be able to significantly alter acquisition sequences, but it does appear to increase the rate at which learners acquire the language.

There is comparatively little research concerning the effect of instruction in the English article system. Sajavaara (cited in Larsen-Freeman and Long 1991) found "a disturbed difficulty order in the **elicited speech** of secondary-school Finnish EFL students, articles being notably lower" (p. 305). This may have been due to the fact that, like Japanese, Polish, Farsi, and many other languages, Finnish has a different mechanism for expressing the functions of the English articles. However, it does not explain why studies of Japanese subjects (e.g., Makino 1979) found no such disturbed order.

Pica (1983, 1985) found strong correlations in difficulty order for native-Spanish-speaking subjects in naturalistic, instructed, and mixed settings (naturalistic plus instructed), leading her to conclude that instruction appeared to trigger the oversuppliance of grammatical morphology and the inhibition of ungrammatical, **pidgin**-like constructions, though she cautioned against drawing conclusions about the rate of acquisition from this data. She found that the acquisition of the article *a*, unlike the plural *-s* and progressive *-ing* morphemes, appeared not to be influenced by instruction. She attributed this to the relative difficulty of the structure, which depends on a variety of linguistic and **extralinguistic factors** (e.g., first or **subsequent mention** in the discourse, degree of familiarity, etc.) and suggested that, for this reason, teaching the article *a* might be excluded from classroom instruction so that "increased attention can be given to items more responsive to classroom presentation and practice" (1985: 214). However, she noted that the instruction of *a* "had not been sequenced or organized according to prefabricated constructions or grammatical contexts, but instead through presentation of rules for **first mention** and **specificity**" (p. 218), suggesting that a more systematic presentation might have produced different results.

There is other evidence that the individual articles have different patterns of acquisition. Huebner (1983) found that his uninstructed Hmong subject overused and overgeneralized with the article *the;* Master (1987) found a similar result with speakers of languages with no article system (e.g., Japanese), but not with speakers of languages that have article systems (e.g., German), whereas neither group showed overgeneralization or overuse with *a*. Furthermore, certain functions of the article system appeared to be more readily acquired than others. For example, *the* with subsequent mention nouns (e.g., John bought a book yesterday. *The* book cost $20.) attained higher accuracy levels than *the* with **ranking adjectives** (e.g., *the largest, the next*). ∅ with plural **count nouns** (e.g., ∅ *books*) attained higher accuracy levels than ∅ with **noncount nouns** (e.g., ∅ *paint*). In other words, not only do the individual articles appear to be acquired at different stages, but each has different levels of difficulty.

Ellis (1990) and Larsen-Freeman and Long (1991) have assembled a convincing body of evidence supporting the efficacy of grammatical instruction in general. Although there are not many studies concerning the effect of article instruction per se, an awareness of forms that contribute little to communicative effectiveness may be necessary to make sure that learners, especially adults, acquire them (Zobl 1985). When formal instruction serves primarily to bring such forms to awareness, rather than to provide an immediate means of acquiring a specific element of syntax, it "speeds up learning *in the long term* and helps to prevent the kind of grammatical fossilization found in naturalistic adult learners" (Ellis 1990: 169).

The purpose of the present study is to investigate whether the teaching of multiple aspects of the English article system by means of systematic instruction can accelerate learning as demonstrated by the ability to make grammatical choices on a reliable article test administered at the end of the instructional sequence.[2]

Method

This study is a quasi-experimental, pretest/posttest, **control group** design. It is quasi-experimental because the subjects were not randomly assigned to groups but rather belonged to classes that were formed as a result of performance on an ESL placement examination. The subjects in the study were all students enrolled in a series of university-level courses devoted to the teaching of academic writing skills. The classes met three

2 The use of an objective test to measure acquisition requires some justification. The subjects were given the test without prior announcement and they were only given enough time to answer without deliberating upon their responses. It was hoped that the test would thus reflect their spontaneous knowledge. A better way to test acquisition would be to analyze extended spontaneous spoken or written discourse. However, when this was attempted with the subjects' entrance and exit compositions, it was found that the range of article usage inspired by the composition topics was too narrow to be of use. The only way to access the subjects' knowledge in several areas was to design an instrument that reflected a broad range of article usage.

times per week during the ten-week quarter, and all the subjects were taking a normal schedule of other academic classes at the same time.

Testing instrument

The test consists of 58 items, reflecting the entire range of article usage in English (see Appendix A). The test is divided into two parts. The first is a list of items containing a single blank in either a single sentence or a pair of sentences for **discourse-dependent** subsequent-mention conditions; for example:

Carlos is _____ student at our university.
Once there were many trees here. Now, _____ trees are gone.

The second part was an entire paragraph containing single blanks, a portion of which is shown below:

_____ favorite food of _____ jaguar is _____ wild pig. _____ wild pigs move in _____ bands of fifteen to twenty. They have _____ great courage and _____ strength in _____ group. (adapted from Taylor 1956: 186)

The subjects were asked to circle *a, an, the,* or $\emptyset$ on a separate answer sheet. The correct answers contain two instances of *an*, eight of *a*, 18 of $\emptyset$, and 30 of *the*. Five of the 58 items have two possible answers (two allowed *a* or *the*, two allowed $\emptyset$ or *the*, and one allowed *a* or $\emptyset$).

In a preliminary trial of this testing instrument, 75 students at five different levels of the UCLA ESL Service Courses (ESL 33A, 33B, 33C, 35, and 36) took the test in late 1985. With the exception of ESL 35, students were placed into these levels by means of the UCLA ESL Placement Exam (ESLPE), a statistically valid instrument (Henning, Hudson, and Turner 1985). Although, unfortunately, no correlational analyses were undertaken between the actual ESLPE score and the score on the article test, the **mean scores** on the article test increased with assigned level, with the exception of ESL 35, as shown in Figure 1. The lower mean score of the ESL 35 class can be explained by the fact that ESL 35 was a special writing class for those who had failed to move on to ESL 36 because of writing deficiencies. As the article test score increased by level in the other four cases, the lower test score for ESL 35 is a graphic representation of the proficiency level of the student population that was placed into ESL 35 and suggests that these students may have benefited from repeating ESL 33C. Figure 1 also shows that the amount of gain between all but the first and second levels is relatively small.

To determine the statistical **reliability** of the testing instrument, the trial test data were analyzed in two ways: (1) the **point biserial correlation** and 2) the **Kuder-Richardson 20 (KR-20)** and **Kuder-Richardson 21 (KR-21)** reliability measures. The general function of the point biserial

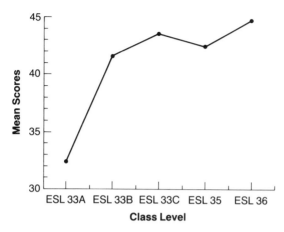

Figure 1

correlation is to determine which items on the test were "good" items. A low point biserial correlation coefficient indicates items tending to be incorrectly answered by otherwise high scorers, and/or tending to be correctly answered by otherwise low scorers. In other words, the analysis indicates which items are suspect in **discriminability** and should therefore be discarded. Point biserial correlation coefficients (r_{pbi}) were computed for each item on the test, which ranged from $-.243$ to $.469$ (see Appendix B). The higher the positive number, the more reliable the item.

The KR-20 is an **internal consistency** method for estimating overall test reliability. Based on the average correlation between pairs of items on the test (or **average item reliability**) and the number of items (these two elements are dependent on the test alone and hence "internal"), it tells us how reliable the test is as a testing instrument. It is only appropriate when all the items in the test measure the same ability. Otherwise, a better indication of reliability is to test and retest with the same instrument (Hatch and Farhady 1982: 248).

Since the items on the article test all test the same ability – i.e., to fill a blank with one of four article options – the KR-20 is appropriate. The test reliability for the full 58 items was .72. Since the KR-20 method is dependent on the number of items and the average item reliability, the optimum reliability can be seen as a trade-off between items with a high point biserial coefficient (r_{pbi}) and the total number of items that make up the test. Figure 2 plots the KR-20 reliability coefficient for differing numbers of items (58, 41, 36, and 27). These numbers (except 58, which represents the entire initial test) were determined by including only those items with an r_{pbi} of .10 and above, .20 and above, and .30 and above, respectively.

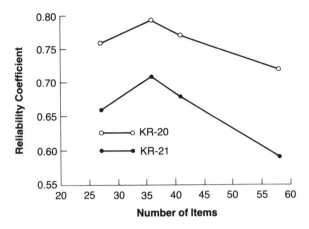

Figure 2

The KR-21 is also an internal consistency method for estimating over-all test reliability. It differs from the KR-20 in that it is based on the number of items, the average score, and the variance of the test scores rather than the item variance, and is thus generally easier to calculate. It is included only to support the KR-20 result. From Figure 2, it is apparent that the 36 items with an r_{pbi} of .20 and above produced the highest reliability coefficient. In order to reap the highest possible KR-20 reliability of .79, items 1, 2, 4, 9, 10, 11, 14, 17, 21, 22, 29, 30, 32, 36, 39, 41, 43, 46, 47, 48, 54, and 57 were not counted when the actual experiment was run. However, those items were left on the test instrument in order to retain the same conditions as were used to derive the reliability coefficient. Figure 3 on page 236 compares the mean scores of the 58-item test with the mean scores of the modified 36-item test. It shows that the results of the more highly reliable 36-item version of the test parallel those of the original 58-item test. The numerical data from which Figure 3 was constructed are provided in Table 1.

TABLE I. DATA FROM THE TRIAL RUN

Class level		N	Mean/58	S.D.	Mean/35	S.D.
ESL 33A	Low intermediate ESL	13	32.38	4.52	23.23	3.87
ESL 33B	Intermediate ESL	17	41.65	4.06	24.29	4.10
ESL 33C	High intermediate ESL	28	43.57	5.54	26.28	5.24
ESL 35	Developmental comp	17	42.47	5.92	25.06	5.34
ESL 36	Intermediate comp	47	44.72	4.95	26.66	3.73

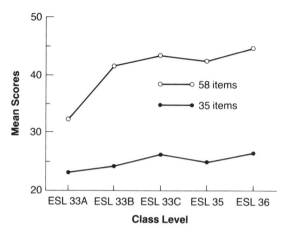

Figure 3

Subjects

The subjects of this study are at the high-intermediate/low-advanced level of instruction, where learners can be assumed to have sufficient linguistic and pragmatic knowledge to be able to focus on this subtle aspect of syntax. The article test was administered to 47 subjects in four ESL 36 classes at UCLA. Fourteen of these subjects (one class) served as the experimental group, 33 (the three other classes) as the control group. The subjects were all nonnative speakers of English, representing 12 native languages, as shown in Table 2. The subjects were asked to indicate how long they had studied English, how long they had been in the United States, and whether they had ever received article instruction before. Years of English ranged from 1 to 13, averaging 7.1. Years in the United States ranged from .5 to 12.5, averaging 5.0. The majority (72%) reported that they had received prior article instruction; 26% reported that they had received no article instruction; 2% did not respond.

Experiment

The article test was administered during the first week of class. The subjects were all given 15 to 20 minutes to complete the test, which was sufficient time to answer all the items (a native speaker taking the test was able to complete it in about five minutes) but not enough for the subjects to ponder their answers. The object was to capture the subjects' spontaneous responses to the items as much as possible. The test administrators, all trained ESL practitioners, were instructed to answer any questions the subjects might have about the vocabulary on the test. The subjects were

TABLE 2. NATIVE LANGUAGES OF SUBJECTS

	S.E. Asia		Middle East		Europe		Other	
Experimental	57%		29%		14%		–	
Control	76%		15%		6%		3%	
	Chinese	8	Arabic	1	Czech	1	Northern Sotho	1
	Filipino	3	Farsi	6	Italian	1		
	Indonesian	2	Hebrew	2	Spanish	2		
	Japanese	2						
	Korean	19						

not told that they were participating in an experiment. They were simply told that they would receive their score on the test within the next two weeks. This constituted the pretest phase of the experiment.

The same article test was administered again during the tenth week of each of the classes. This was considered sufficient time to remove any danger of a **practice effect,** that is, subjects remembering what they had written on the pretest. The same conditions applied as in the pretest, except that subjects were told, after the test, that they would be given their scores and that the test would be gone over in class at the teacher's discretion. This constituted the posttest phase of the experiment. The mean scores were calculated for the control and the experimental groups and subjected to statistical analysis.

Treatment

The classes constituting the control group were university ESL classes, each typically focusing on the writing process and product in producing four essays during the ten-week quarter. However, the teachers consciously refrained from "teaching" the article system, limiting themselves to correcting article misuse on written compositions. One of the three teachers assigned and discussed lessons in Bander (1971) on the articles when asked directly for help by students in the class, but no systematic treatment was undertaken.

The experimental group received systematic article instruction throughout the nine-week (pretest in week 1, posttest in week 10) experiment. The treatment of the article system focused on six major aspects of the system, in the following order (from Master 1986):

1. the **countable-uncountable** and **singular-plural** distinctions
   Example: There is a tree (singular countable) in my garden.
   There are [∅] flowers (plural countable) in my garden.
   There is [∅] grass (uncountable) in my garden.

2. the **indefinite** [a(n), Ø]-**definite** [the] distinction
   Example: There is a tree (indefinite) in my garden. The tree (definite) is
   losing its leaves.
   There are [Ø] flowers (indefinite) in my garden. The flowers (defi-
   nite) are blooming.
3. the **premodified-postmodified** distinction[3]
   Example: A *mangy old cat* (premodified) came into the room.
   The cat *which lives down the street* (postmodified) came into the
   room.
4. the **specific-generic** distinction[4]
   Example: I received a book (specific) for my birthday.
   A book (generic) makes a great gift.
5. the **common noun-proper noun** distinction
   Example: A doctor (common noun) came to see me.
   [Ø] Dr. Smith (proper noun) came to see me.
6. the **idiomatic phrase-nonidiomatic phrase** distinction
   Example: He is always on [Ø] edge. (idiomatic phrase)
   He lives on the edge of town. (nonidiomatic phrase)

Approximately two weeks were devoted to each of the first three distinctions, three weeks total to the last three. An attempt was made to build a
firm foundation with each distinction and to build on that foundation
slowly and carefully, with constant review of earlier phases.

In response to Larsen-Freeman and Long's (1991) call for more precise descriptions as to what constitutes "instruction" in research investigations, the teaching of the first distinction is described in some detail.
The instruction in this study constituted a focus on the second language
itself (i.e., form) rather than an exposure to linguistic features through
the second language (i.e., comprehensible input). The presentation varied between **inductive** and **deductive** approaches, the practice between
discrete sentences and longer segments of discourse, while the entire
instructional schema was an effort to engage the subjects' cognitive skills
in understanding and applying the rules of article usage in a systematic
manner.

3   I have since revised my understanding of the effect of pre- and postmodification
    (Master 1990). While it is true that postmodification often triggers *the*, there are
    many cases where it does not; for example, "I need *a* tutor who can help me with
    my writing" (postmodified). The true determiner of the article is whether the head
    noun is classified, that is, a type or a member of a class, or identified, that is,
    singled out as being known and unique. In the example in the text, "the cat who
    lives down the street" is an identified cat whereas "a tutor who can help me with
    my writing" is a classified tutor, that is, one of many who could do this.
4   I have also revised my understanding and the pedagogical significance of teaching
    the generic-specific distinction because it can be embraced by the classified-identified
    distinction described in note 3. In other words, I no longer believe teaching the
    distinction to be necessary. The example shows specific versus generic *a*, but there is
    also specific versus generic *the* ("The lion ate my sister" versus "The lion lives in
    Africa"), and specific versus generic Ø ("My radiator needs [Ø] water" versus "[Ø]
    Water is necessary for life").

After the identification of the articles in English – *a, the,* and Ø – the subjects were given a short paragraph in which they were to underline the occurrence of *a* or *an,* a phonetic variant of *a* (all exercise samples are from Master 1986).

Time is measured in a variety of ways. A nanosecond is one of the smallest units. An eon is one of the largest. In our daily life we are more interested in time on a human scale. (p. 2)

This inductive exercise led to a discussion of the rule requiring the use of *a* with consonant sounds and *an* with vowel sounds, which was then practiced in a second paragraph in which the subjects were to choose *a* or *an.*

Our solar system, (a an) one-star system of nine planets, was formed approximately 4.5 billion years ago from (a an) universe of cosmic gas and dust. (p. 2)

The subjects were then introduced to Distinction 1, which required a review of both the singular-plural and the countable-uncountable dichotomies. The singular-countable versus plural-countable dichotomy, the easier of the two, requires singular countable nouns (e.g., *a pencil, a desk, an idea*) to take the article *a* and plural countable nouns (e.g., Ø *pencils,* Ø *desks,* Ø *methods*) to take Ø. After a deductive presentation, the subjects were given a list of singular and plural nouns and asked, in pairs, to label the words with the appropriate article, *a* or Ø.

The subjects were next introduced to countable nouns with visible objects in the classroom (e.g., *a pencil, a desk, a book*), then to abstract countable nouns (e.g., *an idea, a problem, a method*) in order to prevent the erroneous association of uncountable with abstract nouns. Visible examples of uncountable nouns, which are always singular, (e.g., Ø *paper,* Ø *paint,* Ø *chalk*) were introduced in a similar fashion before presenting abstract uncountable nouns (e.g., Ø *love,* Ø *life,* Ø *generosity*). The subjects were encouraged to suggest countable and uncountable nouns themselves to test their own hypotheses about the distinction. This led into the most difficult aspect of the countable-uncountable distinction, the fact that most nouns can take either form. **Dual nouns** (e.g., Ø *iron* versus *an iron,* Ø *football* versus *a football,* Ø *man* versus *a man*) are the easiest type to understand because they represent very different entities in the two forms (i.e., a metal versus an appliance, a sport versus a piece of equipment, humankind versus a male human). The subjects, in pairs, were asked to generate a separate sentence for each of the two forms to show that they understood the difference.

The more important generalization about the distinction is that the uncountable form, for example, Ø *stone* (a material), is invariably more general in concept than the countable one, for example, *a stone* (an object). After a brief inductive presentation based on example sentences, the subjects completed an exercise in which they were to label the underlined noun as being either specific or general at the beginning of the sentence and then to indicate whether the same noun was countable or uncountable at the end (answers provided in brackets).

| [spec] | The patient had an infection in her eye. | [count] |
| [gen] | Infection is usually caused by bacteria. | [noncount] |

A discussion of the exercise led subjects to recognize and articulate the link between specific and countable and between general and uncountable. They then further practiced these distinctions in an exercise in which they were to select an appropriate noun phrase.

The sun provides us with (light/a light) _____.
(Football/a football) _____ is popular all over the world.

This was further consolidated in an exercise in which subjects were to choose whether a noun was specific or general (the nouns could all be interpreted in either way), provide the article *a* or ∅, and then to write a definition of the resulting noun phrase.

___ glass   specific general
Definition: [A glass is a container for drinks that is usually made of glass.]

The next phase of Distinction 1 was to provide the subjects with practice shifting a noun from an uncountable to a countable form, and vice versa. After a deductive presentation of the fact that uncountable nouns such as *∅ water* are made countable by making them more specific, i.e., typically by indicating a quantity (e.g., *a gallon of water*), a container (e.g., *a glass of water*), or the smallest particle (e.g., *a drop of water* or *a molecule of water*), practice was provided in an exercise in which the subjects had to find suitable countable noun phrases for several uncountable nouns.

| salt | [a box of salt, a teaspoon of salt, a grain of salt] |
| homework | [a homework assignment, an exercise, a composition] |

Similarly, after a deductive presentation of the fact that countable nouns such as *a chair* are made uncountable by making them more general, typically by placing them in a larger category (e.g., *∅ furniture*), practice was again provided in an exercise in which the subjects had to choose an appropriate uncountable noun for several countable nouns.

| a banana | food | fruit | nutrition |
| a dollar | capital | money | change |

Throughout this practice, the articles ∅ and *a* were continuously shown with the uncountable and the countable forms, respectively, on the blackboard. In order to practice correctly choosing between ∅ and *a*, the subjects were given an exercise in which they were to fill in blanks in a passage with either $\emptyset$ or *a(n)* and to explain the reasons for their choices (alternatives are sometimes possible).

_____ hospital is _____ place for the scientific treatment of _____ sick people. _____ Many modern hospitals are also _____ medical centers where _____ doctor can send _____ patient for _____ examination. (p. 9)

They were then asked to provide missing $\emptyset$ and *a* in a passage with no blanks to remind them that the zero article would not be visible in normal text and to better approximate the task of the student in writing a composition.

Good laboratory is essential for good research. It should have strong table with hard, acid-resistant surface. It should have water faucet and sink with controlled drainage. It should have gas outlet for Bunsen burner. (p. 9)

In this way, a foundation was built in which the subjects developed a degree of self-confidence in their ability to handle this aspect of the article system before moving on to Distinction 2. This foundation included instruction and practice in selecting *a* versus *an,* recognizing that *a(n)* signals a singular noun and $\emptyset$ a plural one, and recognizing that *a(n)* signals a countable noun and $\emptyset$ an uncountable one. *The* was not introduced until Distinction 2.

Distinctions 2 and 3 received instruction at a similar level of detail. Distinctions 4, 5, and 6 received less emphasis due to time limitations and because they are less significant in the realm of article usage. In Distinction 4, generic *a* and *the* are thought to be marked (Raskin 1980: 130), i.e., less frequent and more difficult to learn and use, while the specific article was dealt with in Distinction 2. In Distinction 5, proper nouns do not adhere to the same rules as the articles for common nouns (see Horowitz 1989), and their acquisition in certain contexts (e.g., street names) may depend on individual experience (Master 1987). In Distinction 6, idiomatic phrases are relatively less frequent in the language and, since they are often derived from historical antecedents, their articles are often unpredictable by rule. Nevertheless, all three distinctions were introduced and practiced within the nine-week period of the experiment.

In the experimental group, article instruction was provided throughout the term. In both the experimental and control groups, other aspects of grammar were dealt with as they arose in student papers. These included relative clause structure, the passive voice, parallelism, coordination and subordination, and comparison structures. The total amount of time devoted to teaching the article system in the experimental group was approximately 6 hours (of 30 total). However, the final exam composition scores (rated by the other ESL 36 instructors) showed that the subjects' writing ability was not impaired by this focus on one element of grammar; in fact, the exit composition scores in the experimental group

TABLE 3. RESULTS OF MATCHED GROUPS T-TEST

	Control	*Experimental*
Pretest	X = 26.61	X = 26.79
Posttest	X = 27.24	X = 29.08
Difference	D = .63	D = 2.29
t-value	t = 1.47	t = 2.80* (p < .05)
t_{crit} (.05/2)	(df = 32) = 2.04	(df = 13) = 2.16

averaged 21.23 (S.D. = 1.08) out of 25, whereas the scores in the control group averaged 20.55 (S.D. = 1.49). As far as article use is concerned, the article pretest scores showed the experimental group to average 0.18 percentage points higher than the control group, an insignificant difference; in other words, the experimental group did not appear to have any particular advantage over the control group at the outset.

Hypotheses

RESEARCH (ALTERNATIVE) HYPOTHESIS

Subjects receiving systematic article instruction over a nine-week period in an intermediate ESL composition course will show greater improvement in mean posttest scores than subjects who do not receive systematic instruction over a nine-week period in three parallel ESL composition courses.

NULL HYPOTHESIS

H_o: A. $\mu_1 - \mu_2 \leq 0$
    B. $\mu_3 - \mu_4 \leq 0$
    C. $\mu_1 - \mu_2 \leq \mu_3 - \mu_4$
where μ_1 = mean posttest score for experimental group
    μ_2 = mean pretest score for experimental group
    μ_3 = mean posttest score for control group
    μ_4 = mean pretest score for control group

Results

The mean scores and **t-values** on the article pre- and posttests for the control and experimental groups are given in Table 3. Table 3 shows that the 0.63 increase in mean score shown between the control group pre- and posttest is not **significant at the .05 level**. The 2.29 increase in mean score shown on the experimental group posttest is significant at the .05 and even at the **one-tailed** .02 level (t_{crit} (.025/1,13) = 2.16).[5] This means

5 (t_{crit} (.025/1,13) = 2.16) is interpreted as follows: The minimal t-value (t_{crit}) that is significant at the p = .025 level for a one-tailed result (/1) with 13 degrees of free-

that the null hypothesis can be rejected for the experimental group but not for the control group. In other words, the experimental group showed a significant increase between the pretest score and the posttest score whereas the control group did not. An **unmatched group t-test** confirmed the significance of the difference (**p** < **.05**, one-tailed) between control and experimental posttest scores, although it should be noted that the use of t-tests with **intact** (i.e., nonrandom) **group** designs can have indeterminable effects on probabilities. However, an **effect size** analysis (Stallings, Needels, and Staybrook 1979), which calculates the size of the effect of an experimental treatment based on a comparison of the means and standard deviations for **gain scores** between the experimental and control groups, produced an effect size of 0.664 for the UCLA study. An effect size of 0.5 is considered moderate, 1.0 is considered good (Lynch 1987).

Correlations with Demographic Factors

It was mentioned earlier that all subjects were asked how long they had studied English and how long they had been in the United States. **Pearson product-moment correlations** (r) between the trial and pretest scores and these two factors were performed. The results are shown in Table 4. Table 4 shows that no significant correlation occurs between test scores and years of English or years in the United States. In other words, the test score does not seem to reflect self-reported length of exposure to English instruction or to an English-speaking environment. Finally, all subjects

---

dom is 2.16. The t-value of 2.29, which is the result of the study, is significant because it exceeds this minimal t-value. In the bell-shaped curve of statistical probability, a result is said to be significant only if it lies at the extreme edges (tails) of the curve and is therefore not a product of chance. This is the meaning of *p* (probability). With p < .025, the meaning is that there is less than a 0.025% probability that the result occurred by chance, or that there is a 99.975% probability that the finding did not occur by chance and is therefore a significant result of the treatment.

Results can be either one-tailed or two-tailed. A two-tailed result indicates that the researcher had no idea whether the result would be a positive or a negative one. It is considered to be a somewhat stronger indication of significance since it applies in both possible cases. A one-tailed result suggests that there is an expectation of directionality in the results, that is, that there was reason to believe that the result would be either positive or negative. In the present study, the trial run suggested that article scores increase by proficiency level irrespective of instruction. Therefore, it was assumed that the results of the treatment (systematic instruction) would be likely to increase the score on the test, not decrease it. For this reason, the one-tailed criterion is justified by the trial run.

"Degrees of freedom" (N-1) refers to the number of different pieces of information on which the statistic is based (N = number of students taking the pretest and posttest) minus 1 for the number of sample statistics used in the calculation (only the single mean of the difference between pretest and posttest scores was used). Since 14 students participated in the experimental group, there are 13 degrees of freedom.

TABLE 4. CORRELATION STATISTICS FOR
DEMOGRAPHIC FACTORS

	Years of Eng.	*Years in U.S.*
Trial test (N = 48)		
Mean	6.71	2.86
S.D.	2.90	2.68
r	.1360	−.2812
r_{crit} (.05,46) = .2875		
Pretest (N = 45)		
Mean	7.10	5.00
S.D.	2.95	2.64
r	−.2675	−.2414
r_{crit} (.05,43) = .3044		

were asked whether they had ever received article instruction before. The 34 subjects who answered "yes" to this question obtained a mean score of 26.68 (S.D. = 3.72) on the article pretest. The 12 subjects who answered "no" obtained a mean score of 26.83 (S.D. = 3.40). The difference, subjected to a t-test for independent means, is not significant. In other words, any instruction that the subjects reported to have received prior to the article pretest did not seem to affect their performance on that test.

Discussion

Since the experimental group showed a significant increase between pretest and posttest scores on the article test, the research hypothesis is supported. In other words, the systematic presentation of the article system appears to have had a significant effect in increasing the mean score on the article posttest. Although the amount of increase is relatively small, the increase of 2.29 points shown by the experimental group is 62 percent of a standard deviation and is therefore substantial; furthermore, the trial run of the test demonstrated that the amount of increase in average score between class levels was also quite small.

The similarity in size of the mean experimental pretest and posttest scores (Tables 3 and 6) and the score differences between class levels (Figure 1) may be evidence of a delayed effect, whereas a large difference could have been interpreted as showing an immediate effect. Although this is probably too small an average time difference to count as a true delay, there was a maximum of nine weeks' time between the beginning of instruction and the administration of the posttest. Distinction 1 had the longest delay, Distinction 6 the shortest. The delayed effect was mentioned at the outset because of the fact that the article system is an aspect of grammar that contributes little to communicative effectiveness. Instruction in such grammatical forms is thought to bring the grammatical concepts they represent to the awareness of the learner but not to affect the immediate control of grammatical forms. Ellis (1990) says in this regard: "[F]ormal instruction may have a delayed effect by providing the learner with more or less explicit grammatical concepts, which will later help her to attend to these features in the input and so acquire them procedurally. Learners who receive formal instruction outperform those who do not; that is, they learn more rapidly and they reach higher levels of ultimate achievement" (p. 171).

The lack of correlation between length of study of English, length of time in the United States, and reported prior article instruction is probably due to the impreciseness of the questions designed to elicit demographic data. The length of time one has studied English might represent two years of intensive instruction or two years of classes that met once a week. The length of time in the United States does not indicate that the subject spent all of that time engaging in interactions in English, as many international students spend a great deal of time conversing in their own languages. Finally, whether or not a subject had received prior article instruction does not describe the length or the nature of that instruction. A "yes" response might indicate nothing more than an article exercise done in class years ago. In other words, the demographic data would have been far more useful if they had been more carefully elicited, perhaps through an oral interview rather than by having the subjects fill in a brief questionnaire on the test answer form.

The significant increase in score on the posttest by the experimental group suggests that the article system can indeed be learned and that it is perhaps the *systematic* presentation of the article system that makes the difference. Pieces of information about the system, rather than an approach that teaches the entire system, can often lead to confusion when the student is called upon to produce written text. The reason is that many aspects of the system tend to operate simultaneously, and it is rare to find a text in which only one or two article rules are applied. This explanation is supported by the fact that even when one of the control group instructors assigned a brief description of the articles plus an exercise to his class (unbeknownst to the researcher until after the study), there was no significant effect on the posttest article score for that group.

The significant increase may be partly due to the effort to focus on the functions of the articles as well as their formal characteristics. Widdowson (1988) says in this regard that teaching only the formal linguistic properties is not appropriate in the language classroom. Grammatical

TABLE 5. NATIVE LANGUAGES OF CSUF SUBJECTS

	S.E. Asia	*Middle East*	*Europe*	*Other*
Experimental	78%	–	22%	–
Control	67%	20%	11%	2%
	Chinese 8	Arabic 9	French 1	Urdu 1
	Hmong 1		German 1	
	Indonesian 6		Serbo-Croat 1	
	Japanese 16		Spanish 4	
	Korean 3			
	Malay 1			
	Thai 2			

instruction must focus on the function of grammar as it serves the intended meaning of an utterance.

Language learning *is* essentially grammar learning and it is a mistake to suppose otherwise. This cannot be done by restricting attention to its formal properties, the relations and regularities which make up the internal mechanism of the device. No matter how legitimate an enterprise this might be within the discipline of linguistics (and this is currently a controversial matter), it will not do for language pedagogy. Learners need to realize the *function* of the device as a way of mediating between words and contexts, as a powerful resource for the purposeful achievement of meaning. A communicative approach, properly conceived, does not involve the rejection of grammar. On the contrary, it involves a recognition of its central mediating role in the use and learning of a language. (p. 154)

Replication of the study

The experiment was replicated at the California State University at Fresno (CSUF) in the spring semester of 1988. The same testing instrument was used and the same procedures followed. The differences were that (1) the control group consisted of five ESL classes at different levels rather than classes at the same level as in the UCLA study, and (2) the amount of time between pretest and posttest was fourteen rather than nine weeks.

The experimental group consisted of nine subjects, the control group of 45. The subjects were all nonnative speakers of English representing 13 native languages, as shown in Table 5. The subjects' years of English ranged from 1 to 13 years, average 5.8 (1.3 years less than the average for the UCLA group). Years in the United States ranged from one month to eight years, averaging 0.7 years (4.3 years less than the average for the UCLA group). The majority (67%) reported that they had received prior article instruction; 22% reported that they had received no article in-

TABLE 6. RESULTS OF MATCHED GROUPS T-TEST
(CSUF)

	Control	Experimental
Pretest	X = 19.69	X = 23.80
Posttest	X = 20.76	X = 26.89
Difference	D = 1.07	D = 3.09
t-value	t = 1.39	t = 3.53* (p < .05)
t_{crit} (.05/2)	(df = 44) = 2.02	(df = 8) = 2.31

struction; 11% did not respond (these figures are slightly lower than the UCLA group's 72% yes, 26% no, with 2% nonreporting).

The mean scores and t-values on the article pre- and posttests for the control and experimental groups are shown in Table 6. Table 6 shows that the 1.07 increase in mean score shown between the control group pre- and posttests is not significant at the .05 level. The 3.09 increase in mean score shown between the experimental group pre- and posttests is significant at the .05 and even at the one-tailed .01 level (t_{crit} 0.01/1,8 = 2.90). In other words, the experimental group showed a significant increase between the pretest score and the posttest score whereas the control group did not, confirming the results of the UCLA study.

It should be noted that even though the control groups did not improve by a statistically significant amount,[6] implying that this amount could be accounted for by chance alone, they did indeed increase (by 0.63 points in the UCLA study, by 1.07 points in the CSUF study) rather than decrease. This may be accounted for by the general improvement in article usage that appears to accompany general increase in proficiency level (see Oller and Redding 1972) arising from factors such as exposure to the language inside and outside of the classroom and continued teacher correction of article errors on compositions. In other words, the increase found in both studies suggests that the control groups were progressing at a more or less normal rate in acquiring increasing control of the article system (indeed, the lack of such an increase would have been surprising) and that systematic instruction is a means of accelerating that acquisition by making students aware of and increasing their conscious control of the way the article system works.

In his comprehensive review of research concerning the effect of language instruction versus exposure on language acquisition, Long (1983)

6 In both the UCLA and the CSUF studies, the difference between pretest and posttest scores for the control groups was significant at the one-tailed .10 level. Thus, although a p-level of .05 is considered to be the minimal level of significance, the differences between pre- and posttest scores indicate that there is only a 10% possibility that these scores occurred by chance.

concludes that Krashen and Scarcella's (1978) concept of learning, which assumes that grammatical instruction only benefits the correction mechanism (the monitor) and cannot aid acquisition, must be broadened to include all language-like behavior to allow for the positive effect of instruction in the majority of studies reviewed. The present study suggests that language instruction is beneficial if that instruction is based on a systematic presentation of the material, that is, when the material is presented in a hierarchy of manageable segments with continuous building on what has been taught before.

References

Bander, R. G. 1971. *American English Rhetoric*. New York: Holt, Rinehart & Winston, pp. 122, 350–57.

Celce-Murcia, M. & D. Larsen-Freeman. 1983. *The Grammar Book*. Rowley, Mass.: Newbury House.

Dulay, H., M. Burt & S. Krashen. 1982. *Language Two*. New York: Oxford University Press.

Ellis, R. 1990. *Instructed Second Language Acquisition*. Oxford: Basil Blackwell.

Hatch, E. & H. Farhady. 1982. *Research Design and Statistics for Applied Linguistics*. Rowley, Mass.: Newbury House.

Henning, G., T. Hudson & J. Turner. 1985. Item response theory and the assumption of unidimensionality for language tests. *Language Testing* 2: 141–54.

Higgs, T. V., & R. Clifford. 1982. The push toward communication. In T. V. Higgs (ed.), *Curriculum, Competence, and the Foreign Language Teacher*. Lincolnwood, Ill.: National Textbook Co.

Horowitz, F. E. 1989. ESL and prototype theory: zero vs. definite article with place names. *IRAL* 27(2): 81–98.

Huebner, T. 1983. *A Longitudinal Analysis of the Acquisition of English*. Ann Arbor, Mich.: Karoma Press.

Hulstijn, J. & W. Hulstijn. 1984. Grammatical errors as a function of processing constraints and explicit knowledge. *Language Learning* 34:23–43.

Krashen, S. 1981. *Second Language Acquisition and Second Language Learning*. Oxford: Pergamon Press.

Krashen, S. & R. Scarcella. 1978. On routines and patterns in language acquisition and performance. *Language Learning* 28: 283–300.

Krashen, S. & T. Terrell. 1983. *The Natural Approach: Language Acquisition in the Classroom*. Oxford: Pergamon Press.

Larsen-Freeman, D. & M. H. Long. 1991. *An Introduction to Second Language Acquisition Research*. London: Longman Group.

Long, M. H. 1983. Does second language instruction make a difference? A review of research. *TESOL Quarterly* 17: 359–82.

Lynch, B. 1987. Toward a context-adaptive model for the evaluation of language teaching programs. Unpublished doctoral dissertation, UCLA.

Makino, T. 1979. English morpheme acquisition order of Japanese secondary school students. *TESOL Quarterly* 13: 428.

Master, P. 1986. *Science, Medicine, and Technology: English Grammar and Technical Writing*. Englewood Cliffs, N.J.: Prentice Hall.

1987. *A cross-linguistic interlanguage analysis of the acquisition of the English article system*. Unpublished doctoral dissertation, UCLA.

1990. Teaching the English articles as a binary system. *TESOL Quarterly* 24(3): 461–78.

McEldowney, P. L. 1977. A teaching grammar of the English article system. *IRAL* 15(2): 95–112.

Oller, J. & E. Z. Redding. 1972. Article usage and other language skills. *Language Learning* 21: 85–95.

Pica, T. 1983. Adult acquisition of English as a second language under different conditions of exposure. *Language Learning* 33(4): 465–97.

1985. The selective impact of classroom instruction on second language acquisition. *Applied Linguistics* 6(3): 214–22.

Pienemann, M. 1988. Psychological constraints on the teachability of language. In W. Rutherford & M. Sharwood Smith (eds.), *Grammar and Second Language Teaching*. New York: Newbury House.

Raskin, V. 1980. Determination with and without articles. In J. Van der Auwera (ed.), *The Semantics of Determiners*. Baltimore, Md.: University Park Press.

Sajavaara, K. 1981. The nature of first language transfer: English as L2 in a foreign language setting. Paper presented at the first European-North American Workshop on Cross-Linguistic Second Language Acquisition Research, Lake Arrowhead, Calif.

Schmidt, R. 1983. Interaction, acculturation, and acquisition of communicative competence. In N. Wolfson & E. Judd (eds.), *Sociolinguistics and Second Language Acquisition*, pp. 137–74. Rowley, Mass.: Newbury House.

Spada, N. 1986. The interaction between types of content and type of instruction: some effects on the L2 proficiency of adult learners. *Studies in Second Language Acquisition* 8: 181–99.

Stallings, J., M. Needels & N. Staybrook. 1979. How to change the process of teaching basic reading skills (Research Report, May 1979). Menlo Park, Calif.: Stanford Research Institute.

Taylor, G. (ed.) 1956. *Mastering American English*. New York: McGraw-Hill.

Widdowson, H. 1988. Grammar, nonsense, and learning. In W. Rutherford & M. Sharwood Smith (eds.), *Grammar and Second Language Teaching*. New York: Newbury House.

Zobl, H. 1985. Grammars in search of input and intake. In S. Gass & C. Madden (eds.), *Input in Second Language Acquisition*. Rowley, Mass.: Newbury House.

Appendix A

Article diagnostic test

I. Choose the correct article (a, an, the, ∅) in the following sentences. Mark your answers on the answer sheet only.
   a. There is __1__ orange in that bowl.
   b. Carlos is __2__ student at our university.
   c. What is __3__ sex of your baby? It's __4__ boy!
   d. I always drink __5__ water with my meals.
   e. Is your brother __6__ man enough to join __7__ army?
   f. What is __8__ diameter of __9__ moon?
   g. Once there were many trees here. Now, __10__ trees are gone.
   h. I would like __11__ cup of coffee, please.
   i. My father earns $25,000 __12__ year.
   j. __13__ evening sky was really beautiful.
   k. A man knocked on my door. __14__ man was bleeding.
   l. People who smoke __15__ cigarettes often get lung cancer.
   m. __16__ air in this city is not very clean.
   n. Einstein was __17__ man of great intelligence.
   o. In this family, __18__ first child inherits everything.
   p. Check __19__ rearview mirror before you change lanes.
   q. Smith was appointed __20__ chairman of that committee.
   r. She owns __21__ enormous house in Pasadena.
   s. __22__ fool though he was, he was clever with __23__ money.
   t. That was __24__ worst storm of 1985.
   u. We found __25__ bottles of vodka in every cupboard.
   v. __26__ restaurant in which we ate was quite expensive.
   w. This room has __27__ length of 12 meters.
   x. __28__ copies of rare books should always be preserved.
   y. If you want to read, why don't you turn on __29__ light?
   z. John was hired as __30__ special assistant to Judge Lee.
   aa. I ordered a bottle of wine, but __31__ bottle of wine was too cold.
   bb. Dr. Engelberg, __32__ physician to Marilyn Monroe, would not comment on her death.

II. Choose the correct article (a, an, the, ∅) in the following paragraph.

__33__ Jaguar and __34__ Wild Pig

   When hunters visit __35__ southwestern part of __36__ United States, they often find __37__ large, catlike tracks along __38__ ground. These tracks are made by __39__ spotted jaguar, __40__ greatest hunter of all __41__ North American animals and __42__ largest member of __43__ cat family on __44__ American continent. __45__ most animals have __46__ favorite food. __47__ favorite food of __48__ jaguar is __49__ wild pig. __50__ wild pigs move in __51__ bands of fifteen to twenty. They have __52__ great courage and __53__ strength in __54__ group. I once read __55__ story about __56__ courage and strength of these wild pigs. __57__ story pointed out that these pigs sometimes even attack __58__ human hunters.

Test item data

No.	Answ(s)	Context
*1.	an	There + indef
*2.	a	Sing 1M
3.	the	[+Poss] SPEC postmod
*4.	a	It + indef
5.	Ø	1M noncount
6.	Ø	Ø+ noun + "enough"
7.	the	cultural SH KNOW
8.	the	the + measurement N
*9.	the	world SH KNOW
*10.	the	Plur 2M
*11.	a	1M PART of-phrase
12.	a	a = one
13.	the	world SH KNOW premod
*14.	the	Sing 2M
15.	Ø	1M indef plur
16.	the	SPEC postmod prep phr
*17.	a	GEN DESC postmod
18.	the	SEQUENCE adj
19.	the	special SH KNOW
20.	the,Ø	naming verb
*21.	an	Sing 1M
*22.	Ø	Ø+ noun + "though"
23.	Ø	1M noncount
24.	the	SUPERLATIVE adj
25.	Ø	SPEC PART of-phrase
26.	the	SPEC postmod
27.	a	a + meas noun [−Poss]
*28.	Ø	GEN plur DESC of-phrase
*29.	a,the	1M sing, SH KNOW local
30.	a,Ø	as + a, Ø + profession
31.	the	2M PART of-phrase
*32.	Ø	Ø+ rank or post + "to"
33.	the	GEN abstract
34.	the	GEN abstract
35.	the	1M sing DESC of-phrase [+Poss]
*36.	the	PROP noun title
37.	Ø	GEN concrete plural
*38.	the	SH KNOW world (local)
39.	the	GEN abstract
40.	the	SUPERLATIVE adj
*41.	the,Ø	SPEC limited group, unlimited group

No.	Answ(s)	Context
42.	the	SUPERLATIVE adj.
*43.	the	GEN abstract
44.	the	PROP noun geographical area
45.	Ø	Idiom: Ø + superlative
*46.	a	GEN concrete sing
*47.	the	DESC of-phrase [+Poss]
*48.	the	GEN abstract
49.	the	GEN abstract
50.	Ø	SPEC 1M plur
51.	Ø	SPEC 1M PART of-phrase [−Poss]
52.	Ø	1M noncount
53.	Ø	1M noncount
*54.	a,the	GEN concrete, abstract
55.	a	Sing 1M
56.	the	DESC of-phrase [+Poss]
*57.	the	Sing 2M
58.	Ø	Plur 1M

Key

* = not counted in 36-item test
1M = first mention
2M = subsequent mention
[+Poss] = + **possessive test**
SPEC = specific
GEN = generic
SH KNOW = shared knowledge
PART = partitive
DESC = descriptive
Sing = singular
Plur = plural
postmod = postmodified
meas = measurement
PROP = proper
abstract = class noun (the)
concrete = class representative noun (a,Ø)
indef = indefinite
premod = premodified
adj = adjective
prep = preposition
post = official position

Appendix B

Statistical item data (from trial test)

No.	Item var.	Point biserial	No.	Item var.	Point biserial
1.	0	0	30.	.102	.076
2.	.054	−.210	31.	.019	.297
3.	.037	.303	32.	.037	.090
4.	.019	.091	33.	.250	.283
5.	.087	.210	34.	.249	.311
6.	.178	.302	35.	.232	.404
7.	.054	.231	36.	.037	−.050
8.	.102	.349	37.	.237	.326
9.	.054	.117	38.	.054	.231
10.	.155	.088	39.	.213	.112
11.	.054	.038	40.	.071	.469
12.	.071	.298	41.	0	0
13.	.143	.266	42.	.071	.355
14.	.019	.020	43.	.241	.046
15.	.071	.383	44.	.213	.415
16.	.167	.325	45.	.143	.436
17.	.188	.083	46.	.250	.151
18.	.087	.394	47.	.130	.081
19.	.116	.457	48.	0	0
20.	.143	.324	49.	.197	.395
21.	.188	.178	50.	.241	.365
22.	.102	.104	51.	.249	.434
23.	.226	.302	52.	.247	.324
24.	.071	.199	53.	.188	.231
25.	.197	.334	54.	.054	−.243
26.	.071	.398	55.	.116	.312
27.	.249	.443	56.	.143	.266
28.	.248	.249	57.	0	0
29.	.037	.019	58.	.205	.308

10 Linguistic theory and pedagogic practice

David Nunan

Introduction

One of the major problems confronting language teachers, curriculum designers and materials writers is the selection and sequencing of grammatical content, the integrating of such content with semantic and pragmatic elements, and the selection of an appropriate pedagogy for curriculum implementation. In making choices about what to teach, when and in what way, practitioners can seek guidance from linguistic theory and research.

In this chapter, the implications of theoretical and empirical directions in linguistics for language pedagogy are presented and evaluated. I shall trace some of the major shifts which have occurred in theory and research since the 1960s and indicate ways in which these shifts have been reflected in pedagogic practice. The chapter will focus in particular on linguistic models which have made strong claims to relevance for pedagogy.

The empirical component of the paper takes the form of a case study of the grammatical teaching practices of two language teachers. The data base for the study consists of two classroom sequences in which the teachers are introducing and practising question forms – morphosyntactic items of particular significance to current second language acquisition theory. The implications of the research are presented and discussed.

Theoretical and empirical background

For much of this century, curriculum specialists looked to the contrastive hypothesis for guidance on the selection and sequencing of grammatical items for instruction (James 1980). This hypothesis is predicated on the assumption that a learner's first language will have a significant influence on the acquisition of a second. This influence may take several forms. When particular grammatical items or morphosyntactic subsystems, such as articles, exist in both the first and second language and perform similar functions, it is hypothesised that the acquisition of the item in the second language will be facilitated through a process of positive transfer. When the item exists in both languages but performs different functions, or operates in a different way, it is suggested that learning will be inhibited through a process of negative transfer. For example, it is hypothesised that Spanish L1 speakers learning English will have difficulty with the order of adjective + noun because in Spanish the order is the reverse. If, for example, the unmarked placement of the item in a morphosyntactic string is different, then it is assumed that the first language will interfere with the acquisition of the second. This process is known as negative transfer. A third situation may arise where a particular form exists in the target language but not in the first. For example, a native speaker of English will have difficulty in learning Thai with the system of grammatical classifiers which exists in that language but which does not exist in English. One point of controversy with the contrastive hypothesis is the extent to which the first language influences the acquisition of a second. Estimates of the extent of this influence on interlingual errors range from a high of around ninety per cent, to a low of ten per cent. (See Odlin 1989 for a review and discussion of the relevant literature.)

A major implication of the contrastive hypothesis was that learners from different first language backgrounds will acquire target morphosyntactic items differentially. For curriculum developers, the implication was that different curricula need to be devised for learners from different first language backgrounds. (See, for example, Lado 1957.) However, during the 1970s, the contrastive hypothesis came under strong challenge from a series of empirical investigations into the acquisition of certain grammatical morphemes by learners of English as a second language. These studies were stimulated by Brown (1973), who discovered striking similarities in the order in which three children learning English as their first language acquired certain grammatical morphemes. Contrary to expectations, there seemed to be little relationship between the order in which items were acquired and their frequency of use by the parents.

The best-known, and most frequently cited, morpheme-order studies are by Dulay and Burt (1973, 1974), who found that, like their first language counterparts, children acquiring English as a second language appeared to follow a predetermined order which could not be accounted for by frequency of input. Moreover, children from very different first language backgrounds (Spanish and Chinese) acquired the items in virtually the same order, although the order was different from that found by Brown. Bailey, Madden and Krashen (1974) replicated the studies with adult learners and came up with strikingly similar results.

As a result of these and other investigations, it was concluded that the contrastive hypothesis was an inadequate representation of the second language acquisition process, that acquisition orders were driven by an innate or "inbuilt" syllabus which was impervious to instruction and which was driven by the nature of the target language rather than any contrast between the first and second language.

While most second language acquisition researchers were reluctant to derive claims for pedagogy from their research, others were not so reticent. Based on a selective review of the literature, Dulay, Burt and Krashen (1982) made a series of claims which flew in the face of conventional wisdom. These included the following:

1. Exposure to natural communication in the target language is necessary for the subconscious process to work well. The richer the learner's exposure to the target language, the more rapid and comprehensive learning is likely to be.
2. The influence of the learner's first language is negligible in grammar.
3. Conscious learning and application of grammatical rules have a place in second language learning, but their purpose is different from the subconscious learning which produces native-like fluency.
4. Correction of grammatical errors does not help students avoid these errors.
5. Certain structures are acquired only when learners are mentally ready for them. Exposing a learner to a structure does not guarantee learning. (pp. 261–263)

The net effect of these recommendations was to downplay the role of grammar in the classroom. The efficacy of grammatically structured syllabuses was questioned, as was formal instruction and error correction. (Whether or not such prescriptions actually had any effect on teachers' classroom practices is another issue, and one which could only be settled by investigating what teachers actually do, as opposed to what researchers say they ought to do.)

The early morpheme studies came in for a great deal of criticism during the 1980s. The criticisms were both methodological and substantive. One criticism of particular pertinence to the present discussion was that while the researchers had purportedly identified a certain acquisition order, they were unable to offer any explanatory theory of why the order was as it was.

Despite the criticisms, subsequent research has provided substantial evidence that certain grammatical items appear in a predetermined sequence, and that this sequence does not appear to be alterable by instruction. For example, all learners, regardless of whether they are learning English in a second or foreign language context, and regardless of whether or not they are receiving instruction, appear to progress through four stages on the acquisition of negation:

Stage 1: no + verb	"No work". "No understand".
Stage 2: don't + verb	"I don't like". "He don't can swim".
Stage 3: aux + neg	"She can't go". "He don't stay".
Stage 4: analysed don't	"He didn't stay."

(Although, for a different view on fixed sequences of negation, see Eubank 1990.)

Recently, a hypothesis has been developed and tested which purports to offer an explanatory model of second language acquisition. The model was first applied to German by a group of researchers investigating the development of German as a second language, and was subsequently applied to the analysis of data from learners of English as a second language. The hypothesis is called the multidimensional model, although, as it only contains two dimensions, it would be more accurate to call it the "bidimensional" model. The developers of the model suggest that syntactic and morphological items in a given language can be classified according to whether they are developmental or variational. Developmental items will occur in a learner's productive repertoire in a set sequence, a sequence which is determined by speech processing constraints which limit the amount of material one can hold in short-term memory. In acquiring a second language, learners pass through a series of developmental stages and at any one stage will only be able to use the morphosyntactic items which characterise that stage and lower stages. In contrast with developmental items, variational items are not constrained by limits on short-term memory but may be learned at any time.

According to this model, learning and using language consist of mental operations. In order to speak a language fluently, these must become largely automatic, in the same way as the physical operations in breathing, walking, running and driving a car must become automatic for the actions to be carried out competently. Because speech processing operations are very complex, and because the time available for speaking or comprehending is limited, it is only possible to focus on a limited part of the whole speech processing operation at any one time. Learning a language, then, is a matter of gaining automatic control of these complex mental routines and subroutines.

This model has been applied to English by Johnston (1985). (See also Pienemann and Johnston 1987.) At present, six developmental stages, determined by speech processing constraints, have been described. These are as follows:

Stage 1: Production of single words, phrases and formulae. (Formulae are utterances such as "I don't know" and "What's your name?" which are learned as chunks, and which cannot be broken down into their individual elements.)

Stage 2: Production of simple sequences or "strings" of words following regular word-order rules. For example, Subject + Verb + Object combinations such as "I like rice".

Stage 3: Ability to identify the beginnings and ends of strings of elements and to attach and move elements from the beginning to the end of a string and vice versa. For example, attaching adverbs to the beginning or end of a string, as in "Yesterday, I go home".

Stage 4: Ability to identify and manipulate particular elements within a string. At this stage, the learner can form questions by moving the verb to the beginning of a string, as in "Can you swim?"

Stage 5: Ability to shift elements around in an ordered way within strings, as in "Where are you going tonight?" (Here, in order to form the question, the learner is required to move the *wh-* and *be* elements from within the string, where they would occur in the declarative statement "You are going X, tonight", to the front of the string.)

Stage 6: Ability to break down elements within strings into substrings, and to move elements out of substrings and attach them to other elements. At this stage, learners will be able to do such things as form double subject complements as in "He asked me to go".

It has been argued that this particular model provides clear guidelines for pedagogy. Pienemann (1985, 1987) argues that it is futile to introduce learners to items which are developmentally beyond their current stage of development: "Instruction can only promote language acquisition if the interlanguage is close to the point when the structure to be taught is acquired in the natural setting (so that sufficient processing prerequisites are developed)" (Pienemann 1985). In a number of small-scale experiments, he found that it was impossible to 'override' the developmental order through instruction, and that, further, attempting to force production can be counterproductive, leading learners to adopt avoidance strategies.

Apart from the work of Pienemann, empirical studies investigating the pedagogic applications of the multidimensional model are rare. One such study is reported by Brindley (1989). The investigation sought to test the predictions made by the Pienemann/Johnston model in the area of questions. The researchers collected speech data from a sample of eight learners pre-course using a semi-structured elicitation procedure. This enabled each learner to be assigned to a developmental stage. A teaching program was then implemented that focused on structures predicted by the model to be learnable by each learner according to their stage of development. Post-course speech data were collected and analysed. The analysis led the researchers to the following conclusions:

1. Subjects produced many more questions post-course than pre-course.

2. Learners appeared to progress through the stages in the order predicted by the model, although only two learners progressed from one stage to the next during the course of instruction.

In this section, I have taken a selective look at some of the theory and research relating to morphosyntactic development which have made claims of relevance to pedagogy. I looked in greatest detail at the teachability hypothesis, which asserts that items can only be learned, and should therefore only be taught, when learners are developmentally "ready", because it is predictive as well as descriptive. It also makes strong claims of relevance to pedagogy, arguing that the timing of instruction should be determined by the learner's stage of morphosyntactic development, and that premature instruction may be detrimental to the learner's progress. In the next section, I shall present a study which was carried out to provide data for exploring, in a preliminary fashion, the claims of the teachability hypothesis.

Grammar instruction in the classroom

In this section, I shall present some case study data which will provide a basis for critically evaluating the claims of the teachability hypothesis. The data are taken from a larger investigation of the methodological practices of language teachers reported in Nunan (1991).

Rationale

The purpose of this case study is to examine what happens at the level of pedagogic practice when teachers violate the teachability hypothesis. The study focuses on the teaching of question forms, in particular, *wh*-questions with "do" insertion, because these have been dealt with at some length by proponents of the teachability hypothesis. Johnston (1985) points to the early introduction of such structures in most coursebooks, and contrasts this with the fact that they only emerge in the productive repertoire of the learner at a relatively advanced stage (Johnston 1985: 378).

Subjects

Subjects for the study were two highly experienced teachers working with low-proficiency adult immigrant learners of English as a second language. One of the teachers had formal qualifications in EFL, while the other did not. The two lessons selected for analysis were both grammar lessons in which the pedagogic focus was on the teaching of *wh*-questions with "do" insertion. As we have already seen, the teaching of questions has featured prominently in theoretical and empirical investigations into the acquisition of English morphosyntax.

Type of data and method of analysis

The data for the study consisted of lesson transcripts. From these, teaching sequences in which *wh*-questions with "do" insertion appear were extracted and analysed. The analysis was interpretive rather than statistical. In the next section, selected extracts from the transcripts will be presented, along with interpretive comments on the data.

Data and analysis

EXTRACT I

Context   This extract is taken from a lesson in which the principal pedagogical objective is to prepare students for a day trip on a tourist steam train. The teacher begins the lesson by handing out copies of a timetable and a brochure about the trip. In this extract, the teacher circulates around the room, asking *wh*-questions about the steam train.

T: Now . . . Where do you catch the train? Where do you catch the train? [She points to a student in the front row.]
S: Keswick.
T: Yeah.
   [She turns and writes on the whiteboard "Where do you catch the train?"]
T: Do you know where Keswick is? . . . OK, where do you catch the train? At Keswick. Keswick is near the city – but not the big railway station. It is about, oh, one kilometre – two kilometres from the city, and – the big trains go from Keswick. If you want to catch the train to Melbourne, or to Sydney, or to Alice Springs, you go to Keswick. It's the new railway station. All right. So, where do you catch the train?
   At Keswick.

Comment
In this initial interaction, the teacher asks a *wh*-question and nominates one of the "star" students to answer it, which he does correctly. A side sequence then occurs, in which the teacher provides some experiential content on the location of the station. This interaction could have a number of pedagogical functions – to provide learners with the skills needed to extract information from transport timetables, to drill *wh*-questions, to provide information on the public transport system and so on, and it is worth noting that the students are not told why they are being asked to engage in the question-answer session.

T: Now – what time . . . what time does the train leave?
Ss: Nine. Nine o'clock. Nine p.m. Nine p.m. Nine a.m.
T: [leans over a student and checks the timetable] OK. Depart nine a.m.
   So . . . [She returns to the board.] . . . what can I write here? What time . . .

[She writes "What time" on the board.] What comes next? What
time . . . ?
Does . . . does . . . [She writes "does the train".] . . . does the train . . . yes?

S: (inaudible comment)

T: No. What time does the train . . . ? What's another word for "depart"? –
Leave. What time does the train . . . leave?" [She writes "leave" on the
board.] OK, you, you tell me. . . . It leaves at nine a.m. OK. What time
does it arrive?

S: Er, eleven fifty-eight a.m.

T: [leans over his shoulder and checks his timetable] OK. Now – where does
it arrive at eleven fifty-eight? At Victor Harbour?

Ss: No. Goolwa.

T: No.

Ss: Goolwa. Goolwa.

T: Goolwa. Have a look at your map and see if you can find Goolwa. See if
you can find Goolwa on this map.

S: Near, er, near the Victor Harbour.

T: Near Victor Harbour, yeah. [She writes "What time".] OK, what comes
next? . . . What time . . . ? What's the question? What time . . . ? . . . does
(does)

S: . . . the train arrive . . .

T: Arrive. [She writes "does the train arrive at Goolwa?"] All right, so what
time does the train arrive at Goolwa? OK. What time?

S: Eleven. Eleven. Eleven fifty.

T: Eleven fifty . . . eight. What's another way of saying eleven fifty-eight?
Two minutes to . . . twelve. Yeah, two minutes to twelve. OK.

Comment

In this part of the interaction, the teacher answers most of the questions
herself. The wait time (for example, between asking for a synonym for
"depart" and answering the question) is less than two seconds. In fact,
one of the notable features of the interaction is the relative lack of processing time given for students to answer the questions. This is exacer-
bated by the fact that the questions are beyond their current processing
capacity.

There is evidence in this extract and in other parts of the lesson transcript that *wh*-questions with 'do' insertion are beyond the current production capacity of the learners. This is also borne out by the psycholinguistic
research literature relating to learners at initial proficiency (Pienemann
1985, 1987). However, while the learners have great difficulty providing
the form of the questions, they are capable of answering the teacher's questions appropriately. The most reasonable explanation is that they are either responding to the questions as formulae or are using the key question
words as prompts. Either way, it would seem that the teacher's pedagogic
objective, if not her execution, is a defensible one.

T: Now, where does the train go after Goolwa?

S: Victor Harbour.

T: Victor Harbour. OK. What time does it arrive at Victor Harbour? [There is some inaudible muttering from the students. The teacher frowns and inclines her head toward one of the students.]

T: Twenty-two minutes past twelve. – OK. Then . . . What time does the train leave to come back?

S: Four thirty. Four thirty.

T: Four forty . . . ?

Ss: Four thirty.

T: Four thirty, OK.

S: Half past four p.m.

T: [shakes her head] Half past four, yeah. Not half past four p.m. – Half past four in the afternoon . . . yeah. OK. Now, what time does it get back to Keswick?

S: Er, eight p.m.

S: Eight o'clock in afternoon.

T: OK, so how long does it take to come . . . from Victor Harbour to Keswick?

Comment

The continuation of the interaction reinforces the points which have already been made: The students, when given the opportunity, are quite capable of answering the "unprocessible" questions correctly.

There is a very interesting exchange towards the end of the interaction relating to the issue of "uptake", that is, whether learners learn what teachers teach. The teacher corrects one of the students, pointing out that we say "half past four in the afternoon", not "half past four p.m." Another student "learns" this item, and says (incorrectly) "eight o'clock in the afternoon". (A point which, by the way, goes uncorrected by the teacher – presumably because it is not a central issue on her pedagogic agenda. However, in relation to teachability, it does raise the important point that the learners themselves, their own agendas, interests and preoccupations are important elements in the language learning equation [see the study reported in Nunan 1989].) The centrality of the learner, and the learner's interpretation of what is going on within the teaching/learning process are generally overlooked in research into teachability (Breen 1985).

T: How long does it take?

S: (Three hours)

T: Three and a half hours, is it? Let's have a look. [She checks a timetable.] Yep, that's right.

S: Three a a half hour.

T: So . . . [She writes on the board "How long".] What's the question? How long . . . does . . . it, or the train . . . ? Come on. [She writes "does it take".] What's the word? [points to "take"] How long does it take . . . all right, we can say to go to Victor Harbour. OK [She writes "How long does it take to".] How long does it take to . . . [makes an eliciting motion with her hand] What's the, what's the opposite? To . . . come back. [She writes "come back".] OK.

Comment

Once again, there is compelling evidence that the question forms themselves are beyond the processing capacities of the learners. While they are
capable of providing (generally appropriate) responses to the questions,
they are generally incapable of providing the teacher with the appropriate
formulations – this despite the fact that by now the paradigm has been
built up visually on the board.

The next question is encoded in a complex syntactic structure involving
the conditional, yet the learners are still able to provide an appropriate
response.

T: Now, if you get to Victor Harbour about – what was it – twenty past
twelve . . . and then you leave Victor Harbour at about half past four, how
long do you spend in Victor Harbour? How long do you spend in Victor
Harbour? [She writes "How long do you spend in"]

S: About four hours.

T: About four hours. Yeah. OK. A nice long time. Yeah. Plenty of time. [She
writes, "Victor Harbour".] Now – the bad part – how much does it cost?
Have a look in the brochure and see if you can find the price. . . . Oh, yes,
there it is. You're looking for a word "fares" . . . "fares".

S: Twenty-five . . . twenty-five dollars.

T: Yeah, twenty-five dollars, that's right. . . . Not so good, eh?
[She writes "How much."]

S: Very cheap.

T: Not so cheap. OK, what's the question? How much . . . does . . . it cost?
Yep. How much does it cost? It costs . . . twenty-five dollars . . . for an
adult, for an adult. [She writes, "does it cost?"]
[The board now displays the following:
Where do you catch the train?
What time does the train leave?
What time does the train arrive at Goolwa?
How long does it take to go to Victor Harbour?
How long does it take to come back?
How long do you spend in Victor Harbour?
How much does it cost?]

Comment

Without drawing the attention of the students to the illustrative structures
on the board, the teacher gives them another brochure and timetable, and
asks them to find similar information to that which they have found in
relation to the excursion to Victor Harbour.

General commentary on extract 1   Proponents of the teachability hypothesis would probably claim that extract 1 fails as a piece of pedagogic
interaction, and that it fails because the teacher is dealing with linguistic
content which is unlearnable. I believe that such a conclusion would be

premature and probably unwarranted. Despite the fact that the learners are dealing with syntactic items which they are unable to break down into their constituent elements, they are able to provide semantically appropriate responses to the questions (although, when asked, they are unable to provide the question forms, which would seem to be fairly clear evidence of their unprocessibility).

Pedagogically, the major problem with the interaction is the lack of clarity in relation to the objective of the interaction. Is it to lay out explicitly for the learners the paradigm for *wh*-questions with "do" insertion? Is it to give learners communicative practice in answering *wh*-questions in relation to authentic input data? Is it to prepare learners for an out-of-class learning experience? Was the teacher's purpose transmission, language activation or preparation for a future activity? Did she have all three purposes in mind?

If the teacher had been clear about the objective, and had been able to convey this to the learners in a meaningful way, the interaction would have been more satisfactory from our own position of comfortable retrospectivity. Having laid out the *wh*-question paradigm on the board, the logical next step would be for the teacher to draw the learners' attention to the pattern which has been exhaustively drawn up. However, for reasons which are not entirely clear, she fails to take this final pedagogic step. It may have been that the inability of the students to provide citation forms of the questions made her realise that the form was unlearnable for this particular group. It may have been that she ran out of time and that the desirability of providing further explication fell victim to the exigencies of classroom management. Whatever the reason, the proponents of learnability doubtless argue that, given the unlearnability of the material for learners in question, it is a good thing that the teacher did not draw the paradigm to their attention.

I would argue that if the intention were to introduce learners to the paradigm, then it would have been useful to make the pattern explicit, regardless of the fact that it is patently beyond their current processing capacity. Making salient features of the language which are currently unprocessible could be argued (and has been argued – see Long 1983; Pica 1985; Schmidt and Frota 1986) to be one of the central reasons for undertaking formal instruction, as opposed to picking up a second language naturalistically on the street. Additional support for the explicit treatment of morphosyntactic items which are beyond the current processing capacity of the students comes from the SLA literature itself. Johnston (1985), amongst others, argues that acquisition is driven by formulae, that out of memorised formulae emerge the analysed morphosyntactic items. The big questions here – ones which are rarely raised, let alone answered – relate to the gestation period for acquisition. How far in advance of the learner's current competence should a given item be introduced? The "teachability" proponents suggest that structures should be no more than one stage in advance of the learner's current stage of development – a view which is disputed here. Whatever the answer might be, it seems clear that the avoidance strategy recommended by "teachability" proponents is difficult to support. While the students taking part in the lesson in extract 1 are clearly unable to generate the target structure, it is equally clear that they are comfortable with *wh*-questions and more than capable of responding appropriately to them. Whether they are capable of generating such questions is another matter, one which is taken up in relation to extract 2.

The second extract is taken from a class which is very similar to that in extract 1 (both consist of low-proficiency, newly arrived immigrants). The grammatical focus of the session (teaching *wh*-questions) is also very similar. However, the teacher is quite different, as is her teaching approach.

EXTRACT 2

Context   The teacher is following up on an earlier lesson in which *wh*-questions were introduced and practised. The aim of the lesson is to do further work on these question forms. During the interaction, the teacher and the students are sitting in a large circle. The teacher has some cue cards in her hand. She looks at one of the cards.

T: Let's have question "live". [She gestures with her hand.]
S: What do live?
T: No, not "what", what's the question?
S: Where?
T: Where! Good. Where . . . [She leans forward and gestures with her hands.]
S: Where . . . you . . . live?
T: [gestures encouragingly] He's nearly there. Can you help him?
S: Where . . .
    [The teacher begins counting the words off on her fingers and repeats each word as the student says them.]
S: Where (where) . . . do (do) . . . you (you) . . . live (live)?
T: OK. Listen. [The teacher speaks rapidly and makes sweeping gestures with her hands to indicate the intonation contour.]
    Where d'you live? Where d'you live? Where do you live? Everyone. [She sweeps her hand around the group.]
Ss: Where do you live?

Comment
This particular teacher's style contrasts markedly with Teacher A's whose strategy, when students had difficulty with an item, was to provide the response for them. Teacher B adopts a range of strategies. These include giving the learners time to respond (cf. Rowe 1986 on wait time). She also encourages learners to assist one another. A third strategy employed in this initial interaction is to indicate visually the number of words required by the learner.

T: OK. Victor, please ask Roberto.
S: Where do you live?
T: Where do you live?
S: I live . . . in Smithfield.
T: OK, fine. What's the next question? [consults one of the cards in her hand] "Come from". Er . . . Elizabeth, could you ask Maria, please?
S: Where do you come from?
S: Er . . .
    [Maria hesitates; the teacher gestures vigorously to herself.]
S: Er . . . I'm . . . come. . .
T: No, no, no, "I am"
S: I'm
T: No "I am". [The teacher turns to another student.] Can you help her?
Ss: I . . . come . . . from . . . Chile.

Comment
The next phase in the lesson is to get students questioning each other. Once again, rather than providing the question herself, she encourages the students to help each other.

T: OK, fine. What was number five – the question – "languages"?
Ss: What, er, what . . . what . . . what . . . languages. . .
T: What languages. . .
S: What . . . languages . . . do . . .
T: Do
S: . . . you . . . speak?
T: Yes. What languages do you speak? What languages do you speak? Remember? What languages do you speak? OK, Daniel, ask Pia.
S: What languages do you speak?
S: I speak English.
T: Uh huh. All right. And in your country . . . I speak Viet. . .
S: I speak Vietnamese.
T: Good, I speak Vietnamese. And . . .
S: And . . . And a little . . .
T: And a little English. And a little English. And a little English. And . . . a little [The teacher pauses, gestures and smiles encouragingly at one of the male students.]
S: English.
T: OK. I know you don't like saying you speak a little English. [The students laugh.]

Comment
The teacher continues to introduce new cue words and get students to question each other. She also lightens the tone of the lesson by referring to one student's evident reluctance to say he speaks a little English.

T: What's the next one? [She consults her cards.] Question. "Married" . . . What was the question?

S: Are . . .
S: Are you married?
T: Uh huh, are . . . Ask Rosa, please.
S: Are you married?
S: Yes, I am. This is my wife.
T: This is my. . . ? [The teacher points to one of the male students.]
S: This is my wife.
T: Wife? [laughter]
S: Ah, husband.
T: This is my husband. OK. Have you got. Have you got any children? Have
    you got a pen? Have you got . . . a book? Have you got any brothers or
    sisters? Remember yesterday? OK. Helena, could you ask Victor the ques-
    tion, please?
S: Have you got any brothers, er, sisters?
S: Yes. I've got er two brothers, two sisters.

Comment
Once again, it is evident that *wh*-questions with 'do' insertion are beyond
the processing capacity of these learners. However, in the controlled cli-
mate of the classroom, they are capable, given enough time and support,
to come up with the required question forms. Given the fact that in genuine communicative interactions outside the classroom it is highly unlikely
that the students would be able to form such questions, we need to ask
whether this type of practice is justified. I believe that it is for the reasons
already enumerated. The learners are obtaining formulaic practice in key
areas of morphosyntax.

General commentary on extract 2   In both of the lesson extracts presented and analysed in this chapter, we have seen instructional sequences
in which the teachers violate the teachability hypothesis by presenting
and practising morphosyntactic items which are beyond the processing
capacity of the learners. Despite this, I believe that the lessons are justifiable for the following reasons:

1. It is important for ESL learners such as these to have *wh*-questions
as part of their communicative repertoire, even if such structures are
only learned and used as unanalysed formulae. In any event, it is argued
(by Johnston 1985, among others) that analysed language evolves out of
formulaic language.

2. While we know little about the "gestation" period of language
development, it is reasonable to argue that a major function of instruction is for the teacher to make salient to the learners the ways in which
the language is structured, even if they are not capable of analysing the
language items at that particular point in time. This very point is argued
by Long (1983, 1985); and also by Ellis (1990a), and Rutherford (1987),
in their work on grammatical consciousness-raising.

General commentary on extracts 1 and 2   In both of the classroom extracts analysed here, the learners are presented with morphosyntactic items which are well in advance of their current level of competence. Despite this, the instructional sequences can be justified on the grounds of acquisition, psycholinguistics and pedagogy.

1. **Acquisition.** Indications are that the acquisition process is initiated by target utterances which are, in the first instance, learned as formulae. There is evidence in the second extract that the students are able to manipulate the target utterances through learning them as formulae.

2. **Psycholinguistic.** In psycholinguistic terms, we know that learners do not immediately reproduce productively those items to which they have been exposed. However, in the absence of evidence to the contrary, it is reasonable to assume that learners need, and will benefit from, systematic exposure to target structures over a prolonged period of time. We do not know how long this gestation period is likely to be. No doubt it will be influenced by factors such as the context in which the students are learning, the processing complexity of the target items, and factors associated with the learner, such as degree of communicative need. Evidence does suggest (see, for example, Pica 1985) that making salient to learners structures which are beyond their current processing capacity can facilitate the rate of acquisition. There is also a danger in confusing productive and receptive knowledge (Ellis 1991).

3. **Pedagogical.** From the perspective of communicative language teaching, there is very little that one can do in the classroom, particularly at lower levels of proficiency, without the introduction of relatively late-acquired structures such as question forms. This is another reason for introducing such items as formulae early in the learning process.

Conclusion

The overall purpose of this chapter has been to bring together linguistic theory and research and pedagogic practice. I have chosen to focus on such theory and research which makes claims of relevance to practice. In the first part of the chapter, I reviewed several models which have either influenced pedagogy or which have made strong claims of relevance, focusing in particular on the teachability hypothesis. In the second part of the chapter, I presented a study of grammar teaching in action designed to provide evaluative data on the hypothesis. While I find the research evidence on invariant sequencing convincing, I do not accept the pedagogical implications claimed by proponents of the "teachability" hypothesis. I believe that there are grave dangers of uncritically importing into the classroom conclusions derived from data collected through laboratory-type experiments and other elicitation procedures. I feel that, at this stage, the greatest potential of the research reviewed here lies in areas of language education other than the classroom (one area which comes to mind is that of assessment).

I should like to conclude the chapter by pointing out that in the final analysis all linguistic theories, as well as research conducted in laboratory contexts and simulated settings, must be contested against the reality of genuine classrooms. In such genuine contexts, a range of issues and factors, practical as well as theoretical, will operate to determine what is pedagogically feasible and desirable. The problematic relationship between outcomes from research carried out in laboratory settings and the exigencies of the classroom has been articulated by Ellis (1990b), who expresses scepticism that laboratory research will ever

> produce the definitive answers that some researchers expect – even if they are designed rigorously. . . . There are two principal reasons for this scepticism. First, the instruction-learning relationship is a complex one. It is a variable relationship, probably curvilinear rather than linear. . . . Success, therefore, can be achieved in many ways. Experimental research will provide 'piecemeal understanding' (Allwright 1988) and contribute to theory building, but it will never provide the comprehensive answers upon which pedagogic decisions can be based. Second, a positivistic view of the role of research fails to recognize the intrinsic nature of educational change. Innovation in the classroom can never be just a question of implementing a recommendation derived from research. It is always a process of negotiation, involving the teacher's overall educational ideology, the learners' expectations and preferences and local constraints that determine what is feasible. There is no single pedagogical solution which is applicable in all classrooms. (pp. 67–68)

While I am in no way suggesting that research carried out in laboratory or simulated settings be eschewed by practitioners, I do believe, like Ellis, that research which is intended to inform pedagogy needs, where feasible, be carried out within the language classroom. Where this is not feasible, research outcomes need to be contested and evaluated against the realities of the classroom. In this regard, classroom teachers themselves have a major role to play in collecting and analysing data from their own classroom contexts and situations.

References

Allwright, D. 1988. *Observation in the Language Classroom*. London: Longman.
Bailey, N., C. Madden and S. Krashen. 1974. Is there a "natural sequence" in adult second language learning? *Language Learning* 24: 235–43.

Breen, M. 1985. The social context of language learning: A neglected situation? *Studies in Second Language Acquisition* 7.

Brindley, G. 1989. Learnability in the ESL classroom. Paper presented at the Biennial ATESOL Summer School, University of Sydney, January 1989.

Brown, R. 1973. *A First Language.* Cambridge, Mass.: Harvard University Press.

Dulay, H., and M. Burt. 1973. Should we teach children syntax? *Language Learning* 23: 245–57.

1974. Natural sequences in child second language acquisition. *Language Learning* 24: 37–53.

Dulay, H., M. Burt and S. Krashen. 1982. *Language Two.* New York: Oxford University Press.

Ellis, R. 1990a. Grammatical consciousness-raising. Paper presented at the Annual JALT Convention, Omiya, Japan, November 1990.

1990b. Researching classroom language learning. In C. Brumfit and R. Mitchell (eds.), *Research in the Language Classroom.* London: Modern English Publications.

1991. Grammar teaching – What kind works best for second language acquisition? Paper presented at the Second International Conference on Explorations and Innovations in English Language Teaching Methodology. Bangkok, Thailand, December 1991.

Eubank, L. 1990. Linguistic theory and the acquisition of German negation. In B. VanPatten and J. F. Lee (eds.), *Second Language Acquisition/Foreign Language Learning.* Clevedon Avon: Multilingual Matters.

James, C. 1980. *Contrastive Analysis.* London: Longman.

Johnston, M. 1985. Syntactic and Morphological Progressions in Learner English. Canberra, Australia: Department of Immigration and Ethnic Affairs.

Lado, R. 1957. *Linguistics Across Cultures.* Ann Arbor: University of Michigan Press.

Long, M. 1983. Does instruction make a difference? *TESOL Quarterly* 17: 359–82.

1985. Input and second language acquisition theory. In S. Gass and C. Madden (eds.), *Input in Second Language Acquisition.* Rowley, Mass.: Newbury House.

Nunan, D. 1989. *The Learner-Centered Curriculum.* Cambridge: Cambridge University Press.

1991. *Language Teaching Methodology.* London: Prentice Hall.

Odlin, T. 1989. *Language Transfer.* Cambridge: Cambridge University Press.

Pica, T. 1985. The selective impact of classroom instruction on second language acquisition. *Applied Linguistics* 6(3), 214–22.

Pienemann, M. 1985. Learnability and syllabus construction. In K. Hyltenstam and M. Pienemann (eds.), *Modelling and Assessing Second Language Development.* Clevedon Avon: Multilingual Matters.

1987. Determining the influence of instruction on L2 speech processing. *Australian Review of Applied Linguistics* 10:2, 83–113.

Pienemann, M., and M. Johnston. 1987. Factors influencing the development of language proficiency. In D. Nunan (ed.), *Applying Second Language Acquisition Research.* Adelaide, Australia: National Curriculum Resource Centre.

Rowe, M. 1986. Wait time: Slowing down may be a way of speeding up. *Journal of Teacher Education* 37: 43–50.

Rutherford, W. 1987. *Second Language Grammar Learning and Teaching*. London: Longman.

Schmidt, R., and S. Frota. 1986. Developing basic conversational ability in a second language: a case study of an adult learner of Portuguese. In R. Day (ed.), *Talking to Learn: Conversation in Second Language Acquisition*. Rowley, Mass.: Newbury House.

11 The Introspective Hierarchy: A comparison of intuitions of linguists, teachers, and learners

Terence Odlin

Both in the teaching and the learning of grammatical structures, intuition plays a key role. Teachers use their intuitions about the target language to provide goals for students and to evaluate student performance. Learners have their own intuitions about what does or does not belong to the target language, and changes in such intuitions reflect, however obliquely, their developing competence in the target language. This article considers the hierarchical nature of intuitions in language teaching. In idealized form, the hierarchy of intuitions establishes clearcut degrees of *authority* in judgments: Learners normally defer to the intuitions of teachers, and when teachers are in doubt they defer to the intuitions of grammarians (who may or may not be professional linguists). In reality, the workings of the hierarchy are far more complex. The focus of the article is on one of the problematic aspects of the hierarchy: the fact that there are limitations on the ability of teachers and linguists to provide reliable judgments. This fact has important consequences for everyday practice in language teaching.

On the nature of intuitions

Scholars have long found it difficult to define the term *intuition* in a fully adequate way. Such a definition would imply a satisfactory answer to some of the most intractable philosophical and psychological problems. The nature of knowledge, consciousness, and judgment will certainly be important considerations in any satisfactory account of intuition, but these and other considerations remain controversial (cf. Rorty 1967). For the purposes of this article, however, the following definition is adequate: Intuition is "arriving at decisions or conclusions without explicit or conscious processes of reasoned thinking" (Gregory 1987: 389).

The definition just given is typical of many others in that it alludes to the notions of *consciousness* and *explicitness*. These terms themselves are controversial for many scholars, including second language researchers (cf. Schmidt 1990). As the distinctions between *conscious* and *unconscious* knowledge and *explicit* and *implicit* knowledge have not proven

271

satisfactory to all investigators, alternative distinctions have often been proposed, calling for similar distinctions between *declarative* and *procedural* knowledge, *analyzed* and *unanalyzed* knowledge, *controlled* and *automatic* processing, and *learning* and *acquisition* (Bialystok 1979; Krashen 1981; Bialystok and Ryan 1985; Odlin 1986; Singley and Anderson 1989).

Whichever pair of terms is the most satisfactory, it does seem useful to distinguish between implicit knowledge (or, knowing) and explicit knowledge (knowing about). The former typically denotes the capacity to speak and understand a language. In contrast, *explicit knowledge* implies different capacities, including the ability to judge if a sentence is grammatical or not, to judge whether two words have equivalent meanings, to say how many syllables a word has, and so forth. *Explicit* is a useful descriptor since it suggests that knowledge about language can be verbalized: Language learners can express their intuitions (even when the expression is inaccurate) and linguists can provide explicit descriptions of language and linguistic behavior, including acquisition.

Explicit knowledge is not a unitary concept. Indeed, the range of abilities involved is wide, as the following list of tasks suggests:

- judging acceptability
- locating a deviant feature in a sentence
- correcting a deviant sentence
- proofreading a text
- judging ambiguity in a sentence
- judging the synonymy of words or sentences
- paraphrasing a sentence or text

Most of these are tasks that adult native speakers of a language can perform with little or no training, even if the performance is not always flawless. (Proofreading a text requires that an individual can read, of course, but the other tasks do not presuppose any literacy.) The list is hardly exhaustive: Bialystok and Ryan (1985) discuss a number of tasks especially common in schools, such as identifying grammatical rules involved in distinguishing standard and nonstandard usage.

The abilities just listed play an important role in communication. While explicit knowledge is sometimes thought to be irrelevant to everyday communication, conversations would certainly be more cumbersome, and at times impossible, if we did not have the ability to make corrections (e.g., "Go north – I mean south!"), to request clarifications (e.g., "Excuse me, did you say *fifty* or *fifteen?*"), or to provide interpretations ("Most of the regulations apply only to seniors"). Language teaching would be infinitely more difficult without these abilities or those that make it possible to carry out grammatical analyses such as part-of-speech identifications.

In view of the importance of these everyday abilities, there is surely much more that could be – and some day should be – said about the wide range of intuitions of learners, teachers, and linguists since such intuitions underlie explicit knowledge. However, two types of judgments are especially important and will be the focus of most of the discussion in this article.

Judgments of grammaticality and acceptability

Linguists frequently distinguish between *grammaticality* and *acceptability*. The distinction is a useful one in a number of ways. As seen by linguists, the notion of grammaticality applies to descriptive grammars (as discussed in the introduction to this volume). Thus, to judge the grammaticality of a sentence is to say whether or not the sentence is consistent with the grammar describing the language, regardless of whether speakers consider the sentence to be nonstandard, stylistically inappropriate, or infelicitous in any other way. A judgment about the grammaticality of a structure with English words makes a claim about whether the structure "is English" or "is not English," but the judgment need not make any claim about whether the sentence "is good English" or not. Acceptability judgments, on the other hand, make claims such as whether a structure is standard or nonstandard, whether it is easily understood or not, and whether it is stylistically appropriate or not.

Often there is widespread agreement about the grammaticality of a sentence. For example, nearly all informants in a study by Elliott, Legum, and Thompson (1969) agreed that the following sentence is grammatical:

1. Marcia made cookies this morning and Sara did so this afternoon.

Similarly, a more recent study by Coppetiers (1987) indicates that native speakers of French often concur in their judgments even of problematic sentences.

In such cases, the consistency of the informants' judgments validates the assumption of linguists that some judgments are highly reliable and that they can therefore provide a baseline for analyzing the structures of a language. If such consistency were rare among native speakers, linguists would find it hard or even impossible to justify their use of intuitions in writing descriptive grammars. Moreover, comparisons between native and nonnative speakers would be problematic if there were not considerable homogeneity in the judgments of native speakers. Such consistency exemplifies the first of three principles suggested by Labov (1975) to provide guidelines for introspection:

I. THE CONSENSUS PRINCIPLE: if there is no reason to think otherwise, assume that the judgments of any native speaker are characteristic of all speakers of the language.

Unfortunately, not all cases are so straightforward. Neither linguists nor ordinary native speakers seem able to provide consistently accurate judgments about structures used outside of their dialect area. For example, Trudgill (1984) found that many people (including linguists) at a university in southern England considered the following sentence to be impossible in English:

2. My hair needs washed. (= My hair needs to be washed.)

This construction with *need* is used in some dialects of American and Scottish English, but few of the linguists (all of whom were native speakers) or ordinary native speakers had accurate intuitions about #2 being a possible sentence in English. These results contrast strikingly with those I obtained when I provided this sentence (along with others in Trudgill's study) to native-speaker students at Ohio State University in a written survey. Nearly everyone judged #2 to be possible, and many reported using sentences like it.[1] Such a result is not at all surprising since this structure is common in several parts of Ohio and some neighboring states.

Even if teachers and linguists had a thorough knowledge of dialect differences, introspective judgments would still be problematic in many instances. Numerous difficulties are related to the difference between grammaticality and acceptability. Chomsky (1965) and many other linguists have considered grammaticality to be a correlate of linguistic competence, and acceptability to be one of linguistic performance. Generative grammarians frequently discuss examples that they consider grammatical though not acceptable, as in the following example from Chomsky (1965: 11):

3. The man who the boy who the students recognized pointed out is a friend of mine.

Although many people, including some linguists, would be skeptical that a sentence such as #3 is in fact "possible English" in any sense, the distinction between grammaticality and acceptability has proven useful, as has the distinction between competence and performance discussed in the introduction to this volume.

A multitude of performance factors influence judgments of acceptability. For example, Greenbaum (1988) found that there is a significant correlation between frequency and acceptability: The more frequently a

---

1 The questionnaire and procedure I used were very similar to those described by Trudgill. In the interest of brevity, I have not provided the numerical breakdown of responses in Trudgill's survey or in my own.

structure is used, the more likely it will be given a high acceptability rating. In this sense, the frequency of a sentence structure provides no help in making decisions about grammaticality: A rarely used structure is nevertheless part of the language, as in the case of object-of-comparison relative clauses such as *I see the man that John is taller than*. Aside from frequency, other performance factors can affect judgments, including (1) the presentation order of sentences in a list (Greenbaum 1977; Snow 1975); (2) the discourse contexts in which sentences occur (Heringer 1970); (3) the concreteness of the words in the syntactic structure (Levelt et al. 1977); (4) the perceived linguistic ability of the individual using the sentence (Tucker and Sarofim 1979).

Since many performance factors affect acceptability judgments, linguists can justifiably posit a distinction between acceptability and grammaticality. Sentences that are part of the language are equally grammatical even if differing acceptability judgments are obtained for *I see the man that John is taller than* on the one hand, and *Marcia made cookies this morning and Sara did so this afternoon* on the other. At the same time, however, the notion of "grammaticality judgments" remains problematic (cf. Ringen 1977). The term is certainly widespread, and doubtlessly there exist many judgments that are uncontroversial statements about what is or is not in the grammar of English, Korean, or any other language. Nevertheless, performance factors influence *all* judgments.

If grammaticality judgments, as opposed to acceptability judgments, are really possible, they must be sorted out from the performance factors that can influence them. Such factors affect the judgments of linguists, teachers, and learners, albeit in different ways. Accordingly, there is a need to consider the roles of both performance and competence in distinguishing the judgments of linguists, teachers, and learners in the Introspective Hierarchy.

Linguists' judgments

Teachers often defer to the judgments of linguists. When teachers enroll in graduate courses taught by linguists, when they consult reference books such as *A Concise Grammar of Contemporary English* (Quirk and Greenbaum 1973), or when they seek advice such as that provided by the Oxford Word and Language Service, they give tacit recognition to the greater expertise of linguists. Despite the intellectual authority of linguists, however, there are real limitations on the reliability of their judgments.

In some cases, the limitations on linguists' judgments result from competence factors that also affect nonspecialist judgments. As noted earlier, linguists in southern England often could not recognize that *My hair needs washed* is a possible sentence in English. Such a result is not surprising, since English dialects show a number of syntactic differences, many of them not very well known. If one happens to speak another dialect and is unfamiliar with the differences between dialects, it will sometimes be impossible to determine what speakers of other dialects might or might not say.

There is also no reason to think that linguists are immune to all of the performance factors that affect nonspecialists in their judgments of English sentences. As noted earlier, Chomsky and others consider sentences such as #3 to be grammatical but not acceptable: *The man who the boy who the students recognized pointed out is a friend of mine.* The reason for the unacceptability is clear: Using multiple self-embedded relative clauses such as #3 would surely tax *anyone's* comprehension.

Yet along with the performance factors that affect any person's judgments, some factors seem especially likely to affect "expert" judgments, as seen in studies showing that the judgments of linguists can diverge from those of nonspecialists. Spencer (1973) took sentences from some of the better-known papers by linguists in the 1960s and asked 65 individuals to give grammaticality judgments. Their judgments agreed with those of linguists in only about 50 percent of the cases. Moreover, in the judgments of most sentences, there was a high degree of consensus: On average, fewer than 20 percent of the subjects gave ratings which disagreed with the ratings of other subjects on any given sentence.

There is more than one explanation for such cases of disagreement between the judgments of linguists and those of nonspecialists. In many cases, a linguist "may think that he is dealing with grammaticality but may really be reporting, say, his success in imagining a context in which the example would sound normal" (McCawley 1985: 673). Spencer did not provide any of the specific sentences used in her study, but the following sentence illustrates the problem of context:

4. Please sit in the apple-juice seat.

As Lakoff and Johnson (1980: 12) note, this sentence "makes perfect sense in the context in which it was uttered. An overnight guest came down to breakfast. There were four place settings, three with orange juice and one with apple juice." Out of context, the sentence may well seem unacceptable and even uninterpretable (cf. Blaubergs and Jarrett 1977). In such cases, then, imagination is a performance factor that can affect intuitions of acceptability or grammaticality. Misjudgments of sentences such as #4 are not peculiar to linguists: Anyone might fail to imagine the necessary context. However, there may be an "occupational hazard" in the activity of analyzing syntactic and semantic structures out of context. Carroll, Bever, and Pollock (1981) provide empirical evidence of just such a hazard, and they observe:

Speakers/hearers . . . are not normally aware of the unacceptabilities, presuppositions, and ambiguities in their own utterances, or in the speech of others. In order to have intuitions about acceptability, linguists must almost cease to be behaving speaker/hearers. They must pause and reflect . . . [and] objectify the sentence from all the specific potential functional contexts of its utterance. (p. 370)

Thus, introspections about any sentence out of context may discourage analysts from imagining situations in which a sentence would be acceptable.

Results such as those in Spencer's study do not necessarily confer greater authority on ordinary native speakers when their judgments differ from those of linguists. Despite any consistent differences in the judgments of nonspecialists, one could still argue that the expert knowledge of linguists is more reliable. In intuitions about language (or about other phenomena), a unanimous judgment of nonexperts might be incorrect. However, the problem of authority in judgments is complicated by the fact that neither ordinary speakers nor linguists always agree with each other in their judgments, as seen in studies by Levelt (1972) and Ross (1979). Levelt presented sentences from papers on English syntax to a group of 24 linguists and found that in fewer than half the cases did the judgments of subjects concur with those given in the papers. Each of the linguists was a nonnative speaker of English, but all had advanced training in English and several were English-language specialists. Ross's study, moreover, found similar disagreements among ordinary speakers and also among linguists. For example, there was considerable disagreement about the following sentence:

5. What will the grandfather clock stand between the bed and?

Among nine linguists (all native speakers of English), two found this sentence completely acceptable, two found it marginally possible, and five considered it "absolutely out." Judgments on a number of other sentences concurred somewhat more but still showed considerable disagreement.

Sociolinguists and others have long noted the main theoretical dilemma posed by introspection in linguists. As stated by Labov (1972: 199), "linguists cannot continue to produce theory and data at the same time." That is, in consulting their own intuitions, linguists run the risk of having their theories mislead them about what actually occurs in a language (cf. Ross 1979; Itkonen 1981; Trudgill 1984). Such risks seem unavoidable, however, unless researchers dispensed with intuitions altogether – if that were possible to do, and indeed it is not. Even if abolishing intuition might work, alternative ways of pursuing research have their own problems.[2]

2 One could minimize reliance on intuitions by only looking at text-based materials, for example. However, the nonoccurrence of a sentence type in even a very large corpus in English, for instance, does not guarantee that the sentence type is impossible (cf. Gregg 1989).

Moreover, the problems in judgments do not seem insurmountable as there are ways to control for inaccuracies (Labov 1975; Snow 1975). For example, Labov has proposed the following methodological principles:

I. THE CONSENSUS PRINCIPLE: if there is no reason to think otherwise, assume that the judgments of any native speaker are characteristic of all speakers of the language.
II. THE EXPERIMENTER PRINCIPLE: if there is any disagreement on introspective judgments, the judgments of those who are familiar with the theoretical issues may not be counted as evidence.
III. THE CLEAR CASE PRINCIPLE: disputed judgments should be shown to include at least one consistent pattern in the speech community or be abandoned.

The first principle, which was noted earlier, is one that most linguists would concur with: Nearly all recent syntactic work seems to proceed on similar assumptions. The other two principles, however, are frequently ignored. Theoretical biases – and unconcern about such biases – have sometimes led to amusing splits in judgments, with scholars at one institution favoring one interpretation of a sentence and scholars at another institution favoring a different interpretation (Labov 1972). More recently, a prestigious journal has declared a moratorium on papers dealing with contractions because of widespread disagreement in grammaticality judgments (Birdsong 1989).

Even though Labov's three principles are not always heeded, they do provide a useful start for determining when an acceptability judgment may also be a reliable grammaticality judgment. If and when linguists develop (and heed) a complete set of guidelines, they will be able to make more credible claims about grammaticality (and competence) than is sometimes the case now. Whether or not linguists' judgments become increasingly reliable, their judgments will still fall short of the needs of teachers. For many linguists, their primary concern is grammaticality rather than acceptability, even if their judgments say more about the latter than about the former. However, teachers need to be just as concerned with acceptability as with grammaticality. The implications of this difference will be discussed in the final section.

Teachers' judgments

As teachers defer to the expertise of linguists, learners defer to the linguistic authority of teachers in several ways. For example, learners' questions about what is grammatical (and/or acceptable) imply that they expect the teacher to be able to provide accurate judgments, even if that expectation is not always met in practice. The expert knowledge that a teacher actually has will vary, of course, with the education and experience of the individual. Not surprisingly, variations in background will sometimes lead to variations in judgments, as much of the discussion in this section will suggest. Despite the variation, however, there is some uniformity in teachers' judgments. For example, Birdsong and Kassen (1988) found considerable agreement between two groups of teachers of French about the relative severity of certain errors, one of the groups consisting of native speakers of French and the other of nonnative speakers. In the same study there is also evidence of considerable agreement between these groups of teachers and two groups of learners, although there are methodological problems involved in such comparisons (cf. Birdsong 1989).

Although teachers will agree in some instances, there is considerable evidence that their judgments are not always reliable either with regard to acceptability or to grammaticality. Teachers may be especially prone to judging an ordinary type of sentence negatively (i.e., they may consider it unacceptable), or on the other hand, teachers may misjudge whether a certain type of sentence exists in the language (i.e., they may consider it ungrammatical). The following discussion considers both kinds of misjudgments.

Extreme prescriptivism can lead to questionable judgments of acceptability. Schmidt and McCreary (1977) found discrepancies in judgments of several groups, including two groups of ESL teachers. Each group was presented with pairs of sentences such as the following:

6. a. There's about five minutes left.
6. b. There are about five minutes left.

In the ESL teachers' group consisting of native speakers, a large majority of informants employed #6a in a test of spontaneous usage. However, several of these informants in a subsequent test *reported* that they normally used #6b – in fact, more teachers reported using #6b as opposed to #6a. The discrepancy of such judgments was even more striking when the same informants were asked, on a third test, to judge the "correctness" of the same patterns: Only a small minority of the teachers considered #6a to be correct. In the other group of ESL teachers, who were nonnative speakers of English, there were similar discrepancies, although slightly less than half of the group employed #6a in the test of spontaneous usage.

Another significant fact in this study is that the responses of the native-speaker teachers of ESL were quite similar to responses of native speakers who were not teachers of English. It seems clear that the teachers' performances closely reflected the discrepancy between the forms that ordinary speakers of English use and the forms that they regard as correct. Schmidt and McCreary (1977: 428) thus claim that "all native speakers speak dialects which are in some ways 'non-standard.' " One may doubt whether sentences such as #6a are invariably nonstandard, as discussion further on suggests. Yet whatever the best interpretation of such findings is, the discrepancy in use and judgments indicates that teachers may pass on to learners some judgments that are questionable. ESL students might well be perplexed to hear their teachers (as well as most other native speakers) use forms such as #6a but then to be told that such forms are unacceptable.

Along with misjudgments of acceptability, questionable judgments of grammaticality are also possible and do indeed occur. That is, teachers may not always correctly judge whether a certain type of sentence exists in the language. When teachers are nonnative speakers of English, such misjudgments are not highly unusual. Some of the most notorious examples of misjudgments are found in *New Guide of the Conversation in Portuguese and English* [*sic*] (Carolino 1883), which also appeared in abridged form under the title *English as She Is Spoke* [*sic*] (Carolino 1883/1967). As both titles would suggest, Carolino was not highly proficient in English. In fact, the editor of the 1967 edition speculates that Carolino merely translated by means of a dictionary and had no real knowledge of the language. Still, Carolino had enough confidence to posit rules for English that are, to say the least, unique. For example, he distinguishes between the two forms of the indefinite article in English (*a/an*) by using one (*a*) before *cousin* in referring to any male cousin and the other (*an*) before the same word in referring to any female cousin. Portuguese influence was no doubt the source of this bizarre rule. Carolino's blunders were not confined to illusory distinctions. He also provided as models of usage forms such as the following:

For the comedy
Were you go to theatre yesterday?

Yes, sir; I won't to see the new play in which did owed to play and actress which has not appeared on any theatre.

How you think her?

She has very much grace in the deeds great deal of exactness on the declamation, a constitution very agreable [*sic*], a delight ful [*sic*] voice. (1883: 117–18)

Even though such mistaken intuitions go, one hopes, beyond the normal range seen in language teaching by nonnative speakers, they are not the only manifestation of nonnative proficiency. Judgments by nonnative speakers may vary more than judgments by native speakers, although there is controversy about this supposed difference (cf. Lehiste 1971; Coppetiers 1987; Birdsong 1992). A less controversial characteristic of nonnative judgments is caution: Birdsong (1989) notes a tendency for nonnative speakers to be more reserved in their judgments. Teachers who are nonnative speakers will probably be especially liable to feel uncertain about their judgments.

Even having native-speaker intuitions does not, however, guarantee that judgments will be accurate. Just as linguists may not accurately judge sentences from other dialects, teachers may often err in making such judgments. As mentioned before, native-speaker students at Ohio State were generally able to identify *My hair needs washed* as a possible English sentence. On the other hand, these students (among whom were many ESL teachers) were generally not aware that some native speakers of English use sentences such as the following:

7. Look – is that a man stand there? (Look – is that a man standing there?)

Trudgill (1984) notes that such sentences are common among native speakers in East Anglia, which lies northeast of London.

Such results are hardly surprising. Being a native speaker, a linguist, or a teacher does not guarantee that one will have consistently accurate intuitions about structures outside one's dialect area. In a certain respect, such misjudgments are relatively unimportant. After all, the target language is usually a standard variety and sentences such as *Is that a man stand there?* have not gained widespread recognition or acceptance. On the other hand, teachers should be able to distinguish common cases of grammatical but unacceptable sentences (e.g., *She love him very much*) from those that are neither grammatical nor acceptable: that is, sentences that only a person such as Carolino would use or pseudosentences that no one at all would use. Trudgill's survey and my own indicate that most linguists are aware that *She love him very much* is a possible (albeit nonstandard) English sentence, but the surveys also indicate that many teachers are not aware that such sentences widely occur in nonstandard dialects. Precision in such matters is desirable since the credibility of teachers may suffer if their students encounter a native speaker who says *She love him very much* after they have been told that such sentences do not exist.

Learner judgments

Although caution is certainly necessary, there have been some fairly consistent findings in studies of the intuitions of second language learners. One such finding is, not surprisingly, that more advanced learners tend to be more accurate in their judgments and/or corrections of deviant sentences (e.g., Arthur 1980; Singh, d'Anglejan, and Carroll 1982; Gass 1983; Odlin 1987). This strongly suggests that even though performance factors may make it difficult to pinpoint an individual's specific competence, differences in intuitions reflect different stages of development in the learner's knowledge of a second language.

Further evidence that learner judgments will sometimes reflect interlanguage competence comes from studies of language transfer. Under certain conditions not completely understood, native-language influence appears to affect learner judgments. This influence is evident in several studies in which there have been two or more groups of learners with different languages. For example, White (1985) found that Spanish speakers and French speakers responded quite differently to the following sentence:

8. My sister is very tired because came home late last night.

The absence of a subject pronoun in such a subordinate clause is not grammatical in either English or French. However, Spanish does allow subject pronouns to be omitted in comparable sentences, and the judgments of Spanish speakers seem to have been affected by their native language: In a statistically significant comparison, White found that seven times as many Spanish speakers accepted sentence #8 as did French speakers. In a study of relative clauses, Gass (1979) obtained comparable evidence for transfer, as did Schachter, Tyson, and Diffley (1976), though in the latter study there are some complicating factors. Kellerman (1977, 1978) argues that learner judgments may sometimes reflect subjective assessments about the degree of similarity between the native and the target language. For example, Kellerman (1978) found that Dutch students were reluctant to judge *The cup broke* as grammatical even though a word-for-word translation equivalent exists in Dutch, *'t kopje brak*. Kellerman's explanation for this reluctance is that (1) there are constraints on what can transfer, with idioms being less transferable than some other structures; and (2) such constraints affect learners' judgments (cf. Sjöholm 1983; Odlin 1991). Although Kellerman's arguments are not completely satisfactory, Yip's paper in this volume supports certain claims, since the semantic structure of ergative verbs such as *break* appears to influence learner judgments in such cases.

Findings like those just described make it hard to argue that learner judgments (or any other kind) reflect only performance factors. If performance alone determined learner judgments, it would be hard to explain why learners considered more proficient (according to measures besides judgment tests) so often outperform less proficient students on judgment tests. Likewise, it would be hard to find performance differences that might consistently account for effects that native-language competence has on learners' developing interlanguage competence.

Aside from transfer, the principles of Universal Grammar may inform some judgments. Ritchie (1978) made strong claims for universal influences in a study of Japanese ESL students in which he asked learners to judge the relative acceptability of sentences such as #9b and #9c:

9. a. That [a book by Chomsky] has just come out is not surprising.
9. b. That [a book __] has just come out by Chomsky is not surprising.
9. c. That [a book __] has just come out is not surprising by Chomsky.

While speakers of English may find #9a more acceptable than #9b, #9b will probably seem much more acceptable than #9c. Ritchie and others see the unacceptability (and ungrammaticality) of #9c as due to a principle known as the Right Roof Constraint, which is believed to put limits on the "rightward movement" of units such as prepositional phrases. This hypothesized universal would presumably inform learners' intuitions. That is, even if learners had never encountered a sentence such as #9b (a syntactic pattern that is not especially common), they would sense that it is a much more probable structure in English than is #9c. Ritchie's results do provide some intriguing suggestions of a universal at work. However, there are theoretical and methodological problems in his study that cast serious doubt on the conclusions (Schachter 1989). Moreover, similar problems arise in several other studies investigating possible influences from language universals (Birdsong 1989; Thomas 1989; White 1989). If universal factors inform learner judgments (and they probably do in some ways), researchers are not yet able to provide a convincing explanation.

Several of the studies just cited indicate that learners' intuitions can reflect their competence. However, it would be mistaken to assume that the window provided by intuitions is transparent instead of translucent. That is, the competence which underlies intuitions does exist and is explorable, but performance factors can make it difficult to interpret the nature of that competence (cf. Chaudron 1983; Birdsong 1989; Bley-Vroman 1989; Gregg 1989). Some of the performance factors that affect judgments of native speakers surely affect nonnative judgments also (Odlin 1987). However, these factors probably have greater effects on nonnative judgments, which are especially prone to instability and uncertainty because learners' interlanguage competence is often incomplete.

Recent studies by Ellis (1990, 1991) indicate that previous attempts to gauge such uncertainty have probably underestimated the seriousness of the interpretation problem (cf. Yule, Yanz, and Tsuda 1985; Sorace 1991). In one study by Ellis (1990), Japanese speakers took the same judgment test on two occasions, with two weeks intervening between the first and the second sitting. From the first to the second time, many subjects changed their judgments of sentences such as *The president offered him a job,* even though very few reported any uncertainty about their response (and the test instructions made that option clear). Not all judgments were so unstable; for some sentences, subjects rarely changed their judgments (cf. Beretta and Gass 1991). Nevertheless, the instability in learner judgments on some sentences indicates that uncertainty is one of the key characteristics of learner intuitions. Although research has demonstrated that native speakers can show some of the same uncertainty (Snow 1975), the incomplete knowledge of learners makes such a trait more important and one that teachers need to take into account in second language instruction.

Conclusions

Although linguists and teachers have genuine claims to expertise in their judgments, the evidence reviewed in this paper shows important limitations on the ability of the experts to provide reliable judgments. Few, if any, linguists or teachers have irrefutable intuitions about grammaticality, even though many of their judgments are reliable. Both competence and performance limitations affect expert judgments of grammaticality, and these limitations can likewise affect judgments of acceptability. In linguistics, there is a growing awareness of such limitations, even if some grammarians continue to dodge the epistemological question *What Is a Linguistic Fact?* posed by Labov (1975). In the practice of pedagogical grammar, this question is just as relevant. The authority of teachers in the Introspective Hierarchy lies midway between that of linguists and that of learners. Accordingly, it will be useful to compare the knowledge and goals of teachers and linguists, and also to compare the knowledge and goals of teachers and learners. Such comparisons suggest some important implications.

Teachers and linguists

One implication of the research reviewed in this article is that teachers should sometimes question the authority of linguists' judgments. Although linguists' expertise is greater in certain ways, professional (not to mention amateur) grammarians can and do make mistakes in some of their judgments whether because of ignorance of dialectical variation or because of theoretical biases or because of a performance limitation. Some of these judgment errors will not matter much for language teaching, as in the case of *My hair needs washed,* since such constructions have limited use and acceptability. On the other hand, some judgments involve structures not confined to any particular dialect. Huddleston (1977) considers the following sentence ungrammatical:

10. a. The computer is down by 10:00 tomorrow.

It probably is true that a sentence such as #10a occurs less often than the equivalent sentence marked for future tense:

10. b. The computer will be down by 10:00 tomorrow.

However, no one has to be a novelist in order to imagine a context in which #10a would be likely. For example, in a meeting of computer scientists who finally agree on their plans for maintenance, one of them might say

10. c. OK, we're agreed then. The computer is down by 10:00 tomorrow.

Teachers preparing materials on verb tense might not want to inform their students that #10c is possible, since learners could easily over-generalize and use present tense in contexts requiring the future. On the other hand, teachers should not include #10a as a negative example in explanations of future tense, especially not if their students are proficient enough to notice actual uses of #10c in everyday communication. Even when judgments such as Huddleston's appear in prestigious books and journals, teachers should not forsake their own intuitions.

The limitations on expert knowledge are not the only reason for teachers to be cautious when they consult linguists' judgments. The goals of grammarians usually differ sharply from those of teachers, even though the interests of the two professions overlap. Linguists tend to be concerned more with competence than with performance. In linguistics there has long been a tradition of focusing on language in isolation from the uses it is put to; "language" is a powerful, if sometimes misleading, abstraction, and linguists normally see competence as the basis for any language (cf. Gregg 1989). Thus, putatively grammatical yet definitely unacceptable sentences constitute a legitimate object of study, as in the case of sentence #3 *The man who the boy who the students recognized pointed out is a friend of mine.* Since most teachers have little acquaintance or interest in such structures, their concerns might seem to be narrower. However, just the opposite is true. Like linguists, teachers must be concerned about competence (and grammaticality), but they must also be concerned about performance (and acceptability).

Just what makes sentences acceptable is a more complex problem than what makes sentences grammatical, which itself is hardly an easy problem. Nevertheless, the following are key criteria: (1) well-formedness; (2) ease of processing; (3) appropriateness in context. Well-formedness is roughly equivalent to grammaticality: The sentence must conform to the descriptive rules of the language. Ease of processing clearly excludes sentences such as #3 and favors some structures over others (cf. Schachter and Yip 1990). For example, most English speakers (and listeners!) strongly prefer #11a to #11b:

11. a. It is important that their time should not be wasted.
11. b. That their time should not be wasted is important.

Although sentences such #11b are considered grammatical and do sometimes appear in writing, their complexity makes them seem less acceptable (cf. Erdmann 1988). Appropriateness in context encompasses a wide range of cognitive and sociolinguistic factors. For example, most editors would not countenance sentence #6a (*There's about five minutes left*) in formal writing, but such constructions usually go unnoticed in everyday conversation. If great art is, as sometimes claimed, whatever you can get away with, "standard" (hence, acceptable) usage can be whatever meets with little or no disapproval. This observation may fluster some teachers, who might see it as no more than a clever way of saying that anything goes, that there are no real rules for acceptable speech or writing. Actually, however, rules for contextual appropriateness exist, though they are far more subtle (and in many ways more frustrating) than the principles determining well-formedness and ease of processing. Yet however arcane the rules may be, they are what often inform the judgments of native speakers. As such, rules on appropriateness must have a place in any teaching aimed at helping learners to communicate effectively.

Teachers and learners

In the early stages of acquisition, learners have intuitions considerably different from those of native speakers, as the research discussed in this chapter indicates. Teachers working with learners at these stages have relatively easy demands put on their intuitions. What is grammatical or ungrammatical is often straightforward, as seen in the contrast between the following sentences:

12. a. He can speak English.
12. b. * He can speaks English.

Even in the early stages, however, learners will profit from knowing that they may hear native speakers say sentence #6a, *There's about five minutes left*. Teachers may still feel it necessary to counsel students against using such forms themselves in order to simplify the choices that novice learners make. However, it would be a gross exaggeration for an English teacher to claim that sentences such as #6a are always unacceptable, since such sentences are quite common in everyday speech.

More advanced learners can and should receive detailed information about acceptability. While intermediate and advanced students still produce ungrammatical sentences, they must be increasingly concerned about well-formed but unacceptable sentences, especially in writing. The concept of readability provides a useful point of departure for teachers to make students aware that grammaticality is not a sufficient goal in their writing. One instance of where readability concerns touch on grammar is the use of passive-voice constructions. The traditional advice given to both native and nonnative speakers is, of course, to avoid the passive. Strunk and White (1959: 13), for example, view the active as more concrete than the passive:

13. a. I shall always remember my first visit to Boston.
13. b. My first visit to Boston will always be remembered by me.

Although both are grammatical, most readers would likely find #13a easier than #13b. Yet, as Strunk and White observe, the active is not always preferable to the passive: In some situations, the passive can help to keep readers focused on the topic. If teachers wish to transcend superstitious advice such as "Never use the passive," the problem they face is to say just when the passive might be normal. To a large extent, the problem requires knowing the goals of student writers. If the students are writing theses in the natural sciences, they may need to employ passive-voice constructions more than would students writing theses in history. Yet even in science theses, there are variations in the frequency in the use of the passive. Hanania and Akhtar (1985) found that passives were quite common in the sections describing methods in biology and chemistry theses, whereas other sections, such as the introduction and results, used far fewer passives.[3] It would appear, then, that the readability of passives is closely linked to highly specific discourse goals that writers have.

If readability is a key goal for advanced learners, complex syntactic patterns will inevitably have a place in the syllabus. While obvious difficulties arise for readers in cases such as #11b (*That their time should not be wasted is important*), complex structures often make a text easier to read. Conversely, simple syntax may hurt comprehension: Davison and Kantor (1982) discuss ways in which simplified reading materials can actually make a text more difficult. Such findings suggest that writing instruction must, among other things, encourage learners to experiment with complex sentence patterns. Unless they receive such instruction, learners may never use certain types of sentences. Kleinmann (1978) and Schachter and Hart (1979) found evidence that Arabic speakers seem especially unwilling to use passive-voice verb phrases. More recently,

---

3 I suspect that not all readers will accept my assumption that most of the theses examined by Hanania and Akhtar were competently written: One could argue that the passives in the methods section were unwarranted. Among teachers in the humanities there is often a conviction that writers in the sciences (hard or soft) rarely use language well. There is certainly a lot of murky prose in the sciences – though there is surely a great deal in the humanities as well. With regard to the theses studied by Hanania and Akhtar, responsible writing probably accounts for the variation in the use of passives according to the sections of the theses. If the prose came from inept writers, one would expect to find passive voice occurring just as frequently in the introductions or the results sections as in the methods sections.

Schachter (1988) has claimed that advanced learners produce relatively few sentences showing "movement rules" such as the one responsible for the difference between #11a and #11b (*It is important that their time should not be wasted* and *That their time should not be wasted is important*). In some discourse contexts, avoidance will probably not matter. However, not all contexts make avoidance a desirable option for students. As noted, many science theses rely on the passive voice to describe experimental methods. In such a case, Arabic speakers might encounter special difficulty in writing an acceptable thesis if they have not learned to master passive constructions.

Although avoidance can arise for many reasons, it surely indicates that learners feel uncertain about using a particular structure. To counter uncertainty, teachers should be ready to provide accurate feedback. Instructors who are nonnative speakers no doubt face the greatest challenge, since they may feel insecure about some of their own intuitions. However, accurate feedback will sometimes be a challenge for native-speaker teachers as well. Without careful reflection, anyone may provide misleading judgments and advice such as "Never use passive voice" or "No one ever says *There's about five minutes left*." To have accurate intuitions about acceptability, teachers must consider not only well-formedness but also ease of processing and appropriateness in context.

Taking all three criteria into account will surely lead to more accurate judgments, but teachers (native or nonnative speakers) may feel uncertain about just when and how some structures are used. Learners themselves may be able to help in such cases. For example, many advanced classes of ESL learners could investigate the frequency of passive-voice verb phrases in texts in their field. In his article in this volume, Johns shows how a project using computers has succeeded in helping students to investigate various structures. Students have direct access to texts stored on a data base, and they can search for occurrences of particular structures (e.g., the modal *should*). As Johns observes, this project allows intuition (whether of student or teacher) to be tested in a very concrete way. Such methods can thus lead to new possibilities within the Introspective Hierarchy. Although the judgments of teachers should usually suffice to define the target language, students may help teachers develop more accurate characterizations of the actual target.

References

Arthur, Bradford. 1980. Gauging the boundaries of second language competence: a study of learner judgments. *Language Learning* 30: 177–94.
Beretta, Alan, and Susan Gass. 1991. Indeterminacy and the reliability of grammaticality judgments. Paper presented at Second Language Research Forum, University of Southern California.

Bialystok, Ellen. 1979. Explicit and implicit judgments of grammaticality. *Language Learning* 29: 81–103.

Bialystok, Ellen, and Ellen Ryan. 1985. Toward a definition of metalinguistic skill. *Merrill-Palmer Quarterly* 31: 229–64.

Birdsong, David. 1989. *Metalinguistic Performance and Interlinguistic Competence*. New York: Springer Verlag.

——— 1992. On the evidence of competence differences between natives and near natives. *Language* 68: 706–55.

Birdsong, David, and Margaret Kassen. 1988. Teachers' and students' evaluations of foreign language errors: a meeting of minds? *Modern Language Journal* 72: 1–12.

Blaubergs, Maija, and Kenneth Jarrett. 1977. Semantic anomaly: linguists' intuitions versus interpretation in context. In *Current Themes in Linguistics*, ed. by Fred Eckman. New York: John Wiley.

Bley-Vroman, Robert. 1989. What is the logical problem of foreign language learning? In *Linguistic Perspectives on Second Language Acquisition*, ed. by Susan Gass and Jacquelyn Schachter. Cambridge: Cambridge University Press, 41–68.

Carolino, Pedro. 1883. *New Guide of the Conversation in Portuguese and English*. Boston: James Osgood.

——— 1883/1967. *English as She Is Spoke*. Detroit: Gale Research.

Carroll, John, Thomas Bever, and Chava Pollock. 1981. The non-uniqueness of linguistic intuitions. *Language* 57: 368–83.

Chaudron, Craig. 1983. Research on metalinguistic judgments: a review of theory, methods, and results. *Language Learning* 33: 343–77.

Chomsky, Noam. 1965. *Aspects of the Theory of Syntax*. Cambridge, Mass.: MIT Press.

Coppetiers, René. 1987. Competence differences between native and non-native speakers. *Language* 63(3): 544–73.

Davison, Alice, and Robert Kantor. 1982. On the failure of readability formulas to define readable texts: a case study from adaptations. *Reading Research Quarterly* 17: 187–209.

Ellis, Rod. 1990. Grammaticality judgments and learner variability. In *Variability in Second Language Acquisition: Proceedings of the Tenth Meeting of the Second Language Research Forum*, vol. 1, ed. by Hartmut Burmeister and Patricia Rounds. Eugene, Oreg.: Department of Linguistics, University of Oregon, 25–60.

——— 1991. Grammaticality judgments in second language acquisition. *Studies in Second Language Acquisition* 13(2): 161–86.

Elliott, Dale, Stanley Legum, and Sandra Thompson. 1969. Syntactic variation as linguistic data. In *Papers from the Fifth Chicago Regional Meeting*, ed. by Robert Binnick et al. Chicago: University of Chicago, Department of Linguistics, 52–59.

Erdmann, Peter. 1988. On the principle of "weight" in English. In *On Language: Rhetorica, Phonologica, Syntactica: A Festschrift for Robert P. Stockwell from His Friends and Colleagues*, ed. by Carol Duncan-Rose and Theo Vennemann. London: Routledge, 325–39.

Gass, Susan. 1979. Language transfer and universal grammatical relations. *Language Learning* 29: 327–44.

——— 1983. The development of L2 intuitions. *TESOL Quarterly* 17: 443–52.

Greenbaum, Sidney. 1977. Contextual influence on acceptability judgments. *Linguistics* 187: 5–11.

1988. *Good English and the Grammarian*. London: Longman.

Gregg, Kevin. 1989. Second Language Acquisition theory: a generativist perspective. In *Linguistic Perspectives on Second Language Acquisition,* ed. by Susan Gass and Jacquelyn Schachter. Cambridge: Cambridge University Press, 15–40.

Gregory, Richard (ed.). 1987. *The Oxford Companion to the Mind*. Oxford: Oxford University Press.

Hanania, Edith, and Karima Akhtar. 1985. Verb form and rhetorical function in science writing: a study of MS theses in biology, chemistry, and physics. *ESP Journal* 4: 49–58.

Heringer, James. 1970. Research on negative quantifier dialects. *Papers from the Sixth Regional Meeting, Chicago Linguistics Society.* Chicago: University of Chicago, Department of Linguistics.

Huddleston, Rodney. 1977. The futurate construction. *Linguistic Inquiry* 8(4): 730–36.

Itkonen, Esa. 1981. The concept of linguistic intuition. In *A Festschrift for Native Speaker,* ed. by Florian Coulmas. The Hague: Mouton.

Kellerman, Eric. 1977. Towards a characterisation of the strategy of transfer in second language learning. *Interlanguage Studies Bulletin* 2: 58–145.

1978. Giving learners a break: native language intuitions about transferability. *Working Papers in Bilingualism* 15: 59–92.

Kleinmann, Howard. 1978. The strategy of avoidance in adult second language acquisition. In *Second Language Acquisition Research,* ed. by William Ritchie. New York: Academic Press.

Krashen, Stephen. 1981. *Second Language Acquisition and Second Language Learning.* Oxford: Pergamon Press.

Labov, William. 1972. *Sociolinguistic Patterns.* Philadelphia: University of Pennsylvania Press.

1975. *What Is a Linguistic Fact?* Lisse, The Netherlands: Peter de Ridder.

Lakoff, George, and Mark Johnson. 1980. *Metaphors We Live By.* Chicago: University of Chicago Press.

Lehiste, Ilse. 1971. Grammatical variability and the difference between native and nonnative speakers. In *Papers in Contrastive Linguistics,* ed. by Gerhard Nickel. Cambridge: Cambridge University Press, 69–74.

Levelt, Willem. 1972. Some psychological aspects of linguistic data. *Linguistische Berichte* 17: 19–30.

Levelt, Willem, J. van Gent, A. Haans, and A. Meijers. 1977. Grammaticality, paraphrase, and imagery. In *Acceptability in Language,* ed. by Sidney Greenbaum. The Hague: Mouton.

McCawley, James. 1985. Review of *Grammatical Theory* by F. Newmeyer. *Language* 61: 668–78.

Odlin, Terence. 1986. On the Nature and Use of Explicit Knowledge. *IRAL* 24: 123–44.

1987. Some problems concerning the interpretation of passage correction tests. In *Language Testing Research,* ed. by Kathleen Bailey, Theodore Dale, and Ray Clifford. Monterey, Calif.: Defense Language Institute, 70–77.

1991. Irish English idioms and language transfer. *English World-Wide* 12: 175–93.

Quirk, Randolph, and Sidney Greenbaum. 1973. *A Concise Grammar of Contemporary English*. New York: Harcourt, Brace, Jovanovich.

Ringen, Jon. 1977. On evaluating data concerning linguistic intuition. In *Current Themes in Linguistics,* ed. by Fred Eckman. New York: John Wiley, 145–60.

Ritchie, William. 1978. The right roof constraint in adult-acquired language. In *Second Language Acquisition Research,* ed. by William Ritchie. New York: Academic Press.

Rorty, Richard. 1967. Intuition. *Encyclopedia of Philosophy,* ed. by Paul Edwards. New York: Macmillan.

Ross, John. 1979. Where's English? In *Individual Differences in Language Ability and Language Behavior,* ed. by Charles Fillmore, Daniel Kempler, and William Wang. New York: Academic Press.

Schachter, Jacquelyn. 1988. Second language acquisition and its relationship to Universal Grammar. *Applied Linguistics* 9: 219–35.

1989. A new look at an old classic. *Second-Language Research* 5: 30–42.

Schachter, Jacquelyn, Adele Tyson, and Frank Diffley. 1976. Learner intuitions of grammaticality. *Language Learning* 26: 67–76.

Schachter, Jacquelyn, and Beverly Hart. 1979. An analysis of learner production of English structures. *Georgetown University Papers on Language and Linguistics* 15: 18–75.

Schachter, Jacquelyn, and Virginia Yip. 1990. Grammaticality judgments: why does anyone object to subject extraction? *Studies in Second Language Acquisition* 12(4): 379–92.

Schmidt, Richard. 1990. The role of consciousness in second language learning. *Applied Linguistics* 11(2): 129–58.

Schmidt, Richard, and Carol McCreary. 1977. Standard and superstandard English: recognition and use of prescriptive rules by native and non-native speakers. *TESOL Quarterly* 11: 415–29.

Singh, Rajendra, Alison d'Anglejan, and Susanne Carroll. 1982. Elicitation of Inter-English. *Language Learning* 32: 271–88.

Singley, Mark, and John Anderson. 1989. *The Transfer of Cognitive Skill*. Cambridge, Mass.: Harvard University Press.

Sjöholm, Kaj. 1983. Problems in 'measuring' L2 learning strategies. In *Psycholinguistics and Foreign Language Learning,* ed. by H. Ringbom. Åbo, Finland: Publications of the Research Institute of the Åbo Akademi Foundation, 174–94.

Snow, Catherine. 1975. Linguists as behavioral scientists: towards a methodology for testing linguistic intuitions. Assen, The Netherlands: Van Gorcum, 271–75.

Sorace, Antonella. 1991. Magnitude estimation techniques for the elicitation of non-native acceptability judgments. Paper presented at ALMS: Applied Linguistics at Michigan State, Michigan State University.

Spencer, Nancy. 1973. Differences between linguists and non-linguists in intuitions of grammaticality-acceptability. *Journal of Psycholinguistic Research* 2: 83–98.

Strunk, William, and E. B. White. 1959. *Elements of Style*. New York: Macmillan.

Thomas, Margaret. 1989. The interpretation of English reflexive pronouns by non-native speakers. *Studies in Second Language Acquisition* 11(3): 281–304.

Trudgill, Peter. 1984. *On Dialect*. New York: New York University Press.

Tucker, Richard, and Marian Sarofim. 1979. Investigating linguistic acceptability with Egyptian EFL students. *TESOL Quarterly* 13: 29–39.

White, Lydia. 1985. The PRO-Drop parameter in adult second language acquisition. *Language Learning* 35: 47–62.

  1989. *Universal Grammar in Second Language Acquisition*. Amsterdam: John Benjamins.

Yule, George, Jerry Yanz, and Atsuko Tsuda. 1985. Investigating aspects of the language learner's confidence: an application of the theory of signal detection. *Language Learning* 35(3): 473–88.

12 From printout to handout: Grammar and vocabulary teaching in the context of Data-driven Learning

Tim Johns

In this chapter I shall describe and illustrate on-going work that attempts to synthesise two approaches to language teaching – one basically traditional, and the other more innovative. The setting for the work is the in-session programme of classes offered by the English for Overseas Students Unit at the University of Birmingham to overseas postgraduate students following courses and undertaking research in a wide range of subjects, from Production Engineering to Special Education and from Accountancy to Theology. Students who need help and encouragement can choose from a programme of classes, some of which are defined in terms of language *form* (e.g., Remedial Grammar, Pronunciation) and others in terms of language *function* (e.g., Academic Writing, Social Interaction). The form/function distinction is, however, not adhered to rigidly, and in all classes it is the form/function relationship that is the ultimate object of study in terms of the rules that determine the *interpretation* of form and those that govern the *realisation* of function.

Two examples may help to demonstrate the implications of Figure 1:

1. In the functionally defined academic writing class we emphasise the importance of indicating to the reader the extent to which the writer allies himself/herself with previous writers on the same topic, and in that context we look at the formal devices (e.g., syntactic choice of tense and lexical choice of reporting verb) by which that functional choice is realised.

2. In the formally defined remedial grammar course, the passive recurs as a formal structure at various points in the materials dealing with transitivity and complementation, but the work does not end with the manipulation of form ('Change these sentences into the passive'): Attention is paid also to the choice between active and passive, a choice which involves decisions of 'appropriacy' rather than 'correctness' ('Decide in these contexts whether the marked sentences should be active or passive').

This is a revised version of a paper which first appeared under the same title in the *CALLAustria Newsletter* (July 1990, pp. 14–34), and was reprinted in the University of Birmingham *English Language Research Journal* 4 (Johns 1991b). I am very grateful to Julian Edge and Eugene Winter for their detailed comments on that earlier version: the remaining flaws and follies remain my responsibility.

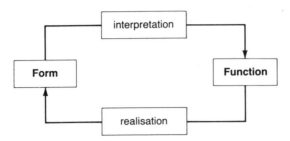

Figure 1   The relationship between form and function in language.

These examples raise the important issue of the nature of the data on which teaching is based. If one is concerned, as in an exercise involving *conversion* between active and passive, with language viewed purely as a formal system, it is understandable that both teacher and student may be satisfied with the constructed and artificial examples that have for so long been the stock-in-trade of textbooks and grammars. On the other hand, if one's focus is language in use, as in an exercise involving *choice* between active and passive, it becomes self-evidently dubious to base the teaching on invented rather than genuine examples. Apart from anything else, the statement by the teacher or materials writer that in such and such contexts the active or passive 'is likely to be used' carries less interest and less conviction than the statement that in such and such contexts the active or passive 'was used' – a statement which can lead to a genuine examination of the reasons (end-weight, cross-referential proximity, etc.) underlying the choice. The use of 'simplified' texts is often recommended as a way of ensuring that the language is authentic in purpose yet within the learner's grasp (Widdowson 1979). However, that procedure is also doubtful in relation to the active/passive choice exercise, since simplification is liable to destroy those very features of the original text (for example, the relative 'weight' of the elements of the message) that account for the choice. In general, it appears that a concern with language function as well as with language form entails a far more extensive use of authentic, unmodified data than has been traditional in language teaching. That, in turn, raises the question of how such data are to be obtained and made available to the learner in such a way that they do not overload his or her linguistic and learning resources.

Among the elective common-core classes provided by the Unit, the most popular is that titled Remedial Grammar, attendance during the autumn term running at well over one hundred per session. A number of reasons can be found for this preference for grammar on the part of our students. Most of them come from an educational background in which language learning is equated with formal grammar learning, and against such a background problems with English are likely to be identified as 'not knowing enough grammar'. That identification may be strengthened by their first contact with the Unit, since all overseas students take a structurally based 130-item Assessment and Diagnostic Test on arrival at the university. The intention of the test is not quite what it appears, since it discounts 'book knowledge' of grammar and pays particular attention to those areas of syntax which are usually either ignored in grammar-based language courses (e.g., transitivity), or handled inadequately (e.g., article usage), the reasoning being that if a student is able to do well on such items, that is likely to be the result of extensive experience of the language used in communication rather than formal learning *about* grammar. Remedial grammar sessions are linked to the areas of grammar identified by the test so that students can identify in advance those that will be of particular use to them. As a result of the way in which the diagnostic areas of the test are defined, we thus commit ourselves to teaching what is often untaught and may, indeed, be unteachable in terms of conventional language teaching methodology.

A further reason for the popularity of grammar sessions may be located in the special situation in which our students find themselves. For a learner of English in a non-English-speaking environment, a major need is to get adequate exposure to English and experience of using English, and what happens in the classroom should be designed to cater for that need. Our students, on the other hand, may feel that they already have more exposure to English than they can comfortably handle: They are, to be sure, 'acquiring' English in Krashen's sense (Krashen 1982), but that acquisition tends to be haphazard and to leave them feeling confused. In this situation, a preference for grammar is in effect a plea for help in overcoming confusion, and it is incumbent on us as language teachers to do two things in responding to it. First, we need to provide adequate opportunities, in classes and in individual consultations, for students to raise problems and queries, which in turn can help us to see the directions which our teaching should take. Second, we should attempt to make our teaching *transferable* in the sense that the strategies developed in the classroom for 'puzzling out' how the language works should also be applicable outside the classroom. The principle of transferability applies throughout the programme: Vocabulary Studies classes, for example, concentrate on strategies for making more effective use of dictionaries, thesauruses and other works of reference; for developing the ability to guess the meaning and use of unknown words from context; and for perceiving the morphological and semantic relationships between families of words.

The last reason for the popularity of grammar lies in the students themselves. They are intelligent, and respond to challenges to their intelligence; and most of them are accustomed to the idea of research and finding things out for themselves. Much use is made of pair work: with students from a large number of different countries and different departments we can make it a class rule that students should sit next to someone from a different country and a different department from their own, so that they can all, in the freer 'information-gap' activities, find out about each others' countries, cultures and subjects. Many overseas students feel isolated, and for them the opportunity offered by such activities to meet and make friends with other people in the same situation gives the classes a social as well as an academic function.

That, then, is the work which we are now reassessing in the light of information technology in general, and the classroom concordancing – or Data-driven Learning (DDL) – approach in particular (for background see Johns 1986, 1988 and 1991a; Tribble and Jones 1990). The DDL approach is innovative in two respects, one technological and one methodological.

The technological background to Data-driven Learning is the remarkable increase over the past ten years in storage capacity and processing speed of affordable microcomputers; the increased availability of ready-made corpora of machine-readable text and the possibilities for automatic entry of corpora via scanners and OCR (optical character recognition) software; and the development for microcomputers of flexible and powerful concordancing programs that are able to recover rapidly from a corpus all the contexts within which a particular linguistic element – word, morpheme or phrase – occurs. In addition to MICROCONCORD (Scott and Johns 1993), these programs include the OCP package from Oxford University Press, WORDCRUNCHER from Brigham Young University, Joseph Rézeau's CONCORDTEACH, and the Longman MINI-CONCORDANCER – see Higgins (1991) for a consumer's report.

The early development of the DDL approach can, perhaps, best be characterised by comparing it with that taken by the Collins Birmingham University International Language Database (COBUILD) project, also in the English Department of Birmingham University (Sinclair 1987). In preparing a range of reference and teaching materials for English as a Foreign Language, COBUILD has made extensive use of KWIC (keyword-in-context) concordance data based on a very large corpus of contemporary English. The materials thereby reflect authentic usage and go a long way towards dispelling the myths and distortions that have arisen from reliance on intuition-based 'armchair' linguistics – myths and distortions that are too easily perpetuated from one generation to another of dictionaries, grammars and coursebooks.

The aim of contextualising and demythologising the language and of making available to the learner information about authentic usage is common to COBUILD and to Data-driven Learning, and the example and ideas of COBUILD have been among the main sources of inspiration for the work reported in this paper. The approaches differ, however, in the use they make of the linguistic evidence. The COBUILD pattern is as follows:

The computer sorts the words in various ways, and delivers information on each word to a team of editors and compilers. They study the words and build up an elaborate profile of their meanings and uses in a database back in the computer. The database is then the primary source of a family of books which will span many years of editorial work. (Sinclair 1987: vii)

The main point to note from this description is the importance of the editorial team in mediating between the learner on one hand and the raw data on the other. What distinguishes the DDL approach is the attempt to cut out the middleman as far as possible and to give direct access to the data so that the learner can take part in building up his or her *own* profiles of meaning and uses. The assumption that underlies this approach is that effective language learning is itself a form of linguistic research, and that the concordance printout offers a unique resource for the stimulation of inductive learning strategies – in particular the strategies of perceiving similarities and differences and of hypothesis formation and testing (Johns 1988).

At the outset, the main use we made in class of concordance printout was reactive, responding to the difficult questions that intelligent students put to their not-always-so-intelligent teachers – for example, 'What is the difference between *therefore* and *hence?*' (Johns 1988) or 'Why aren't all *shoulds* real *shoulds?*' (Johns 1991a); the concordancer allowed the teacher to say 'I'm not sure: let's find out together'. That pattern, with the teacher abandoning the role of expert and taking on that of research organiser, has continued and has proved a powerful stimulus to student enquiry.

The implications of the DDL approach have proved so powerful that they have demanded to be taken into account in rewriting our mainstream teaching materials and bringing them closer to authentic language use. Those implications involve both the *product* of language learning and the *process* of language learning:

1. The evidence thrown up by the data has left no escape from the conclusion that the description of English underlying our teaching, whether homemade or inherited from other teachers and linguists, needs reassessment.
2. Experience in using concordance data reactively has indicated that it could also be used proactively in a more traditional teacher-centred setting, and has suggested also a range of concordance-based exercise types which could have high transferability, helping students to develop inductive strategies that will help them to become better language learners outside the classroom.

Although these conclusions apply across the whole range of our teaching, recent work has concentrated on revision of materials for the classes on Remedial Grammar and Vocabulary Studies, and it is by means of extracts from those materials that I shall try to illustrate these two points.

The main corpus used for the materials under discussion is one of approximately 825,000 words from the weekly journal *New Scientist,* supplemented on occasion by corpora of 1.25 million words from the American computer journal *Byte,* 667,000 words from the *Times* and *Guardian* newspapers, just under half a million words of research papers from the journal *Nature,* and approximately 115,000 words of academic papers in the fields of plant biology and transportation and highway engineering. The *New Scientist* corpus, which was collected in 1984 by Eugene Winter for his research project on Information Structures in English, has both advantages and disadvantages for DDL. On the plus side, it covers a wide range of topics, a range which to a large extent reflects the interests and specialisations of our students. Where a citation contains an obscure reference to organic pesticides, say, or to arms-reduction negotiations, the chances are high that there will be a chemist or a specialist in international relations who can explain the reference to the rest of us. There is also a wide stylistic range from the formal to the semi-formal. On the negative side, the range is weighted rather too heavily for our students towards journalese, and it is necessary on occasion to compensate for that weighting.

The construction of the teaching materials from which the extracts are taken starts with the preparation of a number of computer concordances which are both printed out and saved to disc. After the raw data have been studied and analysed, the concordance files are loaded into a word processor, where citations are selected and the teaching materials built around them. The most important principle that has to be borne in mind in carrying out this work is that the inevitable process of selection should not distort the evidence – that is to say, the concordance extracts chosen should represent as far as possible the full range of linguistic and communicative features of the raw data. There are two main sources of distortion. The first can occur if selection is made on linguistic criteria that are imposed externally – for example, the teacher's preconceptions of what *ought to be* in the data rather than what *is* in the data. The second can occur if selection is made on pedagogic criteria that may in themselves be perfectly justifiable (for example, that preference should be given to citations that are relatively self-contained and self-explanatory) but which have the unforeseen effect of biasing the sample in terms of the forms represented or the meanings that those forms convey. There are three different approaches to the danger of distortion through selection:

1. To know nothing in advance about the data and to make the selection on a purely random basis. That is not the approach that has been taken for the

materials described, but an element of controlled randomness may become necessary as larger corpora become available and the amount of raw data they throw up becomes more massive.

2. To know a great deal about the data in advance of selection and to make the selection in the light of that knowledge. This approach was taken in writing most of the materials described in this chapter, and entailed spending at least as long in preliminary analysis of the syntactic and communicative features of the data as in the writing of the materials themselves.

3. It may be permissible on occasion to select data on a distorting criterion provided that that criterion is made explicit to the learner. For example, Figure 2 shows a concordance of *that*-clauses selected on the criterion that one citation is given for each of 95 monotransitive matrix verbs appearing to the left of the *that*-clause. This criterion distorts the raw data in that it suppresses evidence as to the relative frequency of those verbs; interestingly, the first time the handout was given out in a class, one student made the useful suggestion that this information could be taken into account by dividing the citations into three blocks according to frequency.

In the next part of the chapter I wish to illustrate by means of extracts from the teaching materials prepared within the English for Overseas Students Unit some of the *linguistic* points that emerge from a close study of the *New Scientist* data, and also some of the *pedagogical* approaches that are possible, concentrating on observational/research tasks, exercise types and freer improvisational activities.

Figures 2 and 3 show extracts from the Remedial Grammar materials on Complementation, and present contrasting ways in which observational tasks can be set up. Figure 2 shows a relatively simple task within an 'open' rubric: Students are simply asked to identify the monotransitive verbs that are in the data followed by *that*-clauses, and to raise with the teacher any queries about the verbs or the contexts in which they appear. The presentation of the verbs in context gives students the possibility of working out from that context what the verb means – e.g., the memorably surrealistic context for *vouchsafe* (92) with its (English) policeman chasing a puma in a panda car – and observing any collocational patterns that extend beyond the Verb + *that*-clause – e.g., *There is no reason to expect that* (33) or *I gather that* (40). This presentation seems to the writer superior to the usual strategy in pedagogic grammars of simply listing the verbs that can occur in a particular pattern. Moreover, it appears to be the rule rather than the exception that when students and teacher work together on data within an open rubric (which is the usual condition for reactive DDL) they discover things unobserved and unsuspected by the teacher when the materials were prepared. In this case, for example, we noticed that it was possible to identify pairs of verbs with similar meanings – e.g., *discover* (28) versus *ascertain* (5) – in which one member of the pair is familiar and the other less familiar. We *surmised* (88) that this might be due in part to the

The girl over there	accept(s)		the weather will be even worse tomorrow
The Vice-Chancellor	consider(s)		we should all be given a long holiday
Tim Johns	think(s))		nothing is nicer than a cup of tea
Everyone in the room	know(s)	(that)	one day I shall become Prime Minister
Most experts	believe(s)		we have not been told the whole story
Some of my friends	realise(s)		students find grammar very boring
Overseas students	suspect(s)		the pubs close too early in England

Here, in citations from __New Scientist__ *are some of the verbs we can use in this pattern: identify any verbs that you are interested in or that you are not sure of, and look at the contexts in which they are used.*

```
 1) t. Virtually all biologists now accept that evolution is a fact, and that natural and sexu
 2) hing given away.' Ashagre acknowledges that this is too little. 'We had planned for 170,00
 3) The pilot radioed his plight but added that he would try and land anyway. The scientists a
 4) ear Regulatory Commission. GPU alleges that the commission failed to warn it about the saf
 5) oyalties even after it has ascertained that a piece of Britain contains valuable metals. A
 6) the safe side, it is better to assume that there is no 'no effect' level. And it backs in
 7) ke regularly. Some 23 per cent believe that smoking keeps down weight. This may be another
 8) ces, is at it again. But he is betting that the Department of Health will not prosecute hi
 9) high-density chip alone. Intel boasts that CHMOS (complementary, high-performance, metalo
10) value of the wheat. Bowers calculates that, of the £5950 that the NCC pays, £500 goes in
11) this notion as 'silly', Regan cautions that 'silly sounding ideas sometimes turn out to be
12) m the House of Representatives charged that the EPA 'acted improperly or at a minimum crea
13) Rutherford Appleton Laboratory checked that the telescope was pointing correctly.  One loo
14) rcles, and opponents of the work claim that the cycles are not statistically significant,
15) should be implemented. Hunt commented that his inquiry 'was not concerned with the techno
16) lin, NNC's managing director, conceded that the immediate export prospects were slim, howe
17) nstalled it would be wrong to conclude that the overall impact on jobs has been negative.
18) it. The Apollo missions have confirmed that the Moon is lifeless; all the hopes that Galil
19) the situation, however, I conjectured that in these times of diminishing reactor safety r
20) eim, however, saying that 'we consider that Heim acted in such a way as to reduce the cred
21) t out for themselves.' Marcus contends that responsible manufacturers are already dealing
22) to greater than 400°C, so they decided that they had better cool the reactor.' The cooling
23) tion. The incomparable Nature declared that his was 'a book fit for burning'. But we point
24) ion is poor. Kenneth Baker has decreed that all new cable systems must be compatible, so t
25) ends of the Earth has already demanded that the inquiry be adjourned until the NII has end
26) oductive lines of research demonstrate that ginseng increases the efficiency both of adren
27) airport. Ministers have always denied that the MRP experiment is part of a larger plan.
28) estern Electric says it has discovered that this is not the ideal approach. The patent con
29) nia. More studies are needed to ensure that the baits effectively attract the pest. The se
30) e first place. But Huxley did envisage that selection acted on genes that had more than on
31) University of Birmingham, establishes that, out of 330 servicemen, 27 have suffered from
32) article in Electrical Review estimated that the industry could save £1000-1400 million per
33) poverty. There is no reason to expect that unemployment will recede of its own accord, an
34) d North American conservationists fear that acceptance of the proposals could mean a drama
35) ide, north Wales, last November, feels that the risk is justified. The £25 million plant i
36) on overseas governments, who now find that there are cheaper courses elsewhere in the wor
37) the wilds of Snowdonia and finding out that, though meeting with difficulties, few women i
38) and humiliation, it was easy to forget that one was listening to a teenager, and only a fe
39) the cost of storage. Better to gamble that a private collector would keep the car until i
40) read about the Turin shroud. I gather that the cloth has really been dated, found to be t
41) has asked the government to guarantee that it will continue to buy data for 15 years. Ini
42) d in Palermo, Sicily, last week, heard that observations at Etna were being neglected. Spe
43) emic. Secondly, Rutter evidently holds that any behavioural effects of lead are irrelevant
44) lable only as a hardback. We must hope that the publishers will bring out a paperback. Haw
45) version of these matters is. I imagine that you would also be aware that the only reason t
46) of stern worldwide opposition implies that the Japanese people are not conservation minde
47) , one could read the article and infer that spruce forests aggravate the consequences of a
48) ent. They are not for those who insist that learning must be a serious business and who wo
83) rst people, perhaps the first, to spot that biological polymers would tend to be helical w
84) talised with a restriction stipulating that only the Home secretary can authorise his rele
85) olved in the exhibition, felt strongly that the British neglected technical education. In
87) ments; they were also wrong to suppose that the human skull gives us much information abou
88) magazine included an article surmising that British ships could have been lost because, am
89) lawsuits, but some in Congress suspect that polluting companies are getting off lightly. L
90) entist in the Chicago office testified that changes favourable to Dow 'had been dictated b
91) niversity than on the dole. Some think that the universities would do well to look outward
92) t seemed, with a policeman vouchsafing that he had chased a puma in his panda car. But the
93) otnotes are rewarding. One only wishes that he had spent more time gaining a perspective o
94) he brightest radio sources, worked out that extragalactic sources have a double structure,
95) tion'. At the atoll, Polynesians worry that the radioactivity could be spread beyond Murur
```

Do you notice anything special about the that-clauses following the verbs demand *(25) and* require *(76)?*

Figure 2   Extract from THAT-CLAUSES II [require (76) does not appear].

Look carefully at the following citations from New Scientist . What two features do they have in common?

1) ena from more dubious data, we propose that they should be renamed 'UAPs', for unidentifie
2) hen his advisory committee recommended that last year Depo-Provera should get a licence. C
3) eir drinking water. The EEC recommends that tap water should not contain more than 5 micro
4) he scale of the problem. It recommends that the government should set a firm date for thes
5) olol. The Greenfield report recommends that prescription forms should contain a box, which
6) f the road plan was the recommendation that for half its length it should be routed throug
7) h a name for the strategy. He suggests that the term 'porpoising' should be used to descri
8) put an absolute veto on-any suggestion that Post Office canvassers should be remunerated b

Now look at the following citations. How are they similar to citations 1) - 8)? And how are they different ? Can you explain the difference?

9) sed, and with it, speed. They proposed that Harward create such a super-track tuned to hum
10) ed voice: 'Then will somebody propose that this paper be rejected ir respective of its co
11) under review. An HSE document proposes that GMAG be turned into ACGM--an Advisory Committe
12) apolis. They said: '. . . we recommend that the dose of benoxaprofen be decreased (approxi
13) mistic. The committee also recommended that the government clarify the rules covering the
14) sing plants breaks down. It recommends that France take a second look at following the pol
15) h. The coordinating committee suggests that the appeal panel ask why this change has been
16) of the University of Bristol, suggests that a group of babies be trained to use a 'baby-op

Who can think of the most interesting completions for the following sentences?

1. If I were head of my department I would recommend that all examinations _____

_____

2. When John told me that he had had an argument with his girl-friend I suggested that he

_____

3. As a postgraduate student at the University of Birmingham, I propose that _____

_____

Figure 3   Extract from THAT-CLAUSES I.

search for 'elegant variation' by writers for *New Scientist*. At all events, the hunt for pairs offered a useful five-minute activity for the students, many of whom are preoccupied by the desire to achieve elegant variation in their own writing.

Figure 3, which is based on an insight developed in the course of developing some reactive materials for the modal verb *should* (Johns 1991a), shows a very different observational task from that of Figure 2. Here we have only a small number of citations (16, arranged in two groups of 8) and a 'closed' rubric, which leads students through a fixed chain of inductive reasoning. The chain goes something like this:

1. The features that citations (1)–(8) have in common are, first, that the verbs and nouns to the left of the *that*-clause are very similar in meaning, (indeed *propose* or *proposal* could be substituted for all of them with scarcely any change in meaning) and, second, that they all contain the word *should* in the *that*-clause.
2. Citations (9)–(16) are similar to citations (1)–(8) with respect to the verbs to the left of the *that*-clause. They are different in that the *that*-clauses do not contain the word *should* – instead (and here a small inductive leap is re-

quired) they contain the form of the verb that would follow *should*. In other words, in (9)–(16) *should* 'has been left out'.
3. A further small inductive leap is needed to reach the conclusion that *should* can be left out in (9)–(16) because it is unnecessary (or, in the jargon of linguistics, redundant), its meaning of suggestion/proposal/etc. being already contained within the matrix verb or noun.[1]

Notice that this inductive chain at no point appeals to the notions – more confusing than helpful to my students, and to their teacher too – of the 'putative *should*' for (1)–(8) or of the 'mandative subjunctive' for (9)–(16) (Quirk et al. 1985: 156–57). Notice also that the observational task leads immediately into a quirk improvisation on the theme of proposals, recommendations and suggestions. In such exercises the focus of the task is as much on the message as on the medium. Thus, the second of the improvisational matrices has, on each occasion this material has been used, revealed interesting differences between the women and the men in the class, the women suggesting completions such as '. . . he should apologise to her' and '. . . he buy her a bunch of flowers', and the men preferring advice such as '. . . he should find himself a new one' and '. . . he forget her as quickly as possible'. This freer type of activity forms a central role in these materials, representing the point at which learners can attempt to 'take off' from the data provided by the computer, and create some data of their own, for themselves, and for their own situation.

Figures 4, 6 and 7 show some of the possibilities for gapping exercises (or, more accurately, gapping-with-matching since the correct answers are supplied) based on concordance output.

Figure 4 is taken from materials for the Vocabulary Studies class, which has for many years included work on the sense relations of synonymy, antonymy, hyponymy and converseness as defined by Lyons (1963, 1977). The materials were based on invented examples, and were detectably artificial and removed from authentic usage. Although it is not possible, in basing such work on data, to instruct a concordancer to 'search for all instances of hyponymy', a suitable probe – in this case the phrase *such as* – is able to recover a large number of instances where the writer specifies a relationship between superordinate (e.g., *minerals*) and hyponym or hyponyms (e.g., *limestone, sand, salt, kaolin*). The corpus throws up 646 citations for *such as* from *New Scientist* alone, comprising 574 instances of [superordinate] *such as* [hyponym(s)], and 72 of *such* [superordinate] *as* [hyponym(s)].

1 Since writing the first version of this chapter I have discovered that a very similar treatment of the deletion of *should* in contexts such as this was proposed by William Cobbett (Cobbett 1819). It appears that Cobbett was anxious, as a radical patriot, to eliminate alien notions such as the subjunctive from the description of Modern English. One hundred seventy years later his ambition has yet to be fully realised, as a glance at any half-dozen recent descriptive grammars of English will show.

a) *Find the missing word in the following 10 citations, all of which are taken from the weekly journal* **New Scientist** *-*

1) deviation form the pattern. _____ such as Botswana, Mozambique, Namibia, Swazila

2) was shown a list containing _____ such as 'arm', 'finger' and 'toe'; personality

3) nk estimated in 1970 that in _____ such as Bogota in Columbia, Mexico City, Madra

4) ould have to be converted to _____ such as carbon monoxide for the reduction proc

5) ial status; exploitation of _____, such as limestone, sand, salt and kaolin; the

6) conditions, farmers can sell _____ such as coffee only if high and constant quali

7) not be able to spot nuclear _____, such as Polaris, for example. Both superpowers

8) ding a stockpile of imported _____ such as chromium, cobalt and manganese that ar

9) r innovation in traditional _____, such as steelmaking and clothing, to the tune o

10) and can be met from cheaper _____, such as coal rather than oil. In the long term,

Words   cities, countries, crops, fuels, gases, industries, metals, minerals, weapons, words

...

e) *If you can get all of the last 10 examples right, your English must be very good indeed!*

41) body, into a common sphere. _____ such as cognitive training and coping strategi

42) re based on measurements of _____, such as aluminium-26, chlorine-36, manganese-5

43) uter works' books explaining _____ such as binary numbers and punched cards at a

44) an imporve many scars, birth _____ such as cleft lip, and deep frown lines. So fa

45) on of unexplained technical _____, such as brachyodont and hypsodont, More import

46) onsumption. The report urges _____ such as insulating lofts, walls and ceilings, a

47) osages will control exposed _____, such as aphids on cereals. The ground is less c

48) age we may abstract certain _____, such as rules of grammar, sentence construction

49) easy-going disposal of gross _____ such as pig slurry and creamery wastes. But, ar

50) rto discuss some of Wells's _____, such as George Orwell and Ray Bradbury. Perhaps

Words   concepts, defects, isotopes, measures, pests, pollutants, regularities, successors, terms, therapies

Figure 4   Extract from CLASSIFICATION – SUCH AS.

When one uses data to exemplify a point in a particular linguistic model, one must be ready for a 'backwash' effect from practice to theory, the data making it necessary to take a fresh look at the model itself. That is what happened here. Lyons's discussion of superordinate-hyponym relationships locates knowledge of such relationships in the competence of the ideal native speaker-listener (Chomsky 1965): In that sense they are *given* in the structure of the lexicon. However, the data show many examples of what might be termed hyponymy-in-performance, where the superordinate-hyponym relationship is *created* by the writer within a particular context for a particular purpose (see Figure 5). A structural description of the lexis of English would contain

```
1) eeps", bringing in unwanted passengers, such as oil, herbicides, organic chemicals like
2) age groups had their "tools" for life - such as baby walkers, roller skates and compute
3) e about how far some of the key issues, such as fuel clad ballooning, the integrity of
4) while essential aspects of the project, such as the denuded hillsides and the transport
5) itude and, indeed, the respect of hacks such as myself, who have come to rely on the OH
```

Figure 5   KWIC citations for SUCH AS illustrating hyponymy-in-performance.

the information that *oil* is one of the hyponyms of *fuel* (along with *wood, coal, uranium,* etc.) and would no doubt show also that it enters into other hyponymous relationships (e.g., that it is, together with *grease, graphite,* etc., one of the hyponyms of *lubricant*); however, no such description would or could contain the information that *oil* may be a hyponym of *passenger* (1), nor that a *baby walker* may be a *tool* (2). In the first two citations the writers are setting up metaphors which require the realisation by the reader that in the context of these discourses, *oil, herbicides* and *organic chemicals* may count as *unwanted passengers* in a *chemical sweep* and that *baby walkers, roller skates* and *computers* may, for different *age groups,* be *tools for life.* The important point to note about citation 3 is that although what counts as a (*key*) *issue* must satisfy certain general criteria (e.g., 'an important subject that people are discussing or arguing about' – COBUILD dictionary), particular instances will always depend crucially on the world of discourse created by the text; thus no conceivable dictionary of English could contain the information that *fuel-clad ballooning* is or may be a hyponym of *issue.* Citations 4 and 5 show similar non-dictionary hyponyms, with citation 5 additionally requiring the recognition by the reader of an ironic purpose behind the writer's self-classification as a *hack.*

In writing the materials on Classification, it was decided to use only authentic examples recovered by means of the concordancer, and to take account of hyponymy-in-performance as discussed earlier. For the first exercise, fifty citations for [superordinate] *such as* [hyponym(s)] were selected, graded in order of difficulty into blocks of ten, and gapped on the superordinate. The first and last blocks are shown to indicate the spread of difficulty that is possible when citations are drawn from such a rich source of data, those in the last block being very difficult indeed in respect not only of the vocabulary, but also the knowledge of the world they require – for example, that H. G. Wells, George Orwell and Ray Bradbury were or are all writers of futuristic fiction, Wells being active at the turn of the century and the other two more recently. With graded blocks arranged in this way, the teacher can detect when the exercise is becoming too difficult for most of the students and leave the remaining blocks to be completed by those who wish to do so in their own time, a

Complete the following ten sentences from New Scientist with the adjectives given:

1. There is one small river at Ebenat, but that has become so _____ that the relief workers have to bring in water by tanker.

2. As pits become deeper they must also become wider in order to prevent the sides from becoming so _____ they are unstable.

3. On cold, damp spring days, the streets get so _____ in Centralia, Pennsylvania, that traffic is forced to a standstill until visibility improves.

4. At the moment protein A is so _____ it costs between £5 and £10 a milligram.

5. Scientists have become so _____ with the fine structure of living cells that their manipulation and culture now appear commonplace.

6. Officials are embarrassed by the fact that the total in the fund is still so _____ that, under United Nations rules, none of it can be spent.

7. And on the Links motorway, the 13 kilometres of elevated road at the core of the country's motorway network, repairs are so _____ that the Department of Transport issues weekly press releases.

8. They, the experts, had examined the statistics and concluded that the risk of being killed by an accident in a nuclear power station, or by cancer-causing saccharin in coffee was so _____ that it was 'acceptable'.

9. Meanwhile, the rural housing problem, which affects most people in the Third World, is so _____ that no government has even tried to tackle it on a national scale.

10. However, the languages of science and engineering have become so _____ that communication across the disciplines is difficult to achieve, but there seems to be no reason in principle why this must be so as the concepts are universal.

Adjectives familiar, frequent, immense, low, polluted, scarce, small, smoky, specialised, steep

Figure 6   Extract from THAT-CLAUSES IV.

key being provided at the end of the lesson. Further exercises in the handout cover the structure *such* [superordinate] *as* [hyponym(s)], finding an appropriate hyponym or hyponyms in the context of a particular superordinate, and extended idioms using *such as* – e.g., *There is no such thing as.* . . .

With the materials extract shown in Figure 6, we are back with *that*-clauses – in this case with what are known traditionally as clauses of result – and with the start of a similar gapping exercise, the gap being made on the adjective following *so*. Finding the correct adjective requires an understanding of the whole statement, and for that reason the citations have been taken from a sentence concordance rather than a KWIC concordance as used in the previous extracts. This exercise illustrates an important characteristic of all the exercises in the revised materials, namely that the focus is not on form or form alone, but on the meanings that are realised by form. Notice in this exercise, for example, that the 'wrong' answers do not produce ungrammatical sentences, but sentences with meanings that are in varying degrees bizarre or unusual. What the exercise does *not* do is invite the student to 'commit ungrammaticality', a traditional practice stemming from a preoccupation with purely formal choices that may have much to do with the odium that has, in recent years, attached itself to explicit grammar learning and grammar teaching.

Figure 7 shows one of the many exercises in the materials that deal with noun phrases followed by *that*-clauses. This is an area neglected in traditional pedagogic grammars partly, it appears, as a result of the classification of *that*-clauses following verbs and adjectives as 'complements' and of *that*-clauses following noun phrases as 'post-modifiers', a classification which conceals the close parallelism in structure and meaning between, for example,

He concluded that . . .   He came to the conclusion that . . .
He argued that . . .   He put forward the argument that . . .

As Winter has pointed out (1982), the nouns such as *assumption, belief, claim, conclusion, fact, idea* and so on that occur frequently in this context have a powerful organising function in text as 'replacement items' for the following clause. My students are aware of the importance of these nouns, and of the difficulty they have in using them appropriately, so the product of the exercise is likely to be of value. In addition, this extract shows a concordance-based exercise type – gapping using multiple contexts – that is a powerful stimulus to a process of language learning that involves hypothesis formation and testing, and close attention to meaning and patterns of collocation. In the first item, for example, a plausible initial guess at the missing word is *evidence,* and that does indeed make good sense in the first context given that the *New Scientist* corpus dates from 1983, shortly before the HIV virus was discovered. It works reasonably well also with contexts 2–4, although it is slightly odd in context 3 (Is 'ranking among the most important British mathematicians' a claim for which convincing evidence could be provided?), and biologically unlikely in context 4. It is the last context, however, which shows clearly that *evidence* cannot be the right answer, since there is no way one can be left in evidence or in no evidence. Tests of other possible answers fail even more drastically, while the four instances of *no* before the gap beckon the solver ever onwards towards the correct answer, *doubt.*

Figure 8 shows authentic data being used in another type of matching exercise – here matching two halves of a sentence. Once again, the constraints on possible answers are semantic rather than syntactic, and some fun is to be had with more advanced students from trying to contextualise the false matches. As far as the 'correct' matches are concerned, the sentence formed by matching first half E with second half F illustrates the resonances that can be struck by authentic text – resonances that are almost always lacking in the concocted examples of the textbook. Many of our students come from countries with political systems in which one may well need friends in high places to remain safe, and the

One of the words shown at the end of the exercise has been left out of each of the blocks of five citations from New Scientist *. Can you find which word is missing from each block?*

1) may have patients suffering from AIDS. There seems little
ay in a flush of enthusiasm.' He concluded that he 'had no
h the longest entry of any pure mathematician. There is no
When horses and donkeys are pastured together there is no
riment by F. B. Exner and G. L. Waldbott, I was left in no

that AIDS is caused by an infective agent of some kind. Thi
' that lead should be totally removed from petrol. 'The poin
that Smith ranks among the most important British mathemati
that each species mates preferentially with its own kind. O
that besides being unethical, fluoridation was both ineffec

2) ignificance. Each research group came to a broadly similar
the data sets,' he said, 'one is not inexorably led to the
oan-Kettering Institute in New York to the rather unlikely
ts between October and December 1979, Tunstall came to the
th neither new evidence nor any fresh insights. Their main

: that if there is any link between lead and IQ, it is total
that a negative secular solar radius trend has existed sinc
that the mammalian ovary must be capable of inducing oestru
that Mr X had an IQ of 80 and a reading comprehension age,
, that 'more than ever, the typist of the new era will be th

3) ywhere that DDT has ever killed anybody, yet we have ample
iked the scientific committee to be asked to present clear
ld evolve ways of settling disputes peacefully. Convincing
dded to the copper to get beyond this barrier. There is no
e dementia. Neuroscientists from Baltimore have persuasive

that it has saved millions of lives. We all agree to the ne
that radioactive dumping is damaging before it could recomm
that animals actually do operate this way comes from James
that zinc metal was ever prepared in Africa--it has to be m
that links the disease to an enzyme deficiency in a region

4) of the State Department, government scientists tested the
One test of the
at the periphery gives Hubauer the material to explore the
n the government's case. Several scientists questioned the
fected ones. Allison's paper says: 'We now wish to add the

that these species of Fusaria occur naturally in the region
that unemployment causes morbidity was performed by M. H. B
that extrinsic influences are likely to affect allegiances
that the Vietnamese, Kampuchean and Pathet Lao governments a
that these effector cells kill asexual forms of malaria par

5) This record of televised interviews leaves the
do not understand.' Yet the public is regularly given the
(31 March, p 883) must have given many of its readers the
or touch each other, so new devices are needed to give the
ve just passed a resolution banning Irish jokes, under the

that psychology bears an uncanny resemblance to its next of
that a general solution to the problem of natural-language
that polonium is an abnormal constituent of man's environme
that people are in the room. These could include a tele-sme
that jokes are the enemy of tolerance and affection. The jo

6) to the conservation of wildlife in Britain. The entrenched
tor their mastery. Its professional presentation, and cosy
rs for each one that is known, although we can work on the
this option. But the most serious problem seems to be the
et many theories based on black holes proceed on the tacit

that all reclamation is desirable must be challenged. It is
that there are clear answers, is all very American. A quite
that two faunas that have several animals in common are of
that the load-factor on many lines would be constant. That
that such objects exist in the Universe. One could also poi

7) past 50 years has been hunting chance alignments. The old
amics and electromagnetism go far to bear out the author's
ent minister, Huguene Bouchardeau has retracted an earlier
, that a poor environment causes familial retardation. The
It is difficult to reconcile such findings with Ornstein's

many enthusiasts made that Britain is criss-crossed with le
that special relativity provides 'a foundation on which alm
that the waste had left France. It was 'not impossible' tha
that IQ is heritable appears to provoke controversy at ever
that intuitive non-logical thinking is a function of the ri

8) the lengthy trial proceedings ground to a halt because of
dies on elderly patients. These actions do not support the
ate attack by missiles. Scientology circles were shaken by
the Sellafield works because he insisted on answers to his
eld functioned effectively prior to and during the attack;

that attempts had been made to bribe the jury. A new trial
that Dista Products failed to take appropriate action on th
that L. Ron Hubbard was dead and a group of opportunists we
that the plant's laundry was inefficient and turned out 'cl
that the Exocet missile was mistakenly identified as friend

9) pton, deputy chairman of the Electricity Council takes the
ly interesting in the way that it counters the widely held
e of five. During the 1960's Noam Chomsky popularised the
ther European nations (see chart). The committee takes the
charge leaping across the gap and is more inclined to the

that consumers, and women in particular, could not cope wit
that Los Alamos was dragging its feet over the development
that human languages together share certain universal gramm
that government research projects carried out by private in
that somehow mechanical energy is being converted to light.

10) the answer to the baker's prayer; it counters the popular
indow of the centre's intentions and an affirmation of its
ion materials like cement and steel. But there is a common
ses designed to send medical students back to sleep in the
, to the new-fangled cognitivists, psychologists share the

that all bread is fattening and that white bread is too ref
that computing should be accessible to everyone. The day I w
that low-rise building will increase the urban sprawl. Howe
that they now understand pain mechanisms. Psychology has re
that we do things essentially for ourselves. We manoeuvre i

Nouns allegations, assumption, belief, claim, conclusion, doubt, evidence, hypothesis, impression, view

Figure 7   Extract from THAT-CLAUSES II.

Match the first half of each sentence with the second half. The first match is A-C. Can you find the others?

A	In an exchange of letters in January, tensions rose so high that	A	it can transmit light with very little attenuation.
B	Vitamin E is available from so many food sources that	B	large companies with financial muscle are needed to exploit them.
C	Cocoa cultivation spread so quickly round the world that	C	the two leaders are no longer talking to each other.
D	His only complaint is that the technique is so simple that	D	gravity can no longer hold it together?
E	He had so many appreciative friends in very high places that	E	no normal diet could possibly be deficient in it.
F	The deposits are, in the main, so marginal that	F	he probably considered himself safe.
G	Optical fibre is made of very thin glass, which is flexible and so transparent that	G	other researchers will be able to duplicate it quickly enough to keep up with his group.
H	Today in Western Europe and North America, overt cruelty to domestic animals is rare – so rare that	H	flagrant violation of commonly accepted treatment is newsworthy and universally condemned.
I	And why does any star which is radiating energy not lose so much mass (thanks to E=mc²) that	I	there is 'less heat going into the system than is radiated by the tip of my little finger'.
J	Fred Gillett of the American science team says that despite the sun's heat falling on IRAS, the satellite's insulation is working so well that	J	all the crops derived from a few wild ancestors, so that modern cultivated varieties suffer from a lack of genetic variation.

Figure 8   Extract from THAT-CLAUSES IV.

implications of '. . . *he probably thought himself safe*' (my emphasis) were not lost on them.

Teacher: And what happened to him?
Students: Now he's in prison / He's dead / (Draws finger across throat)

Figure 9 is taken from materials on Article Usage, which focus on the notoriously tricky distinction in English between the Definite Article *the* and Zero (∅). The materials concentrate on two main areas of difficulty:

1. The choice between 'generic' ∅ and 'specific' *the* with plural nouns (materials not shown). It is of course not possible, without a tagged corpus, to concordance the Zero Article directly; however, the use of quantifiers such as *all*, *most* and *some* as probes makes it possible to attack the problem indirectly

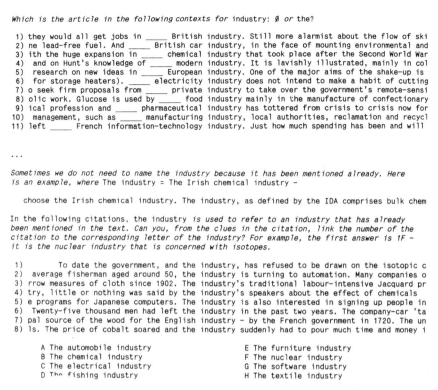

Figure 9   Extracts from DEFINITE ARTICLE PROBLEMS II.

(*all* versus *all* (*of*) *the* – *most* versus *most of the* – *some* versus *some of the* etc.). Experience in using the materials suggests that given carefully graded examples, students can learn to handle not only the clear-cut instances of generic versus specific found in the textbooks, but also the 'fuzzier' examples typical of authentic text.

2. The effect of countability on article usage with singular nouns. Here the probes used are a handful of nouns frequently found in academic discourse that may be countable or uncountable (e.g., *industry, language, trade, society*). Two samples from the materials are shown in the extract, both dealing with the noun *industry:*

    a. Cases where industry (e.g., *∅ British industry, manufacturing industry*) or an industry (e.g., *the chemical industry, the food industry*) is named by means of a Modifier. Some of the examples are fairly easy; others (e.g., *∅ high technology industry* versus *the French information-technology industry*) are more difficult.

    b. Cases where a particular industry is referred to as *the industry* but not named. The task here is a matching exercise, the student having to recover clues as to which industry is being discussed from the limited context of the KWIC citation.

TELL ME WHY

Look at the following short dialogue:

    A   'I have to revise my lecture-notes this weekend.'
    B   'Why do you have to revise your lecture-notes?'
    A   'Because the teacher told us to.'/'In order to pass next week's test.'

Here A says that (s)he has an obligation: B questions it: and A tells B where it comes from. The information in the following citation could be used to make a similar dialogue:

    tion. For instance, <u>the specimen in an electron microscope has to be held in a vacuum</u> to minimise the scattering of the electron

    A   'The specimen in an electron microscope has to be held in a vacuum.'
    B   'Why does it have to be held in a vacuum?'
    A   'In order to minimise the scattering of the electrons.' OR
         'Because the scattering of the electrons must be minimised.'

a) *Construct (with your partner, in your head or on paper as you wish) similar dialogues to the one above for the following citations. For each one, (most of) the information needed to answer the question 'Why?' is already in the citation.*

    1) ed the beam above to drop, by 35 mm. <u>Some other beams have had to be wedged</u> to avoid dropping. The cost of this repair work (which
    2) and wither away. That is not its role in life. <u>Governments have to behave differently.</u> Only then will they win the middle ground,
    3) y and by pH 5 the traps were virtually paralysed. <u>The trap has to be quite acid</u> before it can close. Bennett and Williams suggest
    4) used. Because tin lodes are apt to end at any time, <u>miners have to be continually ready to open up new levels or drives,</u> and to ex
    5) itain <u>people</u> often have good ideas for inventions but then <u>have to sit on the sidelines</u> as no one is prepared to back them. The ro
    6) ls cannot be called marzipan, but it is good.) <u>The kernels have to be de-bittered,</u> for like bitter almonds they contain amygdalin.
    7) ercial winner, and <u>a go-ahead team under Dr John Bather is having to expand</u> to keep pace with the demand. Another service to indus
    8) r a chipmunk or mouse? To find the complete answer, <u>Taylor had to know how much power each member of the menagerie generates</u> as it

b) *In the following citations we cannot find the information needed to answer the question 'Why?' but it is not difficult to think of a suitable answer to that question:*

    three times the energy to convert iron ore <u>(most of which has to be imported nowadays)</u> into steel than to convert ferrous scrap i

    A   'Most of the iron ore has to be imported.'
    B   'Why does it have to be imported?'
    A   'Because domestic supplies are almost exhausted.'

    of the lamps and <u>the very high temperature that the lamps have to run at.</u> Already one firm has developed a 30 W source of this ty

    A   'The lamps have to run at a very high temperature.'
    B   'Why do they have to run at a very high temperature?'
    A   'Otherwise the light won't be bright enough.'

Now try to make your own short dialogues from the following citations:

    9) ement to deposit records (as with books) <u>the institute has had to rely on voluntary donations over the years.</u> Despite this, it has
    10) nt of the word 'contract'. <u>If you've signed a contract you have to fulfill it</u> except in the most desperate circumstances. 'The gen
    11) an 70 years old and in need of modernisation, <u>councils are having to give top priority to repairing more modern buildings.</u> Almost
    12) nefits. Eventually <u>politicians and the general public will have to accept that there will never be full employment again,</u> and will
    13) tteries. Vincent said that <u>a few years ago watch batteries had to be renewed every year.</u> They now last five to seven years, and it
    14) he beaches by D + 1. His lank locks had to be shorn and <u>he had to be kitted-out with battle-dress and ammunition boots.</u> All this t
    15) med priority in seeing the Jupiter satellites. As <u>both men had to use Galilean telescopes,</u> their claims seem unlikely to have been
    16) to make up its own mind. The chances are that <u>Britain will have to find a new place to dump waste by the end of the decade.</u> Britai

Figure 10   Extract from CONTEXTS OF HAVE TO.

Results with the materials are encouraging and indicate that Data-driven Learning may here render teachable – and learnable – what has too often in the past been neither of those things.

The last extract, in Figure 10, illustrates the application of another insight that came from the preliminary study of raw data. It is from some materials which attempt to shed light on the meanings of the modal and semi-modal verbs by focusing on the contexts in which they are used. An interesting feature of the discourse of *have to*, for example, is the number of times the immediate context indicates some sort of explanation or justification of the necessity or obligation expressed by *have to*. That this should be so is not surprising: human beings are liable to ask 'Why?' on being told that something has to be done, and it is natural that writers should anticipate that question on the part of their readers. The exercise asks students to turn that 'frozen interaction' of the written text into a dialogue, using the information given in the citation to provide a justification for the statement made with *have to*.

When the citations without a justification in the immediate context of *have to* were examined more closely, it appeared that in the majority of cases an explanation or justification was not needed since it could be taken as given on the basis of knowledge shared between writer and reader; this gave the possibility of a freer, and more difficult, extension of the dialogue with the students having to provide the justifications themselves. The technique of 'concordance-into-dialogue' used in this exercise has much in common with the question-and-answer methods of text analysis developed by Hoey (1983), and merits further investigation.

Work continues in exploring the possibilities opened up by Data-driven Learning for the teaching and learning of Grammar and Vocabulary. On the one hand there is the practical, down-to-earth business of investigating the different types of observational task and the different types of exercise that can be developed on the basis of concordance output. Data-driven Learning has much in common with other methodological approaches, such as Community Language Learning (Curran 1978) and Grammatical Consciousness-raising (Rutherford 1987), and one line of development would be to borrow some of the techniques employed in those approaches – for example, the use of 'propositional clusters' as advocated by Rutherford. Another possibility, where all the learners have the same L1, is the use of parallel concordances in which the citations for a particular linguistic feature in one language are interleaved with their translation equivalents in a second language (Roussel 1991). At the same time, the 'backwash effect' of practice on theory referred to earlier becomes more and more important, not only in recasting the underlying description of particular grammatical phenomena, but also in the more general sense that the traditional division between distinct 'levels' of language appears increasingly untenable, with Grammar interpreting Lexis on one hand and Discourse on the other (Sinclair 1991). For these reasons, Data-driven Learning remains a methodology in a state of flux and development, and many questions remain unanswered – for example, whether the approach can be adapted for use with beginners or near-beginners. Nevertheless, the general outlines of the methodology seem clear enough to make objective research into its effectiveness both possible and worthwhile. Stevens (1991), for example, has investigated with encouraging results the learning of vocabulary taught by means of concordance-based exercises when compared with more traditional techniques, and his research would certainly be worth replicating for grammar, providing it is borne in mind that DDL influences not only *how* a foreign language is taught, but also *what* is taught.

Of the other questions that research could address, four would appear to be particularly important. The first two relate to the question of the trainability and transferability of language learning strategies. Are students who have been taught to puzzle out features of context in computer-generated concordances significantly more proficient at solving other concordance-based tasks than students who have not been so taught? And are they able to transfer those strategies to other tasks – e.g., puzzling out the meaning of a text in the target language? The third and fourth questions relate to individual differences between language learners (Skehan 1989). Given the possibility of measuring parameters such as aptitude, intelligence, motivation and cognitive style, is success with DDL associated with a particular parameter or parameters? More precisely, is there any association between the parameters of individual difference and a particular style of DDL (e.g., reactive versus proactive; loosely versus tightly defined observational tasks)? Given answers to questions such as these, we shall be able to see more clearly the directions that Data-driven Learning may take in future and its full potential in language teaching methodology.

References

Chomsky, Noam. 1965. *Aspects of the Theory of Syntax*. Cambridge, Mass.: MIT Press.

Cobbett, William. 1819. *A Grammar of the English Language, in a Series of Letters*. London: Thomas Dolby.

Collins COBUILD English Language Dictionary. 1987. London and Glasgow: Collins.

Curran, Charles. 1978. A linguistic model for learning and living in the new age of the person. In *On TESOL '78*. Reprinted in *Innovative Approaches to Language Teaching*, ed. by Robert Blair. Rowley, Mass.: Newbury House (1982).

Higgins, John. 1991. Which concordancer? A comparative review of MS-DOS software. *System* 19: 91–99.

Hoey, Michael. 1983. *On the Surface of Discourse*. London: Allen & Unwin.

Johns, Tim. 1986. Micro-concord: A language-learner's research tool. *System* 14: 151–62.

——— 1988. Whence and whither classroom concordancing? In *Computer Applications in Language Learning*, ed. by Theo Bongaerts, Theo van Els and Herman Wekker. Dordrecht: Foris.

——— 1991a. Should you be persuaded: Two samples of Data-driven Learning. University of Birmingham: *English Language Research Journal* 4: 1–13.

——— 1991b. From printout to handout: Grammar and vocabulary teaching in the context of Data-driven Learning. University of Birmingham: *English Language Research Journal* 4: 27–45.

Krashen, Steven. 1982. *Principles and practice in second language acquisition.* Oxford: Pergamon.

Lyons, John. 1963. *Structural Semantics.* Oxford: Blackwell.

1977. *Semantics I.* Cambridge: Cambridge University Press.

Quirk, Randolph, Sidney Greenbaum, Geoffrey Leech and Jan Svartvik. 1985. *A Comprehensive Grammar of the English Language.* London: Longman.

Roussel, Francine. 1991. Parallel concordances and tonic auxiliaries. University of Birmingham: *English Language Research Journal* 4: 71–101.

Rutherford William, 1987. *Second language grammar: Teaching and learning.* London: Longman.

Scott, Mike, and Tim Johns. 1993. *MICROCONCORD.* Oxford: Oxford University Press.

Sinclair, John (ed.). 1987. *Looking Up: An account of the COBUILD Project in Lexical Computing.* London and Glasgow: Collins.

1991. *Corpus, Concordance, Collocation.* Oxford: Oxford University Press.

Skehan, Peter. 1989. *Individual Differences in Second Language Learning.* London: Arnold.

Stevens, Vance. 1991. Concordance-based Vocabulary Exercises: A viable alternative to gap-filling. University of Birmingham: *English Language Research Journal* 4: 47–61.

Tribble, Chris, and Glyn Jones. 1990. *Concordances in the Classroom.* London: Longman.

Widdowson, Henry. 1979. *Explorations in Applied Linguistics,* vol.1. Oxford: Oxford University Press.

Winter, Eugene. 1982. *Towards a Contextual Grammar of English.* London: Allen & Unwin.

13 *Conclusion*

Terence Odlin

The eleven articles in this volume have, I hope, led readers to arrive at fresh insights about grammar and its role in language teaching. It is possible to have higher hopes: One might imagine that this collection marks the start of the royal road to an ideal pedagogy. Such thinking, however, does indeed seem wishful, perhaps just one more illusion about controversies long heard in the history of language teaching. The following quotations, all from authors cited in Kelly's (1969) *25 Centuries of Language Teaching*, suggest how much of a "consensus" there has been about grammar:

> It is evident that the rules of Grammar can not convey the art of language. . . . How then is language to be acquired? I answer by adopting the mode by which nature teaches children their mother tongue. N. G. Dufief, 1823 (Kelly 1969: 40)

> The idea of those who will have no truck with grammar is the product of a lazy mind which wishes to conceal the fact. And far from being a help to children, it loads them infinitely more than rules, because it deprives them of an aid which would facilitate the understanding of books. P. Nicole, 1670 (Kelly 1969: 219–20)

> . . . for we see most schollers, when they come to the Universities to forget that perfectnesse in their grammars, and most learned men can not say the rules; yet so long as they have full understanding & remembrance to make use in resolving, writing or speaking, this sufficeth. J. Brinsley, 1627 (Kelly 1969: 49)

> First, there must be principles or the light of nature in the scholler, otherwise light is not comprehended out of darknesse. T. Granger, 1616 (Kelly 1969: 219)

All of these positions call to mind recent pronouncements on the role of grammar. Open-minded scholars will acknowedge that each position has at least a grain of truth, but eclecticism can offer no more than a vague guide to practice in the everyday situations that teachers encounter. As Kelly observes, reasonable thinkers such as Erasmus have long recognized the need to balance many pedagogical considerations and to eschew dogmatism. Yet the continuing disagreements about grammar over the centuries should lead modern practitioners to ask the following questions: (1) Has there been any advance in knowledge of sound practice since Erasmus? (2) What can contribute to further progress?

314

If we distinguish knowledge from technology, an affirmative answer to the first question is not so evident. Without question, tape recorders, computers, and video cassettes have enormously expanded the possibilities for good teaching. Even so, the technological revolution of printing led to fewer advances in practice than what a scholar in the time of Erasmus might have hoped for. Printing no doubt made universal literacy (and universal language learning) possible, but it also gave rise to countless dull and misleading textbooks. Where teachers' intuitions have been sound, so have their materials, whether in a textbook or a computer program, and where intuitions have been dubious, so have the materials.

Intuition will always be indispensable, as I suggested in my article in this volume. However, not all intuitions can count as knowledge, so the question remains as to whether there has been any advance in knowledge of sound practice since the Renaissance. If theories of language learning show real advances, then one can argue that highly justifiable applications are now possible. The need for caution should be clear to anyone familiar with the theoretical shifts in linguistics and psychology in this century. Still, only through theories with strong empirical support can practitioners make strong generalizations. In his article in this volume, Little cites the commonplace "There is nothing so practical as a good theory" and then observes:

And yet language teachers are notoriously hostile to theoretical discussion, apparently believing that it has nothing to offer the practitioner in the classroom. Many language teaching handbooks strengthen this prejudice by offering collections of practical hints without any kind of theoretical framework. But unless we have a theory we have no means of moving from specific instances to general principles. That is not to say that language teachers need to be theoreticians themselves; but it is to say that they need to understand the principles on which their practice is based. Otherwise discussion of success and failure in the language classroom can never rise above the level of anecdote, assertion, and counterassertion.

If knowledge of sound practice presupposes a sound theoretical basis – and Little's position seems irrefutable – teachers might well ask what generalizations they can safely assume to be true. A full discussion of possible generalizations is beyond the scope of this volume, but two are evident in the assumptions of every contributor:

1. Second language and first language acquisition are different in some crucial ways.
2. Instruction can make a difference.

The first conclusion seems inevitable if twenty-five years of books, conference volumes, and articles on second language acquisition have anything to show for the all the effort. This conclusion is, of course, quite different from what Dufief claimed in 1823 and what Dulay and Burt (1974) claimed more recently. First and second language acquisition do have some important similarities, but adults learning a second language differ from children both in the advantages and disadvantages they have in language learning (cf. Bley-Vroman 1988; Schachter 1988; Larsen-Freeman and Long 1991). Since the evidence for this difference is so varied and so thoroughgoing, taking Dufief's advice in its most literal form would be risky.

If we cannot expect that adults will closely resemble children in their language learning efforts, the role that teaching can or should play in furthering second language acquisition inevitably becomes crucial. Fortunately, instruction can make a real difference, as the studies by Yip and Master as well those cited in the introduction to this volume indicate. Instructional goals will differ as much as students and classes differ, but any teaching of grammar should help learners to become independent analysts. As I argued in the introduction, students who do not develop such capacities are unlikely to change their interlanguage very much after they have finished their course work. Still, one might always hope, against the evidence, that Dufief was right after all: Perhaps the research has got it wrong once again. Couldn't the right teacher and the right classroom achieve *everything* needed for successful language learning? The question certainly has the appeal that has spawned many utopian philosophies. Yet however seductive the question may be, utopian pedagogies seem no more likely to succeed than have the utopian political systems of this century, systems that have left so many calamities in their wake. Teaching does make a difference, but especially so when it enables learners to continue their learning once a course has ended.

Although theoretical insights can inform sound practice, there remain many areas where the research is at best incomplete (cf. Selinker 1992). One area well worth further investigation is just how learners come to modify their explicit knowledge and their use of grammar. Researchers frequently invoke Krashen (1983) on three conditions for the use of the monitor (i.e., the internal editor that all learners presumably have): time, focus on form, and knowledge of the rule. No doubt these conditions are necessary, even if problematic – one might wonder, for example, just what it means to know a rule, as Westney discussed in his article. Yet contrary to some of those who cite him, Krashen noted that these conditions were *necessary* but not *sufficient*. Another condition, one much less often discussed, is recognizing a given usage in terms of the rule – that is, analyzing a token in terms of a type.

The type-token problem is quite serious, as many teachers who have worked with ESL writers will attest. Students may indeed be able to state a particular rule (e.g., tense in conditional sentences) but not be able to recognize a tense error in a proofreading exercise or, worse still, in their own work. The problem is compounded by the fact that students seem able to identify such errors in some environments but not in others. Textbook exercises can beguile learners into believing that error detection is a simple task. Although such exercises provide a useful start, a much greater challenge for learners is to find a relatively small number of errors in a text that has many well-formed constructions: such tasks lead many learners to go on "witch-hunts," that is, make changes where no changes are needed (cf. Odlin 1987). In these cases, learners mismatch types and tokens, and the psychology of such misperceptions is surely an area that further work on pedagogical grammar should examine more closely.

The type-token problem is only one issue in helping learners to become independent analysts. An even larger, but more amorphous, issue is communicative competence. Indeed, if future work on pedagogical grammar succeeds in advancing practice, as well as theory, in regard to communicative competence, the royal road I speculated about may indeed be open. No one, however, should underestimate the difficulties that remain. As the articles by Nunan, Tomlin, and Hasan and Perrett show, intention, topicality, politeness, and other discourse considerations are often embedded in syntactic structure and in a social context, and all three articles make clear how many controversies remain. Some of these issues may be resolved in a reasonably short time. Nevertheless, patience and curiosity about the unexplored territories will be virtues in demand for a long time to come.

References

Bley-Vroman, Robert. 1988. The fundamental character of foreign language learning. In *Grammar and Second Language Teaching: A Book of Readings,* ed. by William Rutherford and Michael Sharwood Smith. New York: Newbury House.

Dulay, Heidi, and Marina Burt. 1974. Natural sequences in child second language acquisition. *Language Learning* 24: 37–53.

Kelly, Louis. 1969. *25 Centuries of Language Teaching.* Rowley, Mass.: Newbury House.

Krashen, Stephen. 1983. Newmark's "Ignorance Hypothesis' and current second language acquisition theory. In *Language Transfer in Language Learning,* ed. by Susan Gass and Larry Selinker. Rowley, Mass.: Newbury House.

Larsen-Freeman, Diane, and Michael Long. 1991. *An Introduction to Second Language Acquisition Research.* London: Longman.

Odlin, Terence. 1987. Some problems concerning the interpretation of passage correction tests. In *Language Testing Research,* ed. by Kathleen Bailey, Theodore Dale, and Ray Clifford. Monterey, Calif.: Defense Language Institute, 70–77.

Schachter, Jacquelyn. 1988. Second language acquisition and its relation to Universal Grammar. *Applied Linguistics* 9: 219–35.

Selinker, Larry. 1992. *Rediscovering Interlanguage.* London: Longman.

Glossary

acceptability judgment   any claim about whether a structure is standard or nonstandard, whether it is easily understood or not, and/or whether it is stylistically appropriate or not (cf. *grammaticality judgment*).

alternative hypothesis   a hypothesis that states that there is a statistically significant difference, positive or negative, between a sample and the population from which it was drawn. For example, such a hypothesis might state that a certain group of language learners will achieve a score higher than a *mean score* already known for a test of vocabulary knowledge (cf. *null hypothesis*).

aspect   a grammatical category applied to verbs and concerned with how the action is viewed rather than when it occurs (as with tense). English is often considered to have two aspects, progressive and perfective.

Aspects model   a particular type of generative grammar, in which phrase-structure rules and transformational rules were important in specifying sentence structure and interrelations between sentence types such as actives and passives (cf. *PS-rules, transformation*).

average item reliability   Average correlation between pairs of items on a test (cf. *Kuder-Richardson 20*).

causative   a type of verb indicating causation, as seen in *made* in *He made me lose*. Some *inchoative* verbs can acquire a causative sense: e.g., *We grew the tree* (i.e., we caused the tree to grow).

CESL   English as a second language (for the colonised), where English has been "imported" into the learner's community. Compare *MESL*.

clause   a unit of lexicogrammar, approximately the same as simple sentence or T-unit. In the Systemic Functional (SF) model, it is seen as the entry point to the system of choices which specify its full potential.

collocation   the tendency of a word or words to appear in the context of (collocate with) another word significantly more often than would be expected on the basis of chance. For example, the word *twists* frequently collocates with *turns* as in *twists and turns*, even though it can occur independently. Although many collocations are idioms, not all are (e.g., *talk about someone* instead of **talk over someone*).

communicative competence   the ability to communicate successfully in a language in a range of situations.

communicative methodology a general approach to language teaching which concentrates on the use of language as communication rather than on control of the grammatical structures.

Community Language Learning an approach to language teaching with a number of distinctive techniques, all of which involve the students deciding what is to be learned, and the teacher acting as a "linguistic informant."

competence knowledge of language independent of its use (cf. *performance*).

complementation the process of "completing" a phrase or part of a sentence with a complement, as *He became MANAGER, He put the glass ON THE SHELF*, or *I propose TO FINISH THIS SOON*.

comprehensible input speech whose message or intent is readily understandable to the listener.

concordance a collection of all the contexts in which a word or phrase occurs in a particular text or *corpus* of texts. A concordance of a text or corpus shows contexts for all the words in those texts – though in the latter case common grammatical words such as *the* and *of* are usually excluded (cf. *concordancer, concordancing, KWIC concordance*, and *sentence concordance*).

concordancer a program for producing computer *concordances*.

concordancing the production of computer *concordances* by means of a *concordancer*.

context of culture the makeup of the social environment by reference to which members define their sense of ways of being, saying, and doing, and which determines their interpretation of a particular occasion of talk (cf. *context of situation*).

context of situation the significant set of social factors which define the nature of the occasion of talk and with which every linguistic interaction correlates (cf. *context of culture*).

contrastive hypothesis for second or foreign language learners, the ease or difficulty of target language items will be determined by the extent to which the target item is similar to or different from the first language.

control group a group of subjects whose selection and experiences are exactly the same as the experimental group, except that they do not receive the experimental treatment.

corpus a collection of texts containing language, written or spoken, which may be used as a source of information about the language. For computer *concordancing*, the texts must be stored in a standard electronic format that can be recognized by a *concordancer*.

count noun a noun that indicates a discrete object which can be counted and made plural, e.g., *book* (cf. *noncount noun*).

Data-driven Learning (DDL) an approach to language teaching that gives central importance to developing the learner's ability to "puzzle out" how the target language operates from examples of authentic usage. The approach is particularly associated with the use of computer *concordances* in the classroom but can be extended to other situations where the student has to work *inductively* from authentic text.

dativize   for a verb, to occur with an indirect object preceding a direct object, as in *I showed him the results.*

declarative knowledge   conscious *explicit knowledge* about cognitive skills, including language learning and use (cf. *procedural knowledge*).

deductive   describes an explanation or an exercise in which a generalization or rule precedes specific examples or applications of that generalization or rule (cf. *inductive*).

definite   describes a noun whose referent is assumed to be known to the hearer, e.g., *the sun.* Along with the definite article, other ways of signaling definite reference include demonstratives and personal pronouns.

delicacy   degree of detail in the description of any unit. For example, in a system network, reading from left to right, the left-most choices show a "primary degree of delicacy," the right-most are the most delicate. See *system network*.

demographic factors   characteristics of subjects in a study, such as age, nationality, gender, etc.

descriptive   concerned with accurately describing language as actually used (cf. *prescriptive*).

developmental sequence   the "natural" order in which language items or structures are believed to develop in first or second language acquisition.

difficulty order   a ranking of items (e.g., elements of grammar) in the order of the difficulty with which they are acquired. A difficulty order may reflect the "natural" order of a *developmental sequence,* but it can be influenced by factors such as the type of teaching.

direct access model   the hypothesis that learners of a second language have access to the principles of Universal Grammar that are not mediated by knowledge of the native language. This access is believed to be available to all learners, who nevertheless have little ability to articulate the exact nature of the UG principles. In effect, the direct access model hypothesizes that adult language learners have the same access that children putatively do to the principles of UG.

discourse   stretches of language, spoken or written, typically longer than the sentence.

discourse-dependent   describes any syntactic structure that is somehow dependent on information outside the sentence in which the structure occurs. For example, interpreting pronouns such as *she* and *her* often requires understanding who the referent was in a previous sentence: e.g., *Jill went up the hill. She wanted a pail of water.*

discrete sentence   an isolated, decontextualized sentence, as distinguished from a sentence in a paragraph or some other context.

discriminability   the ability of a test item to make reliable distinctions between individual performances on a test.

do-**support**   the obligatory use of *do* as in *Does she know the reason?* or *She doesn't know the reason,* as opposed to *She knows the reason.*

dual noun   noun with clearly distinct count and noncount forms, e.g., *iron* and *an iron* (cf. *count noun* and *noncount noun*).

effect size   size of the effect of an experimental treatment based on a comparison of the *mean scores* and *standard deviations* for gain scores between the experimental and control groups.

elicited speech   speech uttered in response to a controlled stimulus, e.g., a *wh*-question in the past perfect tense, as distinguished from speech that is natural and spontaneous.

ergative verb   a type of intransitive verb, one denoting a situation in which the individual involved in an action has little or no control over it. Thus, *fall* is an ergative verb, whereas *sing* and *eat* are not.

error analysis   the systematic study of learners' errors made in second/foreign languages, in order to discover stages of learning and learning processes.

existential *there*   the use of *there* to highlight the existence of some entity, as in *There's something I want to tell you.*

experiential metafunction   the potential of language to express the speakers' experience of the goings-on – the process, the participant(s), and the circumstances – relevant to it. Realizationally related to *field of discourse* and *transitivity*. See also *ideational metafunction*.

explicit knowledge   the capacity to analyze and talk about language (cf. *implicit knowledge*).

extralinguistic factors   nonlanguage factors that influence communication, e.g., gestures.

field of discourse   the social activity in which the speakers are engaged by using their language on a given occasion of talk. See *mode of discourse* and *tenor of discourse*.

first language   typically the language of primary socialization, which the learner uses to construct her social self (cf. *second language* and *foreign language*).

first mention   describes a noun that is introduced into discourse as a new referent, usually the first time it is mentioned (cf. *subsequent mention*).

foreign language   the language(s) learned to communicate in contexts other than those of the learner's community (cf. *first language* and *second language*).

formulaic utterance   any utterance which is learned and used as an unanalyzed "chunk," such as *What's the time?* or *What's your name?*

While consisting of more than one word, formulae function as single words.

fossilization   the cessation of further linguistic development.

functionalism   in grammatical investigations, the attempt to explain facts about the *use* of language and the *structure* of language with reference to each other. Functionalist studies thus usually emphasize the discourse functions of linguistic structures: e.g., the frequent use of English past tense forms in stories.

functional-notional syllabus   functional-notional syllabuses specify language learning targets in terms of the communicative functions learners should be able to fulfill and the notions, or meanings, they should be able to convey. Examples of functions are "greeting," "asking for permission," "apologizing," "giving instructions," "expressing likes and dislikes." Notions are usually divided into two categories, "general" and "specific." General notions embrace the range of meanings in a language which allow us to achieve the basic conceptual organization without which we cannot construct specific meanings or relate one specific meaning to another. They include notions such as tense, number, and location. Specific notions are usually arranged under such topic headings as "Personal identity," "House and home," "Food and drink," "Clothes and fashion," "Shopping," "Entertainment." When a speaker asks, "Is there a drugstore near here?," she is seeking information (function) about the existence (general notion) of a drugstore (specific notion) in the vicinity (general notion). The fullest functional-notional specifications are those prepared under the aegis of the Council of Europe's modern languages projects.

gain scores   improvement on scores on a test between one administration and the next, e.g., pretest and posttest.

generative rules   sets of rules that aim to "generate" or define all the grammatical sentences of a language in a precise way.

generic   describes a noun that functions as a representative of a group, e.g., *A cat is a mammal,* as distinguished from a specific noun that is an indicator of an actual member of that group, e.g., *I got a cat at the pound yesterday.*

genre   that aspect of the organization of the linguistic interaction which concerns its overall structure; the movements/stages that characterize the type of interaction taking place (cf. *register*).

Government/Binding   the approach to Universal Grammar favored by Noam Chomsky and others. According to GB theory, linguistic knowledge is a mental construct shaped by invariant principles (held to be true for all languages) and by parameters that vary in their "settings" for different languages (e.g., whether the verb normally occurs before or after the direct object).

grammaticality judgment   any claim about whether a structure conforms to the rules of a language as set forth in a *descriptive* grammar of that language. Thus a sentence such as *You was here* is grammatical even though it is nonstandard and, in many contexts, unacceptable (cf. *acceptability judgment*).

higher-level/low-level rules   low-level rules are, roughly, "simple" rules, particularly of morphology and phonology, that are assumed to be easily described and learned; higher-level rules are those of syntax and semantics, in particular, that are more abstract, of wider impact in the grammar, and not so easily described or learned.

hyponym   a semantic construct wherein a term (the hyponym) is subordinate to another term, that is, the superordinate. Thus *house, school,* and *fire station* are all hyponyms of the superordinate *building.*

ideational metafunction   the potential of language to express the speaker's experience of the goings-on and how they might be related to each other, as also other elements of speakers' experience (things, qualities, etc.). Its two aspects are the *experiential* and the *logical metafunction.*

implicit knowledge   the capacity to speak and understand a language (cf. *explicit knowledge*).

inchoative   a type of verb indicating the beginning of a state (e.g., the second verb in *Einstein thought about the problem and suddenly he knew what had to be determined*).

indefinite   describes a noun that is assumed to be new to the hearer (cf. *definite*). Along with *a* and *an,* the absence of an article can be used to signal indefinite reference: e.g., *I see birds.*

inductive   describes an explanation or an exercise in which specific instances are presented or studied in order to discover a generalization (cf. *deductive*).

information focus   an aspect of clause structure realizationally related to the textual metafunction; its structural output is the elements Given and New.

intact group   group of subjects formed on the basis of some criterion such as exam scores or self-selection, e.g., students in a class, as distinguished from a random group.

interlanguage   the linguistic knowledge of second/foreign language learners at any particular stage of development.

internal consistency   reliability determined from a single rather than multiple administrations (cf. *Kuder-Richardson 20* and *Kuder-Richardson 21*).

interpersonal metafunction   the resource of language to express social and personal relations, speakers' assessments and evaluations, and their role-allocating strategies; realizationally related to *tenor of discourse* and *mood, modality.*

keyword   in computer concordancing, any linguistic item that the user of a concordancer instructs the program to search for. In practice, a keyword may be a single word (e.g., *book*), a "skeleton" word (e.g., *n*theless*), a set of words (e.g., *am/is/are/was/were/be/being/been*), a phrase (e.g., *of course*), or even a morpheme (e.g., **ible*).

Kuder-Richardson 20 (KR-20)   internal consistency method for estimating overall test reliability based on the average correlation between pairs of items on the test (or average item reliability) and the number of items.

Kuder-Richardson 21 (KR-21)   internal consistency method for estimating overall test reliability. It differs from the KR-20 in that it is based on the number of items, the average score, and the *variance* of the scores rather than the average item reliability.

KWIC concordance   KWIC is an acronym for "keyword-in-context." A KWIC concordance is one in which each of the citations occupies a single line, with the *keyword* to the right of it. The advantage of the KWIC format is that the central alignment of the keywords allows rapid scanning and comparison of the different contexts.

language function   popularly used to refer to the uses of language, to its general property of being useful for communication (cf. *linguistic functionality* and *metafunctional hypothesis*).

langue   the basic abstract system of language seen in isolation from how it is used; a term first employed technically by Ferdinand de Saussure (cf. *parole*).

learnability   the notion that some principles cause learning to be easy, difficult, or even impossible under certain conditions. Recent discussions of *Universal Grammar* have frequently considered the learnability issue. Similar, but not identical, concerns, are involved in the *teachability hypothesis*.

lexical properties   various features of individual words, such as pronunciation and grammatical functioning.

lexicogrammar   that stratum of language which expresses linguistic meanings and is itself expressed by phonology and/or graphology; the grammar and lexicon of a language. See *semantics, realization,* and *strata.*

linguistic functionality   the social basis of language which permeates its meanings and forms so that it participates in creating and maintaining social systems by enabling social verbal interaction (cf. *language function* and *metafunctional hypothesis*).

logical metafunction   the resource of language to express complex phenomena, both how processes relate to each other by concurrence, dependence, and so on, and how complex classes of things, qualities, and quantities are created by combination, submodification, and so on. See also *ideational metafunction* and *experiential metafunction*.

markedness   the theory that in languages certain words, grammatical structures, and so on (unmarked) are more basic or normal than others (marked) which have more special or restricted uses, as in *dog* (unmarked) versus *bitch* (marked), or (perhaps) the infinitive complement in *I hope to go* (unmarked) versus the *-ing* complement in *I intend going* (marked). Although markedness often lends itself to a binary analysis (i.e., marked/unmarked), many structures require a scalar approach: thus, relative clause patterns can be viewed as "highly marked" or "less marked."

mean score   the average score, that is, the sum of the total scores divided by the number of test takers.

MESL   English as a second language, where the learner has migrated to an English-speaking community (cf. *CESL* and *foreign language*).

metafunctional hypothesis   the hypothesis that social organization is dialectically related to language organization so that the crucial social variables of field, tenor, and mode are expressed by the semantics and lexicogrammar of ideational, interpersonal, and textual metafunctions. See *linguistic functionality*.

metalingual   describes any reflection on or discussion about language. Alternatively, knowledge or terminology that refers to phenomena in language itself is *metalinguistic*.

modality   the system of meanings associated with mental states such as wishes and judgments of possibility, desirability, and so on.

modalization   that part of modality which is concerned specifically with speakers' assessment of probability and usuality. See *modality;* cf. *modulation*.

mode of discourse   one of the three contextual variables, mode is concerned with the semiotic organization of social action and social relation into an intelligible interaction. Realizationally related to textual meaning and wording. See *field of discourse* and *tenor of discourse*.

modulation   that part of modality which is concerned specifically with speakers' judgment of obligation or willingness. See *modality;* cf. *modalization*.

monitor   the conscious linguistic editor of spoken output that is said to be based on learned rather than acquired material.

mood   that aspect of the organization of the lexicogrammar of clause which acts as a resource for speech role allocation, construing the strategies known popularly as *stating, telling, asking, ordering*, and so on. See *tenor of discourse* and *interpersonal metafunction*.

morpheme order studies   a series of investigations carried out in the 1970s into the acquisition of certain grammatical morphemes in English. Although these studies were often considered to be characterizations of *developmental sequences*, they are better viewed as investigations of *difficulty order*.

multidimensional model   a model suggesting that target language items can be categorized according to whether or not *speech processing constraints* affect learning of particular structures at a particular time.

Natural Approach   the name given to Krashen and Terrell's model of second language instruction. Proponents of the model believe that such instruction will encourage the type of language development seen in first language acquisition.

naturalistic language learning   naturalistic language learning is the term used to refer to language learning that proceeds on the basis of the learner's interaction with speakers of the language in question, without the stimulus or support of organized teaching. The *Natural Approach* is only one of the characterizations of such learning.

negative evidence   information that learners might use to determine that certain structures will *not* occur in the target language. According to several recent studies, correction and other types of negative evidence do not suffice to guide learners in distinguishing what is and is not part of the target language.

noncount noun   noun that indicates an amorphous material or mass which cannot be counted and is therefore always singular, e.g., *water, furniture* (cf. *count noun*).

nonidiomatic phrase   a group of words whose individual meanings indicate the meaning of the words together, e.g., *kick the football* as opposed to the idiom *kick the bucket.*

null hypothesis   research hypothesis that states that there is no significant difference between a sample and the population from which it was drawn (cf. *alternative hypothesis*).

one-tailed   describes an expectation of directionality in the results, that is, that there was reason to believe that the relationship between the sample and the population from which it was drawn would be either positive or negative.

p < .05   conventional level of significance indicating that the probability (p) of obtaining the observed result by chance is less than one in twenty.

parole   language use by individual speakers in specific situations. First used as a technical term by Ferdinand de Saussure. See *langue*.

patient   a semantic role indicating a person or thing affected by an action. For example, the word *diamonds* signals the patient in both *The thief took the diamonds* and *The diamonds were taken by the thief,* even though *diamonds* is direct object in the first sentence and subject in the second.

Pearson product-moment correlation   the most common type of correlation showing the relationship (r) between two variables.

performance   the use made by speakers and hearers of their linguistic knowledge (or *competence*) in any specific situation.

periphrastic   describes constructions with more than one word. For example, *did work* in *I did work* is a periphrastic (and also an emphatic) formulation of a past-tense verb phrase, whereas *worked* in *I* *worked* is not. Periphrastic constructions in English are common, as in the use of modals such as *must* and *might,* which normally occur with other verbs in a verb phrase.

phonetic variant   an alternative form dependent on phonetic environment rather than syntactic choice, e.g., indefinite article *a* versus *an,* and the negative prefixes in *illegal* versus *improbable* versus *insufficient.*

pidgin   a new language that develops as a result of language contact between speakers of different languages and that is characterized by radically simplified syntax and lexicon.

pivotal information   the content of a *proposition* signaling a significant event in a text.

point biserial correlation   a correlation that determines which items on a test were "good" items. A low point biserial correlation coefficient (r_{pbi}) indicates items tending to be incorrectly answered by otherwise high scorers, and/or tending to be correctly answered by otherwise low scorers. In other words, the analysis indicates which items are suspect in *discriminability* and should therefore be discarded.

positive evidence   the language that learners are actually exposed to. In contrast to *negative evidence,* this information is believed to be the primary data that learners use to decide what is possible in a language. According to analyses within the *Government/Binding* framework, learners need not only positive evidence but also "access" to the principles of *Universal Grammar* in order to acquire a language.

postmodified   describes head nouns that are followed by descriptive words or phrases within a noun phrase, e.g., *the woman on the bus; the money that was stolen* (cf. *premodified*).

practice effect   a mean gain score that is influenced by familiarity and/or practice in taking the posttest rather than as a result of the experimental treatment.

pragmatic knowledge   knowledge of the appropriate linguistic form to use depending on the situation and the speaker's relationship to the listener.

premodified   describes head nouns that are preceded by descriptive words within a noun phrase, typically adjectives in English, e.g., *a beautiful woman* (cf. *postmodified*).

prescriptive   concerned with recommending how language should be spoken or written (cf. *descriptive*).

primary socialization   the very initial stages of learning one's culture through everyday interaction with members of a close "meaning group." See *first language;* cf. *secondary socialization.*

proactive teaching   describes the traditional situation in which the teacher (aided by syllabus designers, course books, etc.) decides what is to be taught, and how it is to be taught (cf. *reactive teaching*).

procedural knowledge   *implicit knowledge* involved in cognitive skills, including language learning and use (cf. *declarative knowledge*).

product versus process   in the context of language learning, product refers to the target language as a static, complete body of knowledge, and process to the dynamic acquisition of this knowledge, involving a learner's cognitive and communicative strategies.

proposal   the linguistic giving or demanding of goods/services, that is, varieties of offer or order, realized by part of the lexicogrammar of mood. See *mood, tenor of discourse, metafunctional hypothesis;* cf. *proposition.*

proposition   the meaning of statements signaled by clauses or other linguistic structures. See *mood, tenor of discourse, interpersonal metafunction;* cf. *proposal.*

PS-rules   within generative grammar, phrase-structure rules, the type of rules specifying the most basic patterns of clauses, noun phrases, verb phrases, and so on (cf. *transformation*).

quasi-experimental design   an experimental design that includes at least one control group but, rather than randomly assigning subjects to groups as in a true experimental design, usually makes use of intact groups.

ranking adjectives   adjectives that show a rank order in three categories: superlative (e.g., *the largest, the most complicated*); sequence (e.g., *the first, the next*); and unique (e.g., *the same, the only*).

reactive teaching   teaching which takes place in response to the queries and problems of the students, in contrast with *proactive teaching.* One of the possible approaches in *Data-driven Learning,* reactive teaching is also the most important feature of *Community Language Learning.*

realization   the relationship between the various strata of the linguistic theory, whereby each stratum of language is realized by the next below it. Realization relation between the higher strata of grammar, meaning, and context is dialectical and so crucial to the functionality of language. See *strata.*

reciprocal and nonreciprocal communication   in reciprocal communication, which is usually oral and face-to-face, meaning is negotiated by the participants: Each contribution to the interaction is partly shaped by what has already been said and in turn helps to shape what will be said. In nonreciprocal communication, on the other hand, the message is elaborated by the sender without any immediate involvement on the part of the receiver. Examples of nonreciprocal communication are all types of written discourse as well as certain types of spoken discourse: e.g., speeches, lectures, sermons. For instance, a writer sending a letter from Ireland to America does not have the chance to adjust the message once it is mailed, nor does the writer have the benefit of immediate feedback (though, of course, the writer can send a new letter or the reader can phone the writer). It should be noted that nonreciprocal spoken communication often shifts to the reciprocal mode, as when a heckler at a political meeting manages to engage in direct argument with the speaker or when a student interrupts a lecture with a question.

recursivity a property of any generative rule that allows for an infinite number of phrase structures of the same type (e.g., prepositional phrases). Although such rules lead to more complexity in sentence structure than what *descriptive* grammars or *prescriptive* grammars often admit, they have proven useful in developing theories of the creativity of human language.

register the variety of language which correlates with variation in field, tenor, and mode of discourse, severing all aspects of such variation, unlike genre, which refers only to the structural aspects of registral varieties (cf. *genre;* see also *field of discourse, tenor of discourse,* and *mode of discourse;* also *ideational, interpersonal,* and *textual metafunction*).

reliability the extent to which a test produces consistent results when administered under similar conditions.

research hypothesis prediction of a research outcome comparing the relationship between the sample data and the population from which it is drawn (cf. *alternative hypothesis* and *null hypothesis*).

r_{pbi} the point biserial correlation coefficient (cf. *point biserial correlation*).

second language the language(s) which a learner learns in order to participate fully in her own native community, or in an adopted one; as such it could mediate in the secondary socialization of the learner (cf. *first language* and *foreign language*).

second language acquisition the study of the acquisition of second or foreign languages in tutored and naturalistic environments.

secondary socialization learning through interaction about one's culture after the basic patterns of self in relation to society are already established. See *second language* and *foreign language,* and *uncommonsense knowledge;* cf. *primary socialization.*

semantics that stratum of language which represents the total meaning potential of language, i.e., all and only those meanings which can be expressed by language. Choice from this stratum is activated by context; it is expressed or made manifest by choices at the stratum of lexicogrammar and/or phonology. See *lexicogrammar, realization,* and *strata.*

semiosis The process of making and exchanging meaning through symbolic mediation.

semiotic system any system of signs which can be used for semiosis, such that it has at least two strata – content and expression – which are realizationally related. See *semiosis.*

sentence concordance   a *concordance* in which every citation is a sentence in the *corpus* in which the *keyword* appears.

significant at the .05 level   the standard level of statistical significance. For example, two populations may show different mean scores on a vocabulary test, but the difference may not be significant. On the other hand, two other populations may show a difference significant at the .05 level, which means, roughly, that the probability is less than one in twenty that the differences in scores are due to chance.

specific   describes a noun that denotes an actual member of a group, e.g., *I got a cat at the pound yesterday,* as distinguished from a noun that denotes a *generic* concept.

specificity   the noun feature that describes an actual rather than a representative member of a group (cf. *specific*).

speech processing constraints   psychological limitations such as memory capacity, which constrain the mind's ability to use language.

speech role   the part a speaker plays in an interaction vis-à-vis her addressee (e.g., the giver of information). By adopting a speech role, the speaker by implication also allocates some corresponding speech role to the addressee; for example, if the speaker is giver of information, the addressee is positioned as receiver of information. See *mood, proposition,* and *proposal.*

standard deviation (S.D.)   the average variability of all the scores around or deviation from the mean score. The formula for calculating the S.D. involves more than the normal steps in calculating an average.

strata   components of the theory of language description. In the Systemic Functional (SF) model, four strata are recognized: *context, meaning, wording,* and *sound.* These are related by *realization.*

subcategorization   various types of grammatical information associated with the meaning of a particular word. For example, transitive verbs such as *kiss* subcategorize for human subjects and some type of direct object: that is, kissing is normally done by humans, and one must kiss someone or something. Intransitive verbs such as *fall* do not subcategorize for human subjects or for any type of direct object.

subsequent mention   describes a noun that has already been introduced into the discourse and is therefore known or identified (cf. *first mention*).

syllabus design   procedures for selecting, sequencing, and justifying the linguistic and experiential content of language programs.

system network   the paradigmatic organization of language at each stratum as a set of interlocking choices displaying close internal constraints; also the name of the graphic device which materially represents such an organization. See *delicacy.*

t_{crit} the minimum *t-value* that must be obtained in order to claim statistical significance.

t-value   a standardized measure of the distance between the mean of the sample and the mean of the population that helps a researcher decide whether or not to reject the *null hypothesis;* the result of a t-test.

teachability hypothesis   states that certain grammatical items can only be learned (and should only be taught) when the learner is at the developmental stage preceding the item to be taught.

tenor of discourse   the contextual parameter of human relation to which language use must respond. See *mood, modality, interpersonal metafunction.*

textual metafunction   the linguistic resource which enables the expression of the speakers' sense of how what they are saying now is related to what has been already said or what might be expected to be said; realizationally related to the contextual variable *mode* (i.e., the semiotic organization of discourse) and to systems of theme and information focus, as well as cohesion and coherence. See *mode of discourse,* and also *interpersonal* and *ideational metafunction.*

theme   name of a system of choices realizationally related to mode of discourse, and forming part of the lexicogrammatical organization of language which construes the speakers' perspective on what they are "on about" – their point of departure. Also, when written as *Theme,* the name of one element of a two-element structure of the clause as an output of choices in the system of theme, where the other element is known as *Rheme.* See *mode of discourse* and *textual metafunction.*

transformation   within generative grammar, rules that relate the structures of different sentences, for example, actives and passives.

transitivity   the name of a system of choices realizationally related to field of discourse; it construes the speakers' experience of the goings-on in both the external and internal world of observation. The choices of the system specify relations between processes, and the participants and circumstances relevant to those processes. See *field of discourse,* and also *ideational* and *experiential metafunction.*

unaccusative   another term for *ergative verb.*

uncommonsense knowledge   knowledge that persons acquire in the course of living everyday life without any explicit instruction, especially from agencies officially created as part of the state apparatus to educate people. See *primary socialisation* and *secondary socialisation.*

Universal Grammar   the hypothesized set of principles that underlie the grammars of all human languages. Although the term does not necessarily imply analyses developed within the framework of *Government/ Binding* theory, UG is often discussed in terms of such analyses.

unmatched group t-test   a t-test for differences between two independent means.

variance   the average variability of all the scores on a test (or all scores on a test item) in deviation from the *mean* score. The formula for calculating the variance involves more than the steps to compute a mean score.

***wh*-question**   a question that is formed with a *wh*-word, such as *why* and *when* (and including *how*), as opposed to yes/no questions.

zero article   The null article, or absence of an article, represented by the symbol $\emptyset$: e.g., $\emptyset$ *Life is hard;* $\emptyset$ *Cigarettes will harm your health.* Like the indefinite article *a* (or *an*), the zero article is a convention needed to make *generic* statements.

Index

References to English occur on nearly every page and are therefore not listed. In cases of work involving co-authors, only the name of the first author appears in this index.